AMSTERDAM STUDIES IN THE THEORY AND
HISTORY OF LINGUISTIC SCIENCE

E. F. KONRAD KOERNER, *General Editor*

Series IV – CURRENT ISSUES IN LINGUISTIC THEORY

Advisory Editorial Board

Volume 9
Parts I & II

Harry & Patricia Hollien (ed)

Current Issues in the Phonetic Sciences

CURRENT ISSUES IN THE
PHONETIC SCIENCES

Proceedings of the IPS-77 Congress,
Miami Beach, Florida, 17-19th December 1977

Edited by

Harry and Patricia Hollien

University of Florida
Gainesville, Fla.

PART II

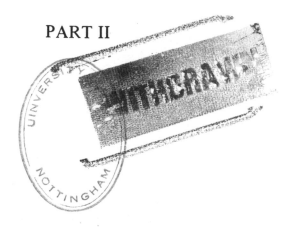

AMSTERDAM / JOHN BENJAMINS B.V.

1979

TABLE OF CONTENTS

PART I

A. HISTORY OF PHONETICS

B. ISSUES OF METHOD AND THEORY IN PHONETICS

C. LARYNGEAL FUNCTION

D. TEMPORAL FACTORS AND QUESTIONS OF INTONATION

TABLE OF CONTENTS

E. PHYSIOLOGICAL AND ACOUSTIC PHONETICS

F. Speech Production

Part II

G. Neurophonetics and Psychopathology

H. Speech Perception

I. SPEECH AND SPEAKER RECOGNITION

TABLE OF CONTENTS

J. The Teaching of Phonetics

K. Children's Speech and Language Acquisition

TABLE OF CONTENTS

TABLE OF CONTENTS

* * * * *

G. NEUROPHONETICS AND PSYCHOPATHOLOGY

DIFFERENTIAL DIAGNOSIS OF NEUROLOGIC AND PSYCHOGENIC VOICE DISORDERS

ARNOLD E. ARONSON
Mayo Clinic

It is possible to infer a disease process by listening to the abnormal voice it produces. However, the ability on the part of medical and other scientists concerned with the voice and its disorders to extract differential diagnostic information from abnormal voice remains in a primitive stage of evolution. The American laryngologist is expert in the diagnosis of structural lesions of the vocal folds when he is able to see the disease by means of laryngoscopic examination. But should the vocal folds appear normal, yet the voice abnormal, the laryngologist loses his bearings and concludes the problem is functional. Yet those of us who have been in a position to sample the voices of focal and systemic laryngeal disease and to compare organic psychogenic voice signs can come to only one critically important conclusion--that there are many organic illnesses producing abnormal voice that do not produce visible abnormalities of the vocal folds.

The two main etiologic categories of abnormal voice in which the vocal folds appear normal to the naked eye are (1) neurologic and (2) psychogenic. The importance of the laryngologist, speech pathologist, psychologist, neurologist, and psychiatrist to be able to infer the etiology of a particular voice abnormality from the sound of the voice is not an academic exercise of voice discription for its own sake. Quite the contrary. To be able to employ the abnormal human voice as a clue to the presence of organic or emotional

illness in its early stages, as well as its more advanced,
can be useful in the differential diagnosis of illness. The
human ear is superbly sensitive to the nuances of voice differences and it is often the human ear alone that can answer
the question, What is the differential diagnostic significance of this patient's voice? Although our subject has to
do with neurologic and psychogenic abnormalities of voice in
which no lesions of the vocal folds can be observed, for contrastive purposes let us review quickly those laryngologic
diseases in which definable lesions do account for abnormal
voice: chronic hypertrophic laryngitis; pedunculated polyp;
sessile polyp; multiple laryngeal polyps; chronic bilateral
polypoid hypertrophic laryngitis; papilloma; leukoplakia;
carcinoma; membranous laryngeal web; bilateral vocal nodules;
unilateral contact ulcer; bilateral contact ulcer; post-
endotrachial anesthesia granulomas; fracture of the larynx;
hemorrhagic polyp; chronic laryngitis.

Aphonia or dysphonia from weakness or incoordination of
the intrinsic or extrinsic muscles of the larynx due to a
lesion in the nervous system is classified, technically, as
a dysarthria. Dysarthria, an umbrella term, refers to all
respiratory, phonatory, resonatory, or articulatory dysfunctions from lesions of the central and/or peripheral nervous
system. And, although it is more common for motor dysphonias
to occur in conjunction with resonatory and articulatory disorders in motor system disease, there are instances in which
abnormal voice occurs either in isolation or is so dominant
as to over-shadow co-existing milder palatopharyngeal and
articulatory malfunctions. A crucial point: The voice disorder that occurs as a manifestation of damage to the motor
system has acoustic characteristics that mirror the neuroana-
tomy and neurophysiology of the neurologic disease. There are
several different points within the central and peripheral
nervous system damage to each of which will result in a different type of muscular dysfunction and consequently, a different phonatory end product. The following classification
of neurologic phonatory disorders relates location of the
lesion to resultant type of muscular dysfunction. Figures 1
through 10 give the dysphonic characteristics found in the
dysarthrias produced by lesions in specific regions of the
nervous system.

We now move on to that often ill-defined territory of
voice disorders subsumed under the term functional or non-
organic voice disorders. One of the main differences between
neurologic and functional voice disorders is that in neurologic, the palatopharyngeal and articulatory musculature are
almost always involved whereas in functional, with rare
exception the disorder is limited to the larynx. To most
people the term functional voice disorder means non-organic.
One is unable to attribute the voice defect to any structural
or neurophysiologic pathology of the laryngeal musculature.
Unfortunately "functional" is used by many clinicians as a
wastebasket term in which are placed all voice disorders for
which no organic explanation is apparent. But there is so
much more specificity to the territory of functional voice
disorders. There are three, perhaps four, major etiologic
subcategories of functional voice disorders into which most
so called nonorganic aphonias or dysphonias can be categorized. They are: vocal abuse, environmental stress, and
self-image related. A fourth category, psychotic mental
states, is recognized but not discussed here.

Voice disorders due to vocal abuse stem from excessive
talking, shouting, singing, coughing, or throat clearing.
The common denominator behind all of these activities is
hyperadduction of the vocal folds and excessive force of
phonation. These misuses cause tissue damage, for example
contact ulcer or vocal nodule. But, the traditional concept
of vocal abuse as a mechanical etiology of contact ulcer and
vocal nodule is an over-simplification because evidence from
many case histories indicates that these individuals, in
addition to abusing their voices, give evidence of dysphoric
emotional states, most often incipient or over anger. These
patients are in such verbal occupations as teaching, sales,
the law, acting or the clergy, and whose voice disorders are
complicated by excess smoking or alcohol consumption. By
personality they are tense, hard-driving, and verbally aggressive. Even children who have vocal nodules in addition to
their screaming, yelling or incessant talking, come from backgrounds in which there is a higher than average incidence of
family pathology. Perhaps the majority of functional voice
disorders are due to environmental stress producing unbeliev-
able varieties of voice symptomatology;muteness;aphonia;either
continuously whispered or interrupted by laryngeal spasms; a

family of dysphonias, some of which are characterized by continuous hoarseness that is not particularly attention getting; the so-called spastic or spasmodic dysphonia of the
adductor type in which there are intermittent moments of
glottal closure and voice arrest; the abductor type, in
which there are intermittent moments of glottal widening
and sudden momentary voice loss.

The classical psychogenic voice disorder is conversion-
whispered speech. A crucial point that needs to be made is
that the patient discussed above who had a dysphonia may be
as classifiable as conversion reaction as the patient with
aphonia. The mechanism of conversion reaction extends to
many different acoustic types of voice. What is meant by conversion reaction? Conversion reaction is a loss of the voluntary motor control or somatic sensation, despite absence of
organic disease. It occurs as a defense against any number
of uncomfortable emotional states arising from unpleasant
and conflict-producing life experiences. It is an unconscious simulation of illness which the patient is usually
convinced is of organic origin and serves the psychologic
purpose of enabling the patient to avoid awareness of emotional conflict, stress, or perhaps failure which would be
emotionally intolerable if faced and dealt with directly. A
multitude of interpersonal problems can be responsible for
conversion aphonia or dysphonia but all have the following
in common. The patient is caught in a conflict between want-
ing but not allowing him or herself to express overtly feelings of anger, fear, or remorse verbally. There is a breakdown in communication between the patient and someone important to him; the patient has something that he is afraid,
ashamed, or doesn't exactly know how to tell.

Perhaps the classic illustration of conversion aphonia
is the following case study. A 26-year-old police officer, on
the force for three years, had never been happy in his work
but never told anyone about his feelings toward his work for
fear of disappointing his parents who had encouraged him to
become a policeman. Always quiet and unaggressive he found it
difficult to lose his temper. On rare occasions where he did
he would shake and become livid with rage. He could not re-
primand motorists or pedestrians because of the strong need

to be liked by everyone. When he came to the clinic he was
aphonic and typically unaware of any relationship between
his feelings about his work and his voice disorder. As is
often true in patients who are ready to relinquish their
sumptoms, symptomatic voice therapy was able to bring his
normal voice back in a brief period. Shortly after his
normal voice returned I asked him how he felt. He said,
"Wonderful, a little funny that it was that easy to get back.
Would it have come back like this if I had just walked in
here without talking to you fellows? Or is it because I
talked to you and the psychiatrist?" I asked him what he
thought was the answer to that question. He said he thought
it was necessary to have talked about his feelings toward
his work, saying, "When I was talking to the other doctors
there was something I brought up, that I started feeling
funny. It was about the police department. The psychiatrist
said,"'You don't really like your job and you are afraid to
tell your family,' and I agreed with him but I felt real
funny." I asked him if talking about it with somebody had
somehow made things different. By this time he had developed
insight into the cause of the problem and volunteered that
from now on he shouldn't be afraid to tell his family how
he feels; that it's his life, that he should be doing something he wants to do, not what others want him to do. Until
now he was unable to admit to himself that he didn't like
the job, that he much preferred his old job, which was that
of a mixer of chemicals for the bleaching of cloth. On that
job he didn't have to say more than 10 words a day and he was
all by himself. He would sing a lot and daydream about money,
and being strong, and I asked him how all of this could be
related to the voice and he said, "Well I don't know, maybe
subconsciously it was the only way I knew of getting away
from there, from being a policeman. Maybe it was my way of
rebelling." I asked him if he thought he would be able to
activate what he had learned here and he finally said, "Now
that I have talked to you fellows and I know that it is because I don't want to tell my parents, maybe now I can tell my
parents because I was always shutting it out before. Maybe it
wouldn't bother them half as much as I think it would."

A third group of psychogenic phonatory disorders relates
to immature personality development in which the dysphonia is

a reflection of the self-image, the voice conforming to the concept that the individual maintains of himself. One sub-group has to do with confused sexual identification, known as mutational falsetto or puberphonia, the failure on the part of the male,and sometimes the female, to make the transition from the higher pitched pre-pubertal voice to the lower pitched adolescent voice. The psychodynamics have not been worked out although those who have written on the subject seem to agree that the male may not have matured emotionally, has more than the usual identification with the female parent and in some cases so serious a failure of male identification that it may border on homosexuality. Occasionally mutational falsetto is associated with failure of physical development during the pubertal stage of physical growth in which the secondary sex characteristics occur later than normal as in hypogonadism. In other instances severe illnesses have occurred precisely during the time when the voice should have been making a change from the higher to the lower pitch, and because of hospitalization and general debilitation, the adolescent fails to make full use of the respiratory and phonatory power that has been developing. The mutational falsetto voice is high in pitch, weak, thin, breathy and hoarse, giving the overall impression of the immaturity, effemiacy, and passiveness. It often breaks downward to a lower pitch level giving a clue to the potentiality for normal voice even though this clue goes unrecognized by the patient. Surfacing now are voice problems associated with transsexualism in which speech clinicians are having to deal with males who have made the surgical and hormonal changes to female and who need to develop a voice more congruent with the feminine role. Infrequently one is confronted by adults whose personality development is so immature that not only does the pitch and inflectional patterns of the voice reveal their need to be identified as someone in the childhood range but their articulation, facial expression and gestures, and entire way of life, reveals the need to remain child-like.

In summary, it can be said that the voice reveals the presence of observable and invisible organic pathology of the larynx or its innervation and most assuredly reveals the

psychopathology of human life. It may be stretching the
point to argue that the voice alone can tell the entire
story. Closer to the truth is that abnormal voice should
be considered as one of many signs and symptoms of organic
and emotional illness that can be used to support or to
controvert the etiologic diagnosis.

SPEECH STUDIES IN PSYCHIATRIC POPULATIONS

JOHN K. DARBY AND ALICE SHERK
Harold D. Chope Hospital and San Mateo
Community Mental Health Center

This summary paper will present an overview of the literature to date on speech analysis of psychiatric populations. We will be focusing on the vocal aspects of speech as revealed by perceptual and instrumental methods. The pathologies reviewed included Schizophrenia and Affective Disorders.

SCHIZOPHRENIA

In considering studies done on schizophrenia, it is important to clarify that this is a broad rubric of disease categorization. The sub-classification,etiology,prognosis, behavioral phenomena, and treatment differ widely depending upon multiple factors involved.We classified the studies under the headings of Childhood Schizophrenia,Adolescent Schizophrenia,and Adult Schizophrenia which cannot be compared one to another due to the diversity of the syndromes.Further, in order to compare studies of populations within these general types of schizophrenia, other factors must be brought into account. For example in the area of childhood schizophrenia there are different syndrome criteria and models in the literature. Particular areas of concern relate to factors such as (1) age of onset, (2) signs of organic involvement, (3) the role of biological/hereditary aspects (4) the import of family dynamics in the illness, (5) I.Q.,(6) developmental history, (7) current level of functioning.The adolescent schizophrenias,

too, are variable, some having their roots in early childhood, others going on to take the form of the adult schizophrenias. The adult schizophrenias represent their own continuum of disease; the traditional methodology breaks out
sub-types as paranoid, catatonic, simple and hebephrenic.
Many researchers have also relied on Langfelt's (1939)
system which breaks the adult schizophrenias into two categories: (1) the chronic process schizophrenia (similar
to Kraepelin's Dementia Praecox), which is felt to have a
more significant biological genetic basis, and (2) acute
reactive schizophrenia where it is felt that environmental
stress factors and family dynamics play a more important
role. The prognosis in these latter cases is much more
favorable, and the behavioral phenomena are quite different.

Childhood Schizophrenia. In a first study, Goldfarb
et al. (1956) compared 12 childhood schizophrenics and six
patients with reactive behavioral disturbances (ages six to
nine). Spontaneous and/or read speech were perceptually
analyzed by a speech pathologist for phonation, rhythm,
intonation, and articulation. The authors found that childhood schizophrenics exceeded reactive behavior disorders in
every category of deviation with the exception of voice
quality. Voice quality in this study referred to nasality,
breathliness, hoarseness, and glottalization. In addition
they noted a "flat" quality which seemed characteristic of
all of the schizophrenic children studied. The schizophrenic
children showed insufficient or inappropriate volume and
pitch changes, and total pitch range was found to be narrowed
with a tendency to excessively high pitch. Inappropriate
rate changes were noted as were excessive prolongation of
sounds, syllables, and words; the latter were felt to be the
basis of the often described "chanting" quality found in the
speech of these children. Finally, articulatory disturbance
was present in both groups; however, the lack of firm lip
closure in the schizophrenic children produced an indistinct
and lax pattern unique to this group.

The second study by Goldfarb et al. (1972) matched 25
controls with 25 schizophrenic children (median age 8 years,
8 months). In this study, significant differences were
found between the two groups in each category analyzed:

volume, pitch, voice quality, rate, phrasing,fluency,stress,
intonation/inflection, articulation, communication of moods,
manner, and attitude. Schizophrenic children showed marked
differences from normals in 50 of the 82 speech and language
faults appraised. However, no single specific clustering
of speech faults uniquely characteristic of childhood schizophrenics was found. It was noted that in a number of voice
and speech elements schizophrenic children showed either too
much or too little of any quality of speech and also diver-
gences in the individual patterns. The authors concluded
that a primary disturbance was evidenced in the control and
regulation of voice and speech communication, and that this
defect in self-regulatory control of speech provided a key
to the impairment in other adaptive functions.

Adolescent Schizophrenia. Adolescent schizophrenia has
been largely ignored by the clinician and research worker in
the past (Loeb, 1969). Kraepelin (1919) stated, "From this
time on (age 15) we see the frequency of Dementia Praecox
increasing with extraordinary rapidity; more than two-thirds
of the cases begin between the fifteenth and thirtieth year."
However, Ostwald (1961, 1963, 1964, 1966) has published research on this population (as well as others). For example,
in 1966, he and Skolnikoff published a study detailing a
number of speech disturbances in a 15 year old adolescent
schizophrenic male with a childhood history of disturbed
reactions to others and poor school performance. In addition, at age 9 the patient manifested a convulsive disorder.
His speech was described as strikingly abnormal. Voice
quality was nasal and indistinct. Articulation was impaired
due to insufficient mouth closure, and consonants sounded
mushy and unclear. Breath control was poor.

Physical action of the mouth and pharynx were studied
radiographically.At times the soft palate did not close off
the nasopharynx resulting in a "fuzzy" nasal sound.Moreover,
spectrographic studies revealed: (1) Frictional noises of
the consonants were missing when the patient enunciated the
word "future," (2) The vowel formant at 2000 Hz kept changing positions, thus "distorting the sound," (3) Lack of
interruption by stop consonants, (4) Exaggerated intonation
pattern, (5) High and prolonged rise of the voice,especially

at the ends of questions, (6) "Dribbling out" of sounds at
the end of sentences, (7) Fusion of emotive noises with
words, and (8) Intermittent prolonged duration of vowel
sounds.

Chevrie-Muller et al. (1971) studied 53 hospitalized
adolescent schizophrenics (age 12-23 years). They used a
complex analytic system (electrologography) involving
oscillograms/glottograms of spontaneous and read speech,
and an age-matched control population. The most striking
finding reported was that the female schizophrenics showed
reduction in frequency deviation (pitch range) relative to
normal females. The males showed a similar trend but not of
statistical significance. The authors suggested that, from
the symptomatic aspect, the female schizophrenics were more
homogeneous than the male population, and this could be one
explanation for the sex difference. Pause times and reading
times were longer in the schizophrenic group but not at a
statistically significant level.Some of their schizophrenic
patients showed extensions of pause times and prolonged
duration of words. They point out a lack of consistent findings here and indicate some variability of findings. They
also suggest that phenothiazine medications may be a significant factor in their results.

Bannister (1972 doctoral thesis) compared eight adolescent schizophrenics to 17 hospitalized non-psychotic patients
and to a control population. The schizophrenic subjects
(seven males and one female) showed significantly reduced
fundamental frequency variability when compared to their
non-psychotic cohorts and the normal controls. It was
further noted that this decrease in fundamental frequency
variability was compatible with Moskowitz's (1951) report
of the results of a perceptual study of schizophrenics where
a monotony in pitch was observed. Bannister noted a contrast
however, with the Saxman and Burk (1968) finding that fundamental frequency deviation for female schizophrenics significantly exceeded that of control speakers on reading.Possible
explanations for the difference were suggested: (1) Psychotropic medication; Saxman and Burk (1968) had removed their
patients from medications 48 hours prior to testing while
other investigators have generally not altered the

psychotropic medication schedule; (2) Differences in diagnosis; (3) Length of hospitalization; (4) Age differential.

Finally, Ostwald (1961, 1963) reported details about a 16 year old girl who entered the hospital in an acute schizophrenic state characterized by withdrawal and apathy. A monotonous sound quality pervaded her speech and acoustic analysis done at the time of admission showed a pattern characteristic of "sharp" voices (see Ostwald, 1963, for definition of four acoustic sterotypes). Following five weeks of hospitalization, psychotropic medication, and therapy, several changes were noted: (1) the Spectral power curve showed a rise in intensity and a reduction in "sharpness"; (2) Formant-3 (at 1430 Hz) showed appreciable change; (3) The voice showed less "compactness"; and (4) Reading had speeded up an average of 0.06 seconds per syllable.

Adult Schizophrenia. Moses (1954) made several clinical observations of schizophrenic voice changes. He suggested similarity to a child's voice due to the marked regression which may be seen. This was described as being of archaic character with primordial attributes. He noted an androgynous character with male patients frequently using "head register" typical of females. Melody was found never to glide but rather to jump intervals without correlation to speech content. He noted inappropriate accents and emphasis and rhythmic repetition of vocal patterns.

Moskowitz (1951) studied a group of 40 schizophrenics (20 ambulatory and 20 hospitalized) and matched them with 40 controls. Subjects were given questions to which they responded, and their recordings were analyzed by means of a perceptual rating scale. He concluded that: (1) Certain voice qualities appeared in the schizophrenic population, such as "monotony, weakness, unsustained auditory gloominess and flat, colorless tone quality"; (2) Male subjects seemed to show a greater degree of "unsustained voice quality"; and (3) White subjects showed more "gloominess" in their voices than black.

Spoerri (1966) studied a population of 350 schizophrenics using both instrumental and clinical measures. He
found the following speech deviations in this population:
(1) dysarticulation (90%), (2)consonant formation deficiency
(56%), (3) beginning of speech (24%), (4) melody (23%),
(5) volume (20%), (6) rhythm (18%), (7) timbre (18%), (8)
register (10%), (9) speed (8%), (10) tone (6%). Spoerri
concluded that: (1) Where intensive social therapy and
medicinal cures are carried out, the number of speech
irregularities are lower; (2) Chronic and demented forms
of schizophrenia show a higher preponderance of speech
deviancy; (3) Characteristic or frequent changes noted
were strain, harshness, register change from chest voice
to falsetto, pitch change from high to low, and dysarticulation. Volume changes between loud and soft were notable;
speed changes were similar to volume with inappropriate
alternations occurring; timbre was gloomy, dull or metallic;
melody was monotonous, and idiosyncratic melodic movement
of syllables occurred; (4) Dement conditions show the greatest distortion of speech, simplest of rhythms, and largest
irregularity of dynamics; in the late stage dysarticulation
is at its worst; (5) Just as there is no such thing as a
schizophrenic language, there can be no typical schizophrenic
speaking voice, and thus it is not possible to make a
diagnosis from the voice change alone; and (6) The deteriorated schizophrenic condition is mirrored in the voice
change.

Saxman and Burk (1968) studied 37 hospitalized schizophrenic females and compared this group to 22 normals. They
analyzed the two groups cross-sectionally by instrumental
analysis of speaking fundamental frequency level (SFF),
fundamental frequency deviation (SD), and mean overall and
sentence reading rates. The group comparisons showed the
schizophrenic population to have a higher mean SFF but not
of statistical significance. The schizophrenic group did,
however show statistically significant differences in having
a slower oral reading rate and a larger SD. The schizophrenic
group was sub-divided into diagnostic types and levels of
severity, and variations were noted between these groups.
The sub-group classification of severity proved useful.
Where significant differences were observed between

schizophrenics and control groups, the mild/moderate/severe
sub-group means were ordered in the direction of difference
such that the severe sub-group represented one extreme and
the control group the other. The authors suggest that these
speech measures may have diagnostic and prognostic implications. They also caution, however, that the changes may
be reflecting severe personality disintegration rather than
constituting speech characteristics unique to the schizophrenic population. As is noted above, Saxman and Burk's
findings of increased fundamental frequency deviation are
in contrast to studies in adolescent schizophrenia by
Chevrie-Muller and Bannister.

AFFECTIVE DISORDERS

Involutional Depressives. Moses (1954) described the
voice of individuals exhibiting depressive symptoms in the
climacteric. Males were reported to lose strength and
volume with the range becoming both narrowed and higher.
Females sometimes showed lowering of range. These changes
were presumably due to the accompanying physiologic changes
of old age rather than the psychotic state.

Darby and Hollien (1977) studied six involutional depressives (ages 50-72) before and after electroconvulisve
treatment. Prior to treatment the voices were characterized
as "dull" and lacking in vitality. Following treatment and
moderate clinical improvement, the voices were judged to have
regained some of their normal vitality in distinction to the
pretreatment "dull" quality. Perceptual analysis by a speech
pathologist showed improvement in articulation and pitch in-
flection (five patients) and stress (four patients). While
listener judgment showed change, it was not striking. Instrumental analysis was also carried out, yet no significant
trends were detected in speech power spectra, fundamental
frequency, fundamental frequency deviation, or speaking rate.
The paucity of significant instrumental findings in this
study is of note. The results would appear to contradict
Ostwald's (1963) findings of increased intensity centered
around 500 Hz following electroconvulsant therapy. The explanation for this most probably relates to a different
type of study approach and a different method of statistical

analysis. First of all, subjects in the Darby and Hollien
study were not compared individually, but as an entire group.
The six pre-treatment power spectral curves were averaged to
one curve and then compared to the averaged post-treatment
curve. Since no significant difference appeared, the selected band frequencies centering around 500 CPS therefore
were not individually compared. Other factors which could
have also been important include: (1) The length of interval between electroconvulsant therapy and recording; (2)
The differences in the diagnostic populations; (3) The
degrees of clinical improvement or mood change; and (4)
The limited number of subjects. At any rate, the need for
further research and clarification is apparent.

Manic Depressive-Manic Phase. Newman and Mather (1938)
described manic patients as "good speakers." Articulation
was described as vigorous. The voice was clear, lively,
and vital. The pitch range was wide with frequent gliding
pitch changes. Emphasis and accent were frequent. Pauses
were rhythmical, but exaggerated in length. Resonance was
oral, pharyngeal. Syntax was described as rich, but loose,
and response initiation was rapid. With improvement of
their condition, the patients showed relaxation of articulation, a narrowing of pitch range, and reduction of emphatic
accent. Pauses and hesitation began to appear. Syntax
tightened up and became more coherent. Finally, Moses (1954)
has described manic voices as exhibiting wide range, uncon-
trolled intensities, fast tempo, and highly dynamic action.

Manic Depressive-Depressed Phase. Ostwald (1961, 1963)
acoustically analyzed a depressed manic depressive 64 year-
old man before and after treatment with electroconvulsant
therapy. The initial acoustic pattern on the spectral power
curve was predominately "flat." Motants three and four were
not clearly defined for reading voice. After treatment,
reading voice and high voice showed strikingly different
curves characterized as "robust" and evidencing more intensity and acoustical energy. The voice showed a loudness
rise of 4.3 sones with the band of maximum increase (2.2
sones) centered at 500 Hz. Reading speech had slowed down
0.06 seconds per syllable.

Manic depressive illness would theoretically provide a most interesting model for voice study for a variety of reasons: (1) It is a disorder which shows oscillation of mood from depressive to normal to manic states with a certain regularity or periodicity; (2) The patterns of change are repetitive and characteristically quite similar for any individual patient; and (3) The opportunity to study the speech changes associated with each state within the same patient could produce some important clues on hypothesis regarding the speech hallmarks of depression and elation.

CONCLUSION

The overview of literature demonstrates a potentially vast field for study. While there are, as yet, very few studies which yield systematic data, the authors feel that a structural foundation for further work is provided by the studies reviewed. The initial difficulty in reviewing these studies had to do with the interdisciplinary nature of the research. Because psychiatry, psychology, speech pathology, and speech science originate from very different roots and lend diverse perspectives to the research, there are often problems in terminology, classification and even research objectives. The studies reviewed demonstrated varying degrees of success in integrating the disciplines. It appears that the most successful approach to resolving these interdisciplinary communication problems will involve active participation by each discipline involved in a given study.

This review demonstrates that while there are as yet no specific clusters of speech disturbances for any given syndrome, there is an indication that specific clusters, trends, or sub-group factors will emerge as products of further research. This potential is one of the most exciting possibilities in the field, and when developed, may yield very significant new information. As a final note, one might speculate that as advances occur, neurobiological and environmental correlates could be identified for various speech parameters.

REFERENCES

Bannister, M. L. (1972). Unpublished Doctoral Diss., Univ. Kansas.

Chevrie-Muller, D., Dodart, F., Sequier-Dermer, N., and Salmon, D. (1971). Folia Phon., 23:401-428.

Darby, J. K. and Hollien, H. (1977). Folia Phon., 29:279-291.

Goldfarb, W., Braunstein, P. and Lorge, I. (1956). Am. J. Orthopsych., 26:544-555.

Goldfarb, W., Goldfarb, N., Braunstein, P. and Scholl, H. (1972). J. Autism Child. Schiz., 2:219-233.

Kraepelin, E. (1919). Edinburgh, E. and S. Livingston.

Loeb, L. (1969). New York, Grune and Stratton.

Moses, P. J. (1954). New York, Grune and Stratton.

Moskowitz, E. (1952). Speech Mono., 19:118-119.

Newman, S. S. and Mather, V. G. (1938). Am. J. Psych., 94:912-942.

Ostwald, P. F. (1961). Arch. Gen. Psych., 5:587-592.

Ostwald, P. F. (1963). Springfield, C. C. Thomas.

Ostwald, P. F. (1964). Dis. Com., XLII.

Ostwald, P. F. and Skolnikoff, A. (1966). Postgrad. Med., 40-49.

Saxman, J. M. and Burk, K. W. (1968). J. Speech Hear. Res., 11:194-203.

Spoerri, T. H. (1966). Arch. Gen. Psych., 14:581-585.

ACOUSTIC COMPARISONS OF PSYCHOTIC AND NON-PSYCHOTIC VOICES

HARRY HOLLIEN AND JOHN K. DARBY
University of Florida and
Harold D. Chope Hospital

Can acute psychosis be detected--and perhaps even identified--solely from analysis of the speech signal? Information provided by Darby and Sherk, in their 1978 literature review, suggest that many clinicians consider this a distinct possibility. If our notion is correct, what elements within the signal are being perceived and identified by these clinicians and what auditory strategies are they using? Other questions can be asked also. Can the relevant speech/voice characteristics be extracted/defined by appropriate apparatus; can they be quantified for analysis? In order to answer these questions, it will be necessary to carry out controlled research of an appropriate nature.

We already have reported one study which was completed under the aegis of our research program in this area (Darby and Hollien, 1977). In that investigation, we analyzed the speech of six patients diagnosed as involutional depressives. Since we were unable to obtain samples produced by these individuals prior to the onset of the disorder, we only were able to study their speech during the course of treatment. That is, we evaluated their speech samples before and after electro-convulsive therapy attempting to identify any speech changes that appeared to be correlated with the disorder and/ or changes resulting from treatment. Our secondary purpose was to compare the results of the laboratory procedures to

subjective evaluations carried out by a speech pathologist.
She used tests commonly accepted within the field of speech
pathology--and ones that roughly paralleled our laboratory
procedures (i.e., fundamental frequency, relative vocal intensity, spectral characteristics and speaking rate). While
the level of agreement between the laboratory measures and
those reported by the speech pathologist was surprisingly
good, neither of the two approaches clearly demonstrated
systematic changes in the speaking behavior of the six subjects as a result of therapy, even though all demonstrated
significant psychological improvement. Some trends were
observed but none were statistically significant.

At this juncture, we initiated a second experiment. Two
larger groups of subjects, diagnosed as exhibiting involutional depression or schizophrenia, were compared to each
other and to a normal group of controls. Three analytical
approaches were utilized in this pilot effort: (1) perceptual (judgements by listeners), (2) acoustic (speaking
fundamental frequency) and (3) temporal (phonation/time
ratios).

                              METHOD

Subjects were 58 individuals, drawn from our developing
data-base, who met our selection criteria. The population
consisted of three groups: Group 1--seven males and eight
females who had been diagnosed as exhibiting involutional
depression (the mean ages by sex were: 59 and 63 years,
respectively); Group 2--12 males and 11 females diagnosed
as acute schizophrenics (mean ages: 24 and 36 years,
respectively) and Group 3--10 males and 10 females (mean
ages: 33 and 26 years, respectively) who exhibited no
psychotic symptoms; this last set of individuals made up the
control group. All subjects read a 132 word standardized
prose passage (Van Riper, 1963).

Three procedures were carried out. First, an experimental (S/R) tape recording, consisting of 8-10 sec. speech
samples of the 58 subjects, was constructed for an aural/
perceptual evaluation. Ten listeners, who exhibited normal
hearing but who had only minimal knowledge of the speech of

psychotics, listened to this tape. They were told that the
recordings consisted of an unequal number of speech samples
drawn from three classes of talkers: involutional depressives, schizophrenics and normals. The listeners were instructed to assign each speaker to one of these three
categories. Second, speaking fundamental frequency (SFF)
data were obtained from FFI-8, the IASCP fundamental frequency indicator (see Hollien and Harrington, 1978). Both
mean SFF and the standard deviation (SD) for the frequency
distributions were obtained. Finally, total-time and
phonation-time data were extracted from the samples by means
of another FFI software subroutine; these data permitted the
calculation of phonation/time ratios (P/T).

RESULTS

The results of the aural/perceptual procedure may be
best understood by examination of Table 1. The listeners
correctly classified the controls as "normal" 88% of the
time, demonstrating that they were able to identify talkers
of that type as non-psychotic. On this basis, it would
appear that the listeners should be able to identify the
psychotic subjects as being "non-normal"; however, such does
not seem to be the case. Specifically, while the depressives
were classified as psychotic about 60% of the time and the
schizophrenics about 70% of the time, the schizophrenics were
thought to be depressives more often than they were correctly
identified (40% vs 29%) and a roughly similar relationship
occurred for the involutional depressives (24% vs 35%).
Indeed, the three-way categorization of the two psychotic
groups (by the listeners) did not depart very greatly from
chance. Additionally, the listeners assigned well over one-
half of all talkers to the "normal" category. In short, it
does not appear that listeners of the type utilized can discriminate accurately between the two types of disorders
studied--even when they previously categorized the talker as
psychotic.

The acoustic data for speaking fundamental frequency
(SFF) can be found in Table 2. For both sexes, the psychotic
groups exhibited lower SFF than did the controls; however,
these differences were not statistically significant. Moreover, all of the values fall within limits expected for

individuals of the respective age groups (see, for example, Hollien and Shipp, 1972). The data relative to variability (S.D.) also failed to exhibit any trends (except for the possibility of a bimodal distribution) and values for all groups fell within normal limits.

Finally, the data for total-time, phonation-time and P/T ratios are presented in Table 3. Here, three relationships may be noted. First, the involutional depressives took substantially longer to read the 132 word passage than did the schizophrenics or the controls. Also, there was substantial difference between P/T ratios for the controls and those for the two psychotic groups. However, the levels for the depressives and schizophrenics were quite similar and data based on this parameter do not appear to discriminate between them. Finally, since the temporal values for the male and female schizophrenics were different, it is possible that there may be measurable sex-related differences for this disorder.

DISCUSSION

The three measurement procedures utilized in this research failed to differentiate systematically between psychotics and controls or between the two clinical populations. The aural/perceptual judgements did result in the correct classification of the controls at an acceptable level and the correct classification of depressives and schizophrenics as psychotic about two thirds of the time. However, this procedure appeared to be insensitive to speech/voice differences between the two clinical groups. The acoustic analysis resulted in slight trends for SFF to be lower for the psychotics than for the controls; however, these differences were not significant--nor were there systematic differences between the depressives and schizophrenics. Hence, it would appear that SFF does not materially shift, as a function of the psychosis, in cross-sectional populations such as these. Finally, the temporal data hinted at some possible differences among the three groups. The normal controls were different from the depressives in total reading time and different from both clinical groups for the P/T ratios. The trends found in these preliminary temporal data are only suggestive in nature; however, they may lead to improved temporal analysis techniques which can be applied to our entire data-base. It is clear that, while this experiment suggested guidelines for future research, it did not provide specific measures for differentiation among and between the groups studied. Further research will have to be carried out if the speech/voice correlates of various psychiatric conditions are to be identified.

REFERENCES

Darby, J. K. and Hollien, H. (1977). Folia Phon., 29:279-291.
Darby, J. K. and Sherk, E. (1978). Amsterdam, John Benjamin AG (in press).
Hollien, H. and Shipp, T. (1972). J. Speech Hear. Res., 15:155-159.
Hollien, H. and Harrington, W. (1978). Occasionally, 2:4-6.
Van Riper, C. (1963). Englewood Cliffs, N. Y., Prentice Hall.

Note: This research was supported in part by NINCDS grant NS-06459 and by a grant from the Scott and White Clinic, Temple, Texas.

Table 1. Summary table of responses by 10 listeners to 8-10 second samples of the speech of the three talker groups. All values are in percent.

Talker Group	N	Listener Response Involutional Depressives	Schizophrenics	Controls
Involutional Depressives	15	35	24	41
Schizophrenics	23	40	29	30
Controls	20	10	2	88

Table 2. Mean speaking fundamental frequency (SFF) in Hz,
standard deviation (SD) in tones and mean age (in
years) for normal, involutional depressive and
schizophrenic subjects.

Subjects	Males				Females			
	N	Mean Age	SFF	SD	N	Mean Age	SFF	SD
Involutional Depressives	7	59	121	1.8	8	63	181	1.5
Schizophrenics	12	24	122	1.2	11	36*	181	1.9
Controls	10	33	127	1.5	10	36	201	1.6

*Age for one subject not available.

Table 3. Total-time, phonation-time and P/T ratios for the
three groups of subjects. (T-T and P-T are in
seconds).

Subjects	Total Time		Phonation Time		P/T Ratio		
	Male	Female	Male	Female	Male	Female	Mean
Involutional Depressives	62.3	60.6	42.2	35.1	.68	.58	.63
Schizophrenics	49.4	57.0	31.9	45.5	.65	.80	.73
Controls	46.1	45.6	37.8	36.5	.82	.80	.81

CEREBELLAR INVOLVEMENT IN MOTOR CONTROL: A CONCEPT

CARL-GUSTAF SÖDERBERG AND TORGNY JENESKOG
University of Umeå

In his Textbook of Medical Physiology (1971) Guyton
points out that the cerebellum has long been called a
silent area of the brain, principally because electrical
excitation of the cerebellum does not cause any sensation
and rarely any motor movement. Yet the function of the
cerebellum is a prerequisite for normal motor movements.
This is inter alia due to the error control performed by
the cerebellum. Basically, the cerebellum is responsible
for coordination of movements as well as maintenance of
balance and muscle tonus. There are connections with
vestibular mechanisms and cranial nerve muclei which are
involved with movements of speech muscles as well as of
the eyes, the neck, the trunk and the limbs. Speech
muscles are consequently affected by cerebellar disorders.
Clinical manifestations of cerebellar dysfunction
include: (1) so-called dyssynergy (inability to coordinate
one muscle system with another, e.g., the phonatory with
the articulatory); (2) dysmetria (movements that are out
of proportion to acts performed); (3) disintegration
(failure of movements that were once acquired); (4) dys-
diadochokinesis (disturbed ability to engage in serial
repetitive movements); (5) intention tremor; (6) mask-like
facies; (7) disturbance of stance and gait; (8) ocular
and head nystagmus; (9) vertigo; (10) headache; (11)
dysarthria; (12) possible associated involvement of
nuclei of cranial nerves V, VI, VII, VIII, IX, X, and XI
(Mysak, 1976).

emphasized by Nyberg-Hansen and Horn (1972), many of the classical symptoms of cerebellar disease (e.g., dyssynergia, dysmetria, dysdiadochokinesia, decomposition of movement, speech disturbances, and even intention tremor) may be only different aspects of ataxia using this broad definition. All of them seem to be the result of the same fundamental defect, namely an error in the force and timing (the spatio-temporal patterns) of muscle activity. All these different symptoms are the result of a deficient regulation of motor activity, and thus there is no paralysis of muscle in cerebellar disease. However, there is slowness in the initiation as well as the termination of also simple motor acts, again a deficiency in the temporal aspects of muscle activity (e.g., Holmes, 1939; Brooks, 1975).

FUNCTIONAL ANATOMY OF THE CEREBELLUM

The subdivision of the cerebellum may be done following several principles (such as phylogenetic or gross-anatomical), but a functional subdivision might be more useful in a discussion of the physiology of the cerebellum. Such a subdivision may be achieved by looking at the organization of inputs to and outputs from the cerebellum. This view is important, because the cerebellar cortex has a rather simple basic structure with only two types of inputs, the climbing fibre system and the mossy fibre system. There is only one output from the cortex--the Purkinje cell axons--and the intrinsic cortical organization is similar all over the cortical layer. This means that the function of different parts of the cerebellum seems to be dependent only upon their afferent and efferent connections, i.e., from where a certain part receives its information and to which part of the nervous system its message is sent.

With these prerequisites the cerebellum has a longitudinal or sagittal organization which divides half of the cerebellum into three major zones with respect to the output from the cortex. These longitudinal zones pass almost through the whole rostro-caudal extent of the cerebellum. The Purkinje cells of a medial zone (hemivermis) project to the fastigial and lateral vestibular nuclei, those of an intermediate part (paravermis) to the anterior and posterior interpositus

nuclei, and finally the Purkinje cells of the most lateral
zone (hemisphere) project to the dentate nucleus (Walberg
and Jansen, 1964; Larsell and Jansen, 1972). In fact the
input organization is more detailed with 8 narrow sagittal
zones in each half of the cerebellum (Voogd, 1964; Oscarsson,
1973, 1976).

FUNCTIONAL LOCALIZATION IN THE CEREBELLUM

Ablation and stimulation experiments in the cat has revealed that each major longitudinal zone of the cerebellum is
concerned with different aspects of motor control, and also
that each zone seem to function more or less independent from
each other. Based upon the results of their now classical
studies, Chambers and Sprague (1955a, b) concluded that
"(a) each medial zone (hemivermal cortex, fastigial and
lateral vestibular nuclei) regulates tone, posture, loco-
motion and equilibrium of the entire body, (b) each intermediate zone (paravermal cortex, anterior and posterior
interpositus nuclei) regulates the spatially organized and
skilled movements of the ipsilateral limbs, and (c) each
lateral zone (hemispherical cortex, dentate nucleus) is
involved in the same skilled and spatially organized movements
of the ipsilateral limbs, but without apparent regulation of
their posture and tone." Thus, referring to the cerebellar
symptoms in man, disturbances of balance and/or equilibrium
as well as nystagmus generally seem to correspond to vermal
lesion symptoms in the cat, while hypotonia and ataxia are
likely to correspond to paravermal and/or hemispherical lesion
symptoms in the cat.

INFORMATION CHANNELS TO AND FROM THE CEREBELLUM

Despite the very detailed knowledge about cerebellar
anatomy and physiology which is available, no one could satisfactorily explain how the cerebellum performs its regulation
of motor acts. However, it is possible that the cerebellum
corrects errors in motor performance by comparing the motor
output to muscles with the actually performed movements
(Oscarsson, 1973). These corrections might be required because of unexpected external events (as changes in load or
resistance), which may interfere with the evolving movement

so that, for a smooth performance, the motor command signal
issued from higher centres might have to be changed (rein-
forced or weakened).

All motor performance relies upon the "correct"
activation (in spatial as well as temporal aspects) of
motoneurones, and the basis of their activation, or inhibi-
tion, is the segmental reflex pathways. There is a great
number of such reflexes originating from sense organs in
muscle, in joint capsules and in skin. Almost all of them
are polysynaptic, i.e., one or more interneurones are involved in the path from primary afferents to motoneurones.
Motor activity elicited from higher centres depends, at
least partly, upon the mobilization of a certain reflex
pattern through activation of some reflex paths and inhibi-
tion of others (Lundberg, 1966, 1975). This seems to be
true for the corticospinal tract from the cerebral motor
cortex as well as for other descending motor systems
originating in the brain stem (rubrospinal, vestibulospinal,
some reticulospinal tracts). When a "motor command signal,"
i.e., a certain spatiotemporal pattern of nerve impulses, is
sent from a motor centre down to the segmental level (brain
stem for the head, brachial and lumbar spinal cord for the
upper and lower extremities, respectively) to influence its
reflex activity, the same signal is also sent to the cerebellum via relays in certain brain stem nuclei (pontine,
lateral reticular, inferior olivary). To inform the cerebellum about the effect of the command signal at the segmental level, there are a great number of ascending pathways,
which seem to carry information to the cerebellum about the
excitability in the different reflex paths. This signal,
the "internal feed-back signal" is thus the same one as that
to the motoneurones themselves, and is the sum of primary
afferent activity and command signal. The internal feed-back
signal is relayed in the same brain stem nuclei as the command
signals. Finally, certain other ascending pathways seem to
transmit information about the performed movement, i.e., give
an "external feed-back signal."

On the basis of these three principal information channels, (1) the motor command signal, (2) the internal feed-back
signal, and (3) the external feed-back signal, the cerebellum

seems to be able to "judge" if the motor act is proceeding correctly. If it is not, going either too fast or too slow, the cerebellum changes its output from the subcortical nuclei, and this changed output (the "correction signal") is sent back to the motor centre, from which the original command signal was started, in order to reinforce or weaken the subsequent aspects of this command signal. With this hypothesis in mind, we may go back to the zonal organization of the cerebellum and recall the inputs and outputs of the different zones. The medial zone receives information from the vestibular organs (command signal) and from the spinal cord (internal and external feed-back signals), and sends information (correction signals) to the lateral vestibular nucleus and the medial reticular formation. In these nuclei originate the vestibulospinal and reticulospinal tracts, respectively, which are mainly engaged in postural motor mechanisms (antigravity muscle activity). The intermediate zone is acted upon from the cerebral motor cortex and from motor centres in the brain stem, e.g., the red nucleus (command signals) as well as from the spinal cord (internal and external feed-back signals). The output from the inter-positus nuclei (correction signals) goes back to the cerebral motor cortex or the red nucleus, from which areas the corti-cospinal and rubrospinal tracts, respectively, originate. These pathways seem to be engaged mostly in voluntary move-ments. To summarize, the medial and intermediate zones seem to be involved in the continuous regulation of motor acts, the former mainly postural and the latter mainly voluntary movements.

The lateral zone has a different organization, pri-marily concerning its input. This comes mainly (via relays in the brain stem) from wide areas of the cerebral cortex, including several association areas (Evarts and Thach, 1969; Kemp and Powell, 1971; Allen and Tsukahara, 1974), and only in scarce amount from the spinal cord. The output from this lateral zone reaches primarily the cerebral motor cortex and is thus capable of influencing the activity of the corti-cospinal tract. It has been suggested that this part of the cerebellum is involved in the planning stage for voluntary

movements, possibly giving the final spatio-temporal "shape"
to the corticospinal command signal (Evarts and Thach, 1969;
Kornhuber, 1973; Allen and Tsukahara, 1974; Evarts, 1975;
Brooks, 1975), a suggestion having support from clinical
as well as experimental investigations. Holmes (1939)
noted delays of 100-200 ms in the initiation of simple
movements in patients with unilateral cerebellar lesions,
when he compared functions in the two arms. Similar delays
in the initiation of simple arm movements in the monkey has
been revealed by Brooks and his colleagues (see Brooks,
1975) using cooling of the dentate nucleus as a method of
interfering temporarily with the cerebellar lateral zone
function.

REFERENCES

Allen, G. I. and Tsukahara, N.   (1974).   Physiol. Rev.,
     54:957-1006.
Brooks, V. B.   (1975).   Canad. J. Neurol. Sci., 2:265-277.
Chambers, W. W. and Sprague, J. G.   (1955a).   J. Comp.
     Neurol., 103:105-129.
Chambers, W. W. and Sprague, J. G.   (1955b).   Arch. Neurol.
     Psychiat., 74:653-680.
Dow, R. S.   (1969). Amsterdam: North-Holland, 392-431.
Evarts, E. V. (1975). Can. J. Phys. Pharma., 53:191-201.
Evarts, E. V. and Thach, W. T.   (1969).   Ann. Rev. Physiol.,
     31:451-498.
Holmes, G.   (1939).   Brain, 62:1-30.
Kemp, J. M. and Powell, J. P. S.   (1971). Phil. Trans. Roy.
     Soc. Lond. B., 262:441-457.
Kornhuber, H. H. (1973). Cambridge, MIT Press, 267-280.
Larsell, O. and Jansen, J. (1972). Minneapolis: U.Minn.Press.
Lundberg, A.   (1966). Stockholm: Almqvist Wiksell, 275-305.
Lundberg, A. (1975). New York: Raven Press, 253-265.
Nyberg-Hansen, R. and Horn, J. (1972). Acta Neurol. Scand.
     48, Suppl. 51:219-245.
Oscarsson, O. (1973). New York: Springer, 339-380.
Oscarsson, O. (1976). Exp. Brain Res. Suppl. 1:36-42.
Rolando, L. (1823). J. Physiol. Exp. 3:95-114.
Voogd, J. (1964). Assen: van Gorcum.
Walberg, F. and Jansen, J. (1964). J. Hirnfors. 6:338-354.

NEURAL MECHANISMS IN SPEECH PRODUCTION

PETER F. MACNEILAGE
University of Texas at Austin

In the first part of this paper I want to consider the neuromuscular stage of speech production--the stage in which the central nervous system instructs the muscles. One reason for interest in the neuromuscular stage of speech production arises from the fact that, although we agree that speech production is a uniquely human phenomenon, we know virtually nothing about the biological basis of this uniqueness. Comparison of the neuromuscular properties of the human speech musculature with those of nonhuman species is one relatively straight forward way of looking for the biological basis of this uniqueness. A second reason for studying the neuromuscular stage is to obtain parametric data on the discharge properties of motoneurons, and the mechanical properties of the muscle contractions that the motoneurons induce. Such data will contribute to the building of models of the operation of this stage of speech production. Perhaps the most basic reason for studying the neuromuscular stages is the reason once given for climbing Mt. Everest: because it is there (not a good enough reason for me in that particular case). Finally, for some of us there is a certain excitement in "listening in" to the ongoing operations of the human nervous system, while we perform our most complex motor function.

For the past few years, Harvey Sussman, Randy Powers, John Westbury and I have been conducting studies on the neuromuscular stage of speech production. Rather than consider our studies and results in detail, it is most appropriate at present to place them in a more general perspective

of present knowledge of the neuromuscular stage of mammalian
motor control.

The cell body of a motorneuron in the brain stem or
the spinal cord, together with its axon, and the muscle
fibers that it innervates is collectively termed the "Motor
Unit." Members of the so-called "pool" of motor units serving any given muscle differ according to their size. The
most important recent hypothesis about the properties of
motor units is the so-called "Size Principle (Henneman et al.,
1965). According to this principle the order of recruitment
(that is, activation) of motor units serving a muscle, together with a number of other functional properties of motor
units is determined by their size. A summary of the size
principle, at the level that one might find in an introductory neurophysiology text can be made by comparing two
hypothetical motor units--large and small. Larger motor
units have larger cell bodies and larger axons, and their
axons innervate more and larger muscle fibers. A number
of functional properties are considered to relate to cell
body size. Larger cell bodies are considered less excit-
able than small ones and are thus recruited into a movement
at higher input levels (that is, later) than small ones.
But once activated, larger cell bodies have greater sensitivity to input changes than small ones. They can be said
to have higher gains. Larger cell bodies also have shorter
afterhyperpolarization (AHP) durations than small ones. For
our purposes AHP duration can be regarded as an index of a
recovery cycle following a motorneuron discharge (a single
firing) so that short AHP durations allow higher discharge
rates. A functional property related to axon diameter is
conduction velocity of the nerve impulse. It is greater in
larger axons.

When the nerve impulse reaches the muscle, it gives
rise to muscle action potentials (MAPs) that propagate along
the muscle fibers. The mechanical consequence of each muscle
action potential is a brief contractile twitch. These
twitches are usually described, for the entire motor unit,
in terms of two main properties; twitch tension, the peak
tension value reached during the twitch, and contraction
time, time from initiation of tension increase to peak

tension. Muscle action potentials and twitch tensions are
greater in larger units as one might surmise from the larger
and more numerous muscle fibers. Contraction time is considered to be shorter in larger units which is functionally
compatible with their short AHP durations and higher discharge rates.

A warning about the size principle is in order before
considering data on speech musculature. As was recently
pointed out by Burke and Edgerton (1975), the size principle is best regarded as "a convenient shorthand that
conveys a good deal of correlated information rather than
as a universal and inflexible rule predicting the output of
a motor unit pool under all conditions" (p. 57). There
are two reasons for this caution. First, synaptic input to
motor units of different sizes may not be uniform, and
this extrinsic factor must be added to the intrinsic factors
just described in attempting to understand the neuromuscular
stage. Second, there is considerable variation in the extent
to which the intrinsic properties are correlated with each
other when different muscles are considered. So I have presented the size principle here as a basis for discussion
rather than as a set of fully agreed upon facts.

Consider now the evidence that pertains directly to
the neuromuscular stage of speech production, beginning at
the mechanical end of the motor unit, and working back toward
the cell body. I want to begin by discussing a study
(MacNeilage et al., 1978) which to our knowledge is the first
to be done on mechanical properties of motor units in speech
musculature. The technique involves recording the force
developed by the entire muscle with a force transducer, and
averaging its output over the period following several
hundred discharges of an individual motor unit (Yemm, 1977).

We measured the mechanical properties of 27 motor units
obtained from the anterior belly of digastric in three experimental subjects, and considered the relation between
these properties and the level of static jaw opening force
at which the units were recruited. Subjects were required
to produce a train of discharges of a motor unit using a
biofeedback paradigm called Motor Unit Training. In this
paradigm subjects continuously monitored the output of an

electrode placed in a muscle by viewing the output on an
oscilloscope and listening to it via a loudspeaker. Subsequently the subject's output was viewed frame by frame
on the oscilloscope screen of a PDP 12 computer and an
observer identified successive examples of the action potential of one motor unit and designated the 10 ms period
immediately preceding it and the 90 ms period immediately
following it as the portion of the force signal to be
averaged.

Measured twitch tensions ranged from .05 to about 5
grams with an average of about 2/3 gram. If one takes into
account the angular relationship between the receptive surface of the transducer and the line of force of the anterior
belly of the digastric, measured values must be approximately doubled to obtain actual values. These twitch tension values are quite comparable to those found by Milner
Brown et al. (1973) in a thumb flexor muscle, but a mean
value of 19 grams has been reported in a foot muscle (Sica
and McComas, 1971) and values ranging from .1 to 205 grams
have been reported for the masseter, with a mean value well
above 20 grams (Goldberg and Derfler, 1977). Incidentally,
it is clear from informal observation that only the smaller
of the units we studied participate in speech gestures.

Consistent with the size principle units tended strongly
to be recruited in order of magnitude of their twitch tensions. So far I do not know any counterexamples of this
finding in studies such as this one that have involved slow
changes in static force level applied to a whole muscle.
But the significance of this finding for the size principle
in general is not entirely clear because of findings in
studies of cat let musculature (Stephens and Stuart, 1975)
and baboon hand musculature (Phillips, 1969) that twitch
tensions of motor units are not positively related to conduction velocities of the motor unit axons. Thus, although
units seem to be recruited in order of magnitude of their
mechanical response they may not be recruited in order of
neuron size. If not, some other principle is required at
the level of the cell body to explain the recruitment order.

Contraction times of the motor units in our study range
from 21 to 56 msec with a mean of 29 msec. These values are

somewhat longer than those reported for cat extraocular
muscle (5-8 ms) (Bach-y-Rita, 1971) and some intrinsic
laryngeal muscles (e.g., 12 ms for the thyroarytenoid)
(Sawashima, 1974). (No human data is available for these
muscles.) But they are shorter than those reported for
human muscles of mastication--the masseter and temporalis
muscles--and other human skeletal muscles. For example,
mean values for masseter and temporalis (Yemm, 1977;
Goldberg and Derfler, 1977) and thumb flexor (Milner Brown
et al., 1973) have been reported in the 50-60 ms range, and
a 60-65 ms range has been reported for the biceps (Buchtal
and Schmalbruch, 1970). There was no sign of the expected
finding from the size principle that later recruited units
would have shorter contraction times. The situation in
the literature regarding this relationship is presently
quite confusing. The inverse relation between size and
contraction time which was incorporated in the size principle as summarized earlier came from studies of cat foot
and leg muscles. But the relation has not been found in the
hand muscle of the baboon (Phillips, 1969). It has been
found in one human hand muscle but not in another. And in
the human masticatory muscles either it has not been found,
or, in the case of two individual subjects, a positive
relation has been found (Yemm, 1977). Furthermore, in one
of the cat leg muscles, the gastrocnemius, the relation is
only found if one lumps together motor units of different
histochemical type in terms of muscle fiber composition.
If these types are analysed separately, only the so-called
"slow" units which are relatively small in size show the
inverse relation between size and contraction time (Stephen
and Stuart, 1975). In larger units no significant relation
was observed. Thus, although differences in typical contraction times across muscles would seem to have obvious
functional significance as they would partly determine the
speed and flexibility with which a muscle can respond, the
role of contraction time within muscles remains to be ex-
plicated.

There is no way to directly determine the physiological
properties of the axon and cell body of motoneurons in human
subjects. We are thus forced into indirect methods of determination with their accompanying problems of inference.

One cell body characteristic we have tried to determine is
AHP duration. In order to do this we accepted the assumption
of Person and Kudina (1972) that AHP durations are indirectly
reflected in the discharge patterns of human motor units dis-
charging at constant rates during natural activation. The
conclusion arose from a study of human thigh muscle. In
this study they found that at relatively low steady discharge rates (rates with mean interspike intervals longer
than 100 msec) successive interspike intervals were un-
correlated with each other. On the other hand, at higher
discharge rates, with mean interspike intervals less than
80 msec, the durations of adjacent intervals were negatively
correlated; that is, there was an alternation of relatively
short and relatively long intervals. They considered that
this alternation occurs when mean discharge interval becomes short because discharges begin to impinge on the AHP
recovery cycle. According to this reasoning AHP durations
of these motor units corresponded to values of mean interspike intervals below which negative correlations within a
spike train would begin to occur. In their study these
intervals ranged from 80-100 msec. We tried to find the
pattern observed by Person and Kudina in a number of cranial
muscles (MacNeilage et al., 1977). In addition we hoped
to be able to determine AHP durations of individual motor
units using the same technique, to determine whether later
recruited units had shorter AHP durations and greater sensitivity to input changes in accordance with the size principle. Experimental subjects were placed in the Motor Unit
Training paradigm in which they were required to discharge
motor units at various steady rates. A total of 1613 two-
second periods of steady discharge were analyzed for 79 motor
units from three subjects. Muscles studied were: Anterior
Belly of Digastric, Masseter, Genioglossus, Orbicularis Oris,
Depressor Labii Inferioris, Quadratus Labii Superioris, and
for comparison purposes, the Biceps. In all cases negative
correlations were observed at the shortest interspike intervals. Regions of crossover to negative correlations ranged
from approximately 55 ms to 35 ms for the cranial muscles.
These crossover regions seem plausible as estimates of AHP
duration. Motor units from cranial muscles are known to
have higher characteristic discharge rates than units in
skeletal muscle, and as AHP duration is considered a de-
terminant of discharge rate the crossover regions would be

expected to be at shorter interspike intervals than the
80-100 ms region found in thigh muscle by Person and
Kudina. As expected, crossover regions in cranial muscles
were at shorter intervals than the crossover region of
approximately 70 ms observed for the biceps.

   We were able to obtain clear crossovers in a few
individual motor units. Unfortunately, we were not able
to obtain cross-overs in enough individual units to test
the hypothesis that later recruited units possessed shorter
AHP durations. However, we were able to indirectly test
the hypothesis that later recruited units show greater sensitivity to input changes. In all 10 cases in which a comparison could be made, the second recruited unit showed
greater changes in output when the subject voluntarily
changed the amount of activation of the muscle than did
the first recruited unit. It has been shown by Kernell
(1966) that larger, later recruited units in cat hind limb
musculature are more sensitive to input changes introduced
directly into the motoneuron cell body by means of a micro-
electrode. In our case, although we assume that the greater
sensitivity of later recruited units is, as Kernell determined for the cat, due to intrinsic properties of the cell
bodies of their motoneurons, we cannot rule out the possibility that they receive relatively greater increases in
input when the subject attempts to activate the muscle more
forcefully.

   I mentioned that one of the aims of the work we have
been describing is the development of models of the neuromuscular stage of speech movement control. We are obviously
still a long way from the model building stage. Nevertheless it might be of interest to consider in a speculative way
one question one question of particular importance in model
building, the question of how many motor units there are in
a muscle and what the size of the muscle fiber component
of the units might be. Let us consider these questions for
the anterior belly of digastric. Let us assume, from the
measurements we have made on twitch tensions, that the mean
twitch tension of a motor is 1.3 grams. Many determinations
have been made in animal studies of the relation between
twitch tensions of motor units and the maximum steady tension

that they can develop. This latter is termed Tetanic Tension. As these estimates center on a tetanus: twitch
ration of 4 or 5:1, let us assume that the mean tetanic
tension of our ABD units is five grams. Many determinations
have been made in animal studies of the tetanic tension
developed by whole muscles, and estimates range from .6 to
4 kg per square centimeter of cross sectional area of the
muscle. Let us assume that the ABD has a value of 2 kg per
square centimeter. Let us also guess that the ABD has a
cross sectional area of about 15 sq mm. That is, 15% of a
square centimeter. Thus, the ABD should develop a tetanic
tension of 15% of 2 kg (namely 300 grams). And we can compute that it would take 60 motor units with an average tension of five grams to produce 300 grams of tension. And we
can compute further that the average cross sectional area
of the fibers of an average sized unit is about 1/4 of a
square millimeter. These calculations ignore the fact that
the twitch tensions of units in the ABD are in all probability not normally distributed. Allowing for the possibility that these estimates of unit number and size might be
wrong by an order of magnitude in either direction, I can
conclude that there may be from 30 to 120 motor units in the
ABD and the average cross sectional area of the fibers of
an average sized unit may be between 1/8 and 1/2 of a square
millimeter. Finally, if the average cross sectional area
of a single muscle fiber is approximately 900 sq microns,
then there may be about 280 muscle fibers in an average
sized unit, give or take an order of magnitude. This
estimate can be compared with an estimate of five fibers
per unit in cat extraocular muscles (Peachey, 1971). (This
is probably an underestimate) and 400-800 fibers in the
medial gastrocnemius of the cat (Burke and Tsairis, 1973).

So far we have done very little work on the behavior
of motor units during actual speech gestures. This is because of a conviction that the information I have already
presented was a necessary base for the understanding of motor
unit behavior in speech gestures. However, we do have some
results (Sussman et al., 1977), and I want to summarize some
of these results now.

We have found evidence from a study of the ABD that
suggests that, as in the isometric case, units are activated

in speech gestures in ascending order of their twitch
tensions. This conclusion was derived indirectly from observation of the amplitudes of the muscle action potentials
and their relation to recruitment order (Olson et al., 1968).
In the case of 6 sets of 3 motor units every later recruited
unit had a higher amplitude than any units that preceded it,
and, in general, amplitude doubled for each successive unit
recruited.

Speech at the movement level consists of a number of
rapid articulatory and phonatory gestures superimposed on
somewhat slower respiratory gestures. Rates of 14 segments
per second, or one segment every 70 msec have been cited for
conversational speech (Lenneberg, 1967). A most important
property of motor units in this context is that they are
extremely sensitive to rate of change of input. Under
steady input conditions it is difficult to obtain discharge
rates higher than 60 impulses per second, and tetanic tension levels, as I mentioned before, are only 4-5 times twitch
tension levels. On the other hand interspike intervals
equivalent to discharge rates of up to 620 i.p.s. have been
observed in monkey extraocular muscles during saccadic movements (Robinson, 1970) and extremely high transient tension levels can be obtained, presumably for the "purpose"
of combating inertia. It will be necessary for us to understand this dynamic sensitivity of motor units in speech
muscles, but at present all we have done is illustrate it.
We have studied a pair of motor units in the ABD under both
the steady input conditions of motor unit training and conditions of rapid input change associated with speech gestures. These two units were recruited at a very similar
static force levels although one unit was consistently recruited later than the other, and, in accordance with the
size principle, was 2.2 times as sensitive to static input
changes. These two units began discharge at similar low
rates and maximal discharge rates reached under motor unit
training remained quite low. On the other hand discharge
rates as computed from the first interspike interval in the
production of the syllable /paep/ were greater than the
maximum under static condition, and significantly greater
for the second recruited unit. In addition during the jaw
opening gesture for /ae/ the second unit showed interspike

intervals equivalent to discharge rates of up to 208 i.p.s. and showed, as expected, a greater dynamic range than the earlier recruited unit.

Finally, for this part of the talk, let me try to give you some idea of what I meant by saying that study of the neuromuscular stage of speech might help us to understand the biological uniqueness of the human speech producer. You have observed that there is a confusing variation of motor unit physiological properties across different species and across different muscles in the same species. Associated with this there is comparably confusing variation of the biochemical properties of muscle fibers that I have so far avoided discussing. I believe we must assume that these variations result from functional specializations and reflect in important ways the biological makeup of different species. Some of these specializations can presently be guessed at with some certainty. To take a straightforward example, contraction times of motor units in rat rib muscles are much shorter than in human rib muscles because rats breathe at faster rates than we do. Take a more complicated example (Burke et al., 1976). The medial gastrocnemius muscle of the cat (and other mammals) is a leg flexor muscle which has a variety of functional roles·for which the motor units of the muscle (and their innervation) seem to be suited. There are a number of small nonfatigueable early recruited units with slow contraction times that can collectively generate the low tension levels sufficient to regulate posture during standing. There is a second set of larger later recruited units with fast contraction times, but also nonfatigueable, that together with the slow units generate enough tension to control walking. Finally, there is a set of large units with fast contraction times, but fatigueable, which with the other two sets can generate the high tension levels required in fight or flight situations. The proposition I am making is that if there has been a development of specialized functions at the neuromuscular stage of the human speech mechanism, this development can be documented by comparison of human data with data from our close nonhuman relations.

(The second part of the oral presentation of this paper
began with a review of evidence for a three-stage view of
the control of speech production. It consisted of an initial
auditory targeting stage, a spatial targeting stage for
some purposes, and a stage of state-dependent movement control based on target information. The material reviewed is
discussed in MacNeilage (1978) and is, therefore, omitted
from the present paper.)

In the remainder of this talk, I want to consider
evidence from the area of aphasia which bears on the three-
stage view of speech movement control, particularly on the
spatial targeting stage. In a fairly casual look at the
literature on aphasia, it is easy to find aphasic syndromes
that appear to involve a breakdown in speech production
primarily at the movement control stage, or at the auditory
targeting stage. Some symptoms of Broca's aphasia can easily
be conceived as resulting from damage to a movement control
system. Speech segment production is slow and laborious
with an appreciable number of distortions of segments and
greatest difficulty with segments that can be considered
most difficult to produce. Although Wernicke's aphasia is
considered to be primarily a disorder of <u>auditory</u> <u>compre-
hension</u>, speech <u>production</u> is characterized by frequent
phonemic substitutions usually called paraphasias, and these
paraphasias can be conceived of as resulting from a defiict
in the auditory targeting stage. There is no simple first
approximation to be made in identification of an aphasic
syndrome that involves a deficit in a spatial targeting
stage of speech production. But on closer examination, I
believe a case can be made that the syndrome named Conduction
Aphasia includes a deficit in spatial targeting. Prior to
making this case a short description of the syndrome is in
order.

In a recent review, Green and Howes (1977) present the
following clinical picture of the linguistic symptoms:
auditory comprehension is normal or mildly impaired; reading
is moderately impaired; speech production is haltingly
fluent; it is moderately too severely impaired, particularly
by phonemic paraphasias and grammatical errors, with most

PETER F. MACNEILAGE

severe impairment in nonspontaneous speech situations
(repetition, naming, oral reading); writing is severely
impaired, but copying is not. There are four reasons why
I believe conduction aphasia may involve a deficit in
spatial targeting. First, the dominant speech production
symptom of phonemic paraphasias is consistent with this view.
Second, conduction aphasia is typically, though not always
associated with apraxia, and apraxia would be expected to
result from a deficit in spatial target function. Third,
the lesions associated with the syndrome are in the parietal
lobe which has traditionally been associated with spatial
functions. Fourth, there is no alternative explanation in
the literature that has a good claim to being preferable to
the one I am suggesting. Let me take up these claims in
reverse order. First, the alternative explanations. Essentially the same view of the neurological basis of conduction
aphasia as the one held by Wernicke when he coined the term
"Conduction Aphasia" is still held today by many theorists,
most prominently by Geschwind. For example, Goodglass and
Geschwind (1977) have stated that: "This syndrome is attributed to the anatomical dissociation of Wernicke's auditory
speech area from Broca's area, thus disabling the guidance
of speech output by auditory input. This effect is thought
to be produced by an interruption of the arcuate fasciculus
--the bundle of nerve fibers that has been identified as
connecting the Wernicke and Broca zones" (pp. 418-419).

Although this hypothesis may be partially correct it
has, in my opinion, major problems associated with the location of the lesion in cases where this has been established.
On the one hand there are reported cases of conduction
aphasia that were not accompanied by damage to the arcuate
fasciculus (Potzl and Stengel, 1937). On the other hand,
all cases of conduction aphasia for which autopsy data has
been presented, have involved damage to the cerebral cortex,
typically quite extensive. A problem with the disconnection
view is that this damage is considered to have no symptomatic
consequences for either linguistic functions or nonlinguistic
functions.

Another hypothesis that has received some attention
is that conduction aphasia involves a deficit in auditory-
verbal short-term memory (Tzortzis and Albert, 1974). This

hypothesis is mainly directed towards explaining the great
difficulty that conduction aphasics have with repetition
of auditory-verbal stimulus material. But the main problem
with this hypothesis is that the speech production problems,
including the phonemic paraphasias, that occur in the
repetition situations, also typically occur in oral reading and in spontaneous speech where short-term memory
demands would not seem to be great.

     In my opinion the neurological evidence as to the
lesion site in conduction aphasia is also consistent with
the hypothesis that it involves a spatial defect. The
supramarginal gyrus of the parietal lobe and/or the temporal
lobe immediately adjacent to it are invariably involved in
conduction aphasia. Green and Howes (1977) summarize the
neuroanatomical data from the 25 cases reported in the literature for which autopsies were performed, in the following
way: "Thirteen cases involved an area extending from the
temporal gyrus to the supramarginal gyrus. In nine cases
the temporal area is spared and the principal damage is to
the supramarginal gyrus. The remaining three cases involve
the temporal area but spare the supramarginal gyrus." Thus,
the general picture is of damage to the perisylvian region,
at the confluence of the temporal and parietal lobes,
centering on the supramarginal gyrus.

     It is well known that a primary role of the parietal
lobe in general is the control of spatial functions. And
in a recent review of constructional apraxia, Warrington
(1969) concluded that whereas the right parietal lobe is
more concerned with spatial perceptual functions, the left
parietal lobe is specialized for spatial functions in the
service of sequential motor behavior.

     More specifically, the supramarginal gyrus itself can
be considered, in terms of its location and its connecti-
vities, to be, in the traditional sense, associative cortex
for the somatic sensory face and upper limb projection areas
immediately anterior to it. It is therefore the area that
one would most expect to be devoted to a space coordinate
system underlying vocal tract movement and upper limb movement.

A number of writers have noted that speech production
disturbances resulting from parietal lobe lesions can
properly be considered within the class of apraxias. These
writers include Hecaen (1967) and Kimura (1976). It is
well accepted that supramarginal gyrus lesions in the left
hemisphere are commonly associated with facial apraxia.
This fact has been specifically commented on by Geschwind
(1965). As noted earlier they are also associated with
severe writing disturbances. This fact is difficult to
interpret, as all aphasic syndromes seem to involve writing
disturbances. Nevertheless, it is consistent with the present hypothesis that this difficulty does not extend to
copying. Copying removes the necessity for unassisted
spatial conceptualization underlying movements in a way
that the stimulus in a speech repetition paradigm does not,
because it is not continuously available. Consequently,
as Geschwind (1965) points out, when required to repeat
words: "The patient often says 'say it again' which may
give the impression of not having heard or comprehended
(p. 627)" (though we know from other evidence that comprehension is minimally impaired). In the present view this
maneuver provides repeated auditory support for the faulty
spatial specification stage.

Supramarginal gyrus lesions are also associated with
what Liepmann (1900) originally called "ideokinetic apraxias"
involving manual control. He considered the disorder to
involve a stage intermediate between "the ideational scheme
of movement" and the "kinetic engram." In accordance with
this notion, ideokinetic apraxia was considered to result
from damage at a site intermediate between the posterior
parietal, and anterior occipital lobes, the supposed locus
of ideational apraxia, and sensorimotor cortex, the site
for "limbkinetic apraxia." The main difficulties with
ideokinetic apraxias lie in carrying out movements to command, or imitation, and in the appropriate handling of
objects. As Brown (1972) puts it: "the alteration concerns partial movements only, these being out of harmony
with the whole." The similarity of these interpretations
to the interpretation of conduction aphasia presented here
is obvious. Some further similarities deserve note. First,

as in conduction aphasia, monitoring of behavior is good,
suggesting intact perceptual functions. Second, just as
spontaneous speech is considered to be better than imitated
speech in conduction aphasia, spontaneous motor behavior is
more efficient than imitation in these apraxias. Finally,
consider the nature of the spatial functions involved in
conduction aphasia and ideokinetic apraxia. Ajuriaguerra
and Tissot (1969) point out that ideomotor apraxia is
"limited to one type of space, namely the space centered
on the body." Speech production also involves movements
within space centered on the body, as MacNeilage (1970)
noted in describing speech targets as "intrinsic." In addition Lashley (1951) notes that when one is asked to write
with the left hand, what remains in common with normal writing is "a reproduction of movements in relation to the space
coordinates of the body."

I have assumed that the paraphasic speech of conduction
aphasics reflects a deficit in spatial targeting. However,
paraphasias are also common in the speech of Broca's
aphasics and Wernicke's aphasics. I had initially thought
that the speech error patterns of conduction aphasics would
directly reflect spatial targeting problems by revealing
a high proportion of place errors and a low proportion of
voicing errors. And I was encouraged to find, in a 1964
analysis of Conduction Aphasia by Dubois et al., the statement that "substitutions from voiced to voiceless consonants
or the reverse are very rare." But in other analyses, for
example, that by Blumstein (1973) and a recent analysis by
Burns and Canter (1977) this pattern of errors is not very
apparent. In retrospect, I believe that although this
pattern should be observed in an occasional patient it
should not necessarily be a typical result. If the assignment of auditory targeting functions to posterior temporal
cortex and the assignment of spatial targeting functions to
the posterior parietal lobe is correct, the following consequences for speech error patterns should follow from
lesions in these regions. Lesions in either temporal cortex
or underlying subcortex should result in paraphasias of all
kinds as either the formulation of auditory targets, or the
transmission of target information should be impaired. If
parietal subcortex alone is involved the same result would

be expected, as is claimed by the proponents of the disconnection syndrome. But if parietal cortex alone was
damaged, errors of place of articulation would be expected
to result from damage to the spatial targeting mechanism
but few voicing errors would be expected because transmission pathways from temporal cortex control would be
unimpaired. This is perhaps being excessively localiza-
tionistic. In addition, pure subcortical or cortical
lesions are by no means common occurrences. Nevertheless
it might be of value to consider the relative amount of
cortical and subcortical damage in conduction aphasics because of the likelihood that cortical and subcortical
structures have different functions.

I have hypothesized that conduction aphasia results at
least partially from damage to a spatial target mechanism.
Arguments are that a targeting deficit would be expected to
result in phonemic paraphasias, the lesion site for conduction aphasia, centering on the posterior parietal lobe,
would be expected to be associated with spatial deficits,
and that other apraxias that probably result from spatial
deficits typically coexist with conduction aphasia. Finally,
I am encouraged to present the hypothesis because of the
absence of other satisfactory hypotheses as to the nature of
the deficit in Conduction Aphasia.

REFERENCES

Ajuriaguerra, J. De and Tissot, R.   (1969).   Amsterdam,
     North-Holland.
Bach-y-Rita, P.   (1971).   New York, Academic Press.
Blumstein, S. A.   (1973). The Hague, Mouton.
Brown, J. W.   (1972).   Springfield, Ill., Charles C. Thomas.
Buchtal, F. and Schmalbruch, H.   (1970).   Acta Physiol. Scand.
     79:435-452.
Burke, R. E. and Tsairis, P.   (1973).   J. Physiol., 234:749-
     765.
Burke, R. E. and Edgerton, V. R.   (1975).   New York,
     Academic Press.
Burke, R. E., Rymer, W. Z. and Walsh, J. V.   (1976).
     J. Neurophysiol, 39:447-458.
Burns, M. S. and Canter, G. J.   (1977).   Brain Lang.
     4:492-507.

Dubois, J., Hecaen, H., Angelergues, H., de Chatelier, R.
    and Marcie, P. (1964). Neuropsych., 2:9.
Geschwind, N. (1965). Brain, 88:585.
Goldberg, L. J. and Derfler, B. (1977). J. Neurophysiol.
    40:879-890.
Goodglass, H. and Geschwind, N. (1976). New York,
    Academic Press.
Green, E. and Howes, D. H. (1977). New York, Academic
    Press, 123.
Hecaen, H. (1967). New York, Grune and Stratton.
Henneman, E., Somjen, G. and Carpenter, D. O. (1965).
    J. Neurophys., 28:569-580.
Kernell, D. (1966). Science, 152:1637-1639.
Kimura, D. (1976). New York, Academic Press, 145-156.
Lashley, K. S. (1951). New York, Wiley.
Lenneberg, E. H. (1967). New York, Wiley.
Liepmann, H. (1900). Mtschr. Psychiat. Neurol., 8:15,
    102, 181.
MacNeilage, P. F. (1970). Psychol. Rev., 77:182.
MacNeilage, P. F. (1978). Child Phon., Percep., Prod.,
    Deviat.
MacNeilage, P. F., Sussman, H. M. and Powers, R. K. (1977).
    J. Phon., 5:135-147.
MacNeilage, P. F., Sussman, H. M. and Westbury, J. R.
    (1978). J. Acoust. Soc. Am. (In press).
Milner-Brown, H. S., Stein, R. B. and Yemm, R. (1973).
    J. Physiol., 230:359-370.
Olson, C. B., Carpenter, D. O. and Henneman, E. (1968).
    Arch. Neurol., 19:591-597.
Peachey, L. (1971). New York, Academic Press, 47-66.
Person, R. S. and Kudina, L. P. (1972). EEG Clin.
    Neurophys., 32:471-483.
Phillips, C. G. (1969). Proc. Roy. Soc. B., 173:141-174.
Potzl, O. and Stengel, E. (1937). Jahrbuch. Psychiat.,
    53:174.
Robinson, D. A. (1970). J. Neurophys., 33:393-404.
Sawashima, M. (1974). The Hague, Mouton and Co., 230-248.
Sica, R. E. P. and McComas, A. J. (1971). J. Neurol.
    Neurosurg. Psychiat., 34:114-120.
Stephens, J. A. and Stuart, D. G. (1975). Brain Res.
    91:177-195.

Sussman, H. M., MacNeilage, P. F. and Powers, R. K.   (1977).
    J. Speech Hear. Res., 21:127-144.
Tzortzis, C. and Albert, M.   (1974).   Neuropsych., 12:355-
    366.
Warrington, E. K.   (1969).   Amsterdam, North-Holland.
Yemm, R.   (1977).   J. Physiol., 265:163-174.

IMPAIRMENT OF VERBAL AND NONVERBAL ORAL MOVEMENTS AFTER LEFT HEMISPHERE DAMAGE

CATHERINE A. MATEER
University of Washington

This paper is based on studies I conducted with Dr. Doreen Kimura at the University of Western Ontario which were concerned with the relationships between verbal and nonverbal oral movement impairment in patients with unilateral hemispheric damage and in patients undergoing thalamic nuclei stimulation. The results of these studies suggest: (1) that all patients demonstrating aphasia, which on one level might be considered an impairment in verbal oral movement, are impaired in the production of nonverbal oral movements as well, (2) that this impairment in complex oral movements, both verbal and nonverbal, suggests a fundamental role of the left hemisphere in the control of certain kinds of motor control, possibly the successive attainment of discrete oral configurations or targets, and may provide the basis of left hemisphere "dominance" for speech and language behaviors and (3) that this asymmetry for neural control of oral motor behavior during speech accepted at a cortical level is also evident lower in the nervous system at at least the level of the thalamus.

Since at least the time of Broca (1861), it has been known that the left hemisphere of the brain is the one primary for speech. Almost as early as this concept was the acceptance of a dichotomy between expressive aphasic deficits (Broca's aphasia or motor aphasia) and receptive aphasic deficits (Wernicke's or sensory aphasia). However, in reality, all aphasic patients have difficulty in speech production at some level. The classification of aphasias into "fluent" and

"nonfluent" speaks to the nature of the impairment in the
production aspects of speech. The speech of nonfluent aphasics
is characterized by effortful, halting production often even
of single phonemes. In contrast, fluent aphasics appear to
produce speech quite easily and effortlessly, but with many
errors in the selection and ordering of sounds and words. The
association with aphasia of defects in the production of nonverbal movements, termed "oral apraxia," has been known since
the time of Hughlings Jackson (1878) who described an aphasic
patient who was unable to protrude his tongue on command but
was observed making spontaneous licking movements. Subsequently, many investigators (DeRenzi, Pieczuro and Vignolo,
1966; Poeck and Kerschensteiner, 1975) have found imitation
of oral movements to be most impaired in Broca's aphasics or
cases of nonfluency. Oral apraxia has not typically, however,
been associated with fluent aphasia and so linguistic rather
than motor impairment explanations have been invoked.

     A major difficulty, however, with studies of nonverbal
oral movement impairment is that tests for oral apraxia have
typically employed only single, relatively simple movements
of the oral musculature such as protruding the lips or
lateralizing the tongue. A fluent aphasic does not have
particular difficulty imitating or producing individual speech
sounds so one might not expect him to have difficulty producing isolated nonspeech movements. Perhaps putting several non-
speech movements together according to some required pattern,
a task at least a step more comparable to the requirements of
speech would result in an impairment in fluent aphasics. This
was the hypothesis put forward in one of the studies to be
discussed. The results suggested that while nonfluent aphasics had difficulty on all types of oral movement, simple and
complex, verbal and nonverbal, fluent aphasics had selective
difficulty with the more complex movements, whether verbal
or not. The results of this study were based on a sample of
62 right handed patients selected on the basis of medical
evidence for unilateral hemispheric lesions of vascular or
neoplastic origin. Patients were classified as aphasic or
nonaphasic on the basis of a cut off score on items selected
from a standard aphasia battery. Aphasic patients were
classified as fluent or nonfluent on the basis of their mean
length of response (temporal as well as semantic aspects

considered). These criteria yielded four patient groups;
21 right hemisphere damaged patients, 21 left hemisphere
damaged nonaphasic patients, 12 left hemisphere damaged
fluent aphasic patients and 8 left hemisphere damaged nonfluent aphasic patients. In addition, 24 age matched non-
neurological control subjects were given all tests.

Three of the tasks were verbal--the imitation of single
phonemes, the imitation of sequences of three different nonmeaningful consonant-vowel combinations, such as /daʃegu/
or /tʃunevoi/ and the imitation of familiar words and phrases.
Two tasks were nonverbal--the imitation of simple oral movements such as tongue protrusion or lateralization and the
imitation of three such movements in a sequence, for example,
tongue lateralization, mouth opening and lip protrusion. As
hypothesized, the nonfluent aphasics were the only group
which was impaired on the imitation of single phonemes or
single oral movements. Significantly, however, the fluent
aphasics, as well as the nonfluent aphasics, were impaired
relative to the nonaphasic left or right hemisphere damaged
patients on the imitation of multiple speech sounds and
multiple nonverbal oral movements. Deficits in coordinating
oral movements appeared to be fundamental to most aphasic
impairments, the meaningfulness of the responses not being
a critical factor in the appearance of the defect.

This impairment was not explicable on the basis of a
memory impairment, since fluent aphasics were as able as
nonaphasic patients to perform a visual sequential memory
task which did not require a complex motor response and to
select and order pictures of the movements which had been
produced. There was also no relationship between sensory
deficits (pressure sensitivity or two point discrimination
thresholds) and impairments on the motor tasks suggesting
that whatever motor skills were being disrupted were not ones
primarily dependent on tactile modes of sensory feedback.
What then were some characteristics of, some clues to the
nature of the impairment? First, the impairment on the multiple oral movements task was a stable one in both fluent and
nonfluent aphasics, rather than a simple delay or reduction in
learning capacity for acquisition of this novel, unfamiliar
task. Although even control subjects did not perform at

ceiling on this task, they, together with right hemisphere
damaged patients and left hemisphere damaged nonaphasic
patients demonstrated typical rising acquisition curves
when three trials were available for correct production of
the movement sequence. That is, when three trials were
available, the nonaphasic groups achieved a mean of 4.67
out of 5 correct movement sequences, three correct movements
in the required order. In contrast, performance of aphasic
patients did not improve over trials, the impairment appearing relatively unalterable over a short period of time. In
fact, only two fluent aphasics produced even one (and then
only one) movement sequence correctly.

The responses on the multiple nonverbal oral movements
task had been videotaped and were further analyzed for the
kind of errors produced on the task. Nonfluent aphasics
produced amorphous, difficult to describe oral movements
continually altering the oral configuration. The remaining
groups produced relatively discrete classifiable responses;
omissions, reversals (two correct movements produced out of
order), unique errors (movements bearing no required ones)
and perseverative errors (movements previously produced but
incorrect in the current context). The groups did not differ
in the percentage of total errors accounted for by omission
errors, reinforcing the idea that the impairment is not related primarily to a memory deficit. Reversal errors also
did not discriminate the groups so it is not that aphasics
produce the correct movements and only sequence them incorrectly. Fluent aphasics, however, produce significantly
more unique errors and perseverative errors. Thus, although
isolated nonverbal oral movements could be produced easily,
the requirement for a change from one target oral configuration to another resulted in an impairment, with a tendency
to reproduce a previously attained target configuration.

Correlations within patients between errors on verbal
and nonverbal oral movements were highly significant: between
single nonverbal and verbal oral movements .89, and between
multiple verbal and nonverbal oral movements .87. When the
recordings of verbal responses on the nonmeaningful syllables
reletition task were analyzed for errors in the same manner
as for errors on the nonverbal oral movements task in a single
patient, the pattern of error type in terms of percentage

per total errors was essentially the same. That is, there
was a high proportion of perseverative errors. Although
such errors have often been classified as substitutions in
previous phonemic analyses, the high frequency of occurrence
of some phonemes as opposed to others in some sense justifies
their categorization as perseverative. Thus, in addition to
the strong correlation between verbal and nonverbal oral
movements in the degree of impairment, there is a strong
correlation between the kinds of errors made on these tasks
within the left hemisphere damaged aphasic group.

Another study using the same subject sample required
(1) the repeated production of a single CV syllable (each
of /ba/, /da/ and /ga/) as rapidly as possible over a 5
second interval and (2) the repeated production of the three
syllable unit/badaga/ over a 5 second interval. Nonfluent
aphasics produced fewer of the same CV syllable over 5 seconds
than the other groups. Fluent aphasics, although able to
produce repeatedly a single CV syllable as accurately and
quickly as the other groups, produced far fewer /badaga/ sequences over the 5 seconds than the nonaphasic patients,
many fluent aphasics being unable to produce even a single
correct /badaga/ sequence. Again, the requirement to move
from one articulatory posture or target oral configuration
to another resulted in impaired performance in the fluent
aphasic patients.

The apparent dissociability in the control of single
and multiple oral movements might suggest at least two
systems operating in the motor control of speech, one which
is involved in the production of relatively discrete oral
movements, perhaps of phonemes, and another operating to
effect transitions from one movement to another in a smooth
and orderly way and probably thus involved in the selection
or programming of movements into longer sequences. The
anatomical areas corresponding to such a schema might be the
anterior speech area for the control of single units and the
posterior speech area for the programming of successive units.
(See Benson, 1967, re: anatomical correlates of fluency
and nonfluency.) MacNeilage's suggestions with regard to a
spatial targeting system operating for speech production
which could provide for the production of oral tract configurations or targets which correspond to particular

acoustic results rather than a system which would code invariant movement patterns for speech production is most
appealing in light of the results of these investigations.
Perhaps it is the ability to achieve successive oral configurations or targets by programming on line the pattern
of muscular activity required for achievement of the target
which is impaired in left hemisphere damaged aphasic aphasic
patients. The impairment on the nonverbal oral movement
task which has no auditory component suggests that auditory
feedback is not integral to such an oral target theory.
Kimura, in reporting that left hemisphere damaged patients
were impaired in the performance of complex manual tasks,
suggested that while the right hemisphere appears to be
specialized for off the body, external spatial judgement and
skill, the left hemisphere might be specialized for an internal, within the body spatial system allowing for the
effective placement and movement of body parts, including both
oral and brachial structures and musculature, in relation to
each other or to a body schema.

The final study which I have only time to mention was
concerned with investigating the effect of electrical stimulation of the left or right ventrolateral nucleus of the thalamus on a motor aspect of speech production. Previous studies
had suggested an asymmetric effect on naming ability per se,
but reports of asymmetric motor effects with thalamic stimulation were inconsistent. Patients undergoing stereotaxic
surgical lesions of VL nucleus (left N=10, right N=12) for
relief of dyskinesias were presented with a task in which
they were required to produce the three syllable phrase
"This is a _____" and the one syllable name of a visually
presented object depicted by a line drawing. On random
presentations, electrical stimulation just below reported
sensory threshold was applied from the onset of the stimulus.
The duration of the verbal response on correct naming trials
was determined from the start of to the completion of the
four syllable utterance. There were no significant difference
in the duration of the verbal responses during stimulation
and nonstimulation trials in the right thalamic electrode
placement group and these trials did not differ from the left
placement nonstimulation trial. Only during left VL stimulation was the duration of the verbal response significantly

longer. This pattern of increased duration is evident in every case of left thalamic stimulation and the subjective impression of the tape reviewer was that increased duration was associated in all cases with increased slurring and articulatory distortion. Thus, the asymmetry in some aspects of oral motor control seen at cortical levels in the brain is evident at the level of the thalamus and this further supports the idea that a fundamental role of the left hemisphere is the mediation of certain aspects of motor activity and skill.

In conclusion, I would like to speculate on the implications of these studies. A left hemisphere based system for the control of complex motor responses requiring a high degree of precision in terms of spatial and temporal organization might provide the current substrate as well as the developmental substrate, in an evolutionary sense, for the highly skilled motor requirements of both speech and dominant hand use. Meaningfulness, symbolic association and familiarity do not seem to be critical factors in the appearance of oral movement defects after left hemisphere damage. What does appear to be critical is the requirement for successive achievement of discrete target oral configurations.

REFERENCES

Benson, F. D. (1967). Cortex, 3:373-394.
Broca, P. (1861). Bulle. Soc. Anat. Paris, 6:330-357.
De Renzi, E., Pieczuro, A. and Vignolo, L. A. (1966). Cortex, 2:50-73.
Kimura, D. and Archibald, Y. (1974). Brain, 97:337-350.
Jackson, J. H. (1878). London, Hodder and Stoughton (Republished 1932).
Mateer, C. and Kimura, D. (1977). Brain Lang., 4:262-276.
Poeck, K. and Kerschensteiner, M. (1975). Cerebral Localiz. Berlin, Springer-Verlag.

PSYCHIATRIC IMPLICATIONS OF SPEECH DISORDER

PETER F. OSTWALD
University of California School of Medicine

The goal of this paper is to review some of the work on speech disturbances which was carried out at the Langley Porter Neuropsychiatric Institute in San Francisco. A much more comprehensive report appears elsewhere (Ostwald, 1977). This work began over 30 years ago, with early formulations about "the social matrix of psychiatry" in terms of theories about human communications (Ruesch and Bateson, 1951). These were followed with attempts to define the complementary functions of "verbal" and "nonverbal" communications (Ruesch and Kees, 1956). Experiments with filtered speech (Starkweather, 1956) had located the nonverbal cues of emotion in the lower reaches (below 1000 Hz) of the acoustical spectrum. My interest was to define more precisely the role of sound in communicating signs and symptoms of disease (Ostwald, 1964).

The first job was to tape-record the vocalizations of psychiatric patients in such a way that accurate acoustical measurements can be made. We did this in a standard noise-and-echo free environment. The microphone was on a stand 10 in. from the patient's mouth. We used an Ampex 601 Tape-Recorder at 7.5 ips. Depending on the design of a particular experiment, we recorded for shorter or longer periods, spontaneous or rehearsed speech. Immediately after each recording, a 1 kHz tone was placed as a calibration signal on the tape. Segments (4-10 sec.) were spliced into loops and run backwards to create an unintelligible noise. This material was then processed by a Scott 420A Sound Analyzer for octave or half-octave band analysis, read with the meter in the "slow setting." Accuracy checks were run occasionally on Bruel

and Kjaer equipment. We were satisfied that our method
would suffice to do the sorts of objective studies we were
interested in (Ostwald, 1960).

MEASUREMENT OF CERTAIN SUBJECTIVE VOCAL QUALITIES

Our first interest was to see what certain subjective
voice qualities looked like when run through a sound analyzer.
Three kinds of voices interested us (we later added a fourth
type, called "robust"). The first was a "sharp voice" that
seemed to stigmatize the sound produced by a very immature,
hysterical young woman (age 22). She sounded very childish,
and as we studied her voice, it occurred to us to compare it
with that of a ten-year old child. There was a regular and
recurring pattern, which resembles the child's voice. It
consisted of two peaks of energy separated by an octave.
Also there were some weekly fluctuations, particularly at
the upper end of the frequency spectrum. We thought that
these changes were consistent with other clinical changes,
especially in her mood, which easily shifted into depression.

Depression is a common finding in psychiatric patients,
and we have sometimes been able to diagnose it over the
telephone. The voice has a peculiarly lifeless "flatness"
to it, and we tried to capture this sound by analyzing the
voice of a 27-year old depressed man. He was seen for six
consecutive weekly interviews, during which there was no
significant clinical improvement. In his case we again saw
the "twin-peaks" effect of an octave separation, but there
is much less variability from week to week, compared to the
patient with a "sharp voice."

We were interested in tracking these acoustical shapes
of patients' voices, and followed a number of patients
through psychotherapy, making observations on (1) the content of their speech, (2) their behavior at the beginning
and the end of interviews, and (3) the voice spectrum, and
trying to find pattern of correlation. These were described
in detail (Ostwald, 1963). One other vocal stereotype
interested us from a diagnostic viewpoint. It is the "hollow"
voice of patients who have organic brain disease. In this
case, we found a dramatic decay of vocal power above 250 Hz.
It differs very clearly from the "sharp" and the "flat" voice.

COMPARISON OF CASES BEFORE AND AFTER TREATMENT

It interested us to see what, if any, relationships there might be between vocal dimensions and treatment conditions. We were convinced, of course, that a good acoustical technique ought to reveal some before and after treatment changes. Clinicians quite routinely listen to their patients' speech in the expectation that cues about emotion are revealed not only by the content, i.e., "what" patients say, but also by their verbal style--"how" they speak (Ostwald, 1965). Because it is burdensome for patients to participate in speech experiments, we decided first to run a study with healthy volunteers. Each of 20 subjects was asked to read a standard sentence, "Joe took father's shoebench out, she was waiting at my door" before and after inhaling from a glass filled with concentrated ammonia solution. This olfactory "stress" produced significant changes of two points along the acoustic frequency spectrum, at 125 Hz. and at 500 Hz. Therefore, we decided to compare these two points, plus two additional points--1,430 Hz. and 5,600 Hz. --in a study of 30 patients admitted to the treatment ward of our hospital. These patients were afflicted with a variety of severe psychiatric illnesses, mostly psychoses. Although it turned out to be far more difficult to tape-record psychotic patients in such a way that accurate acoustical studies could be carried out, we were able to find a number of interesting patterns. The first case is the before-and-after treatment analyses of a 64 year old male patient who was hospitalized during the depressed phase of a manic-depressive psychosis. Approximately three weeks elapsed between the two analyses, and he received five electroconvulsive treatments during this interval. In his case there is a very marked rise in the intensity of his "high" voice. This corresponded with a jovial, almost euphorically aggressive vocal sound which he was able to produce after treatment. But the "low" voice hadn't changed and it was assumed that this "flat" voice indicated the residual of his depression. "Reading" voice, which we used in all cases for the statistical analysis because it provided us with comparable linguistic material, also showed a marked increase. The changes, in both "high" and "reading" voice were in the direction of higher frequency as well as higher intensity. The second case is that of a 16 year old female patient who came to the hospital for treatment of a schizophrenic illness. She was extremely inhibited, almost catatonic. Vocal analysis at the beginning of treatment shows that she emitted very little acoustical energy, and that there was only minimal difference between the lowest, highest and reading levels of her voice. Following a month of treatment, including psychotherapy and an effective neuroleptic agent, the voice was 10 decibels louder, and showed much greater variability. Again, these acoustical manifestations were consistent with other clinical parameters. This patient also showed an increase in word rate of her speech sample after treatment.

We were interested to see whether at this early stage in our research it might be possible to find any correlations between (1) the acoustical measurements of patients' voices before and after treatment and (2) certain clinical descriptive features characterizing the 30 patients as a group. Therefore, we checked to see if changes in the four points measured along the acoustic spectrum--at 125, 500, 1430, and 5600 Hz.--were related to age, sex, diagnostic category (psychotic vs. non-psychotic), form, duration and outcome of treatment. It was reassuring to find that there was an interaction between the treatment variable and the acoustical changes. Both the measurement of loudness and the measurement of change at 500 Hz. correlated with the use of somatic therapy. With electroconvulsive treatment the acoustical changes were in an upward direction while with phenothiazine medication they went down. These findings supported our assumption that the physical analysis of vocal dimensions might provide clinicians with a potentially useful tool in tracking and monitoring changes in the condition of their patients. My colleagues John Starkweather and William Hargreaves at Langley Porter Institute have used an automated technique of vocal analysis (using third-octave band filters sampled every 4 sec.) to study the relationship between voice, mood, and medication (Starkweather, 1964).

SPECTROGRAPHIC STUDY OF VOICE QUALITIES

We have used the sound spectrograph to define some of the acoustical features of voices produced by patients with severe language handicaps related to organic and functional

problems (Ostwald, 1965a). These include so called "paralinguistic" features of the voice, such as harsh, raspy,
whiny and breathy sounds and disturbances in the flow and
continuity of speech (Ostwald, 1964à).

Schizophrenia is perhaps the most challenging issue in
psychiatry today, and it too is a topic that should interest
the phonetician. The late Theodore Spoerri (1964) did an
amazing piece of work in which he carefully described the
speech phenomena associated with psychosis, schizophrenic
psychosis mostly. He separated these into four categories,
pointing the way to a great many problems that need further
clarification. These were: (1) Destruction of speech under
conditions of psychotic upheaval; (2) Reduction of speech
resulting from psychotic emptiness, numbing, and splitting;
(3) neoformation of speech as part of psychotic reconstitu-
tion; and (4) Unique speech phenomena.

Speech spectrography is a very time-consuming method,
and Spoerri was able to apply it to only a small percentage
of his case-load of schizophrenics. In the United States,
where paralinguistic research is pursued by only a very small
number of investigators, acoustic phonetic studies of
schizophrenia has been eclipsed by a much greater emphasis
on the verbal and linguistic pathology of this disease
(Ostwald, 1977a). Our own work is limited to the detailed
investigation of six patients, four males and two females.
One of the males, a 14-year old adolescent in the throes of
a catatonic excitement (Ostwald, 1964, 1964a), produced the
interesting phenomenon which Moses (1954) labelled "schizo-
phonia." He emitted a high, squeaky, childish voice from
the left side of his mouth, and a low-pitched, more adult
sound from his right side.

Another schizophrenic patient kept his mouth open almost
all the time that he spoke, with the result that his speech
sounds were devoid of distinctive features (Ostwald and
Skolniloff, 1966). There was almost no acoustic output
above 1 kHz, his vowels lacked formant structure, and there
was insufficient high frequency noise to make the consonants clear to the listener. As we observed this patient
during various emotional states it became apparent that he

could in fact vocalize energetically, but in doing so he
often made sounds that completely lost the character of
human speech and turned into something more reminiscent of
the screeches, rasps, squacks or growls made by animals.

One of our schizophrenic patients was an eight year old
boy. Often his speech seemed akin to the babblings and
mouthings of babies. There were other times when the boy
produced recognizable fragments of words and sentences, disconnected and without grammatical order, but revealing an
unusually large vocabulary, much of it consisting of words
he had heard but could not use for meaningful communication.
We analyzed the types and found that these various utterances
fell into three categories: (1) Message content, consisted
of words and phrases that were relevant to the social situation and were semantically correct utterances, e.g., "I want
to go out." (2) Slogan content, included words from songs,
rhymes, TV commercials, and other verbal material that the
boy had memorized and would repeat compulsively. (3) Nonsense content contained unintelligible sounds that could not
be deciphered, and also made-up "pseudo-words." This boy
produced a number of different vocal sounds which we called
"normal voice," "screech," and "chant" on the basis of distinguishable paralinguistic features. His "chanting" sing-
song voice was used mostly with slogans, and the "screech"
voice almost exclusively accompanied coherent messages.
Normal vocal behavior was split about 50:50 between message
and nonsense-slogan verbalization. This and other clinical
evidence of disturbances in the relationship between voice
and speech convinced us that one of the most important fields
of investigation is developmental linguistics--the study of
how children learn to manipulate the environment by making
oral sounds.

THE SOUNDS OF INFANCY

Both for theoretical and for practical reasons we
focussed our research on infant vocalization. Psychodynamic
theories often refer disturbances in human behavior to learning processes, wherein individuals experience frustrations,
disappointments, or actual traumas when coping with the
environment. Since speech is a social skill that has to be

acquired during the rapid growth period of childhood, it is commonly assumed that much of what we call "speech pathology" may be developmental in origin. Such an assumption can help us overcome the organic/functional dichotomy, since a derailment of speech development for _any_ reason (e.g., jaw fracture, school phobia, delirium, shyness, etc.) affects both the use of the speech organs and the person's attitudes regarding communication (Ostwald, 1969). Also for practical reasons, since early vocalizations are to such a large extent "preverbal" or "nonverbal" and hence cannot be defined in a dictionary, it seemed logical to turn our acoustical methods in the direction of communication during the first year of life.

The initial effort, a genetic study of infant twins (Ostwald, Freedman and Kurtz, 1962) showed that while acoustical methods gave no greater reliability in terms of distinguishing between groups of babies, they were less time-consuming than the traditional denotation systems employing musical notations and phonetic symbols. However, it was necessary to use a method of continuous sonagraphy to analyze the large amount of data generated by a clinical study of infants. This study focussed on five normal, five borderline, and three severely diseased cases (Ostwald, Phibbs and Fox, 1968). An analysis of 365 cries produced by these babies helped us to confirm the pediatric observation (also made occasionally by mothers and nurses) that in cases of infant distress there may be a significant elevation of vocal pitch.

A VIEW TOWARDS THE FUTURE

At this juncture, I would like to review briefly my ideas regarding where the acoustical study of human sounds might lead. The work I have reported so far deals essentially with various attempts at clinical correlation--i. e., drawing inferences about the relationships between physical shapes of sounds that human beings make, and their observable condition or situation at the time of the soundmaking. It is an attempt to apply certain bioacoustic principles (Busnel, 1963) to human behavior, specifically behavior as it is seen and conceptualized in the practice of psychiatry.

There are certain drawbacks to this method, stemming from
the difficulties we have in making diagnostic remarks about
patients. Psychiatric nosology has a long tradition, going
back several thousand years, that involves high-level abstrac-
tions about the multitude of facts obtained through history-
taking, interviewing, and examining patients and watching
their responses to treatments during the course of illness
(Ostwald, 1968). In the current APA nomenclature there is,
however, only one category describing speech disorders,
called Special Symptoms "for the occasional patient whose
psychopathology is manifested by a single specific symptom."
Unfortunately one so seldom finds a person with just "a
single specific symptom" that even this diagnosis becomes
quite meaningless. Further progress in the diagnostic application of acoustical methodologies will certainly require
the specification of mood states which are the most difficult to quantify of all the variables in clinical psychiatry.

In addition to the diagnostic use, we should think
about therapeutic possibilities inherent in acoustical
methods. One area--the use of acoustical devices for helping deaf or hard-of-hearing patients, has already been explored (Ostwald, 1967). What about the new possibilities
of "bio-feedback?" These methods rely on helping patients
perceive feedback from their internal states by making
these signals more audible or visible (Raskin, 1977). Could
auditory signals be amplified, transformed, or converted in
some useful way? I have experience in only one case, a
patient whose spastic dysphonia was dramatically improved
when he was given a portable microphone and amplifier to
help project his voice. I have often wondered whether the
visual perception of voice, via oscillographic or spectrographic apparatus, could be of benefit to certain patients
afflicted with speech problems, and I believe that some
positive results have been obtained by speech therapists
working with dysarthric, dyslalic, and aphasic patients.

Finally we come to the need for better monitoring of
patients who are in hospitals. The efforts to improve communication in nurseries by monitoring the cries of sick
babies has already been mentioned. It is possible that
similar progress might be made on the wards where adults are

being treated. The danger, however, is that by introducing
more and more mechanical devices into the hospital we tend
to dehumanize medicine. After all, there is no multipurpose
computer that can match the flexibility of the human brain,
and it would be a mistake, at this stage in biomedical research, to use hardware and software to displace trained
clinicians. As was pointed out in a recent eloquent letter
to Science (Weizenbaum, 1977), "The sort of caring that
machines can deliver is very impoverished indeed. It is
certainly incapable of nourishing the emotional processes
which may lead individuals to realizing the possibility of
their being worthy to be affectionately cared about, to care
for themselves, and finally to care for and about others."

Thus, in closing let me emphasize that, in essence, the
psychiatric implications of speech disorders are that there
are patients with serious problems, and that while acoustical
methods may help to clarify something about what these
problems entail, one should not expect miracles in terms of
how such human problems can be solved.

REFERENCES

Busnel, R. G.   (1963). Amsterdam, Elsevier.
Moses, P. (1954). New York, Grune and Stratton.
Ostwald, P. F.   (1960. J. Psychosom. Res. 4:301-305.
Ostwald, P. F.   (1963). Springfield, C. C. Thomas.
Ostwald, P. F.   (1964). The Hague, Mouton.
Ostwald, P. F.   (1964a). Baltimore, Williams and Wilkins.
Ostwald, P. F.   (1965). Sci. Am. 212:82-91.
Ostwald, P. F.   (1965a). J. Neurol. Sci. 2:271-277.
Ostwald, P. F.   (1967). HEW,. #VRA 67-32, 123-128.
Ostwald, P. F.   (1968). Soc. Sci. Info. 7:95-106.
Ostwald, P. F.   (1969). California Research Monograph #10.
Ostwald, P. F.   (1977). New York, Grune and Stratton.
Ostwald, P. F.   (1977a). New York, Spectrum Pub.
Ostwald, P. F., Freedman, D. G. and Kurtz, J. H.   (1962).
    Folia Phon. 14:37-50.
Ostwald, P. F. and Skolnikoff, A. Z.   (1966). Postgrad. Med.
    40:40-49.
Ostwald, P. F., Phibbs, R. and Fox, S.   (1968). Biol.
    Neonatorum 13:68-82.

Ostwald, P. F., Peltzman, P., Greenberg, M. and Meyer, J.
      (1970). Dev. Med. Child Neurol. 12:472-477.
Ostwald, P. F. and Peltzman, P. (1974). Sci. Am. 230:84-90.
Ruesch, J. and Bateson, G. (1951). New York, Norton.
Ruesch, J. and Kees, W. (1956). Berkeley, UC Press.
Raskin, M. (1977). New York, Grune and Stratton.
Spoerri, T. (1964). Basel, Krager.
Starkweather, J. A. (1956). Am. J. Psychol. 69:121-123.
Starkweather, J. A. (1964). Baltimore, Williams and Wilkins,
      424-449.
Wasz-Hockert, O. et al. (1968). London, SIM Pub. #29.
Weizenbaum, J. (1977). Science 198:354.

PHONETIC INDICATIONS OF PSYCHOPATHOLOGY

CLYDE L. ROUSEY
Topeka, Kansas

In <u>Psychopathology of Everyday Life,</u> Freud (1960) discusses at length what he calls slips of the tongue. He made
no differences between "slips of language" (substitutions
of one word for another) and "slips of sounds" (misarticulation of sounds). It is the purpose of this paper to reexamine his discussion of slips of the tongue and to enlarge
and amplify this material within the context of contributions from psychoanalysis and speech pathology. In so doing,
we shall see how sound production can be an indication of
health and psychopathology throughout the course of life.
Many disciplines have difficulty in separating out sound
production from verbal language. As a result, most neurologists and psychiatrists still use the term speech to cover
both forms of behavior. In this regard, the works of Freud
(1953), Head (1926), Goldstein (1948), Hartmann (1951) and
Brain (1961) must be considered as the most influential. The
current predilection to view sound production from a neurological (Darley, Aronson and Brown, 1975) and/or cognitive
(Singh, 1976; Lenneberg, 1975; Segalowitz and Gruber, 1977)
viewpoint also has its basis in the foregoing volumes. Such
a restricted view of necessity may lead to erroneous conclusions in considerations of clinical data. Freud's (1960)
recognition of the psychological meaning of language represented a shift in his view which has generally failed to make
an impact on the classic disciplines of neurology and linguistics. In more recent times, Thass-Thieneman (1967, 1968)

has written an even more definitive work on what we here have
referred to as slips of language.

Freud's insight into psychological determinants did not
appear when he reported inserting the (P) sound in the German
word Affe (ape) so that it becomes Apfe (a nonexistent word)
after he had to repeat the word a second time because his
daughter was not listening or later as he reported his daughter saying Frau Schresinger instead of Frau Schlesinger
because an (L) sound is difficult "to pronounce after a repeated (R)" (Freud, 1960, p. 62). Thus, while the slip of
language in the first instance was understood in dynamic
terms, he seemingly was unable to see that such factors
could be operative in slips of sounds. Although the notion
that a certain sound is difficult to pronounce because it
occurs after another remains popular in linguistic circles,
its validity must be questioned since if such reasoning were
correct, one would expect such types of speech variations to
occur frequently.

The possibility of psychological meaning being an integral part of sound production has been more openly recognized
by others. For example, as early as 1926, Sapir (1926) wrote:
"One of the most interesting unwritten chapters in linguistic
behavior is the expressively symbolic character of sounds,
quite aside from what the words in which they occur mean in
a referential sense. On the properly linguistic plane, sounds
have no meaning, yet if we are to interpret them psychologically, we would find that there is a subtle, though fleeting,
relation between the 'real' value of words and the unconscious
symbolic value of sounds as actually produced by individuals."

Moses (1954) volume while largely ignored by the disciplines of psychology, psychiatry, linguistics and speech
pathology; represents a pioneering effort by a laryngologist
to focus professional attention on the psychological meaning
of sounds. In 1954 and 1961, Greenson firmly placed the
psychology of sound in a psychoanalytic framework. He proposed that sound serves as a discharge function for both
pleasure and pain and both accompany instinctual activities
and is an indicator of affect. Other efforts by Jakobsen
(1960), Ostwald (1963) and Rousey (1965 and 1974) attest to

a slow but consistent growth of interest in the dynamic
meanings of sound. These efforts should be separated from
the frank experimental studies summarized by Mahl and Schulze
(1964) and Scherer (1978). Given the relatively wide dis-
simination in linguistic circles of the foregoing, no effort
will be made presently to review this material.

It is the position of the present author that speech
disturbances as well as normal production of sounds may be
explained within the context of psychoanalytic theory and
are a sign of both normal and pathological personality development. Hartmann (1964) and Anna Freud (1966) provide support
for the psychoanalytic interpretation of behavior such as sound
production. Also Anna Freud (1966) states: "Personally I can
see no difficulty in extending this conviction of certain
fixed relationships existing between surface appearance and id
content from the mental phenomena named above to particular
items of behavior, especially of children, as they can be observed in the areas of play; in hobbies; in the attitude of
illness, food, clothing, etc. I believe, what deters the
majority of analysts from accepting this suggestion is not
so much a disbelief in the validity of the material, but a
reminder of certain phases in the history of psychoanalysis
when such items were used profusely and disadvantageously
for the purpose of symbolic interpretation within analysis,
which is a technical mistake, of course." With this background in mind, the following discussion of the relationship
between speech and psychological development provides the
basis for both a clinical and experimental study of drives,
various aspects of psychological development throughout a
person's life, and for study of intellectual ability up to
and probably through the seventh year.

To begin, it is instructive that a rather striking
parallelism exists between speech development and the
appearance of drives and ego development. For example, in
the first six months of an infant's life, the predominant
speech elements present are vowels (Irwin, 1947, 1948). In
this same period, the hypothesized elements dominant in a
child's psychological life, from a psychoanalytic viewpoint,
are his drives and affective states. In the next six months
of the child's life, there appear all of the consonant sounds.

Roughly, in this same period, psychoanalytic theory contends
there is an intensified development of many ego functions,
such as perception, awareness, adaptive and defensive devices.
Now if the vowels and how they are handled are interpreted as
auditory manifestations of drives and the consonants are considered to reflect the development of the ego, there is a
basis for later translation of deviation of these sounds in
terms of difficulties in object relationship, drive discharge
and affect development. There are some physiological correlates which support making these assumptions regarding the
fundamental psychological meanings of vowels and consonants.
Thus, keeping in mind the differences between consonants and
vowel production, the correct use of consonants is interpreted as reflecting in part the development of ego controls.
If it is remembered that the vowel sounds are hypothesized
as reflecting drive discharge, then the development of consonants in the present theoretical system can be understood
as a way of describing mastery over the infant's instinctual
life.

     Consequently, we would expect psychiatric patients whose
problems center around modulation of instincts to have speech
difficulties centered on vowels, whereas patients whose psychological struggles were at later stages of development
would have speech deviations centering on consonants (Rousey
and Toussieng, 1964; Grimes, 1962; and Green, 1962). The
fact that most speech (sound) difficulties seen by speech
pathologists center on consonants rather than vowels is
understood within the present context as a reflection of
where most psychopathology develops, i.e., in object relationships. In general, voice quality in a person is discernable
in vowel production. An acoustic study of voices of hospitalized patients versus a control group of nonhospitalized
patients (Bannister, 1973) demonstrates significant variations
in the voice (i.e., vowels). Since it is reasonable from a
psychiatric standpoint to assume that hospitalized patients
may have more basic problems with drive expression and modulation, Bannister's findings are interpreted as supporting the
psychological meanings of vowels as presently postulated.
Further support comes from Shervanian's (1959) study which
demonstrated vowels as being the primary focus of sound error

in the autistic child. Utilizing the concept that vowel
production and drive expression are related allows a new
view of voice (i.e., vowel) disturbances found in both
children and adults. Examples of these are the problems of
breathiness, hoarseness and dysphonia. Each of these variations is seen as reflecting various ways of handling sexuality.
For example, the presence of a hoarse voice in the absence of
organic factors is seen as reflecting an attempt at pseudo-
masculinity. The fact that this is a typical voice difficulty
in the oedipal aged boy is viewed as supporting data. In a
similar vein, the common occurrence of breathiness in the
adolescent girl in the absence of organic pathology is seen
as her attempt to temporarily hold her sexual drives in
abeyance until suitable objects are present for their discharge. Finally, the appearance of dysphonia has long been
accepted in psychiatric practice as a potential hysterical
indicator. If one interprets the total or partial loss of
voice within the context of this paper, it would be seen as
a total act of stoppage of expression of sexual drive as it
is discharged by phonation. Freud's description of the onset
of aphonia in the instance of Dora is supportive of this
position.

     In the case of an individual where English becomes the
primary language after speaking some other language since
birth, most sound difficulties seem to occur on vowel sounds.
Since it is reasonable to assume that different cultures
condone and encourage differences in drive expression, it is
viewed as understandable that the person acquiring a new
native tongue has primary sound difficulties with vowels.
Thus, when a psychological as well as physical move to a new
environment has been completed, the foreign dialect problem
diminishes. The impact of various cultures and subcultures
on sound production has been detailed by Labov (1972) as
well as Brown (1969). Their work is seen as providing
further support for the dynamic interpretation of sound
production in so called foreign dialect. With reference to
consonant production, it is important to note the research
by Hall (1962) and Healey (1963). They report that not only
are there no age related pattern of consonant errors in
children, but also that many children produce sounds correctly from the beginning of talking. Research has

demonstrated that all sounds are uttered before the use
of language (Irwin, 1947, 1948) and no person having trouble
with sounds has such trouble in every instance where the
sound is made (McDonald, 1964). Since all of the sounds are
present by one year of age, their incorrect production becomes an indicator of psychopathology (transient or severe)
in object relations while their correct production reflects
a conflict-free development in object relations. Consonants
are thus seen as reflecting vicissitudes in object relationships in the oral, anal, and phallic periods of psychosexual
development. Utilizing Erikson's (1950) conceptualization
of the development of infantile sexuality, the sounds /m/,
/p/, /w/, /h/, /j/, /l/, /n/ and /t/ are hypothesized as
belonging to the oral respiratory-sensory stage, while /b/,
/f/, /k/, /g/ and /d/ are hypothesized as reflecting the
oral-biting stage. The /tʃ/ and /dʒ/ are associated with
the anal-expulsive stage, while the /s/, /r/, / ʃ / and /ʒ/
reflect the anal-retentive stage. The /v/, /θ/, /ð / and the
/z/ are associated with the phallic period.

The placing of the sounds in the various periods stems
from a rather complicated inference process wherein consideration is taken both of the physiological bases for consonant
production and the notion previously advanced that the time
of mastery for consonants for some children under the old
motor maturation theory can be better understood if it is
viewed as an indicator of emotional maturation. For example,
since the /θ/ is produced by protruding the tongue between
the teeth and generally is one of the last consonants to be
mastered by those having trouble with mastery of consonants,
the inference is drawn that this sound is associated with the
phallic period. In contrast, the /f/ made by biting the
lower lip with the teeth is one of the early consonants
mastered under the old notion of the developmental motor
acquisition of sounds. Hence, it is considered as a sound
which is developed during the oral period and belongs to what
Erikson calls the oral-biting stage. To illustrate how disturbances in consonant production can be applied to childhood
psychopathology, consider the substitution of /f/ for /θ/.
Such a sound error is interpreted as related to the child's
disturbed relationship with his or her father. The fundamental relationship of this particular sign to early

father-child relationships has been experimentally studied.
For example, Rousey (1968) in an unpublished paper reported
that in a group of twenty five year olds without fathers as
a result of death, desertion or divorce, sixteen substituted
the /f/ for the /θ/. In another group of twenty five year
olds who were drawn from the same socioeconomic area but who
did have a father present, there were only six who had the
substitution /f/ for /θ/. In that study, no attempt was made
to control for intelligence, neurological dysfunction of any
kind, or quality of the father-child relationship when present
or possible father surrogate when the natural father was
absent. Similarly, LaFon and Rousey (1974) reported that
among eighty delinquent boys ranging in age from nine to
eighteen years, there was a statistically significant relationship between substitution of /f/ for the /θ/ and disturbances in paternal-child relationships. This substitution
is frequent among children of professional parents where the
father must be away from home much of the time as a function
of completing his graduate training. It is also considered
by some observers a "normal" speech deviation among black
children. The clinical facts are that this substitution does
not occur regardless of the race involved when there is a
psychologically positive paternal influence. Within the
proposed theoretical system, its psychological meaning in
terms of a disturbed father-child relationship remains a constant regardless of sex, race or age.

In addition to the dynamic aspects of personality reflected through speech, the presence of sound omissions in
the speech of a young child indicate, where organic factors
such as paralysis of the tongue and lips are excluded, a
slowness in intellectual development or an arrest or regression in development reflecting psychogenic factors. Conversely, the absence of sound omissions in the child of seven
to eight years of age is felt to occur only in a child of
average intelligence. To review briefly, the earlier discussion relating the use of consonants to object relations
and ego development was based on sound substitutions. Relating the use of consonants to intelligence is based on
sound omissions. If the consonant sounds indeed have the
meaning previously ascribed to them of binding the vowels,

i.e., drives, and they generally reflect the level of
psychosexual development, then it could be inferred that the
presence and/or absence of consonants in spoken language
reflects the level of emotional maturation. That is, if the
consonant sound in question is a substitute for the one normally expected, one would infer that there is some organization and maturation of the ego, albeit perhaps a distorted
and a conflictual one. However, if the consonant sound is
absent, one may infer that there is a lower cognitive level
and that this in turn may affect the level of emotional
maturation present. One way to test the validity of this
assertion is to follow the course of development in a
patient presumably retarded. Norris (1974) described a
patient six years and seven months of age whose test achieve-
ments on the WISC were in the 60's (Defective Range) and on
the visual-motor tasks of the Merrill-Palmer an I.Q. of 60
was indicated. However, the speech examination showed speech
patterns devoid of sound omissions with a resulting inference
of at least normal intelligence. After two years of individual psychotherapy plus some work in a special education
class the WISC now yielded markedly different findings. Thus,
the Full Scale I.Q. was 88 to 90, the Verbal I.Q. 91 and the
Performance I.Q. was 86 to 90.

The concept of a genetic assessment of libidinal growth
as a possible indicator of intellectual ability is not
peculiar to the present writer for A. Freud (1965) points
to such a possibility in her metapsychological profile.
While admittedly no standardized scale is known which pin-
points the exact age at which a specific stage of libidinal
growth is supposedly accomplished, there is general agreement
that by the beginning of the educational experience, i.e.,
mastery of reading, etc., which occurs around age seven, some
sort of resolution of the oedipal complex is completed and a
relative channeling of energy through sublimation is focused
on the task of learning. Now, if indeed the mastery of the
consonants does reflect psychosexual development through the
phallic period, and sound substitutions reflect conflict
while sound omissions reflect lack or arrest of cognitive
development, and the period of latency in general occurs
around the time of the beginning of mastery of academic
material, then the absence of sound omissions in the

seven-year-old child seems a reasonable basis for inferring
at least average intelligence. The foregoing concepts have
important ramifications for not only linguistics, but also
for the disciplines of speech pathology wherein correct
sound production is "taught" to replace incorrect sound
production. In other words, one symptom (correct sound
production) is substituted for another symptom (incorrect
sound production). Behavior therapists (Yates, 1958; Ullman
and Krasner, 1965) have long contended that the concept of
symptom substitution is a dead issue. This position was, of
course, necessary for justification of some of their treatment approaches. It is the position of this paper that the
psychiatric problems attendent to symptom substitution are
of crucial importance for the speech pathologist or any other
student of communication. This is highlighted by Rousey and
Diedrich (1974) who found a significant increase in new speech
problems among children who received speech therapy as compared to children with speech disorders who did not receive
speech therapy. This observation raises not only ethical
but also legal issues in the treatment of articulation
problems.

CONCLUSION

In summary, although the usual understanding of speech
production is based on cognitive and neurological factors,
the present paper suggests possibilities for a theoretical
understanding which goes beyond these positions. The elements
of speech when viewed thusly allows description of the discharge and control of one's instinctual life, some of the
defenses, the level of psychosexual development and associated
object relationships, and through a mental age of seven a
gross estimate of intellectual functioning. If a child's
psychological health is developing adequately and the adult
is functioning at a relatively high level of emotional health,
there should be no speech difficulties. Viewing of speech in
this fashion not only allows for tracing in later life of
earlier childhood problems, but also allows for possible early
identification of difficulties in psychological development.

REFERENCES

Bannister, M. (1973). Ph.D. Diss., Univ. Kansas.
Brain, L. (1961). Washington, Butterworths.
Brown, B. (1969). Ph.D. Diss., Univ. of Kansas.
Darley, F., Aronson, A. and Brown, J. (1975). Philadelphia,
    W. B. Saunders Co.
Erikson, E. (1950). New York, W. W. Norton.
Freud, A. (1966). New York, Inter. Univ. Press, 16-27.
Freud, A. (1965). New York, Inter. Univ. Press.
Freud, S. (1953). London, Hogarth Press, 125-245.
Freud, S. (1953). New York, Inter. Univ. Press.
Freud, S. (1960). London, Hogarth, 53-105.
Goldstein (1948). New York, Grune and Stratton.
Green, A. (1962). M. S. Thesis, Purdue Univ.
Greenson, R. (1954). Psychoannal. Quart., 23:234-239.
Greenson, R. (1961). J. Am. Psychoannal. Assoc., 9:79-84.
Grimes, J. (1962). M. A. Thesis, Kansas Univ.
Hall, W. F. (1962). Ph.D. Diss., Univ. Missouri.
Hartmann, H. (1951). New York, Columbia Press.
Hartmann, H. (1964). New York, Inter. Univ. Press, 99-112.
Head, H. (1926). New York, MacMillan.
Healey, W. C. (1963). Ph.D. Diss., Univ. Missouri.
Irwin, O. C. (1947). J. Speech Dis., 12:397-401.
Irwin, O. C. (1948). J. Speech Hear. Dis., 13:31-34.
Jakobsen, R. (1966). New York, Inter. Univ. Press, 124-134.
LaFon, D. N. and Rousey, C. (1974). Springfield, Ill.,
    Charles C. Thomas, 260-266.
Labov, W. (1972). Philadelphia, Univ. of Penn. Press.
Lenneberg, E. H. and Lenneberg, E. (1975). New York,
    Academic Press.
Mahl, G. and Schulze, G. (1964). Baltimore, Williams and
    Wilkens, 466-483.
McDonald, E. (1964). Pittsburgh, Stanwix House.
Moses, P. (1954). New York, Grune and Stratton.
Norris, V. L. (1974). Springfield, Ill., Charles C. Thomas,
    211-227.
Ostwald, P. (1963). Springfield, Ill., Charles C. Thomas.
Rousey, C. and Toussieng, P. (1964). Ment. Hyg., 48:566-
    575.
Rousey, C. and Moriarty, A. (1965). Springfield, Ill.,
    Charles C. Thomas.

Rousey, C.   (1968).   Unpub. manuscript.

Rousey, C. and Diedrich, W.   (1974).   Unpub.

Rousey, C.   (1974).   Springfield, Ill., Charles C. Thomas.

Sapir, E.   (1926).   Ment. Health Bull., 5:1-7.

Scherer, K. R.   (1978).   New York, Plenum Press.

Segalowitz, S. and Gruber, F.   (1977).   New York, Academic
    Press.

Shervanian, C.   (1959).   Ph.D. Diss., Univ. Pittsburgh.

Singh, S.   (1976).   Baltimore: University Park Press.

Thass-Thienemann, T.   (1967).   New York, Washington Square
    Press.

Thass-Thienemann, T.   (1968).   New York, Washington Square
    Press.

Ullmann, L. P. and Krasner, L.   (1965).   New York, Holt,
    Rinehart and Winston.

Yates, A.   (1958).   Psychol. Rev., 65:371-374.

THE PHYSIOLOGY OF CEREBELLAR INVOLVEMENT
IN MOTOR CONTROL

TORGNY JENESKOG AND CARL-GUSTAF SÖDERBERG
University of Umeå

The knowledge of the cerebellum as one important part
of the motor system dates back to 1823, when Rolando concluded from the results of ablation experiments in a number
of animal species, that "cerebellar deficiency was concerned
with motor activity as differentiated from (a) a sensory
function, (b) a function vital to life of the animal, or (c)
the intellectual functions of the brain" (cited from Dow,
1969).

A cerebellar involvement in motor activity may be inferred from the deficiency symptoms resulting from cerebellar
lesions. These symptoms may vary with the localization of
the lesion, but might be described in one or more of the
following points (e.g., Holmes, 1939; Dow, 1969; Nyberg-Hansen
and Horn, 1972): (1) disturbances of balances and/or equilibrium, sometimes without apparent dysfunction in voluntary
motor acts, (2) nystagmus, unvoluntary eye movements usually
associated with unilateral lesions, indicating that eye
muscle control (eye-head coordination) is normally dependent
upon bilateral cerebellar action, (3) hypotonia, i.e., decreased muscle tonus or extremity fixation. This symptom is
most obvious in acute stages and may be compensated for more
or less totally in the stabilized stage of the cerebellar
disease, and (4) ataxia, defined as incoordination or unsteadiness in voluntary as well as postural motor activities. As

The cerebellum accounts for the eurhythmy, the eumetria, the eutaxy, and the diadochokinesia of all phonatory and articulatory movements. Cerebellar dysfunction, then, brings about exaggerated movements of respiration, overloud or interrupted phonation with nystagmic ataxia of the vocal cords, iterative articulation, as well as disturbances of the rhythm and fluency of diction (Luchsinger & Arnold, 1965). Cerebellar disorders in children as a consequence of trauma, cerebellar dysgenesis, cerebellar encephalitis, and Friedreich's hereditary ataxia are said to produce the following signs in the articulatory and phonatory field, viz. slow, laboured, and monotonous articulation along with a jerky irregularity, phonation that may be even more affected than articulation, and, in addition, a strangely explosive way of speaking with pronounced separation of syllables (Worster-Drought, 1968).

Darley, Aronson and Brown (1969) specify three distinct clusters of speech defects among their cerebellar patients: (1) articulatory inaccuracy cluster; (2) prosodic excess cluster; (3) phonatory-prosodic insufficiency cluster. The first category is characterized by imprecise consonants, irregular articulatory breakdowns, and distorted vowels. The second group--prosodic excess cluster--comprises excess and equal stress, prolonged phonemes, prolonged intervals and slow speech rate. The third group--phonatory-prosodic insufficiency cluster--is characterized by a harsh voice, monopitch, and monoloudness. Moreover, lesions of the vermis are, according to Brain and Walton (1969), more likely to lead to articulatory and phonatory disturbances than are lesions of one lobe. They describe articulation as jerky, explosive, and slurred, and phonation as often too loud, with irregular separation between syllables. In respect of unilateral lesions substantial improvement of speech is normally to be expected. Descriptions of ataxic dysarthria are characterized by such terms as slurring, slow and thick, slurring and jerkiness, scanning, staccato, explosive and unintelligible, and, finally, anarthric (Espir and Rose, 1970).

The cerebellum may be influenced by e.g. congenital disorders, familial tendencies, degenerations, neoplasms,

infections, vascular lesions, and metabolic and toxic disturbances (Mysak, 1976). Brain and Walton (1969) point out
that the neoplasms of the cerebellum may be midline cerebellar tumors or tumors of the cerebellar hemisphere. Among
the symptoms of median lesions we find giddiness, unsteadiness on standing, ataxic gait, and muscular hypotonia.
The symptoms of lateral lesions include clumsiness of the
ipsilateral hand, a tendency to stagger to the side of the
lesion, giddiness in shaking or turning the head, pronounced
nystagmus, hypotonia, wide-based gait, and an abnormal attitude of the head (Cp. Mysak, 1976).

Congenital deformities of the cerebellum may be observed through defects (ageneses, dysgeneses) where the
vermis and hemispheres may be absent, the vermis may be
absent without a gross defect of the hemispheres, one hemisphere and part of the vermis may be absent, and the cerebellum may be very small but symmetrically formed. Head
balance and the ability to sit up, stand and walk come late.
There may be an intention tremor of the hands when reaching
for things and a side-to-side sway with frequent falls when
walking. Speech rhythm is frequently affected and there
are signs of scanning or staccato-type patterns whereas
articulation is mostly distinct (Ford, 1966; Mysak, 1976).
Additional symptoms may be underdevelopment of orofacial
muscles, grimacing, drivelling, delayed speech development
as well as slurred and jerky utterance (Espir and Rose, 1970).

Ford (1966) reports four types of hereditary cerebellar
ataxia. They are: (1) Friedreich's ataxia with progressive
degeneration of the spinocerebellar tracts, the corticospinal
tracts, and the posterior columns of the cord. The most
marked early symptoms are unsteadiness of gait, ataxia of the
arms and disturbances in speech; (2) Behr's syndrome, i.e.,
ataxia with spasticity and optic atrophy. The spinocerebellar
tracts, the pyramidal tracts, and the optic nerves have
degenerated. Gait disturbance is first observed and this
is followed by ataxia of the arms, visual disorders together
with optic atrophy, as well as spasticity of the legs; (3)
Familial degeneration of the cerebellar cortex with mental
deficiency in childhood characterized by early symptoms of
varying mental insufficiency, cerebellar ataxia, and nystagmus; (4) Familial cerebello-olivary degeneration in childhood marked by late childhood symptoms of gait disturbance,
ataxia, tremors, and speech difficulties. Generalized

muscular rigidity and mental deterioration are typical of
the late stages of this disease. Finally, Espir and Rose
(1970) comment on the following additional disorders, viz.
multiple sclerosis with slurred, scanning, staccato speech;
idiopathic, cerebellar atrophy starting after 40-50 years;
metabolic and toxic dysfunctions such as hypothyroidism
and alcoholism.

MOTOR ORGANIZATION

In respect of motor organization it is generally considered appropriate to speak of six major levels. These are
accounted for below with modifications commented on at some
length in the experimental paper.

The first or lowest level--the level of the lower motor
neuron--is represented anatomically by the anterior horns
of the spinal cord, for the extremities, and the motor nuclei
of the cranial nerves. This level is described as the final
common pathway. The second level originates in nuclear
masses or in neuronal pools of the brain stem. These give
rise to tracts which project to the lower motor neurons.
This level is called the vestibular-reticular level and
its role is to regulate the reflex activity of the first level
(Darley et al., 1975). Anatomically the third level includes
the basal ganglia and nuclear masses related to them. This
level is known as the extrapyramidal level and could be regarded as a system of relay stations receiving signals from
the motor cortex which it effectuates until new orders are
given. Thus this level is inter alia involved in the sub-
conscious automatic aspects of motor performance. The fourth
level is found in the cerebral motor cortex. This, however, depends on the type of motor activity involved.

The cerebellum is said to represent the fifth level.
It operates as a control device in order to regulate the
precision of responses initiated at the four previous levels.
There is a sixth level as well--the conceptual-programming
level. This is called the highest level of motor organization engaged in part of the planning and programming aspects
of movement including some temporal and spatial aspects.
The remaining planning and programming activity is controlled

by parts of the cerebellum and parts of the basal ganglia.
This specific role of the cerebellum will be further illustrated by the experimental section of our paper.

REFERENCES

Brain, W. R. and Walton, J. N.   (1969).   London.
Darley, F. L., Aronson, A. E. and Brown, J. R.   (1969).
    J. Speech Hear. Res., 12:462-496.
Darley, F. L., Aronson, A. E. and Brown, J. R.   (1975).
    Philadelphia.
Espir, M. L. E. and Rose, C. F.   (1970).   Philadelphia.
Ford, F. R.   (1966).   Springfield, Ill.
Guyton, A. C.   (1971).   Philadelphia.
Luchsinger, R. and Arnold, G.   (1965).   Belmont, California.
Mysak, E. D.   (1976).   Baltimore, Md.
Worster-Drought, C.   (1968).   Dev. Med. Child Neur., 10:
    427-440.

H. SPEECH PERCEPTION

ON THE RECOGNITION OF ISOLATED SPANISH VOWELS

ANA MARIA BORZONE DE MANRIQUE
University of Buenos Aires

In previous studies on the Spanish vowels, it has been observed that these sounds were clearly identified in isolation (Guirao and Manrique, 1975) (Guirao, 1977), but no measurement of their identifiability has been provided as yet. The present work was undertaken in order to verify such observation and to quantify the recognition of isolated Spanish vowels. Current works on the identifiability of vowel sounds in isolation have shown a high score of recognition for Japanese vowels (Guirao, 1977) and a low one for English sounds (Strange et al., 1974). On the other hand, English vowels have proved to be better identifiable when presented in consonantal environment (Verbrugge et al., 1974). One of the conclusions following from the two aforementioned results was that changing spectral vowel patterns were more effective than sustained vowel values as carriers of vowel quality. In order to ascertain if the higher identifiability of medial vowels observed in English is a general phenomena or it is particular to some languages (including English) the identification of Spanish vowels in consonantal environment was also undertaken.

PROCEDURE

The five Spanish vowels /i, e, a, o, u/ were produced both in isolation and in /p-vowel-s/ environment by a panel of 15 untrained talkers which includes ten adults, five male and five female, and five children ranging in age from six to eleven. The talkers were given no special training nor were they asked to record again any sound even if, from the experimenter's standpoint, it did not quite resemble the quality of the one intended. The talkers produced each vowel twice in both conditions, which made a total of 150 isolated vowels and 150 vowels in context. The utterances were recorded on magnetic tape and assembled into two listening tests, one for each condition. In both tests voices were randomly mixed from token to token (mixed condition). This experimental condition was selected in order to avoid the advantage that the familiarity with the speaker's voice may provide for vowel identification. Audio tapes were played on an Ampex AG 440-2 tape recorder and broadcast over a loudspeaker in a partially sound-attenuating room.

Ten undergraduate students for whom the voices were unfamiliar participated in the experiments. They were all native speakers of Argentine Spanish and had no knowledge of other languages. They all listened to the tests in the same order, first in isolated condition, then in context condition. Listeners were asked to identify the vowel sound and to write it down on an answer sheet. A judgment was considered an error if the written vowel was not the one intended by the talker.

RESULTS

Table 1 shows the results, vowel by vowel, of the misidentification of Spanish vowels in isolation together with data for vowels in context. These values represent the average identification errors for ten listeners. The average identification error for isolated vowels is 2.7% while for vowels in context it is 1.1%. The difference between these two averages is not significant.

DISCUSSION

The data reported above confirm the expectation that Spanish vowels in isolation would be accurately recognized. In effect, isolated Spanish vowels have proved to be highly identifiable (97%) even when their recognition was performed under unfavorable experimental conditions. (Untrained talkers and mixed voices). Spanish vowels in context were also very well identified (99%). The identification scores for vowels in isolation and in context conditions are similar enough to allow the conclusion that, at least in Spanish, changing spectral patterns are not superior to sustained values as carriers of vowel quality. Both conditions seem to provide sufficient information about the vowel identity. Comparing these results with those obtained for English vowels, it is clear that Spanish vowels are better recognized than English ones. In effect, for nine English vowels in isolation an identification score of 58% was obtained (Strange et al., 1974) while one of 83% was reported (Verbrugge et al., 1974) for the same vowels in consonantal environment. The difference between Spanish and English results is particularly relevant in isolated condition (97% vs 58%).

One factor that may explain the superior identifiability of isolated vowels in Spanish would be the fact that these sounds have provided to be better separated acoustically than English ones (by their F1 vs F2 values), as it was reported elsewhere (Guirao and Manrique, 1975). However, this observation is based on the analysis of adult voices only. When children utterances are also considered, a certain over-lapping between the acoustic areas of /a-o/ and /o-u/ is observed, as shown by the results of a new series of experiments being carried out at our laboratory at present. Furthermore, the data obtained by filtering natural vowels (Guirao, 1977) show that more information is contained in these sounds than just that provided by the first and second formant frequencies.

On the other hand, the fact that Spanish vowels are perceived in a categorical mode (Manrique and Gurlekian, 1977), contrary to the continuous mode reported for English (Fry et al., 1962), seems to be closely related to their recognition in isolated position since this mode of perception implies a labeling process very near categorical. In effect, Spanish vowels are commonly used in isolation in every day speech since they can form words by themselves which behave as different grammatical categories. Thus Spanish speaking listeners are accustomed to frequently listening to them in that condition and to accurately ascribe the vowel sound to its category in order to understand the message conveyed to them. It seems likely that this functional characteristic of Spanish vowels and the fact that they do not present diphthongized variants are factors that may contribute to make these sounds considerably more intelligible than those of other languages. Furthermore, the present results show that steady-state vowels may be good perceptual targets depending on the characteristics of the language involved.

Thus, for instance, as it was reported above, Japanese vowels, which are quite similar to Spanish ones from an acoustic and functional point of view, are well identified in isolation (Guirao, 1977). These results do not contradict those obtained by Fujimura and Ochiai (1963) in spite of the fact that they showed that isolated vowels were less intelligible than medial ones. The reason for their results lies in the fact that they did not compare the identification of vowels in syllabic context with that of actual vowels pronounced in isolation but with that of vowel segments gated out of CVC syllables.

What Fujimura and Ochiai's results seem to show is that information about medial vowels is distributed over a temporal portion of the syllable longer than the steady-state, a fact that has also been observed for English (Lindblom and Studdert-Kennedy, 1967). The fact that isolated vowels may be accurately identified does not imply that these sounds in context and in isolation are necessarily recognized by exactly the same acoustic cues.

REFERENCES

Fukimura, O. and Ochiai, K.   (1973).   J. Acoust. Soc. Amer., 35:1889(A).

Guirao, M. and Manrique, A. M. B. de.   (1975).   J. Psycholing. Res. 4:17-25.

Guirao, M.   (1977).   Study of Sounds, XVIII.

Lindblom, B. E. and Studdert-Kennedy, M. (1967).   J. Acoust. Soc. Amer. 42:830-843.

Manrique, A. M. B. de. and Gurlekian, J. A.   (1977).   Study of Sounds XVIII.

Strange, W., Verbrugge, R. and Shankweiler, D.   (1974). Haskins Status Report, SR-37/38, 209-216.

Verbrugge, R., Strange, W. and Shankweiler, D.   (1974). Haskins Status Report, SR-37/38, 199-208.

Table 1. Mean percent errors in the identification of each
of the five Spanish vowels in isolation and in
/p-s/ environment.

Spanish Vowels	Percent of Errors	
	In Isolation	In /p-s/ Context
/i/	5.6	0.3
/e/	2	–
/a/	2.6	2.6
/o/	2	2.6
/u/	1.6	–

EXPERIMENTS IN VOICE CONFRONTATION

G. H. BRECKWOLDT
Saint Louis University

Most people accept the fact that in the playback from even the best high-fidelity recording they do not sound their own true self. Numerous speech therapists have resigned themselves to the reality that the patient hears himself differently from the way they, the therapists, hear the patient. From this results the phenomenon of overrating and underrating of progress in therapy. This was studied. It had been noted that some patients of both sexes and a wide age-range, had resented continuing therapy, because they felt that there was no more need for improvement. Their therapists felt differently. Some other patients, also of both sexes and all ages, insisted that therapy had come to a standstill leaving their defect unimproved; while their therapists noted continuing progress and improvement. It was found that, as a rule, the overraters based their judgment on listening to themselves, whereas the underraters based their criticism on hearing themselves from tape recordings. In both cases the basic voice-speech-personality was heard and judged but not the progress of therapy.

While the therapist hears his patient via air-conduction only, the patient hears himself by his own blend of air-bone-conduction (1, 2, 5). The therapist simply does not have a clue as to how exactly the patient hears himself. Speaking of the auditory and visual fields, one could in a sense compare a person's customary self-hearing to his familiar mirror-image and the listening to his own recorded voice to his seeing himself photographically recorded in still and moving pictures.

Through the widespread use of photography most people, from
earliest childhood are accustomed to seeing their photo-
recorded images which represent the closest to how others
see them. In auditory matters, however, the average person's
exposure to hearing his own recorded voice from among other
recorded voices depends on the frequency of hearing one's own
recorded voice played back (11). Obviously, as for example
in radio announcers, habituation plays an important part in
hearing oneself recorded.

One of Holzman's researches into psychological aspects
of voice confrontation shows that a group of bilingual individuals (of Spanish home-language and English acquired
after age sixteen) displays more defensive negation to hearing their recorded native-language voices than to their later-
learned language (7).

According to all relevant psychological researches a
confrontation with one's recorded voice reveals numerous implications. The discrepancy between voice and speech heard
by bone-air-conduction and, on the other hand, by air alone
can, as our initial study shows, lead to a severe therapeutic
handicap in the work with speech and voice defects. The author
therefore designed an instrument which makes it possible to
play back to a speaker (or singer) his recording as a bone-
air-conduction blend corresponding to the natural self-heard
voice. Herewith the difficulty mentioned by Holzman in Novem-
ber 1971 has been overcome. Holzman emphasizes the desir-
ability "to play a person's recorded voice to him in a way
that would approximate the sound he hears when he speaks."
But resignedly he continues "Unfortunately, no one has yet
figured out how this can be done" (8). (n.b.: The under-
linings were added by the author of this paper.) The bone-
air-blending (BAB) instrument not only enables a person to
hear his "natural" voice from his recording, but also simultaneously allows other listeners (e.g., therapists) to hear
the same person (e.g., the patient) the way he hears himself.

The instrumentation consists of known components. In
early experiments (3, 4) recordings were simultaneously made
by a mouth (air) and a throat (larynx and bone (2)) microphone

(see Fig. 1). The latter, i.e., the throat microphone, was abandoned because of its hampering attachment and, more especially, its qualitative shortcomings. Whereas the earlier prototype of the BAB had been geared to the simultaneous air- and throat-microphone recorded material on two-track tape (3, 4), the present instrument can be fed any air-microphone-produced recording (see Fig. 2).

The sound-junction box of the instrument forks the material into the specially constructed BAB head-gear, which consists of a vertical and a horizontal band (see Fig. 3). To these bands are attached with utter flexibility two earphone cups and a bone vibrator (or bonephone). Both earphone and the bonephone have a volume-control. The subject places the earphone cups over his ears and the bonephone to any desired point of bone contact (9, 10), such as the maxilla, teeth, glabella or, as in most cases, the mastoid process (see Fig. 2).

Authors Dirks and Kamm end their article "Bone Vibrator Measurements" (6) with a most provocative comment on headbands: "Questions also arise concerning the advisability of positioning vibrators on the forehead instead of the mastoid process. Unfortunately, the headbands in general use (including the new Radioear P-3333) were not developed for application of the vibrators at the forehead and most likely will not exert 5.4 N static force on an adult head. It appears that locating the new vibrators on the forehead for general use will require further development in headbands. In addition, the new headband developed for application on the mastoid, when used with children will probably not provide a coupling force of 5.4 N. Headbands that are convenient to use and adjustable for heads of all sizes continue to be a desirable but unmet goal."

The BAB headband (Fig. 3) not only meets this goal but, in addition to facilitating all possible positions for the bone vibrator, jointly accommodates the earphone cups. In this way switching of bands for air- and bone-conduction tests can be eliminated once and for all.

At a pre-balanced level the junction box releases the playback material to the three phones of the headgear. The subject now determines whether he wishes to activate both earphones or, as in the average case, only one. He places the bonephone on his preferred bone-contact area. Thereafter he proceeds to manipulate (as a rule conveniently with both hands) the phone volume-controls, until he hears the perfect blend of his own "natural" voice.

Some subjects who heard the bone-air-blend of their own played back recording uttered the wish to listen to some of their favourite singers and music the BAB way. When their request was granted they were startled by what they called "more fullness," "better resonance," "great acoustics," etc. It has been noted that in order to enjoy optimal BAB sound quality the listener automatically keeps the volume at a low and perfectly harmless level. Teenagers, who so frequently play their stereophonic speakers and/or headphones at dangerous sound levels, suddenly realize that basically they are not striving for ever-increasing quantity of sound but for quality.

The only complaint so far heard about the BAB came from a subject who felt discomfort under the bonephone, after the instrument had been used for over one hour. It was found, however, that in this case the junction box had been set at too high an intensity level. This example evidences the BAB as a device preventive of volume abuse.

Experiments in voice confrontation also showed that today's young not only want to hear music but wish to feel it. When they turn their speakers or headphones to thunderous levels, they hope to feel vibrate the floor and furniture or their head and chest. With the BAB the subject receives the craved for vibrations on the touch and feel level but in low and harmless quantity although of optimal quality.

The BAB originally grew out of the need to eliminate the phenomenon of overrating and underrating of therapy progress by the speech or voice patient. In the meantime, in the field of hearing, it has been suggested (4) to introduce the single-unit BAB headgear into audiometry in order to replace the conventional separate headbands used in the testing of air- and bone-conduction.

Wherever natural self-hearing would improve the voice-, speech- or language-training of an individual, there is an obvious need for the implementing of the BAB. Language laboratories, schools of speech, and opera as well as numerous other disciplines in the world of sound may wish to explore the uses of the BAB.

It is somewhat surprising to note that the contemporary sound industry has overlooked the potentiality of bone-conduction. The latter, if correctly blended with air-conduction, gives sound material the dimension of naturalness and self-heardness. Instead, the resourceful and gigantically growing sound industry, these days, is supplying QUADRAphonic speaker and headphone systems to our inaugmentable TWO-ear-system. Before SEXAphonic and OCTOphonic speakers will adorn the various corners of our rooms and six and eight channel headphones our youngsters, it is likely that there will be a reaction to the muchness syndrome of sound bombardment.

REFERENCES

1. Bekesy, G. von. (1949). J. Acoust. Soc. Amer., 21: 217-232.
2. Bekesy, G. von. (1949). New York, McGraw-Hill Book Co., Inc.
3. Breckwoldt, G. H. (1974). Bull. d'Audiophon., Besancon 4:795-798.
4. Breckwoldt, G. H. (1976). Proceed. XVI Internat. Cong. Logo. Phoniat., Basel, S. Karger.
5. Davis, H. and Silverman, S. R. (1970). New York, Holt, Rinehart and Winston.
6. Dirks, D. D., Kamm, C. (1975). J. Speech Hear. Res., XVIII, 28:259.
7. Holzman, P. S., Berger, A., and Rousey, C. (1967). J. Pers. Social Psych. 7:423-428.
8. Holzman, P. S. (1971). Psych. Today. 5:67-69.
9. Panconcelli-Calzia, G. (1934). Die Med. Welt 23:1-12.
10. Panconcelli-Calzia, G. (1934). Vox Phonet. Labor. Univ. Hamburg 20:1-14.
11. Rousey, C. & Holzman, P. S. (1967). J. Pers. Social Psych. 6:464-466.
    Illustrations by
12. Breckwoldt, C., K. H. (1977). St. Louis Univ.

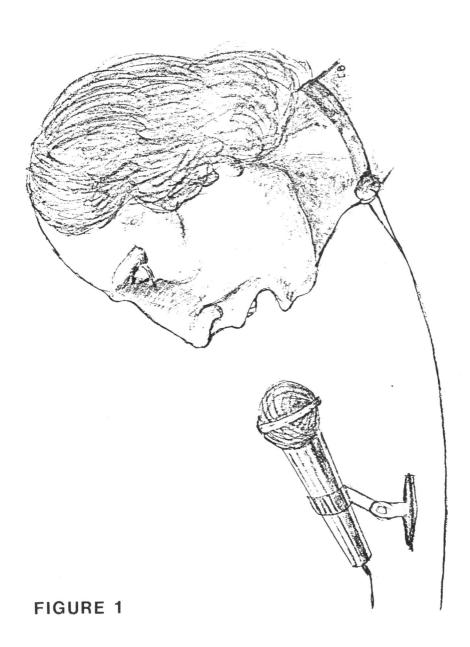

FIGURE 1

FIGURE 2

FIGURE 3

THE EFFECTS OF SEVERAL LINGUISTIC FACTORS ON THE MAGNITUDE OF ERROR IN THE LOCATION OF EXTRANEOUS SOUNDS EMBEDDED IN SPEECH

GLEN L. BULL
University of Virginia

Speech processing, or extraction of meaning from an utterance through analysis of the acoustic signal by a listener, is often supposed to involve several stages of analysis (Savin and Bever, 1970). An interesting question which has been considered in a number of studies is one of the extent to which levels of linguistic analysis correspond to real psychological and physiological processes as opposed to the extent to which they are merely convenient ways of conceptualizing these aspects of the speech event. One means of examining the perceptual process was suggested by Ladefoged and Broadbent (1960), who examined the accuracy with which listeners could determine the phoneme corresponding to an extraneous sound embedded in speech. A similar methology was employed in the present study.

An observer required to locate the position of an extraneous sound embedded in linguistic material is faced with two competing tasks:

1. extraction of meaning from the linguistic material, and

2. location of the position of the extraneous noise in the linguistic material.

Efficient operation of the linguistic mechanism would require that extraction of meaning from the linguistic
material be given first priority under most circumstances.
The present work was based upon two assumptions. The first
was that if a listener is given a linguistic and a nonlinguistic task to perform, the two tasks will be handled
serially. The second assumption was that the accuracy with
which a listener can identify the position of an extraneous
sound embedded in speech should therefore vary as a function
of the linguistic difficulty of the material.

Three types of linguistic materials were selected for
study: meaningful sentences, nonsense sentences, and sequences of syntactically-unrelated words. Three groups of
60 utterances representing the three levels of linguistic
material were constructed. A 25-millisecond burst of wide-
band noise was placed in a position contemporaneous with a
selected phoneme in each utterance. The burst of noise was
placed in the first part of half the utterances and in the
second part of the remaining utterances.

The relative linguistic difficulty of the stimuli within each linguistic level was also considered. Linguistic
difficulty was measured in terms of the ability of listeners
to recall sentences. Three factors which affected recall in
a study by Nichols (1957) were familiarity of vocabulary,
length of utterance in words, and naturalness of phrasing
as ranked by a panel of judges. Meaningful sentences
developed by Nichols were employed as the meaningful utterances in the present experiment. A parallel nonsense sentence from a similar vocabulary and of the same length in
words was created to match each sentence in the group of
meaningful sentences. A similar procedure was used to
create the third group of stimuli, sequences of unrelated
words.

The acoustically recorded stimuli were presented through
headphones to 60 listeners who heard the three groups of
stimuli in different orders. The listeners were required to
mark the judged position of the extraneous sound in each
utterance on typescripts of the utterances. The 10,800
judgments generated in this fashion were scored in the

following way. Discrepancies between the actual and judged
locations of the extraneous sounds were arbitrarily scored
as one point for each letter and each space between a letter
that separated the marked position on the answer sheet from
the spectrographically-determined location of the extraneous
sound. Digraphs which represented a single phoneme were
scored as a single unit and silent letters were ignored;
thus, the "th" in "there" was scored as a single unit and
the final "e" ignored.

A five-way analysis of variance was employed in the
analysis of the data. The main effects considered were:
type of linguistic material, familiarity of vocabulary,
utterance length in words., naturalness of phrasing, and position of the extraneous sound in the utterance. These results
are summarized in the table. The analysis of the data yielded
the following results which exceeded the values required for
significance at the .05 level of confidence. The mean magnitude of errors by listeners was greater in meaningful and nonsense sentences than in sequences of unrelated words.
Accuracy also suffered as the length of utterance increased
and the phrasing became less natural. In those instances,
accuracy of judgments did appear to vary as a function of the
linguistic material employed. This is suggestive of a process
in which the nonlinguistic task is deferred until the later
stages of linguistic analysis. If the linguistic process
lengthens as the utterance becomes longer or the linguistic
material becomes more complex, then the nonlinguistic task
may be affected as a consequence of its deferral. The
accuracy of judgments was not affected by length of utterance
in one instance. Accuracy was not affected by length of utterance when sequences of unrelated words were the stimuli, although accuracy was diminished in longer utterances when meaningful and nonsense sentences were employed, as Figure 1 indicates. One interpretation of this result might be that the
entire utterance is considered as a whole prior to completion
of the linguistic task in the instances of meaningful and
nonsense sentences, but that the utterance is not necessarily
analyzed as a complete unit when the stimulus is a sequence
of unrelated words.

These results, though not conclusive, appear to be consistent with one interpretation of a different series of

experiments. Savin and Bever (1970) presented a series of
recorded syllables to subjects who were required to respond
manually upon detection of either syllable targets or phoneme
targets. A syllable target consisted of a nonsense syllable
in a series of spoken syllables while a phoneme target consisted of a phoneme that comprised part of one of the syllables. Reaction times were faster when subjects were required
to search for syllable targets. In another experiment,
listeners searched lists of three-word sentences for the
presence of either sentences or single-word targets. Reaction
times were faster when listeners were provided with sentence
targets (Bever, 1970). As Foss and Swinney (1973) noted, it
is obvious that this monitoring task is not completed by the
listener until the later stages of linguistic analysis.
McNeil and Lindig (1973) found that the minimum reaction time
occurs whenever the linguistic level of the target and the
search list are the same. For example, if the search list
consisted of a series of three-word sentences, listeners detected the presence of a target sentence more quickly than
they detected a single-word target. McNeil and Lindig concluded that there is a network of processing stages, each of
which can be the focus of attention and observed that
"interesting questions exist concerning the distribution of
attention during speech processing. . ." (McNeil and Lindig,
1973).

In the case of reaction time in response to linguistic
targets the listener has an identification task, but also
has the task, whether stated or unstated, of extracting meaning from the utterance. Evidence to date is consistent with
the possibility that listeners complete some or all of the
analysis necessary to extract meaning from an utterance before they go to other tasks. Listeners appear to attend
to the meaning of the utterance first. Accordingly, the
fastest reaction time could be expected when the linguistic
target matched the level of the linguistic material presented.
If there is a mismatch between the linguistic material and
the linguistic target, the subject may adopt a strategy in
which the larger unit is broken down into its smaller con-
stituents after extraction of meaning, which would account
for the slower reaction time. It is also plausible that the
accuracy of judgments of the location of extraneous sounds
embedded in speech would vary as a function of the linguistic

difficulty of the material, if this task is deferred until
meaning is extracted from the material. If comprehension is
the prime function of the linguistic system, it would not be
surprising to find extraction of meaning from an utterance
undertaken prior to secondary tasks. Experiments involving
both reaction time to linguistic targets as well as experiments requiring judgments of the location of extraneous
sounds embedded in speech provide evidence of a serial
approach to these tasks. The two difference approaches are
consistent with the same interpretation; the listener attempts to understand the meaning of the utterance before he
turns to other tasks.

REFERENCES

Bever, T.   (1970). Amsterdam: North-Holland.
Foss, D. and D. Swinney.   (1973). J. Verbal Learn. Verbal
     Behav. 12:246-257.
Ladefoged, P. and D. Broadbent. (1960). Quart. J. Exper.
     Psych. 12:162-170.
McNeil, D. and K. Lindig. (1973). J. Verbal Learn. Verbal
     Behav. 12:419-430.
Nichols, A. (1957). MA thesis (The Ohio State University).
Savin, H. and T. Bever. (1970). J. Verbal Learn. Verbal
     Behav. 9:295-302.

Table 1. Mean values of the magnitudes of errors resulting
from the location of extraneous sounds in speech
by 60 observers.

| | Level of Linguistic Material | | | |
	Meaningful Sentences	Nonsense Sentences	Word Sequences	Average
Vocabulary				
Familiar	4.6	4.3	3.2	4.0
Intermediate	4.2	4.3	3.3	3.9
Unfamiliar	4.1	3.9	3.2	3.9
Length				
5 words	2.8 ⌉	2.9 ⌉	3.0	2.9 ⌉
9 words	4.2 ⌋	4.2 ⊣	3.0	3.8 ⊣
13 words	4.3 ⌉	4.8 ⌋	3.2	4.1 ⊣
17 words	5.3 ⌋	4.8 ⌉	3.2	4.4 ⌋
21 words	5.0	4.3 ⌋	3.5	4.2
Naturalness				
Natural	4.0 ⌉	–	–	–
Unnatural	4.6 ⌋	–	–	–
Combined Effects	4.3	4.2———————3.2		3.9

Note: A value of 2 would indicate that the mean magnitude of
effor in the placement of the extraneous sound by 60 observers
under the condition specified was one phoneme away from the
target phoneme contemporaneous with the extraneous sound in
the utterance. No values are specified for the condition
"Naturalness" within the Nonsense Sentences or Word Sequences
because those utterances were not rated with respect to that
condition. A vertical or horizontal line connecting two
adjacent means indicates that there was a statistically
significant difference between the two means.

FIGURE 1. INTERACTION OF LINGUISTIC LEVEL (MEANINGFUL SENTENCES, NONSENSE SENTENCES, AND SEQUENCES OF UNRELATED WORDS) AND UTTERANCE LENGTH WITH RESPECT TO THE LOCATION OF EXTRANEOUS SOUNDS IN SPEECH BY OBSERVERS. EVERY TWO UNITS ON THE ORDINATE INDICATE A MEAN MAGNITUDE OF ERROR OF ONE PHONEME AWAY FROM THE TRUE POSITION OF THE EXTRANEOUS SOUND IN THE UTTERANCE.

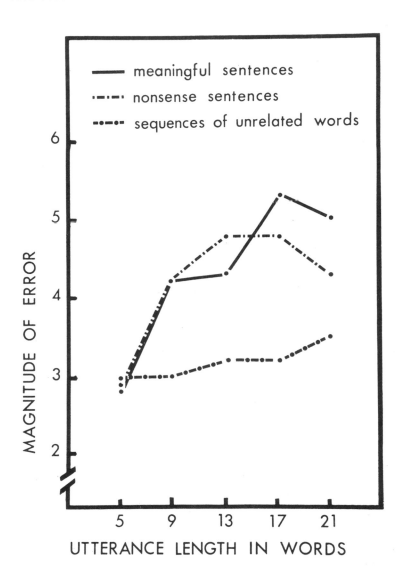

NORMALIZATION INFLUENCES IN THE
PERCEPTION OF SPEECH

CONRAD LARIVIERE
University of Maine

When naturally spoken words are excised from running speech, identification is generally too low for conversational utility. For example, Pickett and Pollack (1963) obtained recognition scores of approximately 55% for single words excerpted from running speech, a figure similar to that reported by Lieberman (1963) for single, non-redundant words. Recognition scores are particularly depressed for words of short duration. Short durations are presumably associated with undershoot of articulatory constrictions (Stevens and House, 1963; Lindblom, 1963; Kent and Moll, 1972; Haggard, 1974; Umeda and Coker, 1974; Giles and Moll, 1975). Combined with variations particular to running speech, such as timing and stress, co-articulatory phenomena may lead to considerable differences in the acoustic cues underlying phonemes and syllables as represented in isolated nonsense syllables vs as represented in running speech.

The identification of excised isolated words markedly improves when speech context is provided. Pickett and Pollack (1963) found that the presence of one or two adjacent words significantly improved the identification of the initially excised word, and Winitz et al. (1973) found high proportions of identification for initially excised words when they occurred in the context of phrase units.

Context is in someway providing normalization cues for the listener. There have been several demonstrations that

physical characteristics of context may play a role in per-
ception--among these characteristics are tempo,formant characteristics of vowels and surrounding transitions, fundamental
frequency contours. Additionally, of course, context may be
providing linguistic cues which help the listener narrow his
response alternatives for the target word.

This investigation represents a pilot study in a series
of experiments which have the long term objective of more
specifically identifying the range of variation in running
speech and the physical and non-physical aspects of context
which serve normalization functions in its perception. In
particular, it involves an investigation of the normalization
function provided by extra-syllabic formant transitions. Co-
articulatory effects have been shown to cross syllable and
word boundaries by many investigators (e.g. Ohman, 1966;
Daniloff and Moll, 1971; Lewis and Daniloff, 1975), and there
is evidence (e.g. Kuehn and Moll, 1972; Lehiste and Shockey,
1972) that extra-syllable phonetic cues, perhaps the leading
and following transitions, are perceptually relevant for consonant identification.

In this experiment, the effect of the immediately adjacent vowels external to some target word was examined in order
to determine their influence on word identification, and the
role of speech context was re-examined by studying the influence of the immediately adjacent words. Errors for the isolated excised words were also examined, with particular emphasis on vowel identification.

PROCEDURE

High quality recording were made of two adult male talkers
reading, in a comfortable manner, 16 paragraphs. Both talkers
were native mid-westerners; they had no formal background in
speech or phonetics, and they were naive concerning the purpose of the experiment.

Each of the 16 paragraphs contained four to five sentences.
A target word was embedded in the next to last sentence of the
paragraph. Target words were of the form CVC or CVCC. Initial
and final consonants were voiceless obstruents. The target

word was either a direct object or a complement. Neighboring
words were usually function words. Words preceding the target word terminated with the vowel / ə /, and words following
the target word began with the vowel / ə /. Target words and
their original sentence frames are shown in Table 1.

From these original recordings, eight excerpts were elec-
tronically gated from each paragraph: (1) The sentence containing the target word. (2) The isolated target word. (3)
The target word and the following vowel. (4) The preceding
vowel and the target word. (5) The preceding vowel, the target vowel, and the following vowel. (6) The preceding word,
target word, and following vowel. (7) The preceding word and
the target word. (8) The target word and the following word.
The procedures for the gating have been described in LaRiviere
et al. (1975). In all instances, a rise-fall time of 10 msec
was used. Spectrographic and oscillographic displays were
used throughout to isolate experimental segments.

Eight different audio listening tapes--one for each ex-
cerpt--were prepared. Each tape consisted of 96 items--16
targets x 2 speakers x 3 repetitions. Order of items was
randomly placed within each list. Each item was separated
by 6 sec. of silence. For each experimental tape, listeners
were 10 undergraduates, all of whom were native American
speakers with normal hearing. All listening was done with
headsets in a sound treated room. Stimuli were presented at
a comfortable level and all subjects listened singly or in
well separated pairs.

The instructions to the listeners spelled out the particular listening task. Each listener was to respond by writing
the sentences or words immediately after presentation. Listeners who were presented the isolated word with one or more
adjoining vowels (conditions 3, 4, and 5) were instructed
that the target word appeared within the context of a vowel
or vowels.

RESULTS

Proportions correct for all conditions and for C_1, V and
C_n (the last consonant) are shown in Table 2. As shown there,

the target word is identified at a near perfect level (.98)
when it appears in the context of a sentence. For the excised word, proportion of correct identification falls to
.75, a value somewhat higher than found in previous investigations.

Although the differences among conditions 2 through 8
appear small, an analysis of variance showed a significant
main effect for conditions ($F_{6,63}$ = 8.99) and talkers ($F_{1,63}$
= 8.99) and talkers ($F_{1,63}$ = 4.06). The condition by talker
interaction was also significant ($F_{6,63}$ = 3.25). Pairwise
comparisons among means were tested using the Scheffe test
(Winer, 1962). Significant differences were obtained between
condition 4 and 6, 2 and 3, 3 and 5, 3 and 6, 3 and 7, and 3
and 8. So, the word plus following vowel condition was significantly depressed relative to most other groups. These
results do not reflect a normalization function for extra-
syllabic formant transition.

As also shown in Table 2, a greater proportion of errors
occur for C_n than for C_1. Errors of final position are apparently the primary contributor to word identification errors.
For condition 2, the proportion of word errors for the 8 words
ending in fricatives and the 8 words ending in stops were
compared. Error rates were not significantly different.

Correct vowel identification was uniformly high. With
the exception of condition 8, correct vowel identification
was less than C_1, but in all cases greater than C_n. In order to examine the influence of consonantal perception on
vowel identification, the distribution of vowel errors was
examined for condition 2 (excised word). The vowel errors
were distributed as follows: Following a C_1 error, .28; preceding a C_n error, .33; for C_1 and C_n error co-occurring,
.04; no consonantal errors, .33. These results suggest that
vowel errors are largely independent of consonantal errors.
However, an interpretation which should not be drawn from
this error distribution is that consonantal context is unimportant in vowel identification.

In a recent experiment by Verbrugge et al.(1976), vowel
identification was compared for destressed syllables appearing

in, and excised from, a carrier sentence. All syllables were
of the form /cVp/, and the carrier sentence was: "The little
/cVp/ chair is read." Each sentence was read rapidly with
stress being placed on the word chair. Under these conditions the vowel was best identified when presented in the context of the entire sentence. (Error rate for the excised
unit was greater than that obtained in the present investigation). Verbrugge et al. concluded that increased identification in the carrier sentence condition resulted from information about talker tempo. It may be the case that
listeners use tempo to normalize information provided by the
formant transitions.

Normalization on the basis of tempo information seems to
be a reasonable hypothesis and deserves further attention.
However, the high level of vowel identification obtained in
the investigation suggest that there are additional factors
which specify vowel perception in running speech. Vowel identification may reflect an analysis by synthesis process in
which "word" and vowel are primary components. Conceivably,
when auditory units are not construed by listeners as words,
vowel identification will reflect normalization schemes as
well as formant information. Not surprisingly, only one
error response in this investigation was a non-word. Under
natural listening conditions, then, the word seems to be a
basic perceptual unit (Fant, 1970; Itahashi et al., 1973).
Words are in turn restricted by sentential context (Miller,
1961). Errors in acoustic processing, then, are corrected by
word identification, which in the context of a sentence will
reflect linguistic information.

Of the 241 word errors for condition 2, 33% involved a
vowel and/or consonantal error, and 67% involved only consonantal errors. An analysis of vowel errors showed that 54%
of them occurred in the presence of consonantal errors in
which the original vowel would not be appropriate, eg. tack -
check. So, in about half the instances, it can be said that
vowel errors may be determined by non-acoustic factors.

These findings suggest that non-acoustic factors will influence vowel identification when listeners have prior knowledge that speech units are words. Accordingly, there is the

possibility that many of the correct identifications obtained
for vowels in this study may simply reflect word constraints.
This factor is difficult to assess in this study because no
regard for this factor guided the initial selection of words.
Another variable which may influence the identification of
excerpted words is frequency of word usage (Howes and Solomon
1951). Each target word in this study was ranked in frequency
using the indexes provided by Thorndike and Lorge (1944) and
Carroll, Davies and Richman (1971). Initially, a comparison
was made between the words most frequently occurring and those
less frequently occurring. Using the Thorndike and Lorge index, words were classified as either AA words (100 or over per
million) or words with frequency values less than AA. Using
the Carroll et al. index, their SFI rankings were employed to
divide the 16 words into high frequency and low frequency
groups. In both indexes, words of high frequency were significantly better identified than words of low frequency. A
rank order correlation was also performed, using SFI rankings
and the number of correct identifications for each word. The
resulting r was .31 (t = 1.22, df = 14, p < .05).

CONCLUSION

The results of this preliminary experiment suggest that the
most useful acoustic information resides within the syllable,
and that this information gets fine tuned by linguistic constraints involving word frequency and what may amount to an
ongoing cloze procedure in the perception of running speech.
A weighting of the contribution of acoustic information and
linguistic information will be a difficult thing to do for
natural, running speech--if indeed listeners use consistent
normalization strategies. Further experiments dealing with
word recovery will require better a priori controls of word
frequency and confusability. Acoustic and linguistic constraints might best be examined using a precursor format
similar to Ladefoged and Broadbent's, so that a given target
word may be preceded, at varying time relationships, by information which is in some cases related and in some cases
not related to the excised words in terms of tempo, intonation, speaker, syntax or semantics.

REFERENCES

Carroll, J. B., Davies, P., and Richman, B. (1971). New
    York: Houghton–Mifflin.
Danniloff, R. G. and Moll, K. (1968). J. Speech Hear.
    Res. 1:707–721.
Fant, G. (1971). STL/QPRS. 1:16–31.
Giles, S. B. and Moll, K. L. (1975). Phonet. 31:206–227.
Haggard, M. (1974). J. Phonet. 2:117–123.
Howes, D. and Soloman, R. L. (1951). J. Exp. Psych. 41:
    401–410.
Itahashi, S., Makino, S., and Kido, K. (1973). IRE Trans.
    Electroacoust. Au–21:239–249.
Kent, R. D. and Moll, K. L. (1972). J. Speech Hear. Res.
    15:453–473.
Kuehn, D. P. and Moll, K. L. (1972). J. Speech Hear. Res.
    15:654–664.
LaRiviere, C., Winitz, H. and Herriman, E. (1975). J. Speech
    Hear. Res. 18:613–622.
Lehiste, I. and Shockey, L. (1972). J. Speech Hear. Res.
    15:500–506.
Lieberman, P. (1963). Lang. Speech. 6:172–187.
Lindblom, B. (1963). J. Acous. Soc. Amer. 34:1773–1781.
Miller, G. (1961). IRE Trans. Inform. Theory 81–83.
Ohman, S. E. G. (1966). J. Acoust. Soc. Amer. 39:151–168.
Pickett, J. and Pollack, I. (1963). Lang. Speech. 6:151–164.
Stevens, K. N. and House, A. S. (1966). J. Speech Hear. Res.
    6:111–128.
Thorndike, E. L. and Lorge, I. (1944). New York: Columbia
    University.
Umeda, N., and Coker, C. H. (1975). J. Phonet. 2:1–5.
Verbrugge, R. R., Strange, W., Shankweiler, D. P., and
    Edman, T. R. (1976). J. Acoust. Soc. Amer. 60:198–212.
Winer, B. J. (1962). New York: McGraw-Hill.
Winitz, H., LaRiviere, C., and Herriman, E. (1973). Phonet.
    27:193–212.

TABLE 1. Target words and the sentence in which they occurred.

Target word	Sentence
talk	He never gave the talk about linguistics.
fight	It was a fight about her boy friend.
pick	One man took the pick assigned for the job.
tack	The boy found the tack under the chair.
course	He had predicted the course of events accurately.
tense	One well known speaker explained the tense of verbs.
sense	The boy had the sense of an older man.
peace	It was the peace among men that was so important.
fife	He put the fife upon the shelf.
seat	He took a seat apart from the group.
calf	He found the calf under a bush.
fake	Therefore, he blessed the fake alone.
feat	The announcer proclaimed the feat about to be performed.
cop	The people told the cop about it.
face	He had the face adorning all his paintings.
farce	The president abhorred the farce of war.

TABLE 2. Proportion correct identification for the target word, and the first consonant (C_1), the vowel (V), and the last consonant (C_n).

Condition	Target Word	C_1	V	C_n
(1) sentence	.98	1.00	1.00	.98
(2) word	.75	.95	.92	.81
(3) word # /ə/	.64	.94	.92	.72
(4) /ə/ # word	.72	.99	.90	.80
(5) /ə/ # word # /ə/	.77	.98	.97	.79
(6) word # word # word	.82	.99	.96	.85
(7) word # word	.80	.98	.95	.84
(8) word # word	.76	.89	.93	.87

SOME PHYSIOLOGICAL INTERPRETATIONS OF THE
PERCEPTION OF VOWEL DURATION ABOVE AND
BELOW THE ONE-PERIOD BOUNDARY

HERBERT R. MASTHOFF
Universität Trier, W. Germany

Since we do not really know, how the speech signal is
processed, a great number of models for the perception of
speech has been developed in the past. It is a general experience that during normal communication conditions, speech
sounds are not always correctly identified or, in other words,
perception errors occur during the communication process. This
has made a point in Lindner's model (1969) for example. Such
errors are mostly due to accompanying noise, distortions or are
evoked by the inattentiveness of the listener. Indeed, a lot
of sounds and noises act upon the ear of which human speech
forms only a part of. Therefore, the selection made by the
listener also forms a potential source of errors.

It is the aim of this paper to show that not only the
factors mentioned above cause perception errors, but that also
some physiological properties of the outer and middle ear are
responsible for typical error patterns, which have been
evaluated under unfavorable conditions, that is, short duration, in the perception test described below.

ACOUSTIC ENERGY AND THE OUTER
AND MIDDLE EAR

Since the auditory transmission mode differs from visual
or tactile transmission, it appears to be possible that this
is a potential error source, too. The external auditory canal
forms the significant part of the outer ear. Besides its

protective function for the middle ear, the external auditory
canal has a natural frequency which ranges from 2000 to 3000
cps. According to Békésy (1960), the peak of pressure increase due to resonance is reached at about 2400 cps. This
means that tones with a frequency between 2000 and 3000 cps
are amplified in the external auditory meatus.

The ossicular chain consisting of malleus, incus and
stapes forms a mechanical connection between the eardrum and
the cochlear fluid. This connection helps to reduce the
pressure loss which would be immense if the transmission
directly took place from the air to the cochlear fluid. The
impeding mass factor is compensated by the special suspension
of the ossicles which are optimally balanced so that it will
keep friction as small as possible. Although the mass factor
is thereby reduced, there is still a loss in transmission
pressure in the middle ear being due to stiffness and being
more or less strong according to the transmitted frequency.
The stiffness factor is produced by the middle ear muscles,
by the ligaments and by the mechanical action of the middle
ear itself. Thus, above the natural frequency of the ossicula
chain a growing dampening of the oscillations can be observed.
At about 2000 cps, the ear ossicles are no longer capable of
oscillating. Transmission is then taken over by bone conduction
It is important though that the natural frequency of the
ossicular chain lies between 800 - 1500 cps.

METHOD

Stimuli. The five German cardinal vowels /i, e, a, o, u/
spoken with a fundamental frequency of 100 cps were the basic
material for the preparation of the stimuli. They were distributed and randomized in 15 groups. Each group represented
a duration unit. The groups were played successively, beginning
with group 1 and ending with group 15. Each vowel occurred
three times in its respective group so that each group consisted of 15 stimuli. The stimuli were separated by a five
second pause to avoid contrastive identification. Figure 2
shows the distribution of the groups with the corresponding
duration. The subjects, consisting of 30 phonetically
unskilled female students (aged 20-25) were asked to
identify the segments, being able to choose /i, e, a, o, u/

and "not identifiable." Table 1 shows the frequencies of F_1
and F_2 for the vowels. The frequencies of the vowels were
measured after the stimuli had been prepared by cross-
sectioning the longest segment (70 ms). The segmentor SEG
IV a), a development of the electronics laboratory at the
University of Trier, was used for the segmenting. This
segmentor works with an almost right-angular time gate.
Further details can be found in a publication of H. Klos/
J. P. Koster (1977), to appear in the Hamburger Phonetische
Beitrage Bd. 24.

RESULTS

The identification rate for each vowel is listed in Table
2. The errors of the 15 groups were analyzed in three
sections with section one comprising the groups 1-7. The
groups 8-13 and 14-15 in section two and three represent the
groups with durations below one period and are distinguished
by the significant increase of errors in group 14 and group
15. It can be seen that there is a considerable difference
in the identification ability among the vowels in the following order: /a, i, o, u, e/. It should be remarked that the
average identification rate of the vowels /i, e, o, u/ and
especially of /a/ is relatively high below the one period
boundary, since at durations below this boundary the sound
wave information is erased, being higher the shorter the
segments are. Also, the hierarchy of the vowels concerning
the identification rate does not change below one period.
Spectrograms which were being made of the 5 ms stimuli showed
that although the curve information is obstructed below one
period, the remaining information is sufficient for building
up formant-like structures.

DISCUSSION

The resonance features and transmission properties of the
outer and middle ear can be related to the results obtained
in the test. Accordingly the extremely high identification
rate of /a/ is achieved by the natural frequency (800-1500
cps) of the ossicular chain. The first formant and the second
formant are within this frequency region. Also there is a
minimum pressure loss during the transmission through the

middle ear at about 1200 cps (Figure 1). The relatively
high scores on /i/ can be attributed to the peak of pressure
increase due to resonance in the meatus at about 2500 cps
being important for the amplification of the second formant.
The vowels /o/ and /u/ suffer a strong transmission loss in
the middle ear with respect to their second formant and have
a moderate loss with respect to their first formant. This
causes the low scores on /o/ and /u/ compared to /i/ and /a/.
However, no explanation from the physiological point of view
was found for the slightly better scores on /o/ in comparison
to /u/. Obviously /e/ has the lowest identification rate of
the five vowels. The reason for this could be seen in the
relatively high transmission pressure loss for the first
formant in the middle ear on one hand, on the other, although
there is a pressure increase peak at about 2600 cps, it is
likely that this increase is compensated by a possible zone
of uncertainty when the oscillations of the ear ossicles stop
at this frequency and bone conduction begins to transmit the
higher frequencies.

CONCLUSION

It has been shown that at least for /i/ and /a/ there are
indications that the identification ability under unfavourable
conditions is influenced by the physiological properties of
the outer and middle ear. Such conditions were created by
presenting very short stimuli to the subject. For /u, o, e/
this is less clear. However, if speech sound identification
depends upon physiological properties of the ear, the construction of machines which are commanded by speech should
not necessarily be based upon human auditive identification
and discrimination abilities, unless the receptive units
would completely correspond to the human decoding mechanism.
On the other hand, when trying to answer the question of
what part of the acoustic information is redundant, the
physiological properties of the ear should be considered,
since the acoustic information is subject to physiological
filtering and amplification processes.

REFERENCES

Békésy, G. von. (1960). New York.
Clasen, B. and Gersic, S. (1975). Hamburg, Buske.
Klinke, R. (1972). München.
Kapal, E.: Gehörsinn. (1960-62). Berlin.
Köster, J-P. and Dreyfus-Graf, J. A. (1976). Hamb. Phon. Beit., 17:35-82.
Lindner, G. (1969). München.
Minifie, Fred D. et al. (1973).New Jersey, Englewood Cliffs.
Møeller, A. R. (1963). J. Acoust. Soc. Am., 35:1526.
Møeller, A. R. (1965). Acta Oto-lary., 60:129.
Klos, H. and Köster, J. P. (1977). HPB 24, Hamburg.

Table 1. Vowel frequencies.

Vowel	F_1	F_2
i	250	2300
e	400	2000
a	850	1200
o	350	800
u	250	700

Table 2. Identification rates.

Vowel	1-7	8-13	14-15
i	89%	87%	43%
e	68%	56%	30%
a	99%	100%	99%
o	84%	62%	35%
u	90%	58%	31%

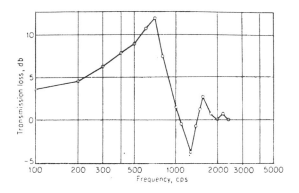

<u>FIGURE 1</u>

Transmission loss in the middle ear
(From: Békésy, 1960)

GROUP	DURATION (ms)
1	70
2	60
3	50
4	40
5	30
6	20
7	10
8	9
9	8
10	7
11	6
12	5
13	4
14	3
15	2

<u>FIGURE 2</u>

PROSODIC EXPECTANCIES IN SPEECH PERCEPTION: IMPLICATIONS OF AN EXPERIMENT ON THE PERCEPTION OF SEGMENTED SPEECH

JOHN OAKESHOTT-TAYLOR
University of Trier

It is well-known that excised words are low in intelligibility. Our own experiments have confirmed this. Words which have been segmented from carrier phrases are generally much less intelligible than when they are heard in their original context (Oakeshott-Taylor, in press). Partially responsible for the lower intelligibility are undoubtedly distortions in the signal caused by the process of segmentation itself. Segmentation will interrupt coarticulated cues, and will introduce unnatural-sounding onsets and offsets which may interfere with the perception of boundary phonemes.

Examination of responses to excised words, however, suggested that these were not the only factors at work. To investigate this possibility, we designed experiments in which segmentation would not interfere with the acoustic cues to the test items. To achieve this objective, we tested the perception of 14 English vowels inserted in a constant /p-ps/ frame. A native speaker of British English spoke two tokens of each vowel in the syllable context; the syllables were also spoken in each of the following three sentences: (a) They can't have been /pVps/. (b) They can't have been /pVps/, can they? and (c) The little /pVps/ can't have been there. We reasoned that by "protecting" the stimulus variable (that is, the vowel) by bilateral syllable context, the integrity of acoustic cues pertaining to the vowel would not be disturbed by the removal of the sentence context. While it is true that coarticulation effects typically extend beyond adjacent segments

the perceptual significance of these effects is minimal
(Lehiste and Shockey, 1972). We may thus assume that listeners to the excised syllables were exposed to the same
range of vowel cues as listeners to contextualized syllables.

The test syllables were presented for identification in
three conditions: "intact," that is, in the context in which
they were originally spoken; "excised," in which the syllables
excised from each of the three sentences were presented in
blocks; and "randomized," in which excised and isolated syllables were presented in random sequence. Results (Fig. 1)
show that identification rates decline when sentence context
is removed, and that a further decline occurs when syllables
are heard in random sequence.

In a second stage of the experiment, the syllables were
subjected to an acoustic analysis. It was found that the
duration, peak intensity and F_0 modulation of the vowel segments, vowel duration as percentage of syllable duration, as
well as formant frequencies, all varied as a function of the
context in which the syllables had been spoken.

Acoustic changes as a function of context suggest an
explanation for the reduced intelligibility of excised and
randomized syllables. An utterance is characterized by
prosodic redundancies. If n-1 syllables of an utterance
have been heard, the prosodic shape of the nth syllable is
very largely predictable. Its pitch and accentuation may
be roughly determined by extrapolating the intonation and
rhythm of the rest of the utterance, while vowel duration
is principally a function of syllable position relative to
pauses (Lindblom and Rapp, 1973). The degree of formant
undershoot may also be derived from vowel duration and accentuation (Lindblom, 1963). We would favour a model of perception in which a listener actively utilizes contextual information to anticipate, or internally compute, the general prosodic outline of words which have not yet been heard (Martin,
1975). Thus the very dramatic changes in the acoustic shape
of a word which occur when a word is spoken in different
types of context are not accompanied by equally dramatic
changes in intelligibility. Rather changes in acoustic shape
(of which durational changes are perhaps the most striking)

can be "normalized" by the listener on the basis of contextual information.

The intelligibility of excised words, on the other hand, would appear to correlate more closely with context conditioned acoustic changes. Excised words are prosodically "anomalous" in that, although heard in isolation, their duration, temporal structure, pitch and intensity patterns are quite untypical of one-word utterances. The suppression of context removes the basis on which a listener can anticipate, and so normalize, the prosodic shape of a word. If, however, words excised from the same carrier phrase are heard in a block, the listener may well be able to build up prosodic expectancies within the stimulus block. This will not be possible with randomized presentation. Here, the duration and other parameters of the stimuli will vary very considerably and unpredictably from one stimulus to the next.

An analysis of error responses in the different conditions revealed a number of trends. Excised syllables (particularly those originally spoken in non-final position) showed an increase in the number of errors on inherently long vowels, accompanied by an increased response bias in favour of short vowels (Fig. 2); there was also an increase in the number of errors on vowels occupying more extreme positions in the vowel space. These trends were accentuated with randomized presentation. This suggests that listeners to the excised and randomized syllables were unable to normalize vowel durations and formant undershoot.

We have extended the procedure outlined above to a study of plosive perception. Plosives were inserted in /CVCs/ syllables in which the vowel nucleus was held constant. These syllables were spoken in isolation and in the three carrier phrases, and were presented for identification in intact, excised and randomized conditions. We found that post-vocalic stops were not perceived differently in the excised and intact conditions. However when citation forms and excised syllables were randomized, we found a marked bias towards voiceless responses to those syllables excised from sentences b and c.

It is known that a major cue to the voicing of a post-vocalic consonant is the duration of a preceding vowel

(Raphael, 1972). An acoustic analysis of our stimuli, however, showed that post-vocalic voicing must be judged in
terms of the relative, not the absolute duration of the
vowel, since the "lengthened" vowels in sentence c were
considerably shorter than the "shortened" vowels of citation
forms. Presumably, when excised syllables were presented in
blocks, listeners could quickly adapt to the durational properties of the stimuli, and could readily discriminate post-
vocalic voicing on the basis of differences in absolute vowel
duration. With randomized presentation, however, absolute
duration varied considerably and unpredictably from stimulus
to stimulus. The--in absolute terms--short vowels in syllables excised from sentences b and c appear to have been perceived against the norm of the physically longer vowels of
citation forms and utterance-final syllables, thus giving
rise to an increase in the number of voiceless responses to
post-vocalic stops.

The results of these two experiments are particularly
suggestive as regards the processing of durational cues. Inasfar as vowel duration is a cue for vowel identity and
post-vocalic voicing, what is important is the relative, not
the absolute, duration of the vowel. Ainsworth (1972) has
proposed a normalization of vowel duration on the basis of
speaking rate (see also Verbrugge et al., 1976). However,
even at a constant subjective speaking rate, very large variations in vowel duration occur as a function of the position
of the syllable in the utterance. It would seem that rules
governing segment durations within an utterance form part of
a language user's "phonetic competence," and are invoked in
perception as well as production. The operation of these
rules allows the listener to ongoing speech to normalize
changes in duration, and thus permits him to extract from
absolute durations information pertaining to the "inherent"
length of a vowel and to the voicing of a following consonant.
Inasfar as the degree of formant undershoot is a function of
vowel shortening, the computation of context-conditioned
changes in duration will also permit the listener to compensate, perceptually, for formant undershoot.

REFERENCES

Ainsworth, W. A.   (1972).   J. Acoust. Soc. Am., 51:648-651.
Lehiste, I. and Shockey, L.   (1972).   J. Speech Hear. Res.,
     15:500-506.
Lindblom, B.   (1963).   J. Acoust. Soc. Am., 35:1773-1781.
Lindblom, B. and Rapp, K.   (1973).   Univ. Stockholm, No. 21.
Martin, J. G.   (1975).   Cohen and Nooteboom (eds.).
     Structure and Process in Speech Perception, 161-177.
Oakeshott-Taylor, J.   (1978).   Hamburger Phonetische
     Beiträge, No. 25.
Raphael, L. J.   (1972).   J. Acoust. Soc. Am., 51:1296-1303.
Verbrugge, R. R., Shankweiler, D., Strange, W. and Edman,
     I. R.   (1976).   Haskins Lab. Stat. Rep., SR-47, 165-170.

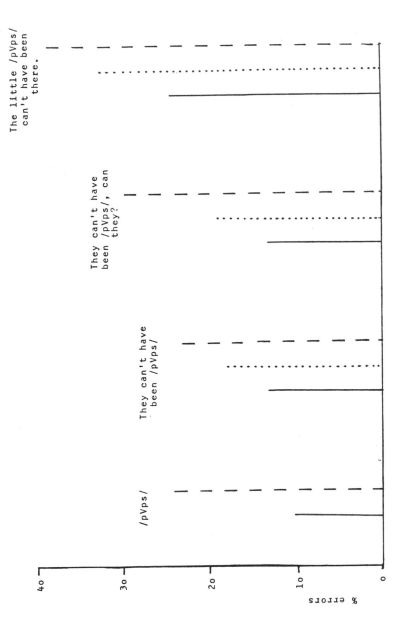

Fig. 1: Percentage error responses to intact (————), excised (•••••) and randomized
(— — —) presentation of syllables spoken in different contexts

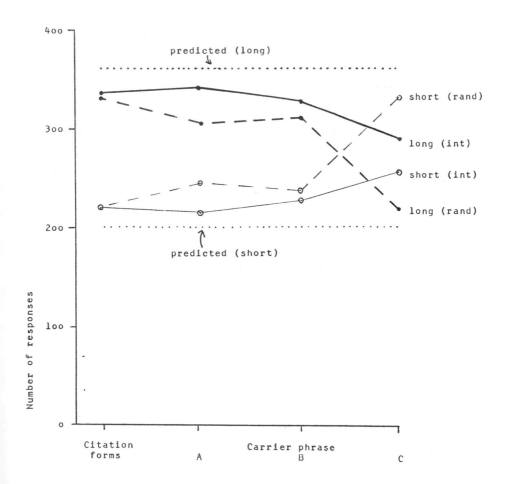

Fig. 2: Number of long and short vowel responses to
         intact and randomized presentation of syllables
         spoken in different contexts. Dotted lines
         show the number of responses which would have
         been expected if subjects had responded randomly.

PERCEPTION OF SPEECH FEATURES BY PERSONS WITH HEARING IMPAIRMENT

JAMES M. PICKETT
Gallaudet College

Speech perception by listeners with severe hearing impairment has not been studied intensively for its psychoacoustic detail. For normal listeners we know fairly well what acoustic pattern cues are used to discriminate the main phonetic features of speech sounds (Liberman et al., 1967). If we had similar knowledge about impaired speech perception we might be able to develop better methods of training hearing-impaired persons to use their remaining auditory capacity. We would also have a better basis for designing new aids for the deaf. The impairments of most crucial concern are cases of moderate and severe sensori-neural damage which typically show deficient perception of speech even under optimum conditions. In this paper we analyze and interpret the results of research studies on the perception of phonetic features by such persons.

Siegenthaler (1954) tested consonant discrimination by hearing-impaired listeners when they were listening at or near their speech reception thresholds. He found that voicing of consonants was discriminated better than place of articulation which, in turn, was perceived better than the stop-fricative and affricative distinctions. This was true for subgroups of the listeners, classified as having "conductive, perceptive, or mixed" impairment, and also for normal listeners. In overall intelligibility, as measured in free-response tests, voiced consonants were more intelligible than unvoiced consonants. In a smaller study Siegenthaler (1949) found that a group of five listeners with flat audiograms, i.e., with relatively constant hearing loss across frequency, discriminated voicing and place equally. In contrast a group of five listeners with sloping audiograms, having better hearing in the low frequencies and poorer hearing above about 1000 Hz, discriminated voicing somewhat better than the flat group. And the sloping group discriminated the place of articulation and the stop-fricative distinctions more poorly than the flat group.

LaBenz (1956) studied speech reception in different frequency regions by listeners with sensorineural hearing loss as compared with normal listeners. The impaired listeners were divided into three classes: sensorineural, mixed, and conductive. The results showed that, for speech limited to frequencies below 500 Hz, the impaired listeners achieved the same average performance (% words correct) as normal listeners. As middle and high frequencies were progressively added to the speech, all listeners obtained progressively higher scores, but the sensorineural listeners lagged behind the mixed cases who, in turn, lagged behind the normal listeners. These results strongly imply that sensorineural listeners as a group use the same low-frequency speech cues as normals and that sensorineural listeners do not make full use of the cues in middle and high-frequency regions.

Oyer and Doudna (1959) analyzed the word responses to W-22 words of a large group of impaired patients with mild to moderate losses. Errors were much more frequent for front vowels than for back vowels; the confusion responses were mostly other front vowels that were close to the stimulus vowel in both the first formant (F1) and the second formant (F2) but unrelated in duration. The consonant confusion patterns, when rearranged, showed better reception of the voicing and manner features than the place features. Initial consonants were received better than final consonants. In subgroups of the patients classified as conductive and non-conductive, reception for general classes of vowels and consonants was uniformly poorer for non-conductives than for conductives although average hearing loss (.5, 1, 2K) was 2.2 dB greater for the conductive subgroup. Confusions were not analyzed for subgroups.

Rosen (1962) analyzed the phoneme confusions of a large group of sensorineural listeners as seen in clinical PB word

tests. The vowel confusions tended to show correct hearing
of F1 and the vowel duration. If we consider only those
vowel confusions in Rosen's data that contributed 10% or
more of all the confusions to a given stimulus vowel, we
suppress the appearance of random confusions and emphasize
the confusions of the poorest listeners; the pattern that
emerges is similar to that found with normal listeners under
noise conditions that mask mainly the middle and high frequencies (Pickett, 1957). Rosen's discrimination scores
(% correct) for individual vowels showed an inverse relation
between vowel discrimination score and the frequency of F1;
that is, discrimination of vowels with low F1 like /i, u, I/
and /ʊ/, was better than for vowels with high F1, like
/ɛ, ɔ, æ/. and /a/.

The consonant confusion patterns of Rosen's sensorineural
listeners were similar to those obtained by Miller and Nicely
(1955) with normal listeners under white noise masking or with
low-pass filtering; the reception of place features was poor
relative to the voicing and nasality features. This similarity
was obtained despite the fact that Rosen's data were from "free
response" tests with words while the data of Miller and Nicely
were from tests where there was a closed set of 16 consonants
in nonsense syllables and these were known to the listeners.

Cox (1969) tested consonant discrimination, using closed
response sets of one-syllable words, with twenty sensorineural
listeners. Initial consonants were tested before the vowels
/i/, /a/, and /u/. Effects of four conditions of filtering
were tested: unfiltered, and low-pass 2000 Hz, 1000 Hz, and
500 Hz. Under all filtered and unfiltered conditions, the
place features of the consonants were much more poorly discriminated than the voicing feature and than the manner features. When the vowel F2 was high, as for /i/, place discrimination was the poorest. Progressive removal of the
frequencies below 2000 Hz reduced discrimination of all features with all three vowels. The voicing feature was discriminated somewhat better than the manner features, with /u/
however, there was little or no difference in this respect.
There were, however, large differences with /i/ between
voicing and manner for speech low-passed at 2000 Hz or below.
Thus, before the vowel /i/, manner features seemed to depend

on the region above 2000 Hz but the voicing feature showed
no dependence on the presence of frequencies above 2000 Hz.

Cox's data for sensorineural listeners are consistent,
at least in general, with data on normal listeners. In
Cox's unfiltered tests, the voicing feature and manner
features were perceived better than the place features; this
was also true for the normal listeners of Miller and Nicely
when listening through low-passing filtering. Another interesting effect in Cox's data is that, when F2 is low, as
with /u/, removing the frequencies above 2000 Hz did not
cause any significant changes in discrimination of any of
the feature categories. However, when F2 was higher, as
with /i/ and /a/, discrimination of all three features,
voicing, place, and manner, was significantly reduced by
removing the frequencies above 2000 Hz, except for the voicing feature with /i/. The reduction was very large for
reception of the manner features with /i/.

Schultz (1964) constructed phoneme confusion matrices
for consonant and vowel responses to the W-22 word test administered clinically to sensorineural listeners who were
classified into four types: (1) Meniere's disease, (2)
acoustic trauma, (3) presbycusic, (4) other sensorineural.
The confusion patterns were more or less similar for the
four types. A rearrangement of Schultz' data reveals the
following relations in perception of the phonetic features.
The error rate for front vowels was nearly twice the error
for back vowels; also confusions tended to match the stimulus
vowel in duration and, except for Meniere's cases and presby-
cusics, confusions tended to match the first formant frequency. In the consonant confusions the error rate was twice
as high for place of articulation as for manner, and manner
errors were nine times as frequent as voicing errors.

Owens et al. (1968a, 1968b) reported an analysis of the
responses of listeners with impaired discrimination to
multiple-choice tests under development for clinical use.
Each test item contained four words as a closed response
set. Vowels were discriminated at a level of 93.6% correct
compared with a chance level of 25%. The error rate for
front vowels was much lower than for back vowels, contrary

to the results of Schultz (1964). Initial consonants were
discriminated better than final consonants. The error rate
for reception of the voicing of consonants was very low,
about 1.5%. Perception of the liquid and nasal features
was very accurate. Lawrence and Byers (1969) tested reception of the voiceless fricatives in initial combination
with /i, e, o/ and /u/, by listeners with high-frequency
sensorineural impairment. Correct reception of these consonants was considerably higher before the two back vowels
/o/ and /u/ (about 95% correct), than before the two front
vowels /i/ and /e/ (about 65% correct). There were no large
differences in reception among the four consonants, although
individual listeners were different in this respect.

Pickett et al. (1972) studied the structure of speech
reception in the range of severe-to-profound sensorineural
impairment. A special version of the Fairbanks-House Modified
Rhyme Test was administered to 99 subjects and the responses
were then analyzed by examining vowel confusions and by
calculating the proportions of responses correct as to feature
for the consonant features of voicing, manner, and place of
articulation, for both initial and final consonants.

The new Rhyme Test consisted of 50 items, 20 testing
initial consonants, 20 testing final consonants, and 10 testing vowels. Each item consisted of six one-syllable response
words chosen as nearly as possible to cover the distinctions
of interest. The stimulus word for each item was chosen at
random from among the six response words; all were one-
syllable words. The 50 stimulus words were recorded and pronounced by an experienced male talker who monitored himself
closely on a VU meter. The Rhyme Test responses of ninety-
nine selected students were analyzed. The basis for selection
was to use the data of all students on which it was possible
to obtain an SRT. The subjects' audiograms and probable
causes of deafness were carefully examined with a view to
grouping the response data for analysis in various ways.
Correlations were run between Rhyme Test score, average
hearing loss, and duration of use of a hearing aid. None
of these approaches looked especially cogent or promising so
we decided to group the responses of the subjects by quartiles
of discrimination ability as measured by the overall Rhyme
Test score.

The results showed that vowels were discriminated
better than initial consonants which, in turn, were discriminated somewhat better than final consonants. The
advantage of vowels was very large. It was also noted that
the poorest group of subjects scored close to chance for
consonants, but still retained some vowel discrimination.
For each different stimulus vowel we also studied how well ·
the vowel was perceived, and how the confusions were distributed over the other vowels especially as related to the
formant frequency relations of the stimulus vowel and the
response vowels. The basic data for this analysis were the
frequencies of response, for each quartile group of listeners, in the correct vowel categories and in the confusion
vowel categories. It was found that the confusions were not
randomly distributed over the available categories of confusion responses but showed definite patterning. In the
responses to the long vowels /i, u, ou, ɔ , æ /, the confusion
patterns for a given stimulus vowel were similar for increasing levels of discrimination, the changes in confusions, consisting more or less of progressive elimination of the confusions typical for the poorest group. The two short vowels
/I,ʌ/ were confused less than the other vowels.

The consonant responses were analyzed to determine how
well certain phonetic features were received by the listeners.
The analysis was made for three features: (1) place of articulation, (2) voicing, and (3) low continuant, i.e., the
occurrence of strong low-frequency energy as in nasals,
liquids, and glides, as opposed to stops and fricatives. The
results of the analysis of feature reception showed that
the place features of both initial and final consonants were
received much more poorly than the voicing feature and the
low-continuant feature. For final consonants voicing was
received somewhat better than the low-continuant feature.
For final consonants voicing was received somewhat better
than the low-continuant feature but these were about equally
received in initial consonants. As a whole, the features of
initial consonants are received better than those of final
consonants. The best subjects receive initial voicing and
low-continuant almost perfectly but still make errors in
hearing the place of articulation for initial consonants.

Taking all results together, the evidence strongly suggests that the second formant region of vowel sounds is not clearly discriminable to sensorineural listeners who show impairment of severe to profound degree. It appears that the first formant position and duration of vowels are well discriminated by all but the more profound cases.

It is well known that discrimination of place of articulation of consonants by normal listeners can be accomplished on the basis of perceiving the transitions in the frequency of the second formant of the adjacent vowel. Our present results how that the place feature is poorly perceived by sensorineural listeners. On the other hand, the consonant features of voicing and of presence or absence of low-continuant energy, may depend on hearing only the gross features of the low-frequency speech patterns. Voicing of consonants may be partially perceived by discriminating vowel durations. It would be interesting, in view of this, to measure the discrimination of sound duration by sensorineural listeners having different degrees of loss. Also there may be amplitude differences in vowel-onset envelope that help to differentiate the voiced and low-continuant consonants from other classes and these differences would be receivable with low-frequency hearing alone, or even through tactual sensation.

The more recent studies have employed modern multidimensional scaling techniques to analyze the dimensionality of speech perception. The dimensions emerging from the multidimensional analysis of errors for heard consonants have turned out to be interpretable on the basis of the classic phonetic or phonological features of speech, thus indicating that the analysis yields dimensions consistent with the acoustics of speech production and with Miller and Nicely's (1955) informational analysis of consonant confusions. Shepard applied the technique to the Miller and Nicely data and to vowel perception data, and confirmed the feature-dimensionality of previous analyses (see Shepard, 1972). The main advantages of multidimensional scaling are three: (1) no particular dimensionality is assumed a priori, as must be done when using an information analysis or in scoring responses to calculate percent reception of features; (2) the individual subject's use of each emerged perceptual dimension

can be measured; (3) direct perceptual ratings of stimulus
similarity can be used as input data for analysis; this has
the advantage that only a few judgment responses per stimulus-
pair are needed instead of the many recognition responses to
each stimulus that are necessary to build up enough confusions
to calculate indices of confusion that may be taken as similarity values. However, confusion indices may also be used
as input data, thus allowing comparison of emerged perceptual
dimensions on the basis of both recognition responses and
similarity judgments.

Rating judgments and multidimensional scaling were used
by Walden and Montgomery (1975) to study the perceptual
dimensions of consonants for normal listeners and for impaired listeners with either flat or sloping audiometric
contour. The method elicited similarity judgments from the
listeners for all possible pairs of the English consonants
(except for the affricates /č/, /ǰ/, and fricative /h/).
The consonants were spoken in initial position before the
vowel /a/ by a male talker. A multidimensional scaling procedure, INDSCAL, was then applied to the rating data of each
subject, to arrive at a group consonant space in three dimensions and in four dimensions. The spatial distributions
of the consonants in the 3- and 4-dimensional solutions were
interpretable according to three or four of the distinctive
features: sonorant/non-sonorant, sibilant/non-sibilant,
continuant/stop, place of articulation, nasal/non-nasal, and
liquid-glide/non-liquid-glide. In addition to group spaces
the scaling procedure also gave individual weighting values
which describe the degree to which each subject used each
dimension in his similarity judging. The dimensional plots
of the consonants for the listener groups showed the operation of the feature-dimensions as follows: the dimensions
used by the normal listeners were stop, sonorant, and place;
the dimensions of the impaired listeners with flat contour
were stop, sonorant, and sibilant; the dimensions of the impaired listeners with sloping contour were liquid-glide,
nasality, and sibilant.

It is especially interesting to see that the place
feature does not seem to function in the similarity judgments of the impaired listeners. This result parallels that

of the earlier studies which used a consonant recognition
task and anslysis of confusions (Oyer and Doudna, 1959;
Rosen, 1962; Schultz, 1964; Cox, 1969; Pickett et al., 1972).
One important cue to place of consonant articulation is in
the differences in transition of the second formant. In
respect to the voicing feature of consonants the results of
similarity judgments do not parallel those of the consonant
recognition studies. Walden and Montgomery found no evidence
of similarity judgment according to the dimension of consonant voicing whereas this dimension is very well-preserved
in the recognition confusions of all types of listeners in
all the previous studies. A study of the rated similarity
of consonant pairs when spoken and rated in similarity
(Peters, 1963) also indicated that consonant voicing was
not a strong dimension of similarity. Shepard (1972) pointed
out that the task of consonant recognition may involve a
different use of perceptual sensitivity to consonant dimensions than does the task of similarity judgment. We believe
that the requirement on the listener of coming to a single
decision in order to recognize a consonant would cause him
to process the acoustic patterns differently from what he
may do when he must merely judge similarity. Students of
speech perception now postulate that the normal process
involves an early transformation of the auditory patterns
into phoneme features and a tentative phoneme string (Pisoni
and Sawusch, 1975). This would be the process for word-
or syllable-recognition as well. For a similarity judgment,
however, the listener may elect to compare the speech-
patterns presented on the basis of acoustic similarity, or
on a phoneme-feature basis, or both.

Walden and his colleagues recognized this problem and
carried out an experiment (Walden et al., 1977) to determine
the extent to which listeners may employ the "strategy" of
encoding the received stimuli as phonemes and judging stimulus
similarity essentially on the basis of the similarity of the
phoneme perceived rather than on acoustic sound pattern. To
the degree that phoneme errors are made this would tend to
bias the dimensional structure away from the perceptual
weighting of those dimensions which are subject to confusion
in recognition. As an example (from Walden et al, 1977),
suppose the pair ba, da is presented for a similarity

judgment and the listener perceived <u>va</u> instead of <u>ba</u>. Then
he would render a judgment on the basis of the similarity
of <u>va</u> and <u>da</u> and there would be a lower similarity because
these two differ in both place and manner of production
whereas <u>ba</u> and <u>da</u> differ only in place. Thus the manner
similarity of <u>ba, da</u> receives a lower-than-deserved rating.
In forming a matrix of similarity judgments, the assignment
of the low rating to the stimuli consonants presented would
tend to reflect the nature of the degraded perception in
contrast to an assignment on the basis of the perceived consonants which would tend to reflect the dimensions of actual
perception.

     In the experiment the listeners, after·hearing a pair
of consonants, first made a similarity judgment and then wrote
down an identification for each consonant. .Various types of
matrices were constructed and analyzed for dimensionality.
Comparisons between the dimensionality of the matrix types
indicated that the listeners had employed phoneme-labeling
which differentially affected the apparent strength/importance
of the different perceived dimensions. Hearing-impaired listeners of two types were employed, congenital cases who were
impaired from birth and "adventitious" cases who had considerable normal-hearing experience before being deafened. It was
expected that the influence of the phoneme-labeling strategy
would differ in that the listeners with no normal-hearing
experience would have a distorted dimensionality of phoneme-
similarity reflecting the ever-present auditory distortion of
their hearing loss.

     The results showed evidence of phoneme labeling. One
line of evidence was derived by comparing the dimensions of
the similarity matrix of the stimulus consonants with that of
the matrix of the consonants as heard in the recognition responses. The listeners' stimulus matrices had strong dimensions of low-frequency similarity, namely voicing, nasality,
and liquid/glide, whereas the response matrices had strong
dimensions of manner of articulation as stop/fricative, and
sibilancy. As further evidence the similarity matrix of the
correct responses was separated out as a "standard" similarity
structure and it was found that the remaining response matrix
correlated with the standard but the remaining stimulus matrix

did not. Both hearing-impaired groups showed a response
matrix dimensionality somewhat like that of normal listeners,
judging sibilant and/or fricative consonant responses to be
very different from non-sibilant or non-fricative, and also
stops from continuants, but with little similarity differentiation between nasal and stop for the congenital listeners
who on the whole had less hearing in the high frequencies
than did the adventitious.

Danhauer and Singh (1975b) report a study on 12 sensorineural listeners having residual hearing of the "low-
pass" type, i.e., listeners who had fairly normal hearing in
the low frequencies, up to a given frequency, and then a
steep decline in hearing level above that frequency. The
stimulus consonants (C) were intervocalic spoken by a male
speaker in the carrier-utterance [ʌCIl]; C was one of the
stops, fricatives, or affricates of General American English
(16 different consonants); nasal, liquid, and glide consonants were not employed. Listeners' similarity judgments
were analyzed by INDSCAL multidimensional scaling.

Three different judgment tasks were used. One was a
triadic task (ABX) where the listener heard three different
stimulus consonants (at C in the carrier-utterance) and had
to judge whether the third consonant was more similar to the
first or to the second consonant. For example, when he heard
the triad ʌbIl, ʌpIl, ʌsIl, he had to judge whether the third
consonant, s̲ was more similar to the first, b̲, or the second,
p̲. The other two judgment tasks employed pair-comparison
where the listener heard a pair of stimulus consonants, e.g.,
ʌbIl, ʌpIl, and had to rate their similarity. Two rating
methods were used, one in which subject chose a whole number
from 1 through 7, and another in which he assigned a number
on any scale he chose, to represent similarity. The first
pair-comparison method of judgment is the same as used by
Walden and Montgomery, and the other pair-comparison was
similar; the ABX method, however, is quite different. We believe the ABX method would tend much more to encourage the
listener to transform the A and B stimuli into phonemes, stored
for later comparison with phoneme X.

Danhauer and Singh's (1975b) subjects were divided into
three groups of four listeners, which groups we will call LP500

LP2000, and LP4000 where LP means low-pass, and 500, 2000,
and 4000 refer to the approximate "cut-off" frequency in
Hertz of the audiogram of each subject, above which there
was a steep decline in hearing level. Each group listened
to the stimuli under two conditions, one where the stimuli
were played back from a high-fidelity recording of the
spoken stimuli, and a second condition where the original
recorded signal was played back and re-recorded after filtering by a low-pass filter having the same cut-off frequency
as one of the listener group audiograms. The filter cut-off
slopes were greater than 52 dB per octave. Each filtered
recording was then played back only to its matching listener-
group. Comparison of results with and without filtering
would then reflect primarily the effect of the listeners' use
of their seemingly poor high-frequency hearing. The results
of Danhauer and Singh (1975b) indicate the following. First,
there is a confirmation of the lack of place as a strong dimension. Secondly, with the ABX method the voicing dimension
was preponderantly strong only for the LP500 group with filter
ing! The no-filtering condition with LP500 listeners reduced
the weight of voicing in the ABX method and produced a strong
weighting of a sibilant-continuant-stop dimension corresponding to the individual listener's degree of high-frequency
hearing at 3 kHz and above. The pair-comparison methods
reduced the weighting of the voicing dimension by the LP500
subjects. The other LP groups, having more-extended mid-
and high-frequency hearing, exhibited preponderant weighting
of sibilance.

Lawarre and Danhauer (1976) carried out a rating study
similar to that of Walden and Montgomery (1975); here again
voicing did not emerge as a strong dimension of consonant perception. The effective dimensions for the hearing impaired,
namely sibilant, plosive, and nasal/liquid-glide, did not
apportion as might be predicted between the flat and sloping
groups, as they more or less had for Walden and Montgomery
(1975). Place was a weak feature.

The evidence from confusion analyses suggests that noise-
burst frequency discrimination, a cue for place discrimination
of unvoiced stops, is poor for some sensorineural listeners
and that this should be tested with controlled synthetic

stimuli. Revoile et al. (1977) have reported some initial
experimental data on this problem. Nasal-glide and glide-
stop confusions, which would implicate poor discrimination
of the speed of formant transitions, also occur for sensorineural listeners, but with weaker confusion tendency
than for the place confusions. Probably only those with
the poorest hearing will be deficient in speed-of-transition
discrimination.

In general the data in the literature indicate that the
confusion proportions of the major types of features shifts
with degree of discrimination deficit. Confusions of place
are predominant in the responses of mildly impaired listeners
and they make few confusions of voicing or nasality. At the
other extreme, severely impaired (but not totally deaf) listeners make almost as many confusions of voicing and nasality
as of place.

Plomp (1978) has recently presented a framework of
predictive relations, for speech reception performance by
the hearing-impaired, that take into account the interfering
effects of noise. It is a curious fact that there is not a
great deal of systematic description of the effects of noise
and frequency-limitation on speech reception by impaired
listeners. Boothroyd (1967) has studied speech-feature reception under various filter conditions and Plomp is carrying
out experiments with noise.

As is well known there is a progressive decline in hearing levels with increasing age especially in the high frequencies and especially after the age of 50 years. Studies
of elderly populations in the files of hearing clinics show
that there is, correlated with hearing decline, a decline in
speech-reception capacity with age, even with the optimum
degree of amplification (for example, Jerger, 1973). However,
studies of non-clinical populations, although showing the
usual aging decline in hearing levels, show little or no
significant relation between age and speech reception under
optimum degree of amplification (Blumenfeld et al., 1969;
Hallerman and Plath, 1971).

There are two major studies of auditory frequency-
discrimination as a function of age. Hallerman and Plath

report no correlation between age and pure-tone frequency
discrimination, using the "warble" or frequency-modulating
technique. Konig (1957) tested a similar non-clinical population, using pairs of tones to which the subject reported
whether the second tone was lower or higher in pitch. This
task showed a decrement in pitch discrimination with age
which might have involved a central factor in memory for the ˋ
sensation-changes to be responded to as "lower" and "higher."

It is certain that there are central functions in speech
reception which may be expected to deteriorate with age in
addition to the declines attributable to aging in the peripheral sensorineural mechanism (Schuknecht, 1964). Farrimond
(1961) found that, to predict the effects of age on sentence
reception, it was necessary to factor out the state of the
subject's vocabulary and his grammatical cognition ability.

Finally, we have been interested in a new trend, in
thinking and research on normal speech perception, toward
the principle that it is the dynamically changing aspects
of the speech spectrum-patterns that are the basic auditory
cues (Shankweiler et al., 1975). Of course it has been known
for a long time that specific formant transitions are cues
to place of articulation (direction of F2 transition) and to
voicing/unvoicing (presence or absence of F1 transition).
However it has not been emphasized that cues change greatly
depending on the dynamics of the context. Particularly the
rate and style of utterance can drastically change a syllable
pattern, yet it is perceived as the same syllable. In other
words a listener must be able to hear, as the basic auditory
information, the relations of rate and frequency within the
formant transition patterns and other transitional spectrum-
patterns. These relations are then used for a perceptual
transform that normalizes for variations in rate, style, and
individual aspects of talker articulation. Thus the final
recognition of the phonemes of a syllable depends, auditorily,
on preservation of the spectral dynamics of the received
speech signal.

. Conclusions. From the studies reviewed we draw the
following general conclusions:
   1. The phonetic features used by deaf listeners to perceive and discriminate speech sounds are the same as those

used by normal listeners. This conclusion was also drawn
by Siegenthaler (1954).

2. Sensorineural listeners have better residual reception for low-frequency speech patterns, such as voicing,
nasal murmurs, and the first formant of vowels, than for
the middle- and high-frequency patterns, such as the bursts
of noise after unvoiced stops, the fricative consonants, and
the second, and higher vowel formants.

3. The superiority of low-frequency pattern reception
holds over a rather wide range of degrees and types of sensorineural impairment.

4. Initial consonants are perceived better than final
consonants by hearing-impaired listeners.

5. Vowel discrimination is better than consonant discrimination for severely-impaired, sensorineural listeners.

6. Sensorineural listeners can better discriminate the
second-formant information in speech when the formant is low;
that is, in back vowels as opposed to front vowels.

7. Mildly impaired listeners with flat audiograms may
receive mid-frequency patterns, distinguishing place of consonant articulation, about as well as they do low-frequency
patterns (Siegenthaler, 1949).

REFERENCES

Blumenfeld et al. (1969). J. Speech Hear. Res., 12, 210-
    212.
Boothroyd, A. (1967). Audiology, 6, 136-145.
Cox, B. P. (1969). Ph.D. Dissertation, University of
    Pittsburgh, Pa.
Danhauer & Singh. (1975b). Multidimensional Speech Per-
    ception by the Hearing Impaired, University Park Press,
    Baltimore, Maryland.
Farrimond, T. (1961). Gerontologia, 5, 65-87.
Hallerman & Plath. (1971). Hals-Nas-Ohrheilk, 19, 26-32.
Jerger, J. (1973). Adv. Oto-Rhino-Laryngol., 20, 115-124
    (Basel).
Konig, E. (1957). Acta Otolaryngol., 48, 475-489 (Stock-
    holm).
LaBenz, P. (1956). Volta Bur. Reprint No. 683, Volta
    Bureau, Wash., D. C.

Lawarre & Danhauer. (1976). Paper MM17, 91st Meeting, Acoustical Society of America, April, 1976.

Lawrence & Byers. (1969). J. Speech Hear. Res., 12, 426-434.

Liberman et al. (1967). Psychol. Rev., 74, 431-461.

Miller & Nicely. (1955). J. Acoust. Soc. Am., 27, 338-352.

Owens et al. (1968a). J. Speech Hear. Res., 11, 648-655.

Owens et al. (1968b). J. Speech Hear. Res., 11, 656-667.

Oyer & Doudna. (1959). Arch. Otolaryngol., 70, 357-364.

Peters, R. W. (1963). J. Acoust. Soc. Am., 35, 1985-1989.

Pickett, J. M. (1957). J. Acoust. Soc. Am., 29, 613-620.

Pickett et al. (1972). International Symposium on Speech Communication Ability & Profound Deafness (G. Fant, Ed.), A. G. Bell Assoc., Wash. D. C., 119-133.

Pisoni & Sawusch. (1975). In Proc. Symposium on Dynamic Aspects of Speech Perception (Cohen, A., & Nooteboom, S. Eds.), Springer-Verlag, New York.

Plomp, R. (1978). J. Acoust. Soc. Am., 63, 533-549.

Rosen, J. (1962). Ph.D. Thesis, Stanford University, Palo Alto, California.

Schuknecht, H. (1964). Arch. Otolaryngol., 80, 369-382.

Schultz, M. C. (1964). J. Aud. Res., 4, 1-14.

Shankweiler et al. (1975). In Perceiving, Acting & Comprehending: Toward an Ecological Psychology (Shaw, R., & Bransford, J., Eds.), Lawrence Erlbaum Assoc., Hillsdale, New Jersey.

Shepard, R. N. (1972). Chapter 4 in Human Communication: A Unified View (David, E., & Denes, P., Eds.), McGraw-Hill, New York.

Siegenthaler, B. M. (1949). J. Speech. Hear. Dis., 14, 111-118.

Siegenthaler, B. M. (1954). Speech Monogr. 21, 39-45.

Walden & Montgomery. (1975). J. Speech Hear. Res., 18, 444-455.

Walden, Brian E. et al. (1977). Army Audiology & Speech Center, Walter Reed Army Medical Center, Washington, D. C. 20012.

AUDITORY PHONETICS

HERBERT PILCH
University of Massachusetts

INTRODUCTION

Auditory Phonetics vs. Articulatory and Acoustic Phonetics.

Assertion. Auditory judgments are the most elementary
judgments in phonetics. Evidence: (i) Even the most sophisticated acoustic and articulatory research (such as into voice
onset time) presupposes certain auditory judgments. (ii) Phonetic knowledge is passed on through oral transmission. (iii)
Communication is ordinarily through listening.

Assertion. The auditory judgments are ordinarily categorized as articulatory or acoustic imitation labels (distinctive features). The latter are speculative. Only very
few isolated auditory categories are used, such as the hiss
and hush. Evidence: Loss of the hiss and hush distinction in
aphasia. This is established on the basis of listening, not
of studying tongue movement or spectrograms. Consequently,
description in terms of apico-alveolar vs. lamino-alveolar
fricatives is less reliable than in terms of hiss and hush.

Auditory Categories

Problem. Find a network of auditory parameters comparable
to the existing networks of articulatory and acoustic parameters. This is to transcend the speculative status of imitation
labels and distinctive features. Solution: On the basis of
the noise vocabulary of English, three dimensions of auditory

perception are distinguished: (i) Time Characteristics:
instantaneous (burst, flap, pop, snap), brief (creak, swish,
zoom), fluttery (crackle, patter, sputter) and continuous
(buzz, hum, rustle).   (ii) Timbre: bright ≠ dark, dull ≠
clear, thin ≠ full, soft ≠ hard.   (iii) Resonance: ring
(clank, twang, thump), hum (buzz, hum, rasp), rustle (crackle,
hiss, swish) and rasp (creak, screech, snarl).

   The time characteristics vocabulary is applicable to the
classes of stops (instantaneous), glides, lax vowels, retroflex vowels (all brief), trills (fluttery), continuants
(continuous), to the subclasses of explosives (bursts), im-
plosives (snaps), flaps (time interval zero between onset and
offglide), double stops (silent non-zero interval), double
fricatives (rustling non-zero interval).   The timbre vocabulary is applicable to voice qualities, such as the soft quality
of the extra-high concave-fall pitch pattern of English.
The resonance vocabulary cuts across the established acoustic/
articulatory classes of periodic/voiced vs. stochastic/voice-
less, characterizing the vocoids (ringing), liquids, nasals,
voiced "frictionless fricatives" (all humming), voiced friction
noise fricatives (buzzing), voiceless sibilants and affricates
(hissing/hushing), other voiceless fricatives (rustling), voice
stops (thumping), voiceless stops (thudding).

   The auditory categorization solves certain phonetic puzzle
of long standing: (i) The phonetic specification of lax/tense
vowels as brief vs. continuous (see above). (ii) the typologi-
cal fact that lax (but not tense) vowels are necessarily followed by a final consonant (in the Germanic languages). (iii)
The specification of voice qualities. (iv) The paradox of
the "frictionless fricatives" (such as the frictionless allophones of /v ð z/ in English, see above). (v) The fact that
no (articulatory) difference of cavity shape is correlated
with the auditory difference between English vowels such as
/i/ ≠ /e/ ≠ /ə/ (as in bid, bed, bud).

The Auditory Text

   Problem: Are specific auditory events (phonemes) necessarily recognizable on the basis of auditory parameters only?
Answer: Yes, in the laboratory test situation; No, in ordinar
discourse. Definition: When we listen to such ordinary

discourse for analytical purposes, it constitutes an AUDITORY
TEXT ("Abhortext"). <u>Elaboration on answer</u>: Assertion:
Phonemes adjacent in auditory space often overlap in auditory texts. In addition to auditory clues, we have to draw
on our lexical knowledge to determine which phoneme we
"actually hear." <u>Evidence</u>: English /p/ and /tw/, /n/ and
/nt/, /k/ and /s̆/.

<u>Assertion</u>: The phonemic indeterminacy of the auditory
text requires editorial conjecture (in addition to the listener's phonemic and lexico-syntactic knowledge). Evidence:
(i) English /aijɨ/ conjectured as either <u>and you</u> or <u>I just</u>.
(ii) The dialectologist calls upon the native speaker to help
him transcribe an auditory text (familiar experience). This
is because successful conjecture requires communicational
experience in a cultural context in addition to linguistic
knowledge (as editors of ancient texts are well aware).

Phonetic Hearing

<u>Problem</u>: Does our network of auditory parameters (see
section above) reflect a unique partition of auditory space,
presumably one innate in the human species? The current
theory of phonetic transcription appears indeed to assume
that: (i) The international phonetic alphabet does reflect
such a unique partition. (ii) The sound systems of languages
constitute subsets of this partition. <u>Answer</u>: These assumptions are false. They are motivated not empirically, but
culturally by European writing habits. For instance, the
Chinese and European partitions of auditory space differ to
the point that there is, in the Chinese tradition, nothing
comparable to European vowels, and that pitch patterns appear
as central in the Chinese tradition, but as marginal at best
in the European tradition. <u>Elaboration on answer</u>: <u>Assertion</u>:
Different phonemic systems constitute so many different partitions of auditory space (not just different subsets of a single
partition). They constitute as many different AUDITORY CATE-
GORIZATIONS which the learner must acquire separately for each
language. <u>Evidence</u>: (i) Nobody can learn from a narrow
transcription how to pronounce a foreign language--because the
language has its own partition of auditory space, not the partition implicit in the transcription. (ii) Nobody is able at
the first attempt to properly transcribe an unknown language--

because the language has its own partition of auditory space, not the partition implicit in the transcription. (iii) Phonemic deafness, in aphasia, entails not loss of hearing, but loss of auditory categorization. This shows that hearing and auditory categorization (for linguistic purposes) are two different things. Conclusion: We distinguish between three different modes of auditory perception: (i) AUDIOLOGICAL hearing (biological property of the human species), (ii) PHONEMIC listening (learned individually for every phonemic system), (iii) EDITORIAL understanding (learned individually through cultural experience with a language).

Auditory Analysis

Problem: In the absence of a "natural" partition of auditory space (see preceding section), what does the parameter network of auditory phonetics specify? Answer: We specify, in a coherent manner, the different partitions imposed by phonemic systems. Elaboration on answer: Empirical Motivation of Parameters: The parameters of auditory phonetics hale from two sources: (i) Culturally pre-established auditory categorization (such as the noise vocabulary of English, see section (1) above; writing habits, see section (3) above). (ii) Phonemic experience with different languages (such as with the tones of Chinese). Example: Pitch is a pre-established category of music and audiology. It is modified in auditory phonetics on the basis of phonemic experience by: (i) Reducing the diapason to very few (relative) pitch levels. (ii) Adding the opposition convex ≠ concave to circumscribe rises and falls (as for English and French, demonstration tape), thus: concave - fall /⌐ /, concave - rise /⌐ /, convex - fall /⌐ / and convex - rise /⌐ /. Validity of Parameters: Auditory parameters should at least specify phonemic distinctions. They do not fully specify auditory impressions. Examples: (i) Finnish and Lettish have the same inventories of pitch patterns in terms of auditory specification. Yet auditory texts sound different in the two languages impressionistically. This does not detract from the validity of the specifications. (ii) One cannot recognize the tones of Mandarin in an auditory text impressionistically on the basis of the auditory (or other phonetic) specification only. Yet the latter is sufficient for the (phonemic) tone

distinctions of Mandarin. <u>Procedure</u>: (i) Listen to several
auditory events and decide whether they sound the same or
different. (ii) Listen for recurrent differences. This
implies setting up classes of phonetic events and thereby a
language-specific auditory categorization. (iii) Neglect
non-recurrent differences. (iv) Once the recurrent differences have been recognized (but no sooner), they can be
characterized in terms of auditory (and other phonetic)
parameters.

This procedure reflects the two fundamental assumptions
of phonetics as formulated by E. Zwirner, namely that phonetic
elements are (i) distinguishable (see procedural step (i)
above, (ii) classifiable (see procedural steps (ii), (iii)
above). <u>Note</u>: The reverse procedure--first listen for pre-
classified phonetic events (such as rising and falling pitches)
then check on their distinctivity--is widely described in textbooks. It is unrealistic in practice.

THE EFFECT OF LABOV'S FIVE PHONOLOGICAL VARIABLES ON PERCEIVED LISTENER JUDGEMENT

IRWIN RONSON
City University of New York

As a result of a more sophisticated and accurate concept of language by linguists, phoneticians, speech pathologists, and hopefully, informed teachers and laymen --speech differences (particularly of some Black speakers) are no longer considered to be speech disorders. Much of our brave new world of thinking has come out of the hard work of the 1960's and early 1970's, and was based on the scholarship of sociolinguistic research done by Labov, Stewart, Taylor, Shuy, Williams, Baratz, etc....just to name a few. Whether the nonmainstream speech of some black speakers speaking "Black English" is viewed through a "difference" model (Baratz, 1968) or not, we have come a long way and it is reasonable to expect that no profes- sional linguist or speech pathologist would view such speech through a "deficit" model. Unfortunately though, the negative connotation attached to many nonprestige dia- lects exists despite the linguistic competence of that very dialect (Williams, 1970; Fromkin and Rodman, 1974). As Shuy and Fasold (1973) have stated, such stigma can affect the speaker's own aspirations as he/she attempts to climb up the ladder of social mobility. This is particularly true of many community college students in New York City. According to Wolfram and Fasold (1974), even professionals might more easily accept regional dialects as adequate language systems than low prestige social dialects, and

Williams (1970) has described some teachers negative attitudes of "unsureness and reticence" as psychological correlates to low prestige speech. Wolfram and Fasold (1974)
also reinforce the point that there is still much misunder-
standing about language varieties that are based on social
distinctions. Race, sex, religion, social class, etc. are
complexly woven into social dialects and it is perhaps
predictable that the business and professional world is
sometimes unwilling to accept low prestige dialects. Needless to say, the speaker of such a "basilect"--to use
William Stewart's term--is at a disadvantage when he com-
petes in the marketplace. There is no good beating our
collective phonetic breasts about linguistic competence
when in the real world speakers of a more standard or
prestigious dialect arbitrarily accept their own dialect as
"the only way to speak." In short, as Labov (1966) has well
demonstrated in his historical work on the social stratifi-
cation of English in New York City, speech is indeed an
extension of social class position.

It would also be comforting to conclude that we educators have done our job well and that the general populace has
absorbed the language message that we all speak subsets of
the same set of language, and that the subsets intersect
much more than they do not: phonologically, lexically, and
syntactically. We would also like to conclude that the
formula of "dialect$_1$=dialect$_2$=dialect$_3$ has been learned.
However, this conclusion is still only in the stage of
"devoutly to be wished." What is, unfortunately, still true
is that value judgements about dialects are often taken
seriously (Dillard, 1973) and probably too often are used
as factors concerning decisions in education and employment.
There seems to be no doubt that the dialect spoken by people
of high status is accorded greater esteem than the dialect
spoken by those of lower socioeconomic or ethnic status.
Consequently, there still appears to be a need for teachers
to rationally and linguistically discuss social and regional
dialects with elementary, junior and senior high school,
and college students; it would be productive to acknowledge
social realities. At Bronx Community College of the City
University of New York, our Voice and Diction, Phonetics,
and Fundamentals of Communication courses do have such discussion units built into each syllabus. It is our intention

to provide students with the intellectual understanding as
well as the opportunity and option of acquiring a prestige
dialect--what we refer to as "business and professional
speech." In a reality bound way we try to offer the student
the opportunity to become bidialectal, if he or she wants
to. In New York City many of the speakers of low prestige
dialects belong to Black or Hispanic minorities and their
speech can serve as one more reason not to get a job or
promotion, because some employers may equate dialectal
difference with job performance deficiency. While it would
be foolhardy to expect racial or ethnic prejudice to vanish
just because a speaker uses a more prestigious dialect, nonetheless, it can provide one less reason to discriminate!

The present study relating linguistic variables to perceived listener evaluation was born out of the theoretical
position stated in the above discussion. There is a practical
need to determine what linguistic variables should be stressed
in order to get maximum return from efforts directed toward
the optional acquisition of more prestigious speech. In
other words, what should we emphasize in Voice & Diction and
Applied Phonetics courses designed to help students get, as
Arthur Bronstein of Lehman College of CUNY has put it,
"speech that fits?" Labov (1966), in The Social Stratifica-
tion of English in New York City, has described five phonological variables: /θ/,/ð/,/æ/,/ɔ/,/r/ which he found to
be highly correlated with the speakers' social status and,
consequently, prestige dialect. It was the purpose of this
experiment to test the hypothesis that adult college speakers'
"improvement" on those specific phonological variables would
be reflected in higher perceived judgements of dialect status
by other peer group listeners.

METHOD

Subjects. The subjects were 20 Black community college
students of low locioeconomic status who registered for an
elective Voice and Diction course as part of their college
work. Low socioeconomic status was inferred from a demo-
graphic student profile report published by the Bronx Community College Office of Institutional Research (Eagle,
1977). For example, 72% of the students come from the Bronx

and 22% come from the Harlem and Washington Heights sections
of Manhatten. Both of these sections of New York City
represent poorer areas and deteriorating employment situations. There were 10 male and 10 female subjects, and
their age ranged from 19 to 52 years with a mean of 27.5
years. Each subject was tested to have normal hearing and
to be free from any speech disorder.

Test Material. The five phonological variables /θ/,
/ð/,/æ/,/ɔ/, /r/ were embedded in test sentences, and there
were four tokens of each phonological variable in each test
sentence. For example, /æ/: "Nancy went to ask the man
for a costume mask." The test sentences were typed on cards
for the speaker subjects to read and tape recordings of
these spoken sentences served as the samples for the listeners to rate. Thus, the test sentences were controlled
for semantic and syntactic factors in both the pre- and
post-test conditions, and only surface structure served as
the independent variable.

Procedure. Each of the five test sentences containing
the phonological variables: /θ/,/ð/,/æ/,/ɔ/,/r/ was typed
on a 5"x8" card and was presented in a random order to each
of the 20 speaker subjects. Their responses were tape recorded on a Wollensak model #2620 cassette recorder and then
played back to 40 listeners who rated the speakers. This
was done at the beginning of the semester and constituted
the pre-condition. The speaker subjects were then given
intensive training on the specific phonological variables:
/θ/,/ð/,/æ/,/ɔ/,/r/ for about six weeks in a voice and
diction class that met two hours per week. While general
course work concerning theory of voice and speech production
(respiration, phonation, etc.) was discussed, there were no
other linguistic variables specifically taught. The method
of instruction stressed kinesthetic and auditory sense
modalities, utilizing the distinctive features of place,
manner, and voicing. The students practiced the sounds in
isolation, words, and sentences; they engaged in conversation and reading aloud activities for class practice sessions.
They were assigned specific material to be practiced at
"home" and used our college's Speech Lab Tutorial for additional help with a Speech tutor. After about six weeks the
speaker subjects were then tape recorded again as they read

the same five test sentences containing the same phonological
variables for the post-condition. The listeners then rated
the speakers again. The time interval between pre- and post-
test conditions for the listeners' ratings was approximately
nine weeks. Perceived listener judgements of the speakers'
speech were made by 40 naive listeners--other college students
who were not speech majors and who had not taken voice and
diction or phonetics courses. The listeners were all enrolled
in and selected from a pool of four freshman "Fundamentals of
Interpersonal Communications" courses. The 40 listeners were
controlled as follows: one listener group was comprised of
Black students (N=20), and the other listener group was comprised of White students (N=20). In addition, there was an
equal number of males and females in each of the Black and
White listener groups (N=10 for each). The listeners heard
the tape recorded response readings of the speakers in both
pre- and post-test conditions and were instructed to rate
the speakers on a 1-5 scale, where 1 indicated low prestige
speech and 5 indicated high prestige speech. Score sheets
were provided and clarifications of procedure were made as
necessary. The mean score for each speaker was arrived at
by averaging the marked scores by the listener raters. For
example, the score given to speaker #1 by all 40 listeners
was determined by averaging the total ratings marked by each
of the 40 listeners. An Error Analysis of the speakers in
the pre- and post-test condition was also performed in order
to determine the amount of speech performance change by the
speakers. The term "error" is used in this study strictly
to describe phonetic change and not to prescriptively communicate any general value judgement about dialects. The
phonetic parameters described in Labov (1972, pp. 72-78)
were adapted for use to determine so-called errors. An
error was scored when two examiners (the experimenter and
one other Professor of Speech) agreed that the speaker's
tape recorded sample of /ð/, for example, had deviated from
the categorical perception of a linguadental voiced fricative
and had approached the category of the lingua-alveolar voiced
stop, /d/. That is, if the speaker said dem instead of them,
it was classified as an error.

RESULTS

Error Analysis of Phonological Variables. The total
number and rank order of errors for the five phonological
variables: /θ/,/δ/,/æ/,/ɔ/,/ r/ for the 20 Black speaker
subjects in the pre- and post-test condition is shown in
Table 1.   There was a total number of 171 errors made by the
20 speakers in the pre-condition.   After six weeks of concentrated teaching and learning, the errors were reduced to
a total of 94.   This represents a total error reduction of
45%.   In the pre-condition, the rank order of phonetic errors
(from most to least) was: /θ/with 43 errors, /æ/ and /ɔ/
both with 33 errors, and /δ/ and / r/ both with 31 errors.
In the post-condition, the rank order of phonetic errors
(from most to least) was: /æ/ with 24 errors, /δ/ with 20
errors, / r/ with 19 errors, /ɔ/ with 16 errors, and /θ/ with
15 errors.   The /θ/ phoneme resulted in the most change,
resulting in a complete reversal of rank order in total
number of errors.   /θ/ was the phoneme with the most errors
(43) in the pre-condition and the least errors (15) in the
pre-condition.

Table 2 shows the total number of phonological errors for
each speaker and for each of the sub groups of male and female
speakers, pre- and post-test conditions.   While the male
speakers had more errors than the female speakers (94 vs. 77)
in the pre-condition, they manifested less total errors in
the post-condition (42 vs. 52).   An inspection of the data
also reveals that the rank order of errors for individuals
as well as for the sub groups of male and female differed
from the overall rank order when all subjects were combined.
The male group's rank order according to number of errors
(most to least) was: /θ/,/ r/,/δ/,/æ/,/ɔ/ in the pre-condition, and /δ/,/θ/,/r/,/æ/,/ɔ/ in the post-condition.   The
female group's rank order of errors was /ɔ/,/æ/,/θ/,/δ/,/r/
in the pre-condition and /æ/,/ɔ/,/ r/, /δ/,/θ/ in the post-
condition.

Ratings of Speakers by Listeners.   Table 3 shows the mean
rating and standard deviation scores of 20 Black speakers by
40 listeners who were categorized into nine groupings for the
pre- and post-test conditions.   Nine separate single factor

analyses of variance (Edwards, 1967) were performed to compare the pre- and post-condition for each of the listener
groups. Statistical significance was·found for all nine
groups. It is clear that the 45% reduction in phonological
errors by the 20 speakers between the pre- and post-condition
was reflected in the listeners' ratings of those speakers.
An inspection of the mean scores of the speakers between
conditions all show a statistically significant increase in
rating regardless of how the listeners were sub grouped,
i.e., Black-White, male-female, etc. Table 4 shows the mean
rating score for each of the 20 Black speakers rated by 40
listeners in the pre- and post-test condition. It is interesting to note that despite the significant increase in scores
between pre- and post-test for all speakers as a group, there
were still some speakers who showed an actual decrease in
rating scores, i.e., speakers #9, 12, and 19.

DISCUSSION

The results of this experiment indicate that (1) speakers
did "improve" their production of the five phonological
variables: $/\theta/$, $/\delta/$, $/æ/$, $/ɔ/$, $/r/$ and (2) such improvement
was reflected in significantly higher ratings for prestige
speech by other peer group listeners. It is reasonable to
infer, therefore, that low socioeconomic college students
can acquire a more' prestigious speech pattern by changing
their production of the five phonological variables found
by Labov (1966) to be highly correlated with socioeconomic
status. It may also be inferred that intensive teaching of
these specific sounds will be reflected in higher perceived
judgements of dialect status by other peer group listeners
as well as by a general population. In this experiment this
occurred regardless of ethnic or sex gender factors. It is
interesting to note that Taylor (1973), in a study of
teachers, also found no significant differences between
Black and White or male and female language attitudes--in
his case, toward questions concerning structure and utility
of Black English dialect.

The present results should be carefully considered with
regard to the limits of the present study concerning situational context. When Labov (1966) investigated the relationship between linguistic variables and socioeconomic status,

he also considered five stylistic situation variables:
A-casual speech, B-formal interview, C-reading aloud,
D-word lists, and D'-minimal pair word lists. The significant outcome of the present study was performed within the
limits of situation variable C-reading aloud. Further research is recommended to include other situation variables.
It is also recommended that teachers utilize the contextual
styles described by Labov (1966) and Joos (1967) when
teaching Voice & Diction or "Applied" Phonetics courses in
which speech change is a goal. One may also note from this
study that improvement on the five phonological variables is
a differential response. As Table 2 shows, both males and
females, and some individuals within each speaker sub group
differed in the amount of error reduction. For example, the
male group had more errors (94) than the female group (77)
in the pre-condition, but ended up with less errors (42)
than the females (52) in the post-condition. It is also
evident from Table 2 that some individual speakers' rank
order of errors differed from the rank order of errors
reported for the group as a whole. Obviously, individuali-
zation of teaching methods is indicated, and this writer is
in agreement with the proposals of Gordan (1975) to indivi-
dualize speech improvement in the community college.

It might also have been predicted that, compared to the
vowel sounds, the two consonants as a class of sounds would
have been more easily changed due to the palpable nature of
their articulation. But this was not so. The errors for
/ɔ/ reduced considerably (52% error reduction), placing it
second in rank for the least number of errors in the post-
condition. One explanation for this might be that the
students found it easier to reduce the excessive liprounding,
tension, and duration features which were the critical
factors stressed in the teaching method for /ɔ/. It is
perhaps understandable why the postvocalic and preconsonantal
/ r/ might have been easy to learn (39% error reduction),
since what was demanded was a more simple addition of part
of a speech segment that already existed in the speakers'
phonemic inventory. It appears that speakers had the most
difficulty learning to make the finer lingual adjustment
necessary to produce the more prestigious /æ/ sound (27%

error reduction). It is suggested that this data (see Table 1) may be useful to instructors in determining teaching strategy.

In summary, it is reasonable to assume that the positive results of this experiment can be generalized to groups of speakers other than to the specific group of Black speakers used in the present study. In New York City there are many low socioeconomic groups such as Italian, Irish, Jewish, Hispanic, Greek, etc., who want to acquire a more prestigious "business and professional" dialect. There seems every reason to believe that others may well profit by concentrating on Labov's five phonological variables. As Wolfram (1970) has stated in reference to teaching standard English, "...we must adopt an attitude and methodology which will take full advantage of what we know about the nature of language systems and language differences." The present study demonstrated that it is profitable to delve into sociolinguistic research, apply it, and make it work!

REFERENCES

Baratz, J. C. (1968). Asha, 143-145.

Bentley, R. H., and Crawford, S. D. (1973). Glenview, Ill., Scott, Foresman and Co.

Dillard, J. L. (1973). Glenview, Ill., Scott, Foresman and Co.

Eagle, N. (1977). New York, Bronx Comm. College.

Edwards, A. L. (1967). New York, Holt, Rinehart and Winston.

Fromkin, V. and Rodman, R. (1974). New York, Holt, Rinehart, and Winston.

Gordon, M. J. (1975). Speech Teach., 24:78-81.

Hymes, D. (1973). Daedalus, 102:59-86.

Joos, M. (1967). New York, Harcourt, Brace and World.

Labov, W. (1966). Washington, Cent. Appl. Ling.

Labov, W. (1972). Philadelphia, Univ. of Penn. Press.

Laffey, J. L. and Shuy, R. (1973). Newark, Inter. Read. Assoc.

Miller, G. A. (1951). New York, McGraw-Hill Co.

Shuy, R. W. and Fasold, R. W. (1973). Washington, Georgetown Univ. Press.

Taylor, O. L. (1973). Washington, Georgetown Univ. Press.
Williams, F. (1970). J. Speech Hear. Res., 13:472–488.
Wolfram, W. (1970). Speech Teach., 19:177–184.
Wolfram, W. and Fasold, R. W. (1974). Englewood Cliffs,
     Prentice-Hall.

Table 1. Error analysis: total and rank order of errors
          for five phonological variables /θ ʒ æ ɔ r / by
          twenty Black speakers. Pre- and post-test
          conditions.

	Pre-test		Post-test			
	Phono-logical Variable	Number of Errors	Phono-logical Variable	Number of Errors	Errors Reduced Number	Percent
Most Errors	θ	43	æ	24	9	27
	æ	33	ð	20	11	35
	ɔ	33	r	19	12	39
	ʒ	31	ɔ	16	17	52
Least Errors	r	31	θ	15	28	65
	Total	171		94	77	45

Table 2. Error analysis for each of twenty Black speakers reading five sentences, each sentence containing four test items of the phonological variables /θ ð æ ɔ r/. Pre- and post-test conditions.

Subjects	θ	ð	æ	ɔ	r	Total Errors	θ	ð	æ	ɔ	r	Total Errors	Percent Reduction
Male Speakers													
1	2	2	2	2	3	11	3	3	1	0	0	7	
2	3	2	1	1	2	9	1	1	1	2	1	6	
3	2	2	2	2	2	10	0	1	0	0	0	1	
4	3	2	1	2	2	10	2	1	0	1	2	6	
5	4	2	2	0	0	8	2	1	0	0	1	4	
6	2	1	1	1	3	8	0	1	1	0	2	4	
7	3	2	3	2	2	12	0	2	1	0	1	3	
8	3	1	2	2	2	10	0	0	1	1	1	3	
9	2	2	1	1	2	8	1	1	0	0	0	2	
10	2	2	1	1	2	8	2	1	1	0	1	5	
Sub-Total	26	18	16	14	20	94	11	12	6	4	9	42	55%
Female Speakers													
11	2	1	2	2	3	10	0	3	3	3	2	11	
12	2	2	2	2	0	8	0	1	3	2	0	6	
13	0	0	0	2	0	2	0	0	0	0	0	0	
14	2	0	2	2	1	7	0	0	2	2	2	6	
15	2	1	1	3	1	8	0	1	0	1	0	2	
16	1	2	1	1	2	7	0	0	1	0	1	2	
17	3	3	3	2	2	13	1	1	3	2	2	9	
18	1	2	2	3	2	10	1	1	2	1	1	6	
19	2	2	2	2	0	8	1	1	4	1	2	9	
20	2	0	2	0	0	4	1	0	0	0	0	1	
Sub-Total	17	13	17	19	11	77	4	8	18	12	10	52	32%
Group Total	43	31	33	33	31	171	15	20	24	16	19	94	45%

754 IRWIN RONSON

Table 3. Mean rating of twenty Black speakers by listeners. Pre- and post-test conditions.

		Pre-test		Post-test		
Group	N	Mean	SD	Mean	SD	P
All	40	2.52	.67	3.11	.51	.01
Black	20	2.53	.75	3.18	.54	.01
White	20	2.50	.53	3.03	.53	.01
Female	20	2.54	.66	3.19	.55	.01
Male	20	2.49	.68	3.03	.49	.01
Black Female	10	2.52	.74	3.30	.55	.001
Black Male	10	2.53	.77	3.07	.57	.05
White Female	10	2.55	.64	3.06	.58	.05
White Male	10	2.46	.62	2.99	.50	.01

Table 4. Mean rating for each of 20 Black speakers by 40 listeners (20 Black; 20 White). Pre-and post-test conditions.

Speakers	Pre-test Score	Post-test Score
1	2.25	3.25
2	2.75	3.15
3	2.38	3.33
4	2.60	2.63
5	2.15	2.58
6	2.70	3.45
7	1.55	3.71
8	1.40	3.18
9	2.68	2.53
10	2.30	2.88
11	2.30	2.73
12	3.88	3.63
13	4.15	4.40
14	2.85	3.33
15	2.65	3.48
16	1.65	2.67
17	3.05	3.08
18	1.78	2.35
19	2.73	2.43
20	2.55	3.50
Average score:	2.52	3.11

CROSS-LANGUAGE DIFFERENCES IN THE PERCEPTUAL USE OF VOICING CUES

WILLY SERNICLAES AND PIERRE BEJSTER
Institut de Phonétique
Université Libre de Bruxelles

Current research on cross-language differences in voicing perception starts out from the point that the voiced-
voiceless distinction essentially depends on one single dimension which is allegedly common to all languages (Lisker and
Abramson, 1964, 1971). For initial stops, this dimension
would be voice onset time (VOT), i.e., the interval of time
separating the release of the stop from the onset of the
laryngeal vibrations. In each language, the voicing distinction would take place in a specific location of the perceptual phonetic boundary on the VOT dimension, according to
acoustical measurements of voiced and voiceless stops in the
language concerned. If VOT is shown to be a relevant cue in
most of the languages studied (for English, Spanish and Thai:
Lisker and Abramson, 1970; for Korean: Abramson and Lisker,
1971; for Kikuyu: Streeter, 1976; for Lebanese Arabic: Yeni-
Komshian et al., 1977), there is no systematic correspondance
between phonetic boundaries and production data.

In our opinion, this lack of correspondance between perceptual and acoustic data is due to the interference of other
voicing cues, the basic assumption of a major cue or dimension
being inadequate. The claim for a multidimensional approach
to cross-language differences in voicing perception is largely
supported by results obtained within specific languages. Identification responses to stimuli produced either by selective
modification of natural syllables (Wajskop and Sweerts, 1973;
Serniclaes, 1976a; Williams, 1977), or by covariation of

different cues by means of synthetic speech (Summerfield and
Haggard, 1974; Stevens and Klatt, 1974; Massaro and Cohen,
1976) make it clear that voicing perception basically depends
on the joint effect of several cues.

In this respect, it can be assumed that cross-language
differences in voicing perception are, at least partially,
due to a specific weighting of the cues as a function of the
listener's linguistic experience. As a consequence, the location of the phonetic boundary on a single cue-continuum no
longer constitutes an adequate criterion for characterizing
cross-language differences since this location depends both
on the perceptual processing of this cue and on the weighting
of the constant cues included in the stimuli. Rather than
the absolute location of the phonetic boundary, it is the
magnitude of the shift of this boundary which constitutes a
convenient criterion for shift of this boundary which constitutes a convenient criterion for investigating cross-
language differences in voicing perception. Indeed, the
weighting of the cues is reflected in the magnitude of the
boundary shift induced by systematic covariation of these cues

The hypothesis of a language-specific weighting of the
voicing cue will be investigated here by a comparison of the
perceptual roles of prevoicing and VOT in both English and
French. The reasons of this choice are as follows: (1)
prevoicing and VOT are independently processed and as such are
more likely to be given different perceptual weightings; (2)
at the production level, prevoicing is more reliable in French
whereas VOT is equally discriminant in both languages, and can
thus be used to compare the boundary shifts arising from
prevoicing.

METHOD

Stimuli. A set of syllables ambiguous as between /pi/
and /bi/ were generated from an OVE III synthetizer. The
stimuli variated both in VOT (seven values ranging from 0 to
60 msec., in 10 msec. steps) and prevoicing, this cue being
either present or absent for each VOT value. The prevoicing
was given a duration of 120 ms (10 periods with F_o constant
at 83 Hz). The levels of prevoicing and of the aspiration

noise used to simulate VOT was -15 dB relative to the peak
amplitude in the vowel. The overall duration of vowel and
VOT was held constant at 200 msec. Both F_0 (120 Hz) and F_1
(275 Hz) were constant in the vowel.

Subjects. Ten English and ten French speaking subjects
took part at the experiment. Among the English speaking subjects, seven originated from U.K. and lived in Belgium since
a few years. These subjects were at various degrees familiar
with French language. The three remaining subjects were
unilingual English-American speakers.

Procedure. Using the 14 (seven VOT x two prevoicing)
stimuli, two randomized series were set up. Each stimulus
appeared 15 times in each series. After a short preparation,
the subjects heard the series through headphones in a sound-
proof booth. They were paid for the task which was to identify
the syllables and write their answers on a response sheet.

RESULTS

The preliminary examination of the individual identification scores of the ten French listeners who took part in this
experiment made it clear that, for eight of them, there is a
simultaneous effect of both cues. For these two residual subjects the scores were either 0% or 100% voiceless responses
depending on the presence/absence of prevoicing. This contrasts with the results of a large majority of French listeners
(8/10) for whom there is a consistent effect of VOT on perceptual responses. The same kind of heterogeneity appeared
in the group of English listeners. For two of these subjects,
the pattern of responses is largely conditioned by the
presence/absence of prevoicing. Though this effect is lower
in absolute terms to that observed for the two non-conforming
French speakers, it contradicts the general tendency that
appears in the results for the English speakers (8/10 in this
experiment), that is, a larger effect of VOT relative to prevoicing. These heterogeneities might obscure the relationship
between average identification scores and VOT. Therefore, the
examination of this aspect of the result will be made by
averaging a subset of data corresponding to the eight listeners
who show homogeneous tendencies in each group (Figure 2). On

the other hand, the effect of prevoicing will be judged from
the overall averages taken from the whole set of data
(2x10 listeners - Figure 1).

Prevoicing. The presence of prevoicing has a clearcut
effect on the average identification score of each group
(Figure 1) (in each case, the X^2 for independent samples
(Siegel, 1956) is significant at p < .001). However, the
decrease in the percentage of voiceless responses is larger
for the data corresponding to the French listeners (Figure 1).
In support of an interaction between prevoicing and language
group, it should be noticed that, when prevoicing is absent,
the difference between identification responses of English and
French listeners is significant (X^2 for independent samples,
p < .001) whereas this difference does not attain significance
when prevoicing is present.

VOT. When based on the average results of a homogeneous
subset of (8 out of 10) English listeners, the percentage of
voiceless responses increased regularly as a function of VOT
lengthening (Figure 2). Paradoxally, the average identification curves relative to the homogeneous subset of (8 out of
10) French listeners is much more irregular (this effect is
more noticeable where prevoicing is present in the stimuli
(see Figure 2). More specifically, there is a flattening of
the identification curves for VOT values exceeding 20 or 30
msec.

DISCUSSION

The Role of Prevoicing and VOT in French. Prevoicing
and VOT are shown to be relevant cues in voicing perception
for most of the French listeners who took in the experiment
(Figure 2). In order to assess the relative importance of
these cues, a convenient procedure is to compare the magnitude
of their perceptual effects with their acoustic ranges in
natural speech (Serniclaes, 1976b). As shown in Figure 2,
the presence of 120 msec. prevoicing involves a shift of the
phonetic boundary of about 20 msec. VOT. This does not imply
that VOT has any greater perceptual effectiveness because the
difference in VOT between voiced and voiceless stops in
natural speech is considerably lower than the difference in

prevoicing. As shown by previous results (Serniclaes, 1976b), the better perceptual discriminability of VOT compensates for its weaker acoustical differentiation, and this argues in favour of an equivalent perceptual weighting of each of these cues.

The identification responses of the French listeners indicate, after the two subjects who are not responsive to VOT have been eliminated (see Figure 2 - condition with pre-voicing), that for values of VOT exceeding 20 or 30 msec., the lengthening of this cue remains almost without effect. This aspect of the results is similar to a phonomenon which appeared in a previous work (Serniclaes, 1976b; Beeckmans, 1977), that is, an increased perceptual discriminability in a range of values close to the acoustic boundary for French stops, whereas elsewhere--for values covering the voiced and voiceless categories--there is a strong decrease in dis- criminability. These variations in discriminability do not follow the location of the voice/voiceless phonetic boundary and, in this respect, they are interpreted as reflecting the existence of non-linearities in the perceptual measurement of VOT. More specifically, we made the hypothesis that relation-ship between acoustical and perceptual values of VOT shows itself as an ogive centered around the neutral value of this cue, whereas the upper and lower ends would correspond to voiced and voiceless categories. In other words, we assume that the perceptual analysis of VOT is characterized by a threshold, the location of which is independent of the phonetic boundary. In this respect, the flattening which appears in the identification functions of the French listeners would be due to the lower discriminability associated to a range of VOT covering or exceeding the voiceless category.

The Role of Prevoicing and VOT in English. The average results corresponding to the ten English listeners who took part at this experiment indicate that prevoicing and VOT both constitute relevant cues (Figure 1), i.e., significantly modifying the labelling behavior of the subjects. However, the perceptual roles of these cues are far from being equiva-lent. Apart from two subjects for whom prevoicing plays a very important role, VOT is given a much higher perceptual weight than prevoicing, a fact which is reflected by the

proximity of identification curves corresponding to the two conditions of prevoicing (see Figure 2). For English listeners
there is no flattening of the identification curves, similar
to the one found for French listeners. However, as the
identification scores are very high for VOT values of 20/30
msec., this does not mean that there are no differences in
discriminability for English speakers somewhere between 0 and
30 msec. VOT.

    Cross-Linguistic Differences in Voicing Perception. For
French listeners, the shift of the phonetic boundary induced
by prevoicing exceeds 20 ms, whereas the effect only attains
about 5ms for English listeners (Figure 1). The perceptual
role of prevoicing is thus undoubtedly more important in
French, a fact which is in accordance with the more frequent
use of this cue in the production of the voiced stops in this
latter language. Depending on the presence/absence of prevoicing, the ranking of English and French boundaries is reversed (Figures 1 and 2). This aspect of the results clearly
demonstrates that the absolute location of the phonetic
boundary does not furnish an adequate criterion for investigating cross-linguistic differences, since this location depends on the whole set of cues contained in the stimuli, and
differentially weighted according to language. In our opinion,
this differential weighting of the cues is responsible for the
discrepancy between acoustical and perceptual boundaries which
often appears when the usual methodology is used in cross-
language investigations. Indeed, a crucial factor in the
interpretation of these experiments is the relation to the
neutralization of the cues which are kept constant in the
stimuli and there is no guarantee that this condition is
fulfilled since, as this experiment shows, a minor cue in
one language can attain considerable importance in another.

    Besides the differential weighting of cues, other levels
of the perceptual identification process could also depend on
the listener's native language. Incidentally, the results of
French subjects taking part in this experiment have emphasized
the previously observed phenomenon of ranges of lower/higher
discriminability along the VOT continuum. If, as we have
assumed, the higher discriminability range reflects the presence of a cue-threshold for VOT, then would its location be

language-specific? At first glance, the answer to this
question would be negative because the location of the VOT-
threshold is compatible with the acoustic neutral value for
VOT in French which differs largely from that characterizing
English. However, to the extent that VOT is a complex variable including various parameters, such as burst intensity,
the direct comparison of temporal measurements of VOT is not
sufficient in locating the neutral values of different
languages.

CONCLUSIONS

By comparing the perceptual effects of prevoicing and
VOT in English and French, it has been shown that there are
large cross-language differences in the perceptual weightings
of the voicing cues, in accordance with their use at production level. As a consequence, the current procedure used in
cross-language investigations, which is to compare the absolute
locations of phonetic boundaries between languages, is no
longer adequate. Besides the differential weighting of the
cues, the question of language-specific characteristics in
cue measurement is raised.

REFERENCES

Abramson, A. S. and Lisker, L.   (1971).   Proc. Int. Cong. Phon.
     Sci., 439-446.
Beeckmans, R.   (1977).   R. A. Inst. de Phon., Bruxelles,
     11/1:69-82.
Lisker, L. and Abramson, A. S.   (1964).   Word, 20:384-422.
Lisker, L. and Abramson, A. S.   (1970).   Proc. Int. Cong. Phon.
     Sci., 563-567.
Lisker, L. and Abramson, A. S.   (1971).   Lang., 47:767-785.
Massaro, D. W. and Cohen, M. M.   (1976).   J. Acoust. Soc. Am.,
     60:704-717.
Serniclaes, W.   (1976a).   Proc. SCS-74, 3:87-94.
Serniclaes, W.   (1976b).   R. A. Inst. de Phon., Bruxelles,
     10/1:83-104.
Siegel, S.   (1956).   New York, MacGraw-Hill, 104-111.
Stevens, K. N. and Klatt,D. (1974).   J. Acoust. Soc. Am.,
     55:653-659.

762   WILLY SERNICLAES AND PIERRE BEJSTER

Streeter, L.A.(1976). J. of Phone., 4:43-49.
Summerfield, A. Q. and Haggard, M. P. (1974). J. of Phone., 2:279-295.
Wajskop, M. and Sweerts, J. (1973). J. of Phone., 1:121-130.
Williams. (1977). J. of Phone., 5:169-184.
Yeni-Komshian, G. H., Caramazza, A. and Preston, M. S. (1977). J. of Phone., 5:35-48.

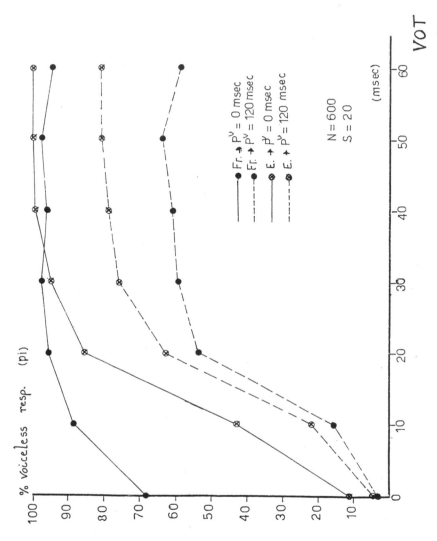

figure 1

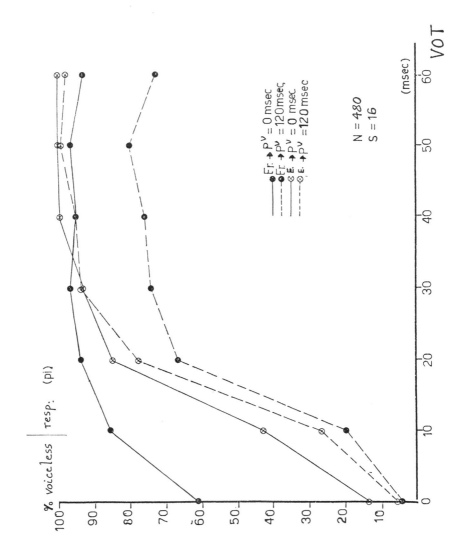

figure 2

PREVOICING AS A PERCEPTUAL CUE IN FRENCH

WILLY SERNICLAES AND MAX WAJSKOP
University of Bruxelles

In traditional phonetic descriptions, the voiced/
voiceless distinction wholly depends on the presence/absence
of glottal vibrations during the closure (Hockett, 1960).
Differing in this respect to some other languages, the acoustical analysis of French homorganic stops seems to support these
kinds of descriptions. The case of prevocalic stops is particularly clear-cut in this respect. In French, prevoicing is
nearly always present during the closure of a voiced initial
stop, whereas in English, for instance, this cue is often lacking (Zlatin, 1974). On these grounds, it could be argued that
prevoicing probably constitutes a major cue in French. However
results of perceptual investigations show that, besides glottal
vibrations during the closure, there are other cues--such as
burst intensity, burst duration (VOT), F_1 transition characteristics...--which are relevant for voicing identification
(Wajskop & Sweerts, 1973). Moreover, it may be assumed that
prevoicing does not even play a major role since, at least one
of the other cues, i.e., VOT,is given a perceptual weight equal
to that of prevoicing (Serniclaes, 1976). Apart from prevoicing
and VOT, the relative importance, and even the nature, of voicing cues in CV frames are not well documented. An index of the
perceptual contribution of prevoicing relative to the whole set
of other cues is given by the proportion in which prevoicing
is able to modify the voiced identity of stops in natural CV
French syllables. Therefore prevoicing was edited from voiced
stops embedded in 45 CV syllables corresponding to 9 phonetic
contexts uttered by 5 speakers native of French and the resulting segments were presented for identification to a set of 10
French listeners.

METHOD

Stimuli. A set of 18 CV syllables was produced by 5
male native speakers of French. The stop consonant (c) was
either /b/, /d/, /g/ or /p/, /t/, /k/ and the vowel /v/, one
of the 3 cardinal vowels - /a/, /i/, /u/. These 90 sequences,
recorded with the usual precautions, were digitalized (at a
frequency of 20 kHz) and copied onto LINC tapes of a PDP-12
computer. Using the CISA program (Jospa & Serniclaes, 1975)
prevoicing was then edited from the 45 syllables including
the voiced stops.

Procedure. Both the 45/voiced stop + V /sequences from
which prevoicing had been edited and 18 unmodified CV sequences, representing the chosen phonetic contexts and selected in
similar proportions from amongst the utterances of the 5 speak
ers, were used for an identification experiment. Each of these
63 sequences appeared 5 times in a pseudo-random series of 315
items. The stimuli were ordered in such a way that each of
the voiced stops without prevoicing was preceded in equivalent
proportions by unmodified voiced and voiceless stops.

Subjects. Ten subjects, all native speakers of French,
took part in the experiment. After a short period preparation,
they heard the series through headphones in a sound-proof
booth. The subjects were paid for the task which was to identify the syllables and write their responses on an answer-sheet

RESULTS AND DISCUSSION

The mean identification score for voiced stops from
which prevoicing had been removed was 43% voiceless responses.
Prevoicing is thus an important cue since its absence modifies
the voiced character of the stop in a little less than half of
the cases. However, it should be clear that the identification
score obtained (43%) does not indicate the relative weight of
prevoicing versus the whole set of other cues. Indeed, in the
syllables used as stimuli for this experiment, prevoicing was
given an extreme voiceless value, whereas the other cues were
probably much more variable. The variability of the effect
induced by removing prevoicing was considerable (m = 43%,
SD = 34%). Of the 45 syllables, 17 collected less than 25%
voiceless responses and 9 collected more than 75% voiceless

responses. This variability may be accounted for in two
different ways. One way is to assume that it is due to the
systematic effects of the various factors involved in the
stimuli (such as phonetic context). Another way is to attribute this variability to random variations of the other voicing cues included in the stimuli.

   Influence of phonetic context and individual differences
on identification scores. The effects of place of articulation (/b/, /d/, /g/), following vowel (/a/, /i/, /u/) speakers
(10) and listeners (5) on identification responses were tested
by analysis of variance. Results indicate that three factors
(place, speakers and listeners) are significant ($p < .005$)
while the fourth (vowel) has a less clear-cut effect ($p < .100$)
Apart from the interaction between place and vowel, all
others, i.e., those involving random factors (speakers and
listeners), are significant ($p < .005$). Amongst these effects,
only the one due to listeners can be accorded an unambiguous
interpretation. This effect has undoubtedly a perceptual
origin in that it reflects individual differences in the relative weighting of prevoicing/other cues. The other effects
may either be perceptually or acoustically determined. A
perceptual determination would consist of a reweighting of
prevoicing/other cues according to the perceived identity of
other features (place of articulation of the consonant or
following vowel). On the other hand, an acoustical determination indicates that the effects are due to variations in the
acoustic values of the voicing cues induced by the changing
of context. This latter interpretation is much simpler since
it does not call for a hypothesis of contextual interaction
at the perceptual level.

   Relationships between cues and contexts. Evidence in
support of an acoustical determination of the contextual variations appears from the examination of the nature of the effects
due to place of articulation and vowel (Fig. 1). As can be
seen, the removal of prevoicing has an increasing effect from
velars to dentals, and from dentals to labials (Fig. 1).
These differences are probably due to the emphasizing of F_o
and F_1 characteristics favoring voiced responses, i.e., pitch-
skip (Haggard et al., 1970) or low F_o at voice onset (Massaro
& Cohen, 1976); F_1 transition (Stevens & Klatt, 1974) or low

F_1 at voice onset (Summerfield & Haggard, 1977), from /b/ to
/g/. The reason for this is that low F_O and F_1 characterizing prevoicing are more persistent after /g/ than after
/d/ or /b/ since it is known that the duration of the movement of the articulator that forms the closure is greatest
for the tongue body, less for the tongue tip, and the least
for the lips.   A similar account may be alleged for the
vowel effect (Fig. 1) characterized by an increased score of
voiceless responses when the following vowel is /a/. For
this vowel, laryngeal vibration occur in conditions that
differ widely from those characterizing prevoicing. As a
consequence, the acoustical characteristics of prevoicing
continue for a shorter period into the vowel /a/ than it is
the case for /i/ and /u/. The relatively low scores of
voiceless responses in these latter contexts would thus be
due to an emphasis of F_O and F_1 characteristics favoring voiced
responses.   Inasfar as F_O and F_1 act as voicing cues by
reflecting the characteristics of laryngeal vibrations with
a closed vocal tract, another parameter, intensity of voice
onset--or intensity rise--might also constitute a cue for
voicing. Taking account of this potential cue would then
reinforce the hypothesis of an acoustical determination of
the contextual effects obtained in this experiment.   In this
examination of the relationship between cues and contexts,
VOT must also be taken into account since it is an important
perceptual cue for French listeners (Serniclaes, 1976). As
VOT increases for backward places of articulation (Lisker &
Abramson, 1964) and closed vocalic contexts (Serniclaes &
Bejster, 1974), the contextual effects linked to VOT go
against the tendencies shown by identification responses in
this experiment (Fig. 1). From this, it must be concluded
that the effects of VOT diminish the influence of F_O, F_1 and,
presumably, intensity characteristics as determinants of
contextual differences.

   Acoustical measurements of the cues. Depending on
place of articulation of the consonant and following vowel,
there are differences both between F_O, F_1 and intensity (I)
at voice onset and between the rate and extent of the transitions of these parameters. However, a close examination of
the nature of these contextual effects makes it clear that
differences at voice onset are, on the whole, more systematic.

As a consequence, we have chosen to measure the values of these parameters at voice onset. These values will, together with VOT, be related to the identification scores for each syllable. VOT was measured on spectrograms in the usual way, i.e., as the difference between the release transient of the stop and the first period of regular laryngeal vibrations. In doubtful cases--when there happened to be simultaneous high frequency noise and regular voicing--a further criterion was provided by comparing the relative amplitude of the sample both below and above 500 Hz. This kind of analysis was performed by a computer-program on the digitalized syllables (at a frequency of 20 kHz). Intensity at voice onset was measured by the same program. F_0 at voice onset was measured by a frequency detector (Landercy & Van Marcke, 1973) values obtained were checked by measuring the length of the first period visualized on computer scope. F_1 at voice onset was measured on spectrograms. Values obtained were checked by a computer analysis using the covariance method.

Relationships between cues and identification respones. The relationships between the identification scores of the 45 syllables (3 places of articulation x 3 vowels x 5 speakers) and each of the 4 cues measured (F_0, F_1, I at voice onset, and VOT) were evaluated by Kendall - τ correlation coefficients. Significant correlations were found for F_0, F_1 and intensity at voice onset (p < .01). The relationship with identification scores is particularly consistent for Intensity and F_0. The scatter diagrams corresponding to these 2 cues are shown at Fig. 2 (Intensity) and at Fig. 3 (F_0). Although the relationship is not wholly apparent in each case (Fig. 2 and Fig. 3), it is nevertheless noticeable that such a relationship emerges in spite of the various disturbing influences of the concurrent cues.

CONCLUSIONS

These relationships between acoustic values of the cues and identification scores argue in favor of an acoustical rather than perceptual, determination of the contextual effects which appear in our results. The question which is then raised is how these cues combine--together with other cues, of temporal nature (Wajskop, 1977)--to ensure an acoustical invariance for voicing perception across speakers and contexts. Together with prevoicing, F_o, F_1 and intensity at voice onset are probably not independently processed since these cues reflect the same articulatory state of the glottis. The combination of these four cues would then form a property similar to that of absence/presence of an abrupt consonant onset, as described by Williams (1977). However, this property would not constitute the sole bases for identifying the voiced character of the stops. Indeed, a cue such as VOT has been shown to be perceptually independent of prevoicing (Serniclaes, 1976). In this respect, voicing identification would result from the contribution of different acoustic properties, each being constituted by the combination of several cues.

REFERENCES

Haggard, H., Ambler, S. and Callow, M. (1970). J. Acoust. Soc. Am., 47:613-617.

Hockett, C. (1960). New York: Macmillan Co.

Jospa, P. and Serniclaes, W. (1975). Rev. Phon. Appl., 33/34:37-49.

Landercy, A. and Van Marcke, R. (1973). R. A. Inst. de Phon. Bruxelles, 7/2:69-88.

Lisker, L. and Abramson, A. S. (1964). Word, 20:384-422.

Massaro, D. W. and Cohen, M. M. (1976). J. Acoust. Soc. Am., 60:704-717.

Serniclaes, W. and Bejster, P. (1974). GALF. 5mes J. Etude du groupe "Comm. Parl." I:10-18.

Serniclaes, W. (1976). R. A. Inst. de Phon., Bruxelles, 10/1:83-104.

Stevens, K. N. and Klatt, D. H. (1974). J. Acoust. Soc. Am., 55:653-659.

Summerfield, A. Q. and Haggard, M. P. (1977). Haskins Lab., SR 49:1-36.

Wajskop, M. and Sweerts, J. (1973). J. Phon., 1:121-130.

Wajskop, M. (1977). IPS-77.

Williams, (1977). J. Phon., 5:169-184.

Zlatin, M. A. (1974). J. Acoust. Soc. Am., 56:981-994.

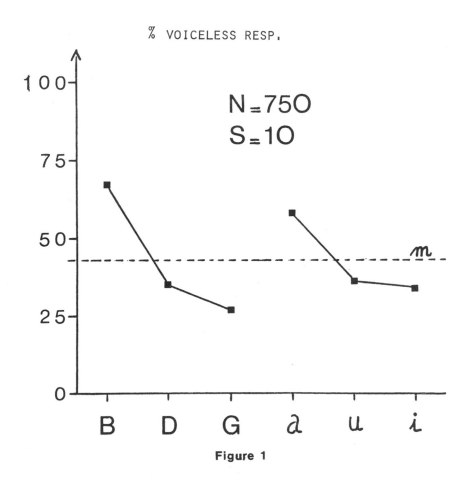

Figure 1

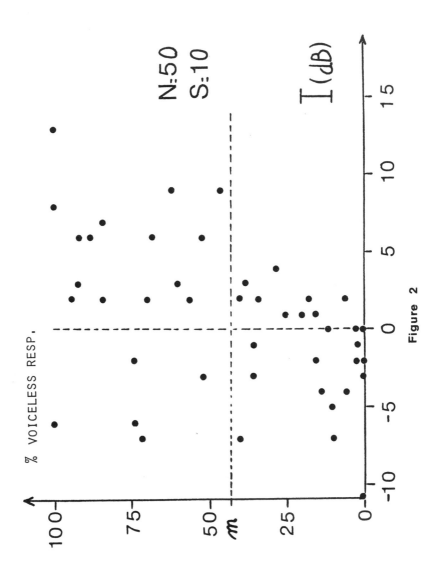

Figure 2

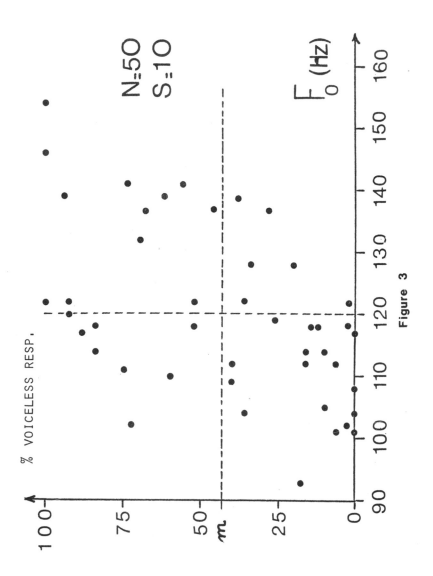

Figure 3

INTELLIGIBILITY OF TIME-ALTERED SENTENTIAL MESSAGES AS A FUNCTION OF CONTRALATERAL MASKING

DEBRA M. VAN ORT, DANIEL S. BEASLEY AND LINDA L. RIENSCHE
Memphis State University and
University of New Mexico

There has been increasing interest in recent years in the nature of the perceptual processing of speech as related to temporal factors. Of particular interest has been the study and application of time-altered speech as a measure of the temporal nature of speech perception using time-compressed monosyllabic stimuli with normal and abnormal populations of various age groups (Beasley and Maki, 1976; Beasley and Freeman, 1977). Konkle and Beasley (1976) studied the effects of contralateral masking on the perception of time-compressed monosyllabic stimuli. They argued that the presentation of a masker to the non-test ear may result in the appearance of an ear laterality effect, which normally did not occur when employing time-compressed speech stimuli. Konkle and Beasley found that neither contralaterally presented white noise nor speech noise had a significant effect on the intelligibility of the time-compressed monosyllabic stimuli. However, a multi-talker contralateral masker presented at 60 dB SPL and 90 dB SPL had a progressively significant effect on monosyllables time-compressed to 60% of original duration. Further the use of the multi-talker masker was associated with a significant right ear advantage when the masker was presented at both 60 dB and 90 dB SPL, when the stimuli were compressed by 60%. Also, there was a significant effect when the multi-talker masker was time-compressed by 60% and presented at 90 dB SPL, but not when presented at 60 dB SPL. Konkle and Beasley suggested, with the natural speech masker, that the

multitalker "dichotic" listening task required the speech
processor to simultaneously analyze the linguistic features
of several natural messages in order to decipher the primary
message. In turn, the multitalker masker, when compressed,
was less linguistically "natural" and thus less "competitive,"
resulting in a significant impact when presented at 90 dB
SPL. Thus, it appeared that the ear laterality effect was
closely tied to the linguistic nature of both the message
and masker, results which have been supported in other research dealing with dichotic listening tasks (Berlin and
McNeil, 1976).

In order to effectively delineate the nature of the
processing of language and temporal factors, however, it is
necessary to employ stimuli that are linguistically more
relevant to natural speech, for example, sentences and sen-
tential-like material. Beasley, Bratt, and Rintelmann (1977)
found a significant decrease in intelligibility of the revised CID sentences (Harris, 1961) when the sentences were
time-compressed to 60% and 70% of original duration. The
pattern of degradation as a function of time-compression was
similar to that of monosyllabic stimuli (Beasley, Schwimmer
and Rintelmann, 1972). The improved intelligibility for the
sentences compared to the monosyllabic stimuli was attributed
to greater linguistic redundancy inherent in the sentences.

Haggard and Parkinson (1972) studied ear laterality
effects associated with normal sentences presented with 90 dB
contralateral multitalker masker. They found no significant
right ear effect, a result comparable to the 0% time-compressed condition of the Konkle and Beasley study using monosyllables. However, it is possible that sentential stimuli
may very well yield laterality effects if the stimuly and
masker are made more difficult to process, for example, time
compressed. The purpose of the present investigation, therefore, was to determine the effect that natural and time-
compressed multitalker maskers presented at 60 dB and 90 dB
SPL would have upon the perception of sentences time compressed to 0% (i.e., normal), 40%, and 70% of normal duration.

METHOD

The Revised CID Sentence Lists, time-compressed by
0%, 40%, and 70%, were presented to forty normal hearing
subjects under two conditions of contralateral masking:
multitalker (MT) and multitalker time-compressed by 60%
(MT60%). Responses for each condition were obtained for an
equal number of right and left ears.

Subjects. The listeners in this investigation consisted
of forty young adults, selected from a university population,
whose hearing was assessed to be within normal limits. Each
subject was randomly assigned to one of four experimental
conditions. Within each group of ten subjects, five right
ears and five left ears were randomly selected to receive
the test stimuli. In order to qualify for the investigation,
each subject was required to pass a pure-tone sweep frequency
screening test administered bilaterally at 20 dB Hearing
Threshold Level (HTL) (re: ANSI, 1969) at octave intervals
ranging from 250 Hz to 8000 Hz.

Stimulus Materials. The Revised CID Sentence Lists used
by Beasley, Bratt, and Rintelmann (1977) (Harris et al., 1961)
were the sentential speech stimuli used in this study. The
five lists (B, F, G, I, and J) were time-compressed to 0%,
40%, and 70% of original duration. The multitalker maskers
consisted of four male talkers simultaneously reading a
passage about the general scope of psychology (James, 1973).
These maskers, multitalker and multitalker time-compressed,
consisted of the tape recorded material generated and used
by Konkle and Beasley (1976).

Apparatus. Subjects were tested individually in an IAC
1200 series sound-treated test suite. The pure-tone screening
was accomplished with a commercial portable audiometer
(Beltone Model 10-D) which supplied the signal to TDH-49
earphones housed in MX 41/AR cushions. The calibration of
the audiometer was checked every two days during the investigation in order to assure compliance with the standards
specified by ANSI (1969). The speech and masking stimuli were
presented via high quality tape recorders connected to a
speech audiometer (Grason-Stadler 162) through TDH-49 earphones

mounted in MX 41/AR cushions. The level of a 1000 Hz
calibration tone recorded on the tapes was adjusted to
-2 VU for all stimulus conditions. Before each testing
session, the speech audiometer, including earphone and
cushion, was calibrated with an artificial ear assembly
(Bruel and Kjaer type 4152) using a condensor microphone
(Bruel and Kjaer type 4144) and a sound level meter (Bruel
and Kjaer type 2204).

Procedures. After the pure-tone screening test, each
subject was randomly assigned to one of the four time-
compression/masker intensity conditions so that there were
ten listeners for each of the time compression and masker
intensity level combinations. The time-compressed Revised
CID Sentence lists were administered at the single intensity
level of 75 dB SPL (re: 0.0002 dyne/cm^2). Contralateral
maskers were presented at intensity levels of 60 and 90 dB
SPL (re: 0.002 dyne/cm^2). Each subject received five lists,
one at each of the time-compression/masker type and intensity
levels specified by the particular experimental condition.
The first list, however, was always presented at 0% time compression with no contralateral masking in order to provide a
baseline for the following more difficult listening task.
The order of presentation of the five lists was rotated
within each group. Regardless of test ear, the time compressed
stimuli was presented via the left earphone with the masker
stimuli presented from the right earphone. The ambient noise
level in the test room was sufficiently low (48 dB SPL, C-
scale via a Bruel and Kjaer type 2204 sound level meter) so
as not to interfere with the test results. Standardized
instructions were provided in written form and also read
orally by the examiner, with the subject required to write
down the appropriate response on the forms provided. A
fifteen second response time was allowed between each sentence
presentation.

Analysis. The individual word responses of each subject
were hand-scored by the experimenters using a key word procedure and then converted to percentage correct scores. For
each subject, five such percentage scores were obtained, one
score for each sentence list administered.

RESULTS

The results indicated that there was a dramatic decrease
in intelligibility at 70% time compression. The several
factors studied showed little differences at 0% and 40% time
compression. Thus, the remainder of the results section will
focus upon the effects of the multitalker masker when the
stimuli were compressed to 70% of original duration. The
scores at 70% time compression were significantly reduced
under the several masking conditions used in the present study
when compared to the monotic listening scores obtained by
Beasley et al. (1977). Generally, the scores for the natural
multitalker masker were better than the overall scores for
the multitalker/time-compressed masker. As can be observed
in Figure 1, however, this effect was due primarily to the
better scores under the 60 dB SPL natural masker condition.
That is, there was a greater decrease in mean scores from the
60 dB SPL to the 90 dB SPL condition for the natural multitalker masker (68.4 to 56.4) than for the multitalker time-
compressed masker (56.2 to 56.3).

When collapsed over all conditions, ear differences were
insignificant (85.5=L, 85.3=R). However, there was a trend
for ear differences to appear as a function of masking type
and intensity. More specifically, using the multitalker
masker, as shown in Figure 2, there was a left ear advantage
under both the 60 dB and 90 dB SPL conditions. However, as
shown in Figure 3, there was a slight right ear advantage
under both the 60 dB and 90 dB SPL conditions for the multi-
talker/time-compressed masker. In addition, ear differences,
whether left ear or right ear advantages, were greater under
the 90 dB SPL condition than the 60 dB SPL condition.

DISCUSSION

The results of the present investigation are consistent
with earlier investigations related to time-compressed speech.
That is, for all conditions, the intelligibility of the
sentences remained normal until the sentences were compressed
to 70% of original duration, whereby there was a dramatic
decrease in subject scores. The decrease in scores as a function of time-compression has been attributed to the decrease

in the temporal redundancy of the speech signal (Beasley and Maki, 1976), thereby taxing the central auditory processing system as it attempts to process the incoming information. The decrease in the scores for the 70% time-compressed condition in this study was significantly greater than that observed by Beasley, Bratt, and Rintelmann (1977), and reflects the effect that the masking had upon the intelligibility of the sentences. However, it is interesting to observe that the contralateral maskers had little or no effect on the responses in the 0% and 40% condition, suggesting that contralateral masking in the form of multitalker "babble" can be usefully employed in the study and application of time-altered speech stimuli.

In general, the higher intensity 90 dB SPL multitalker natural masker had a greater effect upon subjects' responses at 70% time compression than did the 60% dB SPL masker for the natural masker condition. On the other hand, the multitalker time-compressed masker had equally debilitating effects for both the 60 dB and 90 dB SPL presentation levels. These results suggest that the intensity level of the masker has a significant effect upon the intelligibility of speech and language, as expected. However, this effect is magnified if the natural speech masker is temporally distorted. These effects of masking may be attributed to cross-over phenomenon from the masked to unmasked ear. This argument could be applied to the 90 dB condition, but it is unlikely to apply to the 60 dB condition, in that the 60 dB SPL condition was more depressed with the time-compressed masker than the natural speech masker. Thus, while crossover may account for a part of the results, apparently time-compressing the natural speech masker also had a significant effect upon the intelligibility of the sentences.

These results are further supported by the ear effects observed in this study. The scores for both the left and right ears under the 60 dB SPL condition were better in the natural masker condition than in the time-compressed masker condition. However, at 90 dB SPL, the average scores for the two ears were about the same for both types of maskers. Again, crossover effects are unlikely to totally account for this effect, in that the scores for both ears were better under the natural masker condition than the compressed masker condition at 60 dB SPL. Apparently, the distorted prosodic nature and intelligibility of the time-compressed contralateral masker has a significant effect upon the processing of the time-compressed stimuli. Speculatively, this effect could be attributed to a number of factors, including the possibility that the subject's attention to the distorted stimuli was less distracted by the natural masker. That is, the subject could readily "tune-out" the natural masker and concentrate upon the time-compressed stimuli. However, when a time-compressed masker was used, there may be greater interference because the masker and the stimuli are more similar, i.e., both being temporally distorted natural speech. This contention has been supported by Berlin and McNeil (1976), although the exact nature of the interference, whether psychological or physiological or both, is subject to debate.

The trend for ear laterality effects, particularly reflected in the 90 dB SPL condition for both maskers, was interesting and, in fact, somewhat puzzling. The trend for a right ear advantage for the time-compressed masker condition can be accounted for using the arguments traditionally proposed for dichotic listening effects. That is, when the auditory processing systems for each ear were adequately taxed, a right ear advantage appeared, thereby reflecting the linguistic processing nature of the left hemisphere. However, the trend for a left ear effect using the natural masker is more difficult to explain. Parsimoniously, it might be suggested that the natural masker tended to overload the auditory processing associated with the right ear, thereby resulting in a decrease in the right ear scores. That is, the right ear was forced to attend to and sort out two very different signals and thus was overburdened with this task. The left ear, on the other hand, may have been less affected by a signal in the non-test ear, and, in fact, the linguistic processing capabilities of the left ear may have been enhanced by the inhibiting linguistic information to the left hemisphere. That is, the right hemisphere (left ear) has been shown to have linguistic functions other than those associated with prosody (Searlemann, 1977) and thus these verbal processing functions may very well have been artificially enhanced by inhibiting the need to employ verbal processing by the left hemisphere. Nevertheless, for whatever reason, it does appear that ear laterality effects can be shown to occur with sentential material when the system is adequately taxed. Equally important, information pertaining to these effects, if they are real, may contribute to modification of current theories pertaining to ear laterality and consequent cereberal dominance for verbal and non-verbal material. For example, it may be, as Berlin (1976) has suggested, that ear laterality is related to the more general nature of the stimulus signal than simply whether one hemisphere is dominant for language and the other for non-language processing. It is possible that the left hemisphere, which perhaps is more linguistically sophisticated, may be less able to withstand verbal abuse than the more prosodically-oriented right hemisphere. This would suggest that the right hemisphere is "stronger" in a sense than the left hemisphere, a suggestion supported by the contention that analysis of prosodic cues for perception develop earlier than verbal linguistic cues. That is, what perhaps is earliest to develop and is more phylogenetically basic to perceptual processing, namely prosody, is also the less subject to linguistic insult.

REFERENCES

Beasley, D., Bratt, G. and Rintelmann, W. (1976)., Paper at Amer. Sp. Hear. Assoc., Houston.

Beasley, D. and Freeman, B. (1977). New York, Grune and Stratton.

Beasley, D. and Maki, J. (1976). New York, Academic Press.

Beasley, D., Schwimmer, S. and Rintelmann, W. (1972). J. Speech Hear. Res., 15:340-350.

Berlin, C. and McNeil. (1976). New York, Academic Press.

Haggard, M. and Parkinson, A. (1971). Quat. J. of Exp. Psychol., 23:168-177.

Harris, J., Haines, H., Kelsey, P. and Clack, T. (1961). J. Aud. Res., 1:357-381.

Konkle, D. and Beasley, D. Paper at Amer. Sp. Hear. Assoc., Houston.

Searleman, A. (1977). Psychol. Bull., 84:503-528.

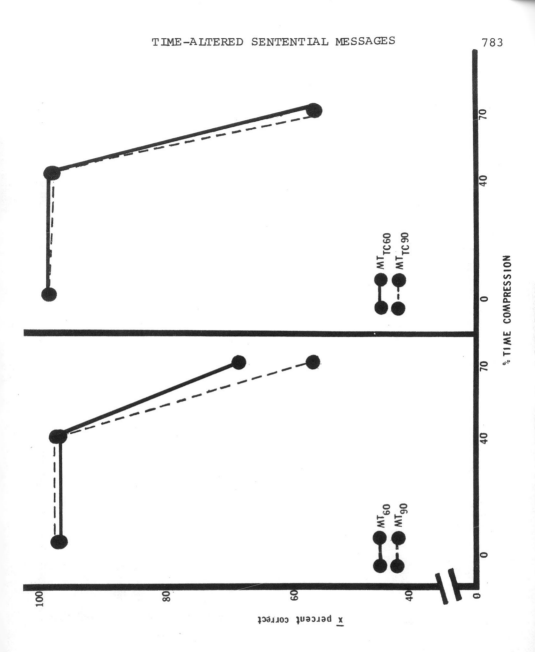

Figure 1:   Mean percent correct scores for the Revised CID
            sentence lists at each percentage of time compression
            and each contralateral masking condition.

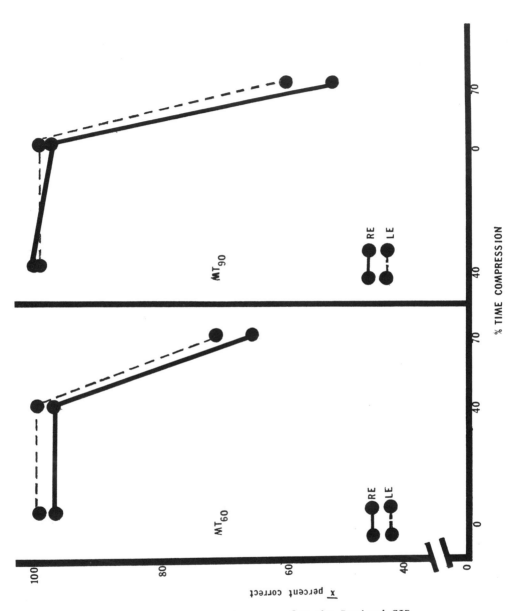

Figure 2: Mean percent correct scores for the Revised CID
sentence lists at each percentage of time compression
for right and left ears with the multitalker masker
at 60 and 90 dB SPL.

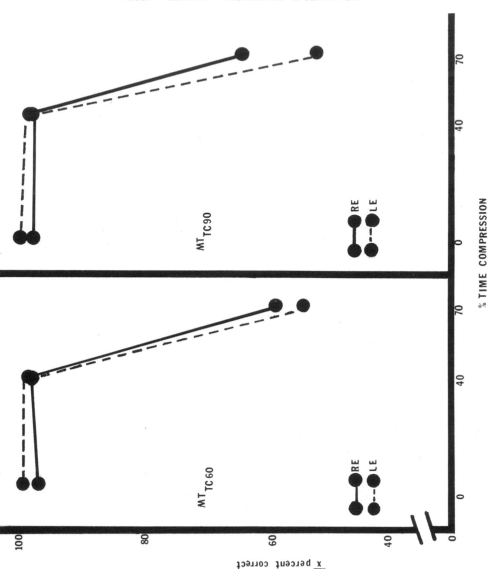

Figure 3:   Mean percent correct scores for the Revised CID
            sentence lists at each percentage of time compression
            for right and left ears with the multitalker/time-
            compressed masker at 60 and 90 dB SPL.

THE PERCEPTION OF DISTINCTIVE FEATURES

MICHEL VIEL
Université de Paris-Sorbonne

Towards the Phonological Study of Perception.

This paper is the second of a series on the same subject. The first was entitled "Pour une phonologie de la
perception" (towards a phonological study of perception).
This article dealt with the results of three tests which were
each put to approximately 200 people. I will briefly summarize a few aspects of this paper. The aim of this first
series of experiments--as indeed that of the second series
which is the object of the present paper--was to see how a
person perceives the phonological system of his mother tongue
as described by articulatory and acoustic phonetics.

My approach was very empirical. Before drawing up the
tests, I talked with a certain number of people--all literate
but untrained in phonetics--about the intuition they had of
the sounds of their language. Originally I did not know if
people had an intuition of their phonological system. Several
linguists I talked to were rather sceptical about this.
Indeed my experience as a teacher of phonetics and of English
as a foreign language should have warned me not to venture
into such a field. I have so often corrected students' papers
in which /m/ and /n/ are called fricatives and /f/ and /v/
nasals that I should have known better than to go beyond the
limits of the phonetics of phoneticians. On the other hand,
I had the feeling that people must have some intuitive knowledge of phonology. My argument was that if, for instance,

each of the voiced consonants was not felt to belong to the
class which linguists call voiced consonants, those consonants
should not react in the same way to sound change whether
diachronic or synchronic. After I had spent several hours
in private conversations with some 20 people, I decided that
this field was worth further investigation. I chose to study
French consonants, leaving aside the sonorants. This left me
with 12 consonants: /p t k f s s̆/, /b d g v z z̆/. I further
decided to focus the attention of my informants on the feature
(voice).

I cannot go into the details of the difficulties I encountered in drawing up the tests and in dealing with the
informants. In a few words: (1) The tests should be easy
because one cannot expect too great of an effort of the
informants. Furthermore informants can be very touchy and
are anxious to give what they believe is the "correct"
answer. (2) The tests should be easy to process. For these
two reasons, I dismissed the idea of questions implying
worded answers.

In the first test, the informants had to pick six out
of 18 pairs of consonants the terms of which they felt to be
"closer" to each other than the terms of the other 12. Out
of the 66 possible pairs I had preselected the six voiced vs
voiceless pairs plus 12 other pairs chosen at random. The
results showed that the first six (/p b, f v,/ etc.) were
selected in a proportion far superior to the other (/z t,
d k,/ etc.). In the second test, I gave six series of three
pairs each, such as /fv/, /fg/ and /fs/. I asked my informants to circle the simplest pair and to cross out the most
complicated. Again the results were fairly consistent with
what one could have expected of a trained phonetician. The
third test was slightly different. As I had previously
focussed my attention on the feature (voice), this time I
asked my informants which term of the pair /p/ and /b/, or
/f/ and /v/, etc. was the simpler if any. Voiceless consonants as a whole were not considered simpler than voiced--
at least not to a significant degree. The results were:
voiceless = 50.48%, voiced = 49.51%; or rather voiceless
43.20%, voiced = 42.40%, none = 14.30%. On the other hand
it appeared that there was a strict coincidence between the

simplicity of each term and its frequency, taking the table
of Delattre (1965: p. 97) as a reference.

The Four Tests (T1, T2, T3, T4).

This research led me to think that the field of phonological perception was pregnant with information but the
results of my first investigation were extremely fragmentary
and to a certain extent disconnected. So I decided to investigate phonological perception in a more systematic way.
Taking temporarily for granted distinctive features as defined in Chomsky and Halle (1968), I decided to study the
four features which suffice to define the 12 non-sonorant
consonants of French. I followed the method adopted in the
first test of the first series: circling a certain number
of pairs with "related" terms out of a larger group. Altogether, as I have stated, the 12 consonants of French make up
66 different pairs. In my preliminary inquiry, I had become
aware that this number was far too large for my informants
to work upon. So I decided to isolate each feature in turn
by dividing each test into two parts, A and B. For instance,
in T1A I took only the stop consonants while in T1B there were
only fricatives. Thus the test would teach nothing about the
feature (continuant) but the number of pairs would fall from
66 to 15 in each part. In the same way (voice) is neutralized
in T2; (coronal), in T3; and (anterior), in T4.

My informants, undergraduates whose subjects range from
musicology to English, all untrained in phonetics, were presented with the following text. (To save space, I have
limited this illustration to T1; T2, T3 and T4 being strictly
parallel.) See Figures 1 and 2.

RESULTS

The results of the tests are given in the following
Tables 1-4. Notice that the informants had to pick three
out of 15 pairs in T1, T2 and T3; seven out of 28 pairs in
T4, and two out of six pairs in T4B. So there was a 20%
chance of picking each pair at random in T1, T2 and T3; a
25% chance in T4A, and a 33.33% chance in T4B. Leaving aside
bilinguals and foreigners, the number of answers was respectively 139, 178, 181 and 174.

Analysis of results. The results were examined from
two points of view: (1) Are they consistent? (2) Are they
predictable according to the theory of distinctive features?
With respect to the consistency of the results, it seems that
they are consistent in three, and perhaps even four, different ways.

Consistency within each part of the test. To a very
great extent the "score" of each pair is inversely proportional to the number of feature differences. For example,
in T1A /b, d/ (one difference in feature signs) comes before
/p, d/ (two differences in feature signs) with 51.07% to
24.46%; in T2A /s, š/ (one difference in feature signs)
comes before /f, š/ (two differences in feature signs) with
65.16% to 47.75%. There are discrepancies in this principle
but the number of regularities is far superior to the number
of exceptions. It is true that consistency is not so obvious
in the lower part of the scale as in the higher part. The
reason is probably that some informants make a random selec-
tion--which cannot be helped. I do not think that the selection of /b, k/ = 2.87% (two differences in feature signs) in
T1A compared to /p, k/ = 2.15% (one difference in feature
signs) necessarily reflects the intuition of the informants.
The chance of selecting either pair has proved to be extremely
low. Hence the fact that one pair is circled four times, and
the other only three, is not conclusive.

Internal consistency of each test. To a very great extent part A matches part B. For example, voiced vs voiceless
pairs are number 1, 3 and 4 in T1A, and 1, 2 and 3 in T1B.

Consistency of the tests among themselves. The same
pairs have approximately the same position in all the tests
in which they are present. Voice vs voiceless pairs are
given positions number 1, 3 and 4 in T1A, and 1, 2, 3 in T1B;
1, 2, 3 in T3A, and 1, 2, 4 in T3B; 1, 2, 3, 4 in T4A, and
1 and 2 in T4B. /s, š/ is number 4 in T1B, 1 in T2A, 3 in
T3B. /b, d/ is number 2 in T1A, 1 in T2B, 5 in T4A (number 1
if you leave aside the four voiced vs voiceless pairs).

A special case of internal consistency. The following
figures from T1A taken separately contradict the principle
of consistency outlined above: (1) /p, d/ = 24.46%, /p, t/
= 8.63%; (2) /b, k/ = 2.87%, /p, k/ = 2.15%. Now there is a
kind of consistency in this incoherence, i.e.: (3) /b, d/ =

51.07%, /p, d/ = 24.46%, /p, t/ = 8.63%; (4) /b, g/ = 9.35%,
/p, g/ = 7.91%, /p, k/ = 2.15%. It is as if the feature
(+ voice) acted as a factor of cohesion. Several similar
examples can be found in the tests. A tentative explanation
for this phenomenon is suggested below.

    Relationship between the results of the tests and the
theory of distinctive features. The results of the tests
cannot be predicted according to the theory of distinctive
features as developed in Jakobson, Fant and Halle (1951) and
Chomsky and Halle (1968). If features were felt to be
logically equivalent, /p, b/ should be put on a par with
/p, f/ or /p, k/. This is never the case. Voiced vs voiceless pairs all occupy the first positions except for number 2
in T1A /b, d/ and number 3 in T3B /s, š/. On the other hand
pairs with a difference in the sign of the feature (continuant) occupy the last seven positions in T2A, the last six
positions in T1B, the last six positions (but one) in T3A,
all eight last positions in T3B, the last 12 positions in
T4A, and all four last positions in T4B.

    I suggested earlier that the number of differences in
feature signs was inversely proportional to the score of the
pairs considered. This is true of pairs taken two by two when
they have a common basis: for instance /t, d/ comes before
/p, d/. However, to account for the systematic difference in
the treatment of the features (voice) and (continuant) we have
to consider that (voice) is a superficial feature, and (continuant) a deep one. The model of features that I put forward
is related to the one which is introduced at the beginning of
Halle (1959) but which seems to have been dismissed in Halle's
later works.

(continuant)   −   +

(voice)   − /   +   − /   +
            p   b   f   v

792   MICHEL VIEL

It is very likely that the figures of the tests are predictable both from the number of differences in feature signs and
the number of nodes. In the above diagram, /p/ is one node
away from /b/, and two nodes away from /f/. The difference
in the number of nodes probably has a greater effect than
the difference in feature signs. Consequently /p, f/ and
/p, v/ will basically be felt to be "2 nodes away," and this
somehow "blurs" the extra-difference in feature signs.
(/p, v/ in fact comes before /p, f/ in T3 and T4.) Notice
that another explanation for this is suggested below. The
features (coronal) and (anterior) are half-way between
(continuant) and (voice). In my preceding paper, I ven-
tured the hypothesis that (anterior) was deeper than
(coronal). I am not so sure now. I rather think that
(anterior) and (coronal) work together as one feature only.
If such is the case, a number of discrepancies disappear,
for instance the position of /p, k/, number 15 in T1A as
compared to /t, k/, number 9.

     Perception and markedness. It seems plausible that
markedness in the sense of Chomsky and Halle (1968) plays
a role in the perception of features. We have already
noticed that when the feature (+ voice) was present, the
chance of selecting the pair was greater than when it was
absent to such an extent that (+ voice) vs (- voice) pairs
often came before equivalent (- voice) vs (- voice) pairs:
/p, v/ has a higher score than /p, f/. A striking example
is given by the feature (+ continuant). In T2A, the three
pairs whose terms are (+ continuant) are number 1, 2 and 3;
in T2B they are only number 2, 5 and 8 but these figures can
be accounted for by a sort of clash with (+ voice) which is
common to all the consonants in this part of the test; in
T3A the only (+ continuant) pair is number 2; in T3B these
pairs are number 1, 2, 3, 5, 6, 7; in T4A they are number
2, 4, 7, 11, 12, 16 (out of 28), and in T4B the only (+ continuant) pair in number 1. It is as if a marked feature
were a factor of cohesion. However I cannot expand on this
idea because inasmuch as the features (anterior) and
(coronal) are not felt to be satisfactory, this leaves a
blank as far as the feature "place of articulation" is concerned.

CONCLUSION

I believe that my figures are reliable. However the suggestions that I have made are only tentative. These suggestions can be summarized as follows: (1) There is a relationship between the number of differences of feature signs in two sounds and the perception of these sounds; (2) Features are perceived according to a hierarchical order, and (3) A marked feature is a factor of cohesion between two sounds (marked sounds sound more alike than their unmarked counterparts). Needless to say I am no way near making these suggestions as a mathematical law. At this stage of my research I cannot say that such a law is out of the question but neither can I say that it is possible. Tentative as my conclusions may be, they do show that the field of phonological perception deserves further study. New material will soon be collected. This is only the second paper in a series on the subject.

REFERENCES

Chomsky, N. and Halle, M. (1968). New York, Harper and
    Row.
Delattre, P. (1965). Heidelberg, Julius Groos Verlag.
Halle, M. (1959). The Hague, Mouton.
Jakobson, R., Fant, G. and Halle, M. (1952). Cambridge,
    Mass., M.I.T. Press.
Viel, M. (1978). "Pour une phonologie de la perception,"
    Travaux du CIEREC, XXII, 23-46, Saint-Etienne.

A (– continuant)

Differences in feature signs			Pairs	Circles	Percentage of circles
voice			p b	113	81.29
	cor		b d	71	51.07
voice			k g	63	45.32
voice			t d	59	42.44
voice	cor		p d	34	24.46
		ant	b g	13	9.35
	cor		p t	12	8.63
voice		ant	p g	11	7.91
voice	cor		b t	10	7.19
	cor	ant	t k	9	6.47
	cor	ant	d g	6	4.31
voice	cor	ant	t g	5	3.59
voice	cor	ant	d k	5	3.59
voice		ant	b k	4	2.87
		ant	p k	3	2.15

B (+ continuant)

Differences in feature signs			Pairs	Circles	Percentage of circles
voice			f v	77	55.39
voice			š ž	73	52.51
voice			s z	71	51.07
		ant	s š	32	23.02
	cor	ant	f š	28	20.14
voice		ant	š z	19	13.66
		ant	z ž	19	13.66
	cor	ant	v ž	17	12.23
voice	cor	ant	v š	16	11.51
	cor		v z	14	10.07
	cor		f s	14	10.07
voice	cor		f z	14	10.07
voice		ant	s ž	8	5.75
voice	cor		v s	8	5.75
voice	cor	ant	f ž	6	4.31

Table 1. Test-I (T1); (number of answers: 139).

A (− voice)						B (+ voice)					
Differences in feature signs			Pairs	Circles	Percentage of circles	Differences in feature signs			Pairs	Circles	Percentage of circles
cont	cor	ant				cont	cor	ant			
		ant	s š	116	65.16		cor		b d	71	39.88
	cor	ant	f š	85	47.75		cor	ant	z ž	66	37.07
	cor		f s	65	36.51	cont			b v	66	37.07
	cor	ant	t k	49	27.52		cor	ant	d g	49	27.52
	cor		p t	46	25.84		cor		v z	43	24.15
cont		ant	t s	30	16.85	cont	cor		g ž	39	21.91
		ant	p k	25	14.04		cor	ant	b g	33	18.53
cont			t s	23	12.92		cor	ant	v ž	33	18.53
cont	cor		k š	23	12.92	cont		ant	g v	26	14.60
cont			p f	18	10.11	cont	cor	ant	g z	26	14.60
cont	cor		t f	16	8.98	cont	cor		d v	22	12.35
cont	cor	ant	p š	16	8.98	cont			d z	17	9.55
cont		ant	k f	9	5.05	cont	cor		b z	15	8.42
cont	cor		p s	8	4.49	cont	cor	ant	b ž	15	8.42
cont	cor	ant	k s	5	2.80	cont		ant	d z	13	7.30

Table 2. Test 2 (T2); (number of answers: 178).

A (– coronal) Differences in feature signs	Pairs	Circles	Percentage of circles	B (+ coronal) Differences in feature signs	Pairs	Circles	Percentage of circles
voice	p b	107	59.11	voice	s z	101	55.80
voice	f v	84	46.40	voice	š ž	81	44.75
voice	k g	70	38.67	ant	s š	78	43.09
cont	b v	53	29.28	voice	t d	69	38.12
ant	p k	41	22.65	ant	z ž	56	30.93
cont ant	g v	27	14.91	voice ant	š z	40	22.09
voice cont	p v	27	14.91	voice ant	s ž	28	15.46
ant	b g	25	13.81	voice cont ant	d š	20	11.04
voice ant	p g	20	11.04	cont ant	t š	13	7.18
cont	p f	18	9.94	cont	t s	12	6.62
voice cont ant	k v	18	9.94	voice cont	t z	11	6.07
voice cont ant	g f	17	9.39	cont	d z	10	5.52
voice cont	b f	13	7.18	cont ant	d ž	9	4.97
cont ant	k f	12	6.62	voice cont ant	t ž	9	4.97
voice ant	b k	11	6.07	voice cont	d s	6	3.31

Table 3. Test 3 (T3); (number of answers: 181).

A (+ anterior)

Differences in feature signs			Pairs	Circles	Percentage of circles
voice			p b	154	88.50
voice			s z	137	78.73
voice			t d	136	78.16
voice			f v	121	69.54
		cor	b d	110	63.21
	cont		b v	74	42.52
		cor	f s	70	40.22
voice		cor	p d	61	35.05
		cor	p t	48	27.58
voice		cor	b t	42	24.13
		cor	v z	34	19.54
voice		cor	z f	26	14.94
voice	cont		p v	26	14.94
	cont	cor	d v	25	14.36
	cont	cor	t f	20	11.49
voice		cor	v s	18	10.34
	cont		p f	16	9.19
voice	cont	cor	t v	15	8.62
	cont		d z	15	8.62
	cont		t s	14	8.04
voice	cont		b f	13	7.47
voice	cont		d s	10	5.74
voice	cont		t z	10	5.74
voice	cont	cor	d f	8	4.59
	cont	cor	p s	8	4.59
	cont	cor	b z	5	2.87
voice	cont	cor	b s	5	2.87
voice	cont	cor	p z	3	1.72

B (- anterior)

Differences in feature signs			Pairs	Circles	Percentage of circles
voice			š ž	123	70.68
voice			k g	105	60.34
	cont	cor	g ǰ	54	31.03
voice	cont	cor	g š	26	14.94
voice	cont	cor	k ž	21	12.06
	cont	cor	k š	19	10.91

Table 4. Test 4 (T4); (number of answers: 174).

INQUIRY ABOUT THE PERCEPTION OF THE SOUNDS OF SPEECH

One has a fairly good knowledge of the way sounds are produced by the organs of speech as well as of their acoustic qualities. However, very little is known about the way they are perceived by the ear.

The object of the present test is to show how the phonetic relationship between French consonants is perceived by the linguistic consciousness of the speakers.

15 pairs of consonants are given at the back of this sheet. You are asked to circle the 3 pairs whose terms seem to sound most alike. It should be clear that the test is about pronunciation, and that

 k = k in képi as well as c before a, o, u
   (car, cor, cure) and qu- (quart);

 g = g before a, o, u (gare, gomme, gueux);

 j = j in Jean as well as g before e and i (gens, gîte).

You are advised to produce a so-called "mute" e after the consonant, i.e., to take it as if you had to deal with ve / che, te / che, ke / che, etc.

Purposefully there are no models of "correct" answers because since the test is about the way you perceive speech sounds, each spontaneous answer is a correct answer. There are no winners and losers in the test. You simply have to think that if you had to deal with colours and choose between white and grey on the one hand, and say red and green on the other hand, you would probably say that white and grey look more alike than red and green. The white-and-grey pair would therefore be circled. Thank you for your attention.

If French is not your mother tongue or if you are bilingual, please say so and state which is your mother tongue or your second mother tongue: If you have studied stenography, please say so: Don't do the test if you happen to have a technical knowledge of articulatory or acoustic phonetics.

Figure 1

A.   Circle the 3 pairs whose terms seem most alike to you.

k	p	g	t	d
g	d	d	g	k

b	d	b	k	p
g	t	k	t	b

b	t	p	b	p
t	p	k	d	g

B.   Circle the 3 pairs whose terms seem most alike to you.

ch	v	j	f	f
v	z	s	z	v

ch	s	s	j	ch
j	ch	f	r	z

ch	v	v	z	z
f	j	s	s	j

Figure 2

I. SPEECH AND SPEAKER RECOGNITION

SOME STEPS IN PERFORMANCE EVALUATION OF THE DAWID SPEECH RECOGNITION SYSTEM

R. D. GLAVE
Universität Bonn

The present paper firstly deals with a brief discussion of some basic considerations connected with the problem of performance evaluation of speech recognition systems. In the second part some concrete results from performance experiments with the DAWID system are presented. The DAWID speech recognition system is basically a real-time isolated word recognition system. It consists of a (hardware-) parameter analyzer (PA) (Friedrich et al., 1971), and a (software-) parameter classifier (PC) (Bierfert, 1978), running a PDP 15. With regard to the well-defined task of the present DAWID system, namely, to identify given sets of isolated spoken words, performance evaluation of such a system seems to reveal no or only few methodological problems: performance depends upon the relative number of correctly identified words, i.e.,the "recognition score." In fact, some of our experiments have to do with the calculation of recognition indices (Glave,1977a) of whole word-identification. However, there is some reason to measure the "performance" (Glave,1976c) in quite a different manner, namely if the evaluation strategy does not aim at the recognition task of the system per se, but at the performance of stages of the recognition process. This procedure gives information not only about that the system works, but in addition, how it works with respect to certain defined aspects of the recognition process.

According to this difference, we will further distinguish between TPE (Task Performance Evaluation) and PPE (Process Performance Evaluation). The first type yields data about the

mean performance of the whole system; with respect to what
kind of variables are involved in the test procedure, one
will get information about functional dependencies, for
instance, between the size of the vocabulary and the mean
performance indices (Glave, 1977a), the kind and number of
speakers, and so on. It must be emphasized that TPE does
not need (and therefore the results do not reflect) any information about the recognition process itself, for instance,
what kind of 'units' are derived by certain well-defined
operations --whether these units are phonetically interpretable,
or can only be labelled by pure operational definitions. The
main information we need in TPE amounts to the definition of
the variables, and the real identification output. In TPE we
describe the performance of our system solely on the basis of
word-identification, -nonidentification, and -permutation.

In order to fulfil the second type of performance
evaluation, the PPE, we need some processing--specific hypotheses, we need properly formulated questions which are--in
the widest sense--concerned with the question, how "successfully" the system operates on a certain processing stage; for
instance, what kind of phonetically interpretable operations
are performed by the system in some well-defined part of the
recognition process. Despite the fact that acoustically derived units cannot be phonemes at all (because there is no
one-to-one relation between information in the acoustic signal
and units resulting from linguistic analysis), we could say:
on the acoustic level the system performance is as good as it
reliably derives units which can be used to identify the
"same" referent word (in a verifiable definition), and to discriminate between "different" words. Thus, performance results
derived from phonetically interpretable experimental variables
are of basic interest in PPE experiments. We may want to know
for instance, whether some specific phonetic segments are
relatable to operationally defined system-units,in other words
whether phonetic hypotheses can be verified by means of
analytically described observations of the output (the 'reactions') of the system or of parts of it.

PPE experiments can concern quite different processing
levels. Of course, as long as a system makes only (or
essentially) use of acoustical information, and is blind

regarding any higher level sources of knowledge, PPE wil predominantly have to deal with taxonomic performance closely connected with the acoustic event. First of all, we have to decide what stage of the recognition process we are interested in, and what kind of information (for instance, what kind of units) we can intensionally describe as the system's output on that stage. The kind of variables we have to consider in PPE is closely connected with these decisions. The inter-preted output only gives indirect, mediated information about task performance, and thus finally depends upon actual em-pirical evidence.

The previous remarks only touch some aspects of perform-ance evaluation proceeding. Beyond that, it seems that there is need for conceptual clearness about the question what kinds of system "performance" we can take into consideration in prin-cipal. It is the simple question: what are the possible meanings of questions concerning the "capability," the "efficiency," the "performance" of speech recognition (and speech understanding) systems? For instance, is it useful to differentiate between "function test" and "reaction test," or between "system test" and "construction test?" Further explications about these concepts can be found in Ungeheuer (1977).

We will now look at the DAWID system. In fact, at first we made PPE experiments in order to get information about the kind of some processing steps of the DAWID recognition pro-cedure. We began with an experiment about the performance of the parameter classifier FRIC. This software system--developed by H. Bierfert (1978)--supplies the real word differentiating elements of the DAWID system, namely: P, B, F, Z, A, I, U, E and--(A and I are supplied by the software component VOC; Lance, 1976). These elements were intensionally described as: unvoiced plosive (P), voiced plosive (B), unvoiced fricative (F), voiced fricative (Z), A (vowel segment of the quality /ɑ,ɔ/, I (vowel segment of the quality /i,e,y/, U (unspecified initial segment), E (unspecified final segment), and "-" (unspecified transition segment). An experimental question of the type PPE was formulated to verify these phonetic charac-terizations of the DAWID symbols: can the word differentiating units of the parameter classifier (PC) be phonetically interpreted, as they are intensionally labelled?

Figure 1 represents the experimental answer to this question in the case of the DAWID symbol P. We see the frequency
of P indications, evoked by allophonic realizations of unvoiced plosives embedded in natural German words. The numbers indicate different phonetic context: 1 vowel, 2 nasal,
3 liquid, 4 unvoiced plosive, 5 voiced plosive, 6 unvoiced
fricative, 7 voiced fricative. This figure shows that the
identification performance of phonetic segments of the type
'unvoiced plosive' is dependent on allophonic variations,
i.e., variations of position and phonetic context. As
one result of this PPE experiment we could formulate that
the DAWID symbols represent--to a rather high degree--
"quasi-allophonic" sound classes. We favored this adjective
because the phonetic labelling of the DAWID symbols can be
characterized as follows: (1) there exists a linguistic-
phonetic relation (representation of classes of allophones),
and (2) an acoustic-phonetic relation (representation of
phonetic 'regular' features) (Glave et al., 1977). A second
PPE experiment was carried out on the reactions of two so-
called "detectors" of the PA (Glave, unpublished). The question was, to what extent the phonetic qualities /e,i/ and
/a,ɔ/, embedded in different phonetic context, could be detected by these acoustic analyzers, provided that the remaining German segmental qualities would be "ignored" by these
detectors. The material (German words and meaningless two-
syllable words) was systematically built up so as to include
the following vowels: / 'a:/, /'ɑ /, /'ɔ/, /ˈe:/, /'i:/,
/ i /, /'ɛ :/, /'ɛ/, /'o:/, /' y:/, /'y/, /'ɸ :/, /'œ/, /ɑ/, /o/,
/u/, and /ə/.

Figure 2 shows the indication (frequencies in percent)
of one subclass of these vowels by the "AO-detector." The
remaining symbols in Figure 2 mean: M = medial position,
I = initial position, F = final position; d = this vowel
occurred as part of a diphtong. These results indicate that
at quite an early stage of the whole processing some well-
defined performance characteristics can qualitatively and
quantitatively be described, and--within certain limits--can
be predicted. This information can be used, for instance,
as an aid for the pre-selection of the vocabulary of a TPE
experiment. Our PPE paradigm gives information about the
system performance under certain defined phonetic aspects.
The same is scarcely possible on the basis of TPE

experiments. A detailed example of a TPE experiment with
the DAWID system is given (Glave, 1977). The experimental
question was: How successfully can the system identify a
given set of selected German words? During this experiment
a total of 88 different words, belonging to four different
subvocabularies, were spoken by five speakers. The size of
the learning sample was ten utterances per word. Though the
identification task of this experiment was quantitatively
quite modest, the gathering of the speech material and processing of the DAWID data was fairly time-consuming (10000
utterances of the learning phase, 5000 additional utterances
of the working phase). The words were used to build up short
simple sentences of the form PETER VERSENDET ZWANZIG POST-
KARTEN. Each word of such a sentence was spoken in isolation.
The result of this TPE experiment (speaker-independent
analysis of word identification) is shown in Figure 3. This
picture shows discrimination- and identification-indices
(Glave, 1977) of over 90% (of three categories), which means
quite a high mean performance rate. Lancé (unpublished)
reports similar results could be received on the basis of an
increased vocabulary (up to 103 words without subclasses).

We hope to have given some evidence about present no-
tions as to how we are defining and empirically investigating
'the performance' of a speech recognition system. We tried
to show that measuring the performance of such artificial,
pseudo-perceptual systems interacting with man can be regarded under fundamentally different aspects. One cannot
say a priori which is the most relevant one. It surely depends upon the kind of questions you actually have about your
system. According to the present situation in speech recognition research it seems that firstly some more intensive discussion about basic concepts and strategies is required in
order (1) to be able to evaluate experimental performance
paradigms of some concrete system, and (2) to be able to
compare different systems with one another;--this does not
necessarily mean to compare 'machines' with one another, but,
more precisely, to compare the results of interactions (of
machines with man) with one another.

REFERENCES

Friedrich, L., Glave, R. D., Kotten, K., Lohmar, R. P.,
    Reinhard, C., Rupprath, R., Stock, D., Tillmann, H. G.,
    and Vieregge, W. H. (1971). Hamburg, Buske.
Bierfert, H. Phil. Diss., Bonn.
Glave, R. D. (1977). Proc. 9 Int. Cong. Acoust., I 118.
Glave, R. D. (1977a). Niemeyer, Tubingen.
Glave, R. D. (1977b). Niemeyer, Tubingen.
Glave, R. D., Lance, D. (1977). Phonet.
Glave, R. D. (1976). IKP-manuscript (unpublished).
Lancé, D. (1976). IKP-manuscript (unpublished).
Ungeheuer, G. (1977). IKP-manuscript (unpublished).

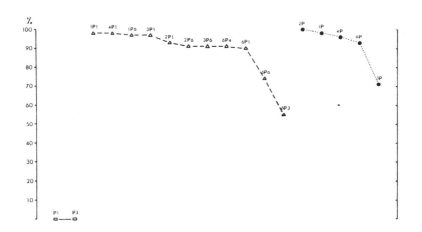

Fig. 1. Frequencies of indications of the DAWID
        symbol P in initial (rectangles), medial
        (triangles), and in final (circles) position

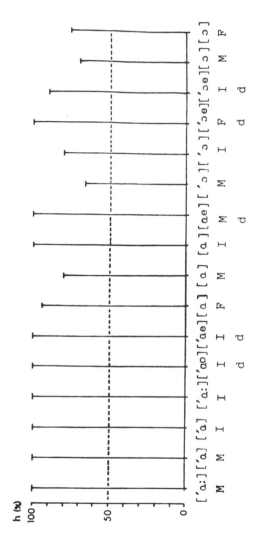

Fig. 2. Relative frequency h (in percent) of "AO" indications

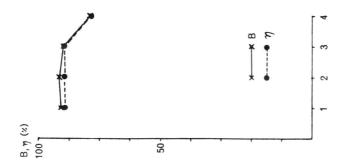

Fig. 3. Performance indices B
and η (in percent) for
four different syntactical
categories

THE EFFECT OF DISGUISE ON SPEAKER IDENTIFICATION FROM SOUND SPECTROGRAMS

KATHLEEN HOULIHAN
University of Minnesota

INTRODUCTION

There are many questions concerning the validity and reliability of speaker identification from sound spectrograms and the admissibility of the so-called "voiceprint" technique as scientific evidence in courts of law. The effect of vocal disguise is one variable that must be investigated before these questions can be answered. In his original report on the "voiceprint" technique, Kersta (1962) claimed extremely high rates of correct speaker identification by visual inspection of sound spectrograms and suggested that accuracy of identification would not be altered by variation in phonetic context, aging, or attempted disguise. Bolt et al. (1970) expressed serious concerns over these claims, and subsequent research has shown that a number of factors, including those discounted by Kersta, do affect accuracy of speaker identification to a significant extent. Tosi et al. (1972) found that identification rates were lower when phonetic context was varied, when the number of reference spectrograms was increased, when open trials (examiners did not know whether or not a match existed) rather than closed trials (examiners knew a match existed) were used, and when non-contemporary rather than contemporary speech samples were examined. Young and Campbell (1967) and Hazen (1973) reported significant reduction in accuracy of identification as a result of variation in phonetic context and decreased duration of the speech sample.

It has also been shown that vocal disguise and other factors significantly alter the speech signal and interfere with spectrographic identification. Endres et al. (1971) found variation in formant structure, fundamental frequency, and other acoustic properties of speech due to the aging process, attempted vocal disguise, and imitation. Williams and Stevens (1972) found similar variation as a result of certain emotional states. Hollien and McGlone (1976) reported less than 25% accuracy of identification in matching spectrograms of disguised voices with those of undisguised voices. Reich et al. (1976) found that five selected disguises (old-age, hoarse, hypernasal, slow-rate, and free disguise) all significantly reduced accuracy of identification, and that certain disguises were more effective than others.

This paper reports the results of two pilot experiments designed to investigate the effects on spectrographic speaker identification of four previously uninvestigated vocal disguises: lowered fundamental frequency, falsetto, whispered, and muffled. The experiments originated as a class project in a seminar on the use of "voiceprints" in speaker identification. Differences between disguised-to-undisguised and within-disguise matchings were examined, and differences in identification rates for female and male voices were considered. The results of these two experiments, within the limits of the design as a class project, are discussed below.

EXPERIMENTAL PROCEDURES

Speakers and spectrograms: In Experiment I, the speakers were the members of an honors seminar on "voiceprints" and consisted of nine female speakers and five male speakers, all undergraduate students at the University of Minnesota of a relatively homogeneous age range and geographical background. These 14 speakers recorded their own voices directly onto a sound spectrograph (Kay Sonagraph model 6061B) and made spectrograms of their own utterances. Spectrograms were made of the sentence "And show the one that you have to me" under each of five voice conditions: undisguised, lowered fundamental frequency, falsetto, whispered, and muffled. For the muffled disguise, speakers were instructed to "cover" their mouths with their hands, but to maintain intelligibility of their speech. The spectrograms were wide-band spectrograms which included the frequency range from 80 Hz to approximately 5000 Hz, and all included amplitude displays. The speakers made three separate sets of spectrograms, each set containing one spectrogram under each of the five voice conditions. The order of the voice conditions was the same in each set. All spectrograms, then, were contemporary samples in that they were made during the same session, but no two samples of the same voice condition were immediately adjacent to each other.

In Experiment II there was more uniformity in the selection of speakers, the number of speakers of each sex, and the production of spectrograms. There were eight female and eight male speakers. The females ranged in age from 20 to 28 years, with a mean age of 23.6 years, and the males ranged in age from 20 to 31 years, with a mean age of 25.3 years. All speakers had lived primarily in the state of Minnesota, with 12 of the 16 from the immediate Twin Cities area. The speakers recorded two series of repetitions of the sentence "There's a bomb in the Main Post Office" in a quiet room on a Uher tape recorded (model 4000 Report IC). Both series consisted of three repetitions of the sentence under each of the five voice conditions used in Experiment I. In this experiment, the muffled disguise was accomplished by having the speakers insert two fingers into their mouths.

Spectrograms of the recordings were prepared by the experimenter on a sound spectrograph. The frequency range used was 80 Hz to approximately 4000 Hz and no amplitude display was included. Spectrograms for the reference sets of "known" speakers were made from the second series of recordings and those for the "unknown" speakers were made for randomly selected speakers for each voice condition from the first series of recordings. As in Experiment I, all spectrograms were contemporary samples.

Examiners and examiner training: The examiners in Experiment I consisted of 21 students from the University of Minnesota. Fourteen were the undergraduate students in an honors seminar who served as the speakers for Experiment I.

Their training consisted of a series of lectures and discussions on phonetics, acoustics, sound spectrography, and
speaker identification from sound spectrograms and a preliminary speaker identification experiment involving six
closed matching tasks, four open matching tasks, four pair
discriminations, and one sorting task. The other seven
examiners were undergraduate and graduate students in an
experimental phonetics course. All had taken at least one
course in general phonetics previously. Their training
consisted of lectures and discussions similar to those
presented to the other 14 examiners, as well as in-class
group matching and pair discrimination tasks and two individual closed matching tasks completed before they began
Experiment I. The seven students from the experimental
phonetics course also served as the examiners for Experiment
II, after they had completed Experiment I, had been advised
of the correctness of their responses, and had re-examined
all the spectrograms from Experiment I. All examiners
worked independently in both experiments.

   Experimental design: The designs of Experiments I and
II were essentially the same. Both involved only closed
trials in which the examiners knew that a match existed.
There were a total of ten sets of reference spectrograms,
five for female voices and five for male voices. The five
sets of spectrograms for each sex corresponded to the five
voice conditions: undisguised, lowered fundamental frequency, falsetto, whispered, and muffled. Each set consisted of one spectrogram of an "unknown" speaker and one
for each of the "known" speakers. The two experiments
differed in the number of "known" speakers--nine female and
five male in Experiment I and eight female and eight male
in Experiment II.

   Each examiner made a total of 18 matches, nine for female
voices and nine for male voices. Of the nine for each sex,
five were within-condition comparisons in which the "unknown"
spectrogram was matched with one of the "known" spectrograms
for the corresponding voice condition, and four were across-
condition comparisons in which the "unknown" spectrogram in
each of the disguised-voice sets was matched with one of the
"known" spectrograms in the undisguised reference set. In

Experiment I no instructions were given to the 21 examiners as to the order of considering each of the ten sets of spectrograms. It was assumed that they all examined the sets in the order listed on the response sheets. However, in Experiment II, each of the seven examiners was instructed to consider the sets in a particular order, randomized separately for each examiner, except that all examiners considered the undisguised sets before the disguised ones.

RESULTS OF EXPERIMENT I

Effect of voice condition: The percent correct for the 21 examiner responses for each task type are presented in Table 1. The table shows results for identification of female voices on the left and of male voices on the right. Within-condition and across-condition tasks are listed separately for each voice condition. In these closed trials, the identification rates were extremely high for within-condition comparisons for both female and male voices, except in the case of the whispered disguise. Identification rates for across-condition comparisons were lower than those for corresponding within-condition comparisons in every case, except for the whispered disguise, where both were low.

In order to determine whether certain of the differences in these identification rates were significant, the Sign Test for Matched Pairs, a non-parametric test that can be used for analysis of small sample sizes, was performed for the pairs shown in Table 2. The p-values shown are those determined after the Bonferonni correction for multiple comparisons. The pairs for which there is a significant difference at the .05 level are marked with asterisks in the table. In the top section of the table, it can be seen that the only significant differences for within-condition comparisons are found in the whisper disguise, in which identification rates are significantly lower than they are for every other voice condition for female voices and for the muffled disguise for male voices. The middle of the table shows that identification rates for across-condition comparisons are significantly lower than those for within-condition comparisons of the same disguise type for the falsetto disguise for female voices and for the muffled disguise for male voices. Finally, the bottom

of the table shows that identification rates for across-
condition comparisons are significantly lower than those
for within-condition comparisons of undisguised voices for
the falsetto, whispered, and muffled disguises for female
voices and for the falsetto and whispered disguises for
male voices.

Sex of speakers: No obvious differences were noted
between the tasks involving spectrograms of female voices
and those involving spectrograms of male voices. However, no
statistical analysis was done, because of the numerical
difference between female and male voices in the reference
sets.

Performance of examiners: Figure 1 shows the overall
performance for all 18 task types of the 21 examiners for
Experiment I. The range is from 39% to 78% correct, with a
mean of 58.6% and a standard deviation of 8.7%.

RESULTS OF EXPERIMENT II

Table 3 shows the results of Experiment II, where there
were seven examiners and eight reference spectrograms for
both female and male voices. Although the small number of
responses for each task type, one for each of the seven
examiners, precluded any statistical analysis, the pattern
of results was approximately the same as in Experiment I.
The identification rate was higher for within-condition
comparisons. However, in this experiment, identification
rates for all within-condition comparisons were approximately
equally high, including those for the whispered disguise.
As in Experiment I, there were no obvious differences between
female and male voices, with the possible exception of the
within-condition comparisons for the falsetto disguise.

DISCUSSION

The results of these experiments suggest that minimally-
trained examiners have little difficulty with spectrographic
speaker identification in closed trials when the spectrograms
are contemporary samples of undisguised voices. These results
are consistent with those reported by Kersta (1962) and Tosi

et al. (1972). However, it appears that the same examiners
have a great deal of difficulty in closed trials with contemporary spectrograms when the spectrograms are of disguised voices. Identification rates drop significantly when
spectrograms of falsetto, whispered, or muffled voices are
matched with those of undisguised voices, although accuracy
of identification does not appear to be affected significantly when the "unknown" voice is in the lowered fundamental
frequency disguise. These results are similar to those reported by Reich et al. (1976) for comparison of disguised to
undisguised spectrograms for other vocal disguises. In
addition, matchings within disguise types, which were not
included in the Reich et al. study, were found to be significantly more difficult than matchings of undisguised
voices only in the case of the whispered disguise in
Experiment I.

Even though the results of Experiment II were not
analyzed statistically, the fact that they show the same
patterns of greater and lesser difficulty of the various
task types is taken to suggest that the results of Experiment I were not influenced by speakers producing their own
spectrograms. It is also taken to suggest that the differences in task types found in Experiment I are largely due
to the effects of the particular disguises, since the speakers
in Experiment II were totally distinct from those in Experiment I.

The results from these pilot studies were based on a
relatively small number of responses--one for each examiner
for each task type. However, the statistical analysis was a
conservative one, so that only differences which were quite
large were considered significant. It is possible, then,
that repetitions of these experiments in which more responses
are collected for each task type will reveal additional
significant differences, especially in the within-disguise
comparisons.

Spectrograms of female voices were included in these
studies in order to examine the belief that female voices
are more difficult to identify than are male voices. The
results presented here certainly do not support this belief.

Although this hypothesis was not tested directly, it is
clear that, in general, identification rates for female
voices were as good as or better than those for male voices.
This was true even in Experiment I, where the number of
reference spectrograms was larger for female speakers than
it was for male speakers, and it has been shown that identification rates decrease as the size of the reference set
increases (Tosi et al., 1972).

The conclusion reached in this study is that more research is needed on identification of disguised voices by
visual inspection of sound spectrograms. Vocal disguise
is likely to be a factor in the forensic use of the "voiceprint" technique, and this study suggests that some but not
all types of disguise interfere with spectrographic speaker
identification, even for within-disguise comparisons in the
case of at least one disguise.

REFERENCES

Bolt, R. H., F. S. Cooper, E. E. David, Jr., P. B. Denes,
    J. M. Pickett, and K. N. Stevens. (1970). J. Acoust.
    Soc. Am., 47:597-612.
Endres, W., W. Bambach, and G. Flosser. (1971). J. Acoust.
    Soc. Am., 49:1842-1848.
Hazen, B. (1973). J. Acoust. Soc. Am., 54:650-660.
Hollien, H. and R. E. McGlone. (1976). J. Crim. Defense,
    2:117-130.
Kersta, L. G. (1962). Nature, 196:1253-1257.
Reich, A. R., K. L. Moll, and J. F. Curtis (1976). J. Acoust.
    Soc. Am., 60:919-925.
Tosi, O. I., H. Oyer, W. Lashbrook, C. Pedrey, J. Nicol, and
    E. Nash. (1972). J. Acoust. Soc. Am., 51:2030-2043.
Williams, C. E. and K. N. Stevens. (1972). J. Acoust. Soc.
    Am., 52:1238-1250.
Young, M. A. and R. A. Campbell. (1967). J. Acoust. Soc.
    Am., 42:1250-1254.

NOTES

[1] Dr. Peter Ladefoged (personal communication) has suggested that inserting two fingers into the mouth should be an
effective disguise because it alters the shape of the
speaker's vocal tract.

ACKNOWLEDGMENTS

I would like to express my sincere thanks to Dr. Jonathan Holt Truex for his invaluable criticisms and advice on all aspects of this study, to Dr. Gerald A. Sanders, Dr. Amy Sheldon, and Marcia Steyaert for their insightful comments, and to the volunteer speakers and examiners for participating in these experiments. I am also grateful to Ed Bedrick of the Statistical Clinic of the Applied Statistics Department of the University of Minnesota for conducting the statistical tests reported here.

FIGURE 1

Experiment I: Score distribution for 18 responses by each of the 21 examiners.

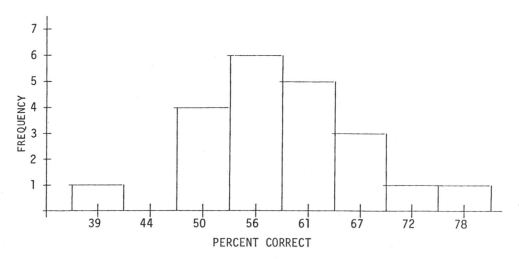

Table 1. Experiment I: Percentage of correct identifications for each task type. (N = 21)

	Female Voices		Male Voices	
	Within-Condition	Across-Condition	Within-Condition	Across-Condition
Undisguised	100	--	95	--
Lowered F_0	86	62	95	57
Falsetto	95	29	90	33
Whispered	5	5	48	14
Muffled	76	19	100	43

Table 2. Experiment I: Summary of statistical analysis of matched pairs of task types. UND--undisguised; LO--lowered fundamental frequency; FA--falsetto; WH--whispered; MU--muffled.

	p-Value	
	Female Voices	Male Voices
Within-Condition		
v. Within-Condition		
UND-UND v. LO-LO	---	---
UND-UND v. FA-FA	---	---
UND-UND v. WH-WH	< .01*	.22
UND-UND v. MU-MU	---	---
LO-LO v. FA-FA	---	---
LO-LO v. WH-WH	< .01*	.22
LO-LO v. MU-MU	---	---
FA-FA v. WH-WH	< .01*	---
FA-FA v. MU-MU	---	---
WH-WH v. MU-MU	< .01*	< .04*
Within-Condition		
v. Across-Condition		
LO-LO v. LO-UND	---	---
FA-FA v. FA-UND	.004*	.14
WH-WH v. WH-UND	---	---
MU-MU v. MU-UND	.14	.02*
UND Within-Condition		
v. Across-Condition		
UND-UND v. LO-UND	.14	---
UND-UND v. FA-UND	< .01*	< .01*
UND-UND v. WH-UND	< .01*	< .01*
UND-UND v. MU-UND	< .01*	.057

Table 3. Experiment II: Percentage of correct identifications for each task type. (N = 7)

	Female Voices		Male Voices	
	Within-Condition	Across-Condition	Within-Condition	Across-Condition
Undisguised	71	--	100	--
Lowered F_0	86	57	100	71
Falsetto	100	43	57	14
Whispered	71	0	71	0
Muffled	86	14	100	14

SPEAKER IDENTIFICATION BY MEANS OF TEMPORAL PARAMETERS: PRELIMINARY DATA

CHARLES C. JOHNSON, JR.
University of Florida

. In general, the most important information contained within the speech signal of an individual is the linguistic message. However, this information is by no means the only data transmitted to the listener by an utterance. Knowledge of the speaker's general emotional state, educational background, geographic origin and/or specific identity may also be provided. All of this relationships are important. However, it is this last information, the speaker's identity, which is the focus of this research.

To date, most speaker identification research has utilized speech parameters drawn from the frequency domain. Nevertheless, some work has been done with the temporal domain. Early work on perceptual speaker identification demonstrated that duration played an important role in the speaker identification process. Later research examining the role of temporal parameters has also shown timing to be of some importance in speaker identification. Sambur (1975), using consonant durations, found that when combined with other parameters very high identification scores were achieved. Doherty (1976) found that temporal parameters yielded low speaker identification scores when used alone. However, when these parameters were combined with his frequency measurements, an overall increase of from 8-26% was produced. This relationship indicates that the temporal domain does contain certain speaker identification related information not available in the frequency domain.

The aim of this study was both to examine more fully
the potential of temporal measurements as speaker identification cues and to develop an extensive set of temporal
parameters. The research consists of two laboratory based
experiments. However, one used normal speaking conditions
while the second introduced voluntary and involuntary speech
distortions. The same set of temporal parameters was used
in both experiments; they were, a time-energy distribution
and a set of voiced/voiceless measurements. These measurements are listed in Table 1.

The time-energy distribution or TED vector is based on
a group of time-by-energy measurements. In general terms,
this analysis depicts the total accumulated time a talker's
speech intensity remains at a specific energy level, relative
to his peak amplitude. It also provides an indication of the
speaker's speech pattern via speech bursts and pause periods.
Specifically, the TED vector uses an analog of the speech
signal which has been filtered, full-wave rectified, integrated, and DC shifted. The signal then was digitized with
a PDP-8i minicomputer and analyzed for duration relative to
these several energy levels.

Initially, the duration of the total speech sample is
measured (see Figure 1). The waveform then is partioned
into ten linearly equal energy levels initiating from the
greatest peak amplitude. At each energy level the number of
speech bursts, mean and standard deviation of the speech
bursts, and the standard deviation of the pause periods were
measured. Mean pause periods and the number of pauses were
not used in the development of this vector since they were
correlative to the speech bursts. However, the total pause
duration was utilized in the articulation/pause-time ratio
parameter of the voiced/ voiceless vector.

The voiced/voiceless speech time (V/VL) vector is composed of three parameters. They are: (1) total phonation
time, (2) total voiceless speech time, and (3) articulation/
pause-time ratio. The phonation time was extracted from the
speech signal via the IASCP FFI-8 linked to the PDP-8i minicomputer. FFI-8 is a digital readout fundamental frequency
tracking device which consists of a group of low-pass filters

with cutoffs at one-half octave intervals coupled to high-speed switching circuts which are controlled by a logic system. FFI produces a string of pulses (each pulse marking the boundary of a fundamental period from a complex speech wave) which are delivered to a PDP-8i computer. An electronic clock marks the time from pulse-to-pulse and these values are processed digitally to yield the geometric mean frequency, standard deviation of the frequency distribution and the total time of phonation. However, only the phonation time data are utilized in this research. The total voiceless speech time was calculated as the difference between the phonation time and the total articulation time, previously computed from the TED vector. The third parameter of this vector is the articulation/pause-time ratio. It was obtained simply as the ratio of articulation-time and total pause-time; both measurements were products of the TED vector.

The first experiment in which the above described temporal parameters were applied used normal or "ideal" recording conditions. Forty adult male speakers were chosen from faculty and students at the University of Florida. Selection criteria included: (a) 18 to 40 years of age, (b) no apparent speech defects, (c) speaker of general American English and (d) no unusual regional or foreign dialects. These minimal requirements yielded a relatively homogeneous population--which permitted initial baseline testing of the temporal parameters and presumably reduced any obvious inter-speaker variations. The subjects read a modernization of "An Apology for Idlers" by Robert Louis Stevenson--an approach that permits the speech samples to be context independent. This passage was chosen because it is relatively long, approximately 600 words, and contains all the phomenes of the English language. Therefore, it provides a good representation of a subject's speech repertoire. Each sample of this experiment was recorded under laboratory conditions in a sound treated chamber and with high quality recording equipment.

The second experiment was also carried out in the laboratory setting. However, speech distortions were introduced into the recording procedure. The purpose of this experiment was to investigate the effects of speaker distortions, both voluntary and involuntary, on the robustness of the temporal vectors. Speakers were 20 male faculty and graduate students from the University of Florida. These subjects were normal speakers of American English 25-45 years-of-age. They exhibited no unusual dialects, speech or voice disorders. The speech materials were the same passage described in the first experiment; so were the recording procedures. However, three speaking conditions were introduced into this procedure: (a) normal speech (control), (b) stress and (c) disguise. Emotional stress can be defined in a number of ways; in this case, it was induced by applying electric shocks, delivered randomly, while the subject was speaking. For the third condition, the subjects were requested to disguise their speech as completely as they could. The only restrictions placed on them were that they could not use a "foreign dialect" or "whisper"; in addition, they were encouraged to use the modal voice register.

RESULTS

The results of the laboratory normal experiment are shown in Table 2. They demonstrate that the TED vector, when used alone, correctly classified the speakers 27.5% of the time. The voice/voiceless vector chose the correct speaker 30% of the time. A combination of the two vectors produced a correct classification score of 37.5%.

The results of the distorted speech experiment may also be seen in Table 2; a discriminant analysis statistical procedure was utilized. Using the normal speech samples as the reference samples, the TED vector correctly matched the stress samples to the normal 21.3% of the time and for the disguised samples, the identification score was 18.8%. The voice/voiceless vector performed at a much lower level, 7.4% for the stress samples and 10.3% for disguise. A combined vector consisting of all the parameters of the TED and V/VL vectors achieved identification scores of 30.9% for the stress condition and 14.7% for the disguise condition.

DISCUSSION

From these results the following relationships may be seen. The TED and V/VL vectors perform about equally in determining a speaker's identity under controlled laboratory conditions, however, the V/VL vector appears to be the more efficient of the two. The V/VL vector did almost as well with three parameters as the TED vector did with over ten times that many. Further analysis is being carried out to determine if some of the TED parameters are not needed to produce the same identification scores. Results of the combined vectors under normal speaking conditions demonstrated an increase in the overall score but, since this increase is small, it seems probable that the information being processed by these two vectors is in some cases duplicated or redundant.

In the second experiment the ability of the two vectors to identify a speaker recorded during stress or disguise was examined. The results showed that the parameters were able to perform this task with varying degrees of success. The TED vector produced correct classifications for the stress condition only about 6% less accurately than for the normal experiment. Under the disguise condition, the degradation in identification scores over the normal experiment was only 9%. This finding would seem to indicate that the information contained within the TED parameters was not greatly modified by stress or disguise. However, this does not seem to be the case with the voice/voiceless vector. The V/VL parameters performed poorly in the stress condition--only slightly above chance level. Therefore, change which occurs in the voice during stress appears to substantially alter the V/VL measurements. The same general argument applies to the disguise condition. The identification score of the combined vectors under the stress condition is greater than the sum of the two vectors used alone. For this stress condition, there appears to be no overlapping of information. That is, in this case it seems that the two sets of measurements are complimenting each other. On the other hand, for the disguise condition, the combined identification scores is less than that of the TED alone and greater than that of the V/VL vector alone. It is unclear at this juncture why such a relationship might occur. Perhaps with further analysis an explanation can be brought forward.

In summary, the two experiments undertaken have demonstrated that the temporal domain of the acoustic signal does
contain some information which aids in the determination of
a speaker's identity from his voice alone. It also is
apparent that this temporal information is not adequate
alone as a speaker identification cue--a finding which would
seem to be in agreement with previous research involved with
speaker identification by temporal data. However, there are
two important points about this research which should be mem-
tioned. First, while the two vectors in this study only produced identification scores of 30-37%, they were reasonably
resistent to changes which occurred during speaker stress.
Second, since these vectors do show resistance to speaker
distortion, they may prove to be a valuable addition to previously developed speaker identification systems based on
the frequency domain.

REFERENCES

Doherty, E. T. (1976). J. Phon., 4:321-326.
Sambur, M. R. (1975). IEEE Trans. Acoust., Speech and
     Signal Process., ASSP-23:169-176.

Table 1. The temporal vectors and their parameters.

Vectors/Parameters	Number
Time-Energy Distribution (TED)	
Number of Speech Bursts	10
Duration Speech Bursts	10
S.D. Duration Speech Bursts	10
Total Speech Time (by Level)	10
S.D. Duration of Period	10
Total Number of TED Parameters	50
Voiced/Voiceless Speech Time (V/VL)	
Total Phonation Time	1
Total Voiceless Speech Time	1
Articulation/Pause-Time Ratio	1
Total Number of V/VL Parameters	3

Table 2. The results of the two experiments. N = 40 for
          normal; N = 20 for distorted.

Vectors	Normal	Stress	Disguise
TED	27.5	21.3	18.8
V/VL	30.0	7.4	10.3
Combined	37.5	30.9	14.7

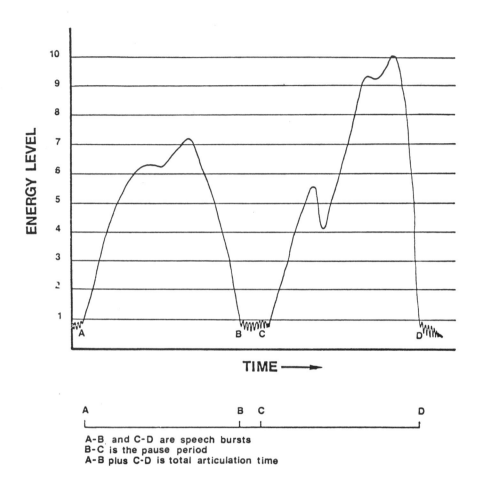

A-B and C-D are speech bursts
B-C is the pause period
A-B plus C-D is total articulation time

Fig. 1.   Schematic representation of a typical energy envelope as generated from the TED equipment configuration.

SOME REMARKS ON DIFFERENT SPEAKER
IDENTIFICATION TECHNIQUES

WOJCIECH MAJEWSKI, JANUSZ ZALEWSKI AND HARRY HOLLIEN
Technical University of Wrocław and
University of Florida

The experiments carried out by several investigators
indicate that automatic speaker recognition (i.e., identification or verification) within small populations of speakers
is feasible, at least under laboratory conditions (Atal, 1976).
However, some of the methods applied to speaker recognition
yield just acceptable scores, while other methods provide quite
satisfactory results. Such a spread of speaker recognition
rates indicates that, by means of the selection of proper
recognition techniques (i.e., identification parameters and
decision rules), recognition efficiency may be considerably
improved. The purpose of this paper is to discuss some of the
problems associated with automatic speaker recognition, to
compare the results obtained by means of different recognition
techniques and, from this base, to draw some conclusions for
future speaker recognition research.

Two distinctly separate operational phases may be distinguished in any automatic speaker recognition experiment.
First, the identification parameters (or a set of parameters)
must be chosen and, secondly, the proper decision criteria
must be applied. Let us consider some of the problems connected
with these phases. A very important problem in speaker recognition is the selection of speaker-dependent parameters of speech.
The general idea is to select--for the purpose of speaker
recognition--those parameters of speech which exhibit low
intraspeaker but high interspeaker variability. Two different
approaches may be distinguished in this regard: the first

utilizes text-independent methods, while the second text-dependent ones. Text-independent methods of speaker recognition are based on long-term statistical analysis procedures which utilize the identification parameters extracted from the speech signal of such duration that the values of those time-averaged parameters remain approximately the same regardless of the text used. Text-dependent methods are based on specific cue material, the duration of which extends from a fraction of a second (in case of phonemes) to a few seconds (in case of sentences).

Both basic approaches to speaker recognition methods have their advantages and disadvantages. The methods based on long-term statistical analyses require relatively long speech samples (an approach which may be inconvenient for practical implementation) but the results are more resistant to the influence of time elapsed between the recordings of the test and reference samples. On the other hand, in the case of text-alignment methods, the text may be relatively short--but usually a time-alignment is required to match the utterances of different durations--and the results obtained are more sensitive to the influence of elapsed time.

Generally, acoustic parameters of speech may be used in the speaker recognition process in one of three forms: (1) as parameters defined as a function of time, (2) as parameters defined as a function of phonetic elements (usually phonemes) and (3) as parameters averaged over time and text. The parameters represented in the last form are obtained through sufficient time-averaging and are used in the case of text-independent methods, while the parameters described by the other two forms are utilized in text-dependent methods. The parameters presented in forms one (i.e., as time-varying parameters) and three (i.e., as time-invariant parameters) are most widely applied in speaker recognition experiments (see, for example, Bricker et al., 1971; Atal, 1974; Furui et al., 1972) than are the parameters presented in form two (i.e., as the parameters obtained for particular phonemes; see Sambur, 1975 and Kashyap, 1976). What may be explained (in part) by this approach is that, applied practically, it would require automatic measurements of speech parameters in particular locations in the utterances and that is a rather difficult task.

As far as the selection of particular speech parameters
is concerned, the chosen parameters should--according to Wolf
(1972)--be efficient in representing the individual voice
features, easy to measure, stable over time, occur naturally
and frequently in speech, change little from one speaking
environment to another and not be susceptible to mimicry. It
is not easy, however, to find speech parameters that simultaneously fulfill all of these conditions and, in practice, a
large variety of parameters extracted directly or indirectly
from the speech wave are utilized for the purpose of speaker
recognition. Among the parameters most widely used are:
vocal intensity, fundamental frequency of phonation, speech
spectrum (both short- and long-term), formant frequencies,
zero crossing rates and predictor coefficients. When the
identification parameters are chosen and associated measurements carried out, i.e., after the first phase of the speaker
recognition process, the second operational phase--classifi-
cation--takes place. In this second phase, decision rules
are applied to assign the parameters extracted from an unknown
speech sample to one of the known speakers (a case of speaker
identification) or to verify that the speech sample was produced by the claimed speaker (a case of speaker verification).

At this point,we will restrict our discussion to the case
of speaker identification, because most of the experiments we
have carried out have been related to that issue (see, among
others: Majewski and Hollien, 1974; Zalewski et al., 1975;
Majewski et al., 1975 and Hollien and Majewski, 1977) and we
are interested in developing a technique that would be suitable
for speaker identification in large populations. Generally,
in order to identify speakers, a decision rule assigns the
unknown speech sample to a speaker on the basis of a minimum
distance between a multidimensional vector representing the
test speech sample and any of the vectors representing the
reference samples. The following measures constitute a group
of decision rules that are most widely used: Euclidean,
Hamming and Mahalanobis distance, cross-correlation coefficient
and minimum prediction residual. The Euclidean distance is a
special case of the Mahalanobis distance; in turn, Mahalanobis
distance together with minimum prediction residual seem to be
the most valuable of the decision rules.

As stated, in the past few years, we have carried out a series of experiments on speaker identification utilizing various decision rules and different parameters derived from the speech signal. The parameters utilized were: fundamental frequency of phonation (Hollien et al., 1975), zero crossing rates (Majewski et al., 1975), long-term speech spectra (Majewski and Hollien, 1974; Zalewski et al., 1975; Hollien and Majewski, 1977; Doherty and Hollien, 1978), linear prediction coefficients (Zalewski et al., 1977) and temporal factors (Johnson, 1978). The decision rules applied were: Euclidean distance (Majewski and Hollien, 1974; Majewski et al., 1975; Majewski and Basztura, 1977; Hollien and Majewski, 1977), Hamming distance, Mahalanobis distance and criteria based on Bayesian model of recognition (Majewski et al., 1975), cross-correlation coefficient (Zalewski et al., 1975) discrimination analysis (Doherty, 1977; Doherty and Hollien, 1978) and minimum prediction residual (Zalewski et al., 1977).

As may be seen from the number of references, long-term speech spectra has been most intensively examined. Utilizing this parameter in speaker identification experiments for relatively large populations of speakers (several groups of 50 American and 50 Polish speakers were involved) and using three decision rules (Euclidean distance, cross-correlation and discriminitive analysis) it was possible to achieve 100% correct identification for the American speakers and 98% for the Poles in contrast to 94 and 96% for the Americans and 96 and 98% for the Poles when either of the first two decision rules were applied separately. On the basis of this experiment it is suggested that a combination of two or more decision rules applied to the same test material (i.e., number of speakers, number of speakers' utterances, number of identification parameters) may result in more powerful identification process than would application of decision rules applied separately.

However, in spite of the successful results obtained under laboratory conditions and for contemporary test and reference speech samples, a review of our results and those of other investigators indicates that further improvement, based on time-averaged parameters, will be difficult to achieve and that neither time-invariant nor time-varying parameters of speech will be sufficient for satisfactory identification in large

populations of speakers. The reason is that, if the number
of speakers to be recognized is large (say 1000 or more), the
exclusive use of gross acoustic parameters is insufficient to
obtain distinctive patterns for all the speakers involved. It
may be possible, however, to solve this problem on the basis of
temporal parameters (Johnson, 1978) or of parameters obtained
selectively for particular phonemes--because in such case, the
feature space used to describe the speakers' patterns will be
augmented by adding a set of phonetic parameters to the acoustic
ones. What should result is a practically unlimited number of
sufficiently distinctive patterns. The number of experiments
dealing with the problem of speaker recognition for large populations is rather limited (some theoretical considerations are
given by Kashyap, 1976) and, because of this, it may be interesting to present some results of an experiment based on the
above cited idea. In this experiment, the speech material consisted of 3000 utterances, including 10 repetitions of six
Polish vowels produced in isolation by 50 male speakers. The
speech signal was pre-emphasized 6 dB per octave; a low-pass
filter, with a 5 kHz cut-off frequency, sampled at a rate of
20 ksamples per second and converted them into digital form
by means of 8 bit A/D converter. A quasistationary segment
of 85 ms duration was taken from each of the utterances and
represented by a vector of p prediction coefficients (in the
primary experiment reported in 1977, p was equal to 12 and,
in the subsequent experiments, p was equal to 16). Using the
Itakura distance measure (1975), i.e., the logarithm of the
ratio of prediction residuals, seven speaker identification
experiments were performed. In the first experiment, speakers
were represented by single vowel LPC vectors and a mean
recognition rate of 81.1% was obtained. In the second experiment, speakers were represented by two repetitions of a given
vowel; in this case, the mean recognition rate was 83.9%.
In the third experiment, when the speakers were represented by
one repetition of two different vowels, the speaker identification score was 95.6%. In the fourth experiment, for two
repetitions of two different vowels, the recognition rate was
97.1%; in the fifth experiment (for one repetition of three
different vowels) the result was 97.9%. In the sixth experi-
ment--two repetitions of three different vowels--the result
was 99.5% and, finally, for one repetition of four different
vowels, a score of 100% correct identification was obtained.
At this point, there appeared to be no need to continue the

experiments by increasing the number of vowels and their repetitions because the population of speakers was too small to show further increase in correct speaker identification scores. Anyway, from the results of these experiments, it may be seen that, with an increase of number of phonetic parameters, there is a substantial increase in speaker recognition rates until the level of 100% of correct identifications is achieved.

There are many other interesting problems and questions related to speaker recognition--such as (1) the problem of contemporary vs. noncontemporary speech samples, (2) laboratory vs. field conditions and/or (3) cooperative vs. noncooperative speakers; however, these problems are beyond the scope of this paper. Hence, on the basis of the presented results and discussion, the following conclusions can be made: (a) The application of several speaker identification techniques combined yields some improvement in speaker recognition rates; (b) A further improvement in speaker recognition rates, within the methods based on time-averaged parameters of speech, seems to be rather difficult to achieve and (c) The consideration of phonetic structure in speaker recognition experiments seems to be a promising way to improve speaker identification scores. Indeed, this approach may lead to a solution of the problem of speaker recognition in large populations of speakers.

REFERENCES

Atal, B. S. (1974). J. Acoust. Soc. Am., 55:1304-1312.
Atal, B. S. (1976). Proc. IEEE, 64:460-475.
Bricker, P. D., et al. (1971). BSTJ, 50:1427-1465.
Doherty, E. T. (1977). J. Phon., 4:321-326.
Doherty, E. T. and Hollien, H. (1978). J. Phon., 6:1-8.
Furui, S., Itakura, F. and Saito, S. (1972). Elect. Commun. Jap., 55A:54-61.
Hollien, H. and Majewski, W. (1977). J. Acoust. Soc. Am., 62:975-980.
Hollien, H., Majewski, W. and Hollien, P. (1975). Inter. Cong Phon. Sci. Abst., Leeds, 337.
Itakura, F. (1975). IEEE Trans. ASSP, 23:67-72.
Johnson, C. C. (1978). Unpub. Ph.D. dissertation, Univ. of Florida.

Kashyap, R. L.   (1976). IEEE Trans. ASSP, 24:481-488.

Majewski, W., Basztura, Cz. and Hollien, H.   (1975). Inter.
    Cong. Phon. Sci. Abst., Leeds, 186.

Majewski, W. and Basztura, Cz.   (1977). Proc. Inter. Cong.
    Acoust., Madrid, 1:438.

Majewski, W. and Hollien, H.   (1974). Speech Commun. Sem.-74,
    3:303-310.

Sambur, M.   (1975). IEEE Trans. ASSP, 23:176-182.

Wolf, J. J.   (1972). J. Acoust. Soc. Am., 51:2044-2055.

Zalewski, J. and Jurkiewicz, J.   (1977). Proc. Inter. Cong.
    Acoust., 4:438.

Zalewski, J., Majewski, W. and Hollien, H.   (1975). Acust.,
    34:20-24.

FURTHER ANALYSIS OF TALKERS WITH SIMILAR SOUNDING VOICES

HOWARD B. ROTHMAN
University of Florida

The problem of speaker identification, i.e., the process by which an individual is recognized or identified (by some means) from the acoustic and temporal features extracted from the speech signals he or she produces, is both complex and controversial. The complexity and controversy become apparent by perusing the scientific literature for the past few years (see, for example, Bolt et al., 1973; Black et al., 1973; and Hollien, 1974). Even so, the determination of an individual's identity solely from the information conveyed by the acoustic speech signal is a familiar everyday experience and one that occurs under a multitude of circumstances. Most, if not all of these, are subjective in nature. Procedures that permit an individual to be recognized or identified objectively and absolutely from speaker dependent features are very difficult to establish and appear to exceed the present state-of-the-art--especially when the identification of an unknown speaker is involved.

Several approaches and considerable scientific effort have been expended on the determination of the validity of speaker identification techniques and/or the development of new ones. Generally, three procedures have been utilized in speaker identification: (1) perceptual (aural), (2) visual (spectrogram matching), and (3) machine recognition. This paper concerns itself with the first two approaches. A review of the literature concerning these approaches will not be provided.

However, Hecker's (1971) assertion that very little is
known of the perceptual and physical correlates of spectrographic speaker homogeneity is still valid. Indeed, there
is a possibility that speakers with similar sounding voices
do not produce similar appearing spectrograms. Accordingly,
a series of investigations designed to examine this issue
have been instituted.

STUDY 1: PERCEPTUAL (AURAL) IDENTIFICATION

Twenty-four talkers (12 pairs) were recorded reading
an extended prose passage. Seven pairs of talkers were re-
lated--i.e., they were either father-son pairs, brothers or
identical twins--and had a long history of being confused with
each other. Seven pairs (fourteen talkers) were recorded
again one week later reading the same passage. Four pairs
(of the seven pairs) were chosen from the original group of
twenty-four talkers based on the fact that the partners exhibited similarities in their long-term speech spectra.Three
of the seven pairs were composed of twins or father-sons.
Four 2-3 sec. speech samples were extracted from the extended
prose passage for each talker and these samples in turn were
grouped according to date of recording, ie,same day or one
week later.All perceptual judgements of contemporary samples
involved contiguous phrases recorded at the same time; the
judgements on contemporary samples involved pairings of the
same phrase and contiguous phrases recorded one week later.
The contiguous phrase shared one word in common with the preceding phrase. The paired samples (contemporary and noncontemporary) were randomized and presented to a panel of 38
listeners for aural/perceptual judgements of similarity or
difference. The entire procedure was replicated by recording all speech samples through a filter bandpass of 250-2700
Hz in order to simulate a telephone passband.

The result of the perceptual procedure can be seen in
Table 1 which presents the mean percent corrent identification
scores for the full passband and the simulated telephone passband conditions.According to Table 1 listeners can identify
two contemporary samples of a single talker's speech (Group 1)
quite easily. The ability to correctly identify non-contemporary samples of a single speaker (Group 2), even when
separated by only a week, results in a sharp drop in correct

identification. The mean percent correct identification
scores for Group 3 are greater than those for Group 2. This
finding indicates that listeners are able to detect some
speaker dependent cues within the acoustic signal which dif-
ferentiates one talker from another. Further,the low scores
obtained for Group 2 indicate that changes occurred in
speakers' acoustic signals over a period of one week. These
changes in the acoustic signal made it difficult for listeners to correctly identify an individual from noncontemporary speech samples. A three way analysis of variance
confirmed the differential effect (significant at the .01
level) of passband, talkers and time on the perceptual
(aural) identification ability of listeners.

STUDY 2: SPECTROGRAPHIC MATCHING

The phrases used in the perceptual (aural) study also
were used for spectrographic matching. That is, matches involving contemporary samples used contiguous phrases; noncontemporary samples were composed of the same phrase as well
as contiguous phrases recorded one week later. Wide band
spectrograms were prepared on a Voice Identification, Inc.,
Series 700 Spectrograph; the frequency resolution used was
0-8 kHz. The spectrograms were presented to six individuals
experienced in spectrographic pattern matching.As a control
condition for the spectrographic matching task and to establish baseline matching ability, duplicate spectrograms were
prepared of one phrase ("they have no curiousity") recorded
by each of the twenty-four original talkers. These were randomized with the additional spectrograms of the same phrase
produced by the fourteen talkers (comprising the seven pairs
chosen from the original group) who recorded the same passage
one week later. The judges knew the phrase but did not know
whether the spectrograms were exact duplicates, contemporary
or noncontemporary. The "exemplar" spectrograms were mounted
on a 45" x 30" card;the spectrograms to be matched were randomized together and presented to each examiner. All examiners, in the pre-test condition,achieved 100% correct matching for the exact duplicates.

A summary table of a two-way ANOVA for the spectrographic
matching task is found in Table 2. The ANOVA confirms, at

the .01 level, that talkers and condition have a significant
effect on the ability to perform identification tasks. Table
3 presents a Duncan's multiple range test which ranks the
scores for all the identification tasks. The means which do
not share the same letter are significantly different at the
.01 level. According to Table 3, the perceptual (aural) task
is a significantly better method for speaker identification
than any of the spectrographic matching tasks. The largest
mean percent correct score for visual matching was obtained
when the same--but noncontemporary phrase was used. However,
there is no significant difference between the mean of 39.22%
obtained by matching the noncontemporary samples of the same
phrases and the mean of 26.25% obtained when matching con-
tiguous/contemporary phrases. A Pearson correlation was performed for all the identification tasks; it showed no correlation between the perceptual (aural) and the spectrographic
(visual) tasks. Further, there is virtually no correlation
among any of the various visual tasks.

A second spectrographic task was done. This time, examiners were asked to make a binary choice; to do so they were
presented with 84 pairs of spectrograms and asked to make a
same or different response to each pair. This approach was
similar to the first aural/perceptual task and was an attempt
to correlate the two tasks: listening and visual matching.
An ANOVA for this last visual spectrographic matching task
again demonstrates that talkers and time had a differential
effect on the visual matching abilities of listeners. For
this task, two groups of examiners were used. One group
(primarily Phoneticians), was experienced in dealing with
acoustic aspects of speech and had many years of experience
in examining spectrographic visualizations of the speech
signal. The second group was composed of some linguists and
both undergraduate and graduate students in speech. All the
students had successfully completed a Speech Acoustics course
and were familiar with the various features of the speech
signal as depicted in spectrograms. A one-way ANOVA and
Duncan's multiple range test confirmed at the .01 level that
training had a differential effect. The experienced group
achieved a mean correct identification score of 58%. The mean
for the relatively naive group was 53%. The means are significantly different at the .05 level. Moreover, a three-way
ANOVA was carried out on the data from the aural/perceptual

and the last visual study. The results show again that
talkers and time are different--and that the two tasks are
different. The largest difference occurs with time; that
is, contemporary versus noncontemporary. When comparing the
auditory and visual tasks the overall means are 70% and 55%,
respectively.

Finally, the results of a Duncan multiple range test
applied to the binary visual task and the combined aural/
visual data demonstrated that the combination of auditory
and visual data produces the highest mean percent correct
score with one exception: there is a reversal for the non-
related pairs. The visual matching task alone produced a
significantly better score than was achieved by the aural/
perceptual listeners. This indicates that there may be some
clues available to the visual examiners that served to differentiate different and non-related talkers. It is impossible to speculate on what these may be even though the
results are intriguing and will be investigated further.
However, overall the auditory method is significantly better
than the visual.

DISCUSSION

The results obtained from the perceptual (aural) and
spectrographic matching studies are clear cut. First, the
perceptual (aural) method of speaker identification is clearly
superior to the spectrographic or "voiceprint" technique.
Second, time (i.e., contemporary or noncontemporary samples)
is an extremely important factor for speaker identification.
Indeed it appears that within the constraints of the population used for these studies (i.e.,adult males chosen for the
similarity of their voices), the time factor seems to be the
most important parameter for speaker identification purposes
The data obtained from the perceptual study indicate a sharp
drop to below a chance level when the speech samples were
recorded one week apart. Clearly then, the "best" situation
for speaker identification purposes will be achieved from 2
speech samples recorded at a single session with a full passband. Equally clear is the fact that these conditions are
impossible to attain in a forensic situation.

It is evident that the studies and data described are not
directly applicable to the Forensic model. A bias was built

into the experimental design when speaker pairs were chosen
on the basis of their being vocally confused with each other
or due to the similarity of their long-term speech spectra.
However, there is no data-base available that allows us to
predict the number of similar sounding voices within a given
population or the probability that they will turn up in a
forensic situation. Further, the recordings used were of a
quality far superior to those obtained in forensic field
situations. Therefore, one can assume that more information
of an acoustic nature was available to the listeners and the
visual judges.

Projecting from the data, and assuming the impossibility
of acquiring an identical phrase produced in a contemporary
time period, it is best to have the same phrase for comparative purposes in a speaker identification task. When the
speech samples are different and noncontemporary the ability
to identify individuals is sharply reduced. This condition
represents the least desirable situation for speaker identification purposes.

Some further points should be considered concerning the
use of spectrograms for speaker identification purposes.
First, most, if not all, of the investigations concerning
spectrographic use for identification of talkers use "examiners"with varied training and background to do pattern matching. Basically, it is the "examiner's" expertise or perhaps
"talent" that is being investigated. Therefore, the process
of identification remains more in the nature of an unferified
and unquantified mystique at least when applied to the forensic situation. Until information becomes available as to
which spectrographic features correlate most clearly or efficiently with a talker's identity, the voiceprint technique
should be considered as similar to the aural/perceptual technique. This latter technique has also defied quantification
and its acceptance is often dependent on the known or pre-
sumed veracity of an individual or on an individual's long-
term acquantance with the voice in question. The difference
between the claims of the voiceprint and aural/perceptual
proponents resides in the fact that the former is in effect
suggesting that his technique and professional opinion be
given extra weight by a jury of lay people due to the
supposed objective, scientific analysis utilized.

Second, the Tosi et al. (1972) study recommends examining the following features for identification purposes: (a) mean frequencies of vowel formants, (b) formant bandwidths, (c) gaps and types of vertical striations, (d) slopes of formants, (e) durations, (f) characteristics of fricatives, and (g) interformant energy. Of these seven features, all can be easily manipulated by the talker and at least two can be altered by the recording process or by the operator of the spectrograph. Consider the following: (1) Disguise can alter, eliminate or obscure formants and alter formant bandwidths; (2) Changes in speaking fundamental frequency can change the distance between vertical situations; (3) The slopes of formant transitions will change with changes in rate of articulation; (4) Fricative information is often lacking in field acquired recordings made at speeds of 15/16 i.p.s.; and (5) Interformant energy can be added to or deleted from the spectrogram by manipulating input intensity, mark level or automatic gain controls. This investigator has not been able to find any published or non-published data which establishes rules for quantifying, measuring or dealing with the above talker or machine variant features of the acoustic signal.

Third, the proponents of the voiceprint technique discuss points of similarity and dissimilarity without specifing the number of points or even what these are, specifically. The questions that most often come to mind are: How many and what types of similarities outweigh a dissimilarity and conversely how many and what types of dissimilarity outweigh a similarity?

Fourth, Dr. Peter Ladefoged (People vs. Law, 1974) and Dr. Oscar Tosi (Singh, 1975) both agreed that the process by which an examiner makes a speaker identification or elimination is highly subjective and, further, that each examiner follows his own processes and establishes his own criteria. Indeed, in People vs. Law, Ladefoged admitted that he does not know how he or anyone else accomplishes the matching task—they just do it! The question that immediately comes to mind is: How do these individuals really know they do it without a verifying statement from an accused that his was the voice in question? In this regard, the Reich et al. (1976) study demonstrated an interaction between task type and error type. This interaction means that a professional examiner must exert some consistent control over the types of errors made. Studies should be conducted to determine the types of errors made by different examiners. Then, those examiners with a propensity for making fewer false identifications and false inclusions should be chosen in order to protect the innocent.

Fifth, positive feedback has been shown to be important to improving the abilities of visual (i.e., spectrographic) examiners. This kind of feedback is difficult to acquire when one is dependent only on the outcome of court cases. The possibility exists that an examiner's criteria for decisions may shift, thereby resulting in more erroneous decisions because of a bias resulting from knowledge of other types of evidence which may or may not be proof positive. Moreover, the Tosi et al. (1972) study indicated that the identification error rate increased as the number of "known" voices or spectrograms increased. Therefore, it appears reasonable to assume that reliability will decrease and error rate will increase as the number of suspects increases.

Finally, the proponents of the voiceprint technique emphasize that a professional examiner fully aware of the consequences of his decision would tend to be extremely conservative in his decision making and would take lots of time in order to arrive at a correct decision. This means that an examiner, if in doubt, would lean towards a "no decision" or an elimination. Yet, Kersta, the father of the method and Nash, the chief disciple, have made errors in courts-of-law. It is impossible to determine if or how many other errors have been made. Therefore, I strongly suggest that one cannot accept the proposition of professional integrity and caution as a guarantee against providing an erroneous judgement.

REFERENCES

Black, J. W., Lashbrook, W., Nash, E., Oyer, H. J., Pedrey, C., Tosi, O. I., and Truby, H. (1973). J. Acoust. Soc. Am., 74:535-537.

Bolt, R. H., Cooper, F. S., David, E. C., Denes, P. B., Pickett, J. M., and Stevens, K. N. (1973). J. Acoust. Soc. Am., 54:531-534.

Hecker, M. H. L. (1971). Am. Speech Hear. Assoc., Mono. 16.
Hollien, H. (1974). J. Acoust. Soc. Am., 56:210-213.
People vs. Law, 114 California Reporter 708-715, California, App. 1974.
Reich, A. R., Moll, K. L. and Curtis, J. F. (1976). J. Acoust. Soc. Amer., 60:919-925.
Tosi, O. (1975). in Measurement Proced. Speech, Hear. Lang. (S. Singh, Ed.), Baltimore, University Park Press, 399-433.
Tosi, O., Oyer, H., Lashbrook, W., Pedrey, C., Nichol, J. and Nash, W. (1972). J. Acoust. Soc. Amer., 51:2030-2043.

Table 1. Mean percent correct identification by listeners (N 38) who did not know the talkers. Group 1 represents speakers paired with their own contiguous samples recorded during a single session; Group 2 represents speakers from Group 1 paired with a sample of themselves (same phrase) (recorded one week later; Group 3 represents speakers when paired with their claimed vocal twin.

Paired Speech Samples	Full Frequency		Telephone Passband	
	Twelve Pairs	Seven Pairs	Twelve Pairs	Seven Pairs
Group 1	94%	92.48%	90.70%	89.58%
Group 2	42%	42.00%	40.30%	40.30%
Group 3	58%	52.06%	56.35%	47.04%

Table 2. Summary table of a two way ANOVA for the spectrographic matching tasks.

Source	Degrees of Freedom	Mean Square	F*
Subject	13	633.52	2.78*
Condition	6	16963.45	74.40*
Error	78	227.99	

Table 3. Duncan's multiple range test for scores on identification tasks. Means with the same letter are not
significantly different; alpha level = .01; N = 15.

Grouping	Mean	Condition
A	100.0	Pretest
B	70.1	Perceptual/Aural
C	39.2	Same phrase/non-contemporary
C DC	26.2	Contiguous/contemporary phrase
D D	22.5	Contiguous/contemporary phrase
E	7.3	Contiguous/non-contemporary phrase
E E	5.3	Contiguous/non-contemporary phrase

PRELIMINARY DATA ON DIALECT IN SPEECH DISGUISE

DONNA A. TATE
University of Florida

Is it possible to determine whether or not a person is disguising their voice? The question actually is a complex one. This study looked at one aspect of that issue--disguise by use of a dialect. Unfortunately there is very little empirical knowledge about either disguise or dialects. In fact, I know of no studies that deal with this particular question of determining if a person is disguising his voice. Labov (1972) does mention a related issue in his study of the Black English Vernacular (BEV). If a Black leaves his native dialect area, and becomes fluent in Standard American English, he later will be able to switch back to a BEV pattern. However, in doing so, this person will retain many Standard forms in his speech. As a result, other Blacks from his native area will identify his speech as artificial BEV.

For the purpose of this study, untrained imposters and trained actors attempted to imitate the accent of natives of North Central Florida who had marked Southern accents. In order to test the success of the disguises, untrained native Southern listeners were asked to determine which of the speakers were real Southerners, and which were imitation Southerners.

METHOD

Subjects: In order to develop the experiment, I utilized three groups of eight male speakers. These groups included native Southerners, untrained imposters, and trained actors.

848   DONNA A. TATE

The native Southern talkers had lived all or most of their
lives in North Central Florida, and had marked Southern accents. The untrained imposters exhibited General American
(or non-Southern) accents. The trained actors also spoke
with a General American accent. Finally, ten untrained
listeners were used as auditors. These individuals were
University of Florida students who either were natives of
Florida or had lived in the state since the age of eight years

   Procedures: For the production of the tape recordings,
high quality laboratory recording equipment and an IAC 1600
sound treated room were utilized. The native Southern speakers were recorded during one session. During this session
they read a modernization of Robert Louis Stevenson's "An
Apology for Idlers" twice, and spoke extemporaneously for one
to two minutes. The combination of the reading and extempora-
neous speech provided a wider range of speech for each talker's
sample--thus allowing better illustrations of his dialect.

   For the untrained imposters there were two recording
sessions. During the first session, they read "An Apology
for Idlers" while speaking in their native dialect. During
the second session, which was at least one day later, these
men first spoke extemporaneously in their native dialect for
one to two minutes. They then listened to samples of native
Southern speech for twenty minutes, but were not permitted to
practice producing the dialect. After this training session,
the imposters attempted to produce imitation Southern speech
while they read "An Apology for Idlers" and spoke extemporaneously for one to two minutes.

   The trained actors also were recorded during two sessions. At the first session they read "An Apology for Idlers"
while speaking in their native dialect. These actors spoke extemporaneously for one to two minutes while using their native
dialect during the beginning of the second recording session,
which was at least one day after the first. They then were
given the option of listening (or not listening) to samples
of native Southern speech for up to twenty minutes. They
also were allowed to practice producing the dialect. After
this training session the actors attempted to produce imitation Southern speech while reading "An Apology for Idlers"
and speaking extemporaneously.

Experimental Samples: For the experiment, I utilized the
two 10-15 sec. samples of speech that best exemplified the
dialect of each native Southern speaker. I also used a 10-15
sec. sample of speech best exemplifying the native dialect of
each of the imposters and actors, and a similar sample of
each of their attempts at imitating Southern speech--i.e.,
those that sounded most Southern. These forty-eight samples
(sixteen samples, each, of the native Southern, imitation
Southern, and General American dialects) were randomized twice
for production of the experimental tape.

Listening Sessions: The listening session was conducted
in a special sound treated perception laboratory, and
utilized high quality equipment. The listeners were informed
that this was a study of disguise. They were asked to determine whether each sample that they heard was native Southern,
imitation Southern, or General American Speech.

RESULTS

The overall results of the study can be seen in Table 1.
As the table shows, the listeners were able to correctly
identify the General American and Southern dialects. In addition, as would be predicted by Labov, they were able to
correctly identify the imitation Southern samples two-thirds
of the time.

The comparative identification of imposters and actors
(while they were attempting to imitate the Southern dialect)
is seen in Table 2. Due to the nature of the speakers'
task, one would expect the actors to be much more successful
than the imposters, resulting in a higher identification of
the actors' imitation Southern dialect as native Southern.
However, this was not the case. While the actors were slightly
better at disguise (being identified as native Southern 37.5%
of the time, as opposed to 30.0% of the time for the imposters),
the difference is not statistically significant.

It is also interesting that, overall, samples of imitation
Southern speech were identified as native Southern one-third
of the time. Thus, we see that most of the time, untrained
native Southern listeners can determine that a speaker is not

Southern, and iş using a Southern dialect as a disguise.
However, even native Southern listeners are not very adept
at making this determination.

As I have already stated, this study investigated one
aspect of the issue of disguise. There is much work still
to be done. As a next step in this research, this experiment
will be repeated with three additional listening groups:
untrained non-Southerners, trained Phoneticians and Linguists.

REFERENCE

Labov, W.   (1972).   Philadelphia, Univ. Pennsylvania Press.

Table 1.   Percent correct listener response by native
           Southerners to three types of dialect.

| | Listener Response | | |
Stimulus	GA	NS	IS
GA	89.7	6.6	3.7
NS	4.4	75.9	19.1
IS	4.4	33.7	61.9

GA = General American
NS = Native Southern
IS = Imitation Southern

Table 2.   Identification of imitation southern talkers.
           N = 32.

| | Percent Response | | |
	IS	NS	GA
Imposters	67.5	30.0	2.5
Actors	56.4	37.5	6.3
Mean	61.9	33.7	4.4

AN OBJECTIVE METHOD OF VOICE IDENTIFICATION

OSCAR TOSI, R. PISANI*, R. DUBES, A. JAIN
Michigan State University and *Institute Galileo Ferraris

Methods of voice identification can be classified into two general groups: subjective and objective. To the first group belong those methods in which a decision concerning whether or not a questioned or "unknown" voice is same or different as one or several "known" voices is produced by a human examiner. Rather, objective methods of voice identification are those in which such a decision is produced by a computer, programmed according to a suitable algorithm. Subjective methods comprise aural examination of voices by the long-term memory process or by the short-term memory process and visual examination of speech spectrograms. Objective methods comprise semiautomatic, automatic and voice authentication systems, with a variable interaction of human examiners in each of them. Methods of voice identification are not exclusive, i.e., two or more different methods can be used concurrently in practical cases. Also subjective methods are not necessarily associated with larger percentage of errors than objective methods. Presently the contrary appears to be true. No doubt that in the future objective methods will be greatly improved, allowing their main assets to be used in legal cases, that is: accurate knowledge of their error percentage, consistency and lack of bias of any kind. Possibly they would be used concurrently with subjective methods in cases from real life, taking the best of the two worlds, by professional, experienced practitioners. For instance, aural methods can disclose better and faster than automatic methods perceptual characteristics of speech such as dialect, type of background noise, selection of the

questioned voice within a sample involving two or more
speakers, etc.

The purpose of this paper is to discuss an automatic
method, text-independent, based on choral speech spectra and
hierarchical talker discrimination. The interest   the
authors in a method strongly text-independent originated in
a practical need from real life case   Indeed, in many occasions related to legal cases it is not feasible to obtain
examplars from suspected persons voices using the same text
as the questioned one. Many methods, including the spectrographic, requires such a condition and therefore they cannot
be used even to attempt an identification or elimination.
To better evaluate the text-independent characteristics of
the method discussed here, two pilot experiments were performed, using not only different texts, but three different
languages as uttered by the 20 speakers involved in these
studies.

The first pilot experiment (Bordone, Dubes, Pisani,
Sacerdote, Tosi, 1974) was performed at the Institute Galileo
Ferraris of Torino, Italy, in 1973, during a sabbatical
leave from Michigan State University. The usage of
choral spectra was suggested by the Director of the Department
of Acoustics of that Institute, Dr. G. Sacerdote, as a better
alternative to the long-term spectra, since the former allows
to obtain similar results as the latter with samples up to
about 1/20 shorter (Tarnoczy, 1958). The three languages
utilized, Piamontes, Italian (Tuscan) and French are fluently
spoken by most native people from Torino, capital of Piemont.

Speech samples were obtained from 20 persons from that
city (14 male and 6 female), within ages 25 and 53 and education ranging from secondary school to university. All speakers
presented no defects or noticeable speech peculiarities. They
recorded three times, within a lapse of one week from each recording session, three 10 minute readings from books and news-
papers, each reading in a different language. Recordings were
obtained in a room with "normal" resonant conditions, using
an internal line and microphone and tape recorder of semi-pro-
fessional quality (Shure #545 and Revox #A700, respectively).
With these samples, eight second loops of choral speech were

AN OBJECTIVE METHOD OF VOICE IDENTIFICATION   853

prepared by using a Samborn #3917 loop tape recorder, a
mixer and a Nagra #IV-5 tape recorder. Choral spectra was
obtained by a system composed of analog instruments, including a B & K analyzer #2107, a B & K level recorder
#2305 and associated devices such as a smoother, an inte-
grator, a chopper, a reset system, etc. as shown in Fig. 1.
The resulting spectra (9 per speaker), consisted of 156
power ordinates within the range of frequencies 63Hz to
6300 Hz, every 4/100 of octave (Fig. 2).

These total 180 choral spectra were transferred to IBM
cards and processed through a CDC 6500 computer, according
to a modified Johnson's hierarchical clustering algorithm.
Each talker was clustered within the same group, within a
5% to a 30% error, accordingly to the various alternative
grouping method tested (connectedness, diameter, average).
This result suggests that talkers possess invariances in
their choral spectrum, regardless of the language used.

The second pilot experiment was performed at the
Michigan State University, utilizing the same exemplars as
in the first one, although not totally. In this opportunity
only 11 talkers were used (6 male and 5 female) and 25 speech
samples as follows: 3 different language samples from 3
talkers; 2 different language samples from 2 talkers and 1
language sample from 3 talkers. The reason for this shortening was double fold: to avoid symetry in the groupings and
to save computer time. In this second pilot experiment,
analog instruments were not used. Original exemplar magnetic
tapes were inputed into a A-D peripheral device, connected to
a PDP 11/40 mini computer. Eight second samples from each
exemplar were digitalized at a rate of 10,000 reading/second
to keep the frequency range from 62 to 4752 Hz. A suitable
program in the CDC 11/40 computer produced choral spectra from
these samples, simulating 76 band pass filters of 6% octave
width (Fig. 3). Each choral spectrum was produced in approximately three minutes. Computer PDP 11/40 was interfaced with
the CDC 6500 in order to process the spectra according to the
hierarchical algorithm mentioned before.

This algorithm consists essentially of comparing any
combination of two spectra i, j, by substracting the power
ordinates A_{ik} and A_{jk} of each similar abscissa k, from 1 to

76 in the present case. A parameter Dif, characterizing
the difference between spectra i and j is then computed, by
two alternative methods:

$$Dij = \sum_{k=1}^{76} Aik - Ajk$$

or

$$Dij = \sqrt{\sum_{k=1}^{76} (Aik - Ajk)^2}$$

In either case it is Dij = Dji and Dii = 0.

Then a 25 x 25 matrix is formed with these parameters
(Fig. 4). Now the smallest Dij is located within the matrix.
The two spectra that originated this Dij are collapsed into a
single spectrum and a new 24 x 24 matrix is formed. The
parameters D for this new matrix are computed accordingly
three alternative methods: (a) connectedness, (b) diameter,
(c) average. A simple example, for a 4 x 4 matrix is offered
in Fig. 4, as an illustration of these three alternative calculations. The process continues by locating the smallest
Dij in the new matrix. Again the two spectra involved are
collapsed, resulting a 23 x 23 matrix, and so on, up to a
final 1x1 matrix.

The series of collapsed matrices produces a dendogram,
indicating groups of most similar spectra, assuming being
produced by the same speaker. Further the 76-dimension of
each collapsed spectra can be reduced by a similar process to
two-dimension, producing a Sheppard grouping graph or alternatively a minimum spanning tree (Fig. 5). All these operations are produced by the computer, yielding a hard copy if
necessary. Examination of Fig. 5 suggests that the choral
spectra method discriminates accurately talkers, irrespective
of the languages they may use.

Research continues in this area. A new experiment,
including commercial telephone line, cassette tape recorder,
spontaneous speech by a group of talkers utilizing only

English, is presently being performed at the Institute of
Voice Identification of the Michigan State University. A
series of open and discrimination tests of voice identification and elimination are programmed. Results will be
available by the middle of 1978.

REFERENCES

Bordone, C., R. Dubes, R. Pisani, G. Sacerdote, and O. Tosi.
      (1974). Presented at Acoust. Soc. Amer. Convention,
      New York.
Tarno'czy, T. (1958). Acust. 8:392-395.

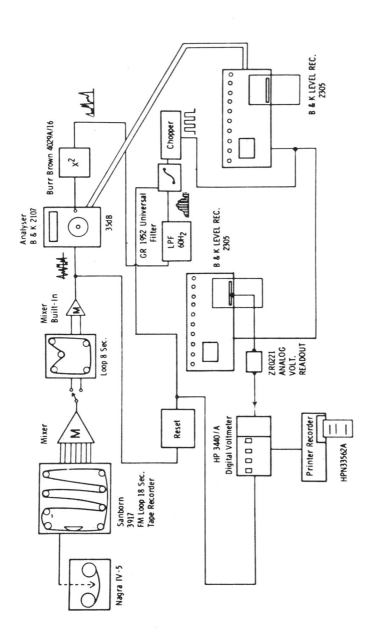

Figure 1.   Analog system used to obtain choral spectra.

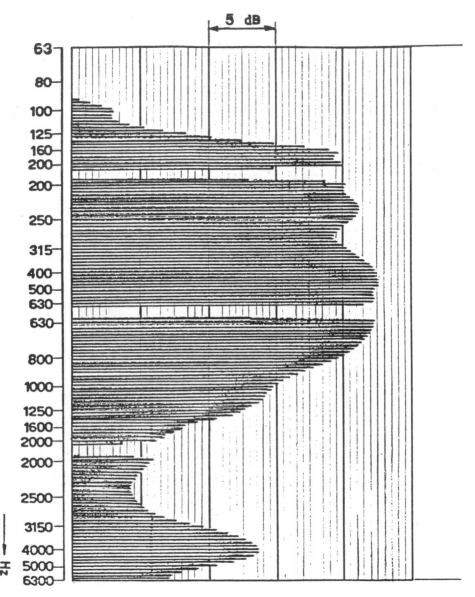

Figure 2.

Choral spectrum from 1 subject speaking
Piamontes, obtained with the analog system of
Figure 1.

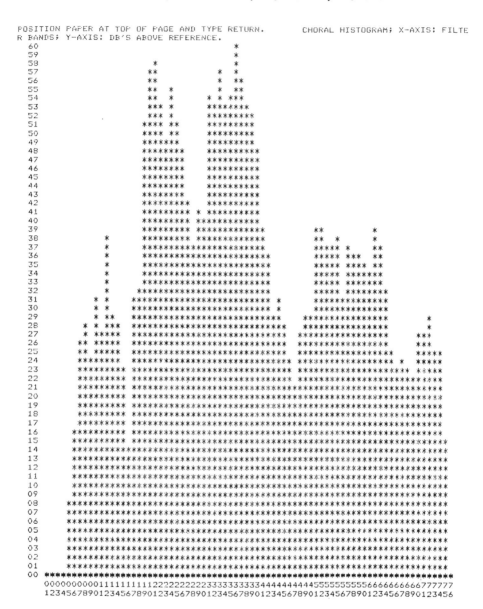

Figure 3.

Choral spectrum from 1 subject speaking French,
obtained through a computer program.

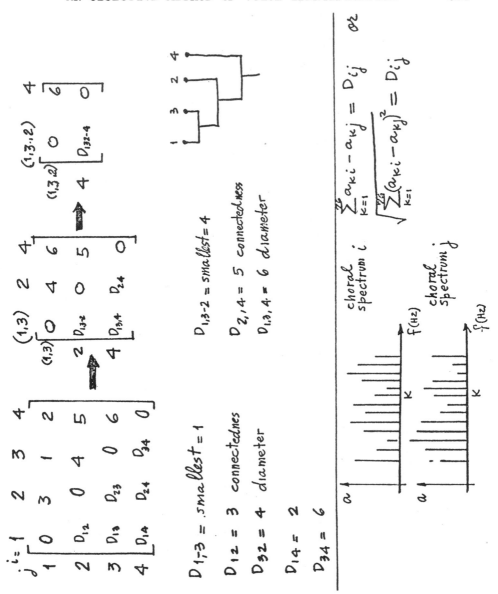

Figure 4.

Example of matrix reduction for computer
hierarchical grouping.

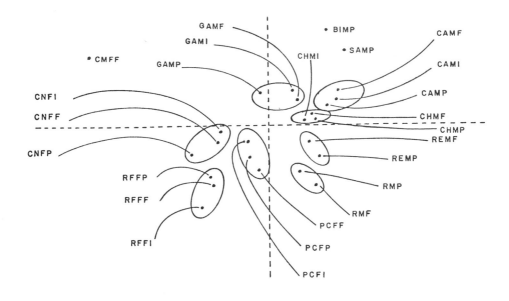

Figure 5a.

Sheppard diagram from hierarchical grouping of
11 talkers, 6 male and 5 female speaking up to
three different languages. Subject GA (male)
spoke French, Italian, and Piamontes each time.
Subjects CH (male), CA (male), CN (female),
RF (female), PC (female), also spoke these
three languages each time. Subjects BI (male),
SA (male), spoke only Piamontes in each recording. Subject CM (female) spoke French only.
Subjects RE (male) and RM (male) spoke French
and Piamontes in each recording.

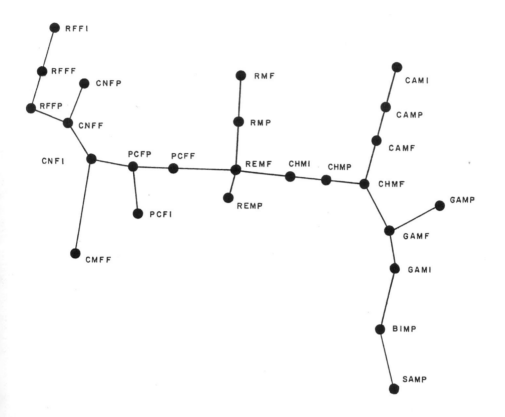

Figure 5b.

Minimum vectorial spanning tree diagram, indicating hierarchical grouping of same subjects as
in Figure 5a.

J. THE TEACHING OF PHONETICS

PHONETICS AND SECOND LANGUAGE TEACHING IN AFRICA

F. O. BENNETT
University of Zambia

In Alan Paton's "Cry the Beloved Country" a key figure
is known as "UM FUND ISI." He is a priest but the Bantu
word used for him as a Reverend or Priest is also the word
for a teacher. It has a very interesting literal meaning
as the three syllables UM - FUND and ISI show. The prefix
UM, also found as MU, is personal. Those who have worked
among Africans at least in Africa South of the Sahara, know
how common are names beginning with MU or sometimes only
M. This is because of the dominance of the personal prefix
--not that any other initial letter is not personal, but
because names have meanings and the personal prefix makes
the meaning clearer. This relationship can be seen also if
we look at the derogatory title once given to the indigenous
people--MUNT, because that is a shortened form of MU - NTU:
a person, as opposed to CI - NTHU: a thing (the /h/ is the
aspiration in correct pronunciation). Now examine again the
Bantu word: UM - FUND = ISI. The word for TEACHER, UM,
equals THE PERSON (WHO); ISI (found in other African
languages as ITSA, ESA or ETSA, etc.) is a causative suffix,
or an intensive. FUND is a basic Bantu root, alternatively
P(H)UNZ meaning LEARN not unlike PUNDIT, PANDIT (Hindi from
Sanskrit) or the borrowed English term FUNDI - perhaps from
Swahili where it means a craftsman. So UM - FUND - ISI is
the person who causes to learn.

UNESCO'S W. J. PLATT adopted this attitude when, as
Deputy Assistant Director-General for Education he introduced

what he called an Initial Learning System. In Southern
Africa, Phonetics is easily introduced in first cycle
education, and in literacy programs, because almost universally (and I speak with a personal knowledge of some dozen
Bantu languages), the dominant vowels are the long singable
vowels. This relationship is the more obvious in Africa
which I soon learned to call "a land of mirth and melody."
Indeed, only Wales--which I had learned to know a little
from a group of brilliant fellow students in Cambridge in
the 30's--was as spontaneously musical.

One of the commonest 'musical interludes' in Southern
Africa is a work scene: a gang of stalwart laborers either
digging in musical unison, or heaving and straining, a little
like sailors who gave us their sea shanties. In this regard,
a short anecdote would appear appropriate. Being compelled
by circumstances to move into direct contact with rural
indigenous people within my first six months in Africa, and
fortunately having a gift for mimicry, I soon became used
to simple conversation and the typical Bantu U (it is of
course the final vowel of the word itself--and the more
fundi among you will note that the syllables are BA - NTU
not BAN - TU). Judge my chagrin on meeting a fellow North
countryman (Yorkshire, one of England's six northern counties)
and being told--in broad Yorkshire and equally deep U's--
"/a nouz wi: a: kumz frum lad/."

Only a short step from this sort of scene, where the
first actors I saw in Natal were true Zulus, are the two
points I wish to make in this paper on Phonetics and Second
Language Learning. First the link between functional
literacy and political expression; secondly, the application of the visual aid of Zulu bead messages to language
learning and in particular, the problem of spelling in
English. However, I first must acknowledge my debt to
Prof. J. Roby Kidd as I worked with his son Ross Kidd at
Evelyn Hone College from 1964 to 1967. While there, I had
live contact with Professor Kidd and was therefore introduced more recently to the International Council for Adult
Education. 'Convergence,' the journal of ICAE, keeps us
informed of world wide developments in adult education and
literacy in both of which spheres language learning is basic.

It is this "digest" of information which has made me personally aware of what I call the level of literacy--or from
another perspective: the ability to learn, which indicates
the heightened value of phonetics as a learning aid.

First, let me discuss the link with political aspirations and expression. "Not passive learners, but active
citizens" is more than a slogan. In Zambia we are still
boiling, not just simmering, with aspirations towards more
freedom and, of course, are kept on the boil because we
are surrounded by large areas of constraint. It is here
that I personally find great joy in advocating the use of
phonetics, because "one symbol, one sound" echoes the
slogan "one man, one vote." I look forward to expanding
this idea in company with the socio-linguists and all who
see literacy campaigns as among the most important in helping man towards freedom from the mind hunger of ignorance.
In this regard, I wish to recognize Frank Laubach who, in
1948, first opened up the unlimited vision of becoming
literate and therefore free.

Closely linked to political aspirations are the legiti-
mate desires of people, especially young people, to be
economically independent; to be capable of earning their
own living. For example, one of the most popular jobs
(especially for the emergent young women of Africa) is
that of secretary. Commercial subjects, formerly only
chosen as a "soft option," are now regularly included in all
secondary schools and, along with colleagues trained as
commercial teachers, I have pioneered the closest possible
linking of the teaching of commercial subjects and the teaching of English. English is increasingly not just English
literature and English language but commercial English or
English in business and more recently communication. This
is more helpful in countries like Zambia where young people
in banks and in business generally may have to communicate
in the several languages of adjacent countries; e.g., French
in Zaire, German still in Namibia, Portuguese in Angola,
Swahili and so on, in East Africa.

Since shorthand (whether Pitman, Gregg or Forkner) is
based on phonetics, there are obvious links between the

disciplines. Shorthand is not yet being used for non-
European languages in Zambia, but I have recommended this
approach--along with the training of secretaries using
the vernaculars for the growing number of businessmen
whose business is mainly with tribal groups. Phonetics
will obviously be the more helpful with the more phonetic
Bantu languages. But the problem remains of the transcription from phonetic shorthand to very unphonetic English.
Thus, as you would expect, I am a member of spelling reform
societies and invariably use the American simplified spelling of words like 'labor' and 'center.'

In a previous section, I referred to my work in Natal,
South Africa, where I lived for 10 years (1953 to 1963) on
the very borders of Zululand itself. It was here that I
first became aware of the unique Zulu use of beads. Many
peoples of the world use beads for trade and decoration,
but only the AmaZulu use beads for communication. I also
link it to the terminology of modern education where
Modern Mathematics introduces sets. In learning situations of many different kinds, I have found most helpful
a gradual build-up of "sets" from the set of letters (A)
the alphabet and (B) the morpheme or phoneme. For the
child or other learner, it is the word: on to sets of
words (a) phrases (b) clauses (c) sentences and more recently
vide Austin and Grime (d) discourses. But most significant
of all is the second set (B) the word, linked to the bead
pattern. For this is linked also to the school of thought
of A. S. Hornby and others which identifies language patterns
and their usage. The simplest examples in English are the
two pairs of sets (i) (a) quite (i) (b) quiet (ii) (a)
unite but (ii) (b) the very opposite 'untie.' One can
readily see that a wrong set or pattern of beads could
easily turn "I love you" into "I love you not"--after all
a slip of the pen can turn a "friend" into a "fiend" or
vice versa. When introducing phonetics in learning groups
I often say: "There can't be spelling mistakes in phonetics."

I come now to my Campaign for Compromise. I propose
that phonetics be taught and used, partly as Pitman has done
with his Initial Teaching Alphabet but without introducing
new symbols. Indeed I go one step further than usual in

compromise, by advocating that students first of all make
and adapt their own Phonetic alphabet a little like the
way everyone does use his own shorthand or speed-writing,
apart from those who have adopted any standard form as
taught in Commercial Schools and Colleges. An alternative
is the Cuisinaire system of 'color phonetics.'

While doing wide reading and research for this paper
I have become aware of the lowering of what I call the
level of literacy, or ability to learn. I have access to
our own College Library as well as to a City Library and
the British Council library and there one finds hundreds
of excellent publications from all parts of the world,
and all walks of life--all in English. By contrast I
have to mark the written work of dozens of students all
in English--all coping with varying degrees of success
with English as an acquired language (sometimes it is
third or fourth, not the second language). There is a
steadily maintained rate of failure in exams, exams mainly
still set and marked in English; because students fail to
understand the question and/or fail to make the examiner
understand their answers. In between the 'high' of the
English of many publications and the 'low' of the level of
literacy of students is the phenomenon of growing inaccuracy
even in the once sacred columns of The Times of London.
Is it the original writers alone who misspell words, or the
proof readers who fail to correct errors--or is it both?
And not only misspellings but grammatical forms that once
would have shocked the ordinary literate reader, let alone
the literati. Here are two recent examples, ostensibly from
the lips of Britain's Minister of Foreign Affairs "I have
drawn your remarks to his attention," referring to the Prime
Minister: then the P.M.'s reply: "You will receive
immediately our view." At least those are the exact words
reproduced by an International News Agency in our Press here.

What, then, is my suggestion; my Campaign for Compromise?
It is a very practical one with two stages. First that whatever clearly conveys a message be accepted as effective communication. Secondly, that phonetics be used more widely
instead of the confusing English spelling. In this way I

have applied phonetics to the learning of English as an
acquired language, with the added help of the Zulu bead
letters in getting the sets of letters more correct in
formal English spelling.

TEACHING BEGINNING PHONETICS IN THE UNITED STATES: SOME BASIC CONSIDERATIONS

JACQUELINE L. BROWN
Ball State University

The primary objectives in most beginning phonetic classes include: (1) familiarizing the students with the International Phonetic Alphabet (IPA), (2) assisting the students in gaining a working knowledge of the application of the IPA, and (3) relating these objectives to the anatomy and physiology of the speech mechanism. It is the purpose of this paper to examine these objectives and suggest possible alternatives and methods for coping with the problems in the classroom.

Students in my classes were given evaluation forms that provided them with the opportunity to respond with regard to structure of the class, problem areas, and valuable class activities. Reference will be made to this study throughout the paper. It should be noted that the student responses were anonymous to avoid any biases that might occur.

One of the first problem areas that must be considered is that of motivation. Lack of motivation, although not specifically related to phonetics, must be considered in teaching something that demands such consistent and concentrated effort on the part of the student. This single aspect must be dealt with before any progress can be expected. Daily quizzes, used by many phonetic teachers in the United States, help to insure regular study as well as a more direct means of communication with the teacher.

Along the same lines, the use of periodic worksheets and exercises seem to provide similar kinds of feedback for the students. According to the class evaluations, students reported that quizzes, exercises and worksheets were very valuable. The students indicated that the individual work put the necessary emphasis on regular study that improved their work. Over 90% of the students indicated that the quizzes and individual work should be continued in future classes.

Another form of practice that can be employed, once the students have learned the IPA, is the transcription of paragraphs, poems, and stories. The use of literature seems to make transcribing a more enjoyable task for the student. These also serve much the same purpose as worksheets, but provide for sentence work that exercises do not. Again, students felt that their overall grade had improved by continuous and extended practice using phonetics.

After considering the problems inherent to learning any new system of communication, it is important to look at the aural problems that are created. In the United States, the teaching of spelling is stressed to a large extent in the primary grades. This extreme emphasis seems to afford many students more difficulty in learning phonetics because of a lack of sound discrimination training. By stressing the aural aspects of phonetics and de-emphasizing orthographic aspects, the student of phonetics in the United States should be aided greatly in learning the International Phonetic Alphabet and how it works.

Since phonetics is a relatively new area of teaching, there are no long established methods that work best but thinking of phonetics as a foreign language seems to offer some strong possibilities. Educators have taught French, German, and Spanish in our schools for several years so why not implement similar methods for the teaching of phonetics. Aural training is widely used in the teaching of foreign language, so a focus on the aural aspects of the IPA need to be foremost in consideration. As mentioned before, students must begin to think in terms of sound and not orthographics. Most students have little if any training in sound discrimination of any kind and so the basics must be considered. With special attention to sound discrimination, the beginning student should then be better able to cope with the sound-symbolization paradigm.

A number of sounds that are closely related in some way almost always cause the students in a beginning class some degree of difficulty. Those consonant pairs that offer the most confusion seem to be the final /s/-/z/ and /θ/-/ð/. There also appears to be a difficulty with the /ɑ/-/ɔ/ as well as /ɝ/-/ɚ/, and /er/ vowel combinations.

The major problem with the consonant pair /s/ and /z/ seems to stem from a strong background and emphasis in orthographics or the inability to put spelling out of their minds. Those students who did have more of a problem with this pair than others were aided in three ways: (1) tapes for aural stimulation, (2) exercises for verbal stimulation, and both of these supplemented with (3) rules regarding the adjacsceny of consonants and pluralization.[1] These methods helped to clear up most of the confusion.

The /θ/ and /ð/ also provided the same kind of problems that /s/ and /z/ did. It seemed that students never realized that the "th" in their language could be voiced or voiceless. Special verbal and aural exercises were implemented to strengthen the concepts of voiced and voiceless in learning new sounds. These exercises were supplemented with the physical tests[2] to further teach the basic concepts of voicing.

The vowels provided still another problem distinct from that of the consonants. There seemed to be little difficulty overall except with those vowels which were closely linked in location on the vowel chart and those readily substituted for each other. The problem seemed to be more prominent in the /ɑ/ and /ɔ/ vowels. The problems with sound discrimination in both of these cases may be distinct to certain regions, however, it seems to plague students from all parts of the country. Students seem to approximate variant sounds thus making the discrimination between the /ɑ/ and /ɔ/ much more difficult for these students. The use of tapes can again be implemented to assist in the aural training necessary to distinguish the sound differences.

The last problem that seems most prevalent among beginning students is the differentiation and use of /ɝ/, /ɚ/,
and /ɛr/. The major reason for this problem again stemming
from a lack of adequate aural training necessary to avoid the
trap set up by the spelling of a word. Students forget to
listen and resort back to their spelling training by substituting the /ɛr/ for the final "er" spellings in their
transcriptions. For example, instead of transcribing mother
/mʌðɚ/ they would transcribe it /mʌðɛr/.

I am sure that there are countless examples of problems
that plague the beginning students, many of which are distinct to the geographic area, the public school training, or
individual environment. However, one major factor seems to
remain constant as a variable in learning ability with regard
to phonetics--listening. A special focus needs to be placed
on aural as well as vocal stimulation and training if the
student is truly to be successful in acquiring an accomplish-
ment in phonetic transcription.

To fill the need for this training, an answer might be
exercises supplemented with tape cassettes for each sound or
sound pair. These tapes could give the necessary auditory
stimulation that the student cannot get on his own. In most
other subjects, a student can go to a book, journal, or other
printed resource, to find the answers to his questions. In
phonetics, however, he must "hear" the answers. The student
must learn to listen. If the student does not have tapes or
aural kinds of learning he may easily fall into learning the
wrong sound or a variant sound merely because the proper
stimulation or reinforcement was not there. These cassettes
or tapes could easily be take the form of a "teaching machine,
if you will. The teaching machines have proven successful in
a number of instances because of not only the sound stimulation, but the immediate reinforcement that can take place
assisting greatly in the education process.

The teaching machine could consist of a tape cassette on
each sound, supplemented with exercises or written transcription. This would operate in much the same manner that teaching
records and tapes work for learning a foreign language only

they would let the student write the sound they hear rather than repeat them. A mini version of this proposed teaching machine was implemented in my classroom with a great deal of success. With a near unanimous reply from the evaluations, students felt this to be one of the most beneficial to their learning.

In our society today, where such emphasis is placed on higher education, more and more students fill the classrooms and fewer and fewer teachers or funds are available. Because of this overloading, classes can reach levels of 80 to 100 students. We, as educators, must continually strive toward the one-to-one relationship with students for the most success. The only feasible way this could be handled is through the cassettes or teaching machines for individual work and feedback; and exercises, quizzes, and transcriptions as a supplement for large classroom work. Although not a replacement for the classroom work, the tapes can serve as an excellent addition that should help to eliminate many of the problems that plague the beginning students.

Many may suggest that this type of individual work is not a workable solution or alternative. Many will argue that students can learn phonetics just as well with a straight lecture-test format. It is at this point that we must decide, as educators, whether we want our students to learn the phonetics or whether we want them to learn it well enough to apply it effectively. The question is up to each one of us.

NOTES

[1] When pluralizing a word, the following rules will apply: (1) If the preceding consonant is voiced the word will end in /z/, (2) If the preceding consonant is voiceless the word will end in /s/, and (3) When the preceding sound is a vowel, the word will end in /z/.

[2] Placing the hand on the throat to feel the buzzing of the voice and placing the fingers in the ears to hear the buzzing for voiced consonants.

NON-ENGLISH PHONE IMITATION AND GENERAL ACADEMIC AND IPA TRANSCRIPTION PERFORMANCE BY MONOLINGUAL ADULTS

RAPHAEL M. HALLER
Illinois State University, Normal

Most speech-language clinicians are trained to use broad International Phonetic Alphabet (IPA) symbols in transcribing phonemic substitutions or additions spoken by communication impaired persons. A hyphen is typically used to specify a phoneme omission and an x to connote a nonphonemic substitution, such as the lateral s. Winitz (4) has recently demonstrated the use of IPA diacritic markers and non-English phones in diagnosis, e.g., to specify the manner and place of articulation of the client's nonphonemic substitution, and in therapy, e.g., to train the client to differentiate between the target phoneme and his error sound. One popular articulation test, the Fisher-Logemann Test of Articulation Competence (1), includes a description of relevant non-English phones in its examiner's manual and recommends their use in place of the nebulous x. Consequently, the writer has begun to train his phonetics students to perceive what he considers relevant narrow phonetic transcription symbols.

In this study 29 monolingual native American English speakers were provided with a practice session in imitating seven non-English phones as part of a phonetics course. One week after this session, the students were provided with an audiotape and an accompanying script in which the same phones appeared in nonstandard productions of familiar words. One week after the listening materials were made available, the class was given an IPA transcription exam based on the script. The rationale underlying this ritual--based on the motor theory of speech perception (2)--was that students would be better able to transcribe non-English phones spoken by the investigator after learning to produce them. The seven non-English phones which were selected represented nonstandard productions which had been observed by the investigator among normally speaking preschool children and articulation defective clients. These phones were /ɫ/, often referred to as the "dark l"; /ɜ/, the predominent British vowel r; /ʔ/, the glottal stop; /ʂ/, the lateral s; and /ʃ/, usually described as either the anterior palatal fricative or the palatal flat fricative. The format during the imitation session consisted of the investigator pronouncing a word first in a standard manner and then in a nonstandard manner employing a non-English phone as the error sound. These words were delivered by live voice. After listening to both pronunciations once, the subject was instructed to imitate the nonstandard version. A response was scored as correct even if the target phoneme was added to the standard phoneme, e.g., /xkʌp/. Five trials were provided for each word and the subject was then asked to judge whether or not he had correctly produced the non-English phone at least one time. The investigator informed the subject whether or not any of the latter's productions had been correct only after the self-evaluation statement had been made.

Table 1 shows the seven words with their associated non-English phones, the number of subjects producing each target phone at least once, the number of total correct productions across subjects and the rank order of the phones' difficulty, the rank of 1 representing the phone which was produced most frequently and by the greatest number of subjects. The glottal stop was the most frequently produced phone, followed in increasing order of difficulty by the voiceless pharyngeal fricative, the British vowel r, the voiced pharyngeal fricative, the lateral s, the "dark l" and the flat palatal fricative. In general, the subjects' self-evaluations of their correct productions were more accurate than their judgments of their consistently incorrect productions. More than half of the subjects failing to produce the "dark l," the lateral s and the flat palatal fricative judged at least one of their productions to be correct.

The rank order of successfully produced phones seems
to be consistent with several observations reported in the
experimental phonetics and dialectology literature. Of the
seven phones measured, only the glottal stop appears in most
dialects serving as an allophone of t or d, as in the pronunciation of country as /kʌʔri/ or in bottle as /baʔl/. Thus
it was expected that this phone would be imitated most often
relative to the others. The rank of 2 for the voiceless pharyngeal ficative and 4 for its voiced cognate may be explained as follows: While the voiceless is nonphonemic in English
it serves as a vegetative sound in such maneuvers as throat
clearing. However, since more supraglottal air pressure
characterizes voiceless consonants than their cognates, it
seems logical that some subjects producing the voiceless member would be unable to generate sufficient aerodynamic force
for the voiced cognate. Physiologically the British vowel r
seems to fall on a continuum between the American English /ɝ/
and the lowest central vowel /ʌ/. Therefore the imitation of
the phone /ɜ/ would not seem to necessitate the violation of
phonological rules. In contrast both s allophones used in
this study seem to violate phonological rules. Only the glide
/l/ in American English requires lateral air emission so the
notion of producing a lateral sibilant would appear to be
bizarre to American speakers. Further the only flat fricatives in American English are dentals so that a palatal flat
fricative would violate the sibilancy rule requiring a
grooved lingual contour. Finally the double articulation required for the "dark l" would seem to be difficult to produce, primarily since--in the investigator's experience--most
adult listeners do not appear to evaluate this phone as nonstandard. These data were compared with the subjects' performance on prior IPA transcription exams given in class and
with the subjects' grade point average (GPA) accumulated at
the end of the previous semester, in an attempt to identify
some factors which might predict student performance in the
course. Table 2 shows the Spearman rank order correlation coefficients and their associated t values resulting from these
comparisons. A statistically significant relationship at the
.01 level was found between non-English phone production and
self-evaluation, irrespective of whether or not the target
phones had been imitated. A significant relationship was also
found between IPA transcription performance in class and GPA.

However, the relationship between IPA transcription performance in class and the non-English phone imitation task
was nonsignificant. These classroom exams had been administered prior to the imitation task and had included standard
and nonstandard word productions, as spoken by the investi-
gator--but not the experimental phones.

The subjects' accuracy in self-evaluating their non-
English phone production might have been due to the phones
selected which were either perceptually similar to or markedly dissimilar from the subjects' own phonological systems.
For example, a subject who failed to reproduce the liquid aspect of the investigator's lateral s could immediately have
perceived the mismatch and rejected the accuracy of his production, despite the absence of a correct or incorrect verbal
evaluation by the investigator. On the other hand the investigator's possible perceptual bias cannot be ruled out. As
Locke and Bookshester (3) have shown, trial-by-trial judgments during a phoneme learning task may be distorted by the
judge's familiarity with the subject's speech efforts. Since
the investigator served as the sole judge, the constancy of
his perceptual phoneme boundaries must be open to question.

The close correspondence between IPA transcription performance in class and GPA may reflect general factors affecting all college coursework such as study time and motivation.
A practical implication of this finding may be that considerable tutorial work in phonetics might be needed for poorly
achieving students.

Finally, the absence of a statistically significant relationship between IPA transcription performance in class and
imitation performance in the lab is open to various interpretations. If phone mimicry mediates between perception and
written transcription, one would expect imitation and transcription performance to be related even though the auditory
stimuli varied. On the other hand students' phonetic transcription performance is a function of many linguistic and
nonlinguistic variables, the identification of which would
seem to require considerable research. Whether the production
and IPA transcription of the same stimuli would be comparable
is a question which the investigator is presently studying.

REFERENCES

1. Fisher, H. B., and Logemann, J. A. (1971). Boston,
       Houghton-Mifflin.
2. Liberman, A. M., Cooper, F. S., Shankweiler, D. P., and
       Studdert-Kennedy, M. (1967). Psychol. Rev. 74:
       431-461.
3. Locke, J. L., and Bookshester, J. (1973). J. Speech
       Hear. Res. 16:667-670.
4. Winitz, H. (1975). Baltimore, University Park Press.

Table 1. Number of subjects (N=29) producing non-English
          phones, number of productions and rank order of
          difficulty.

Target Phone	Standard and Target Productions	Rank Order of Correct Productions	Number of Subjects Producing Phone	Number of Correct Productions
/ʔ/	/baṭ, ba ʔ ḷ/	1	28	125
/x/	/kʌp, xʌp/	2	25	102
/ɝ/	/ɝ θ, ɜ θ/	3	21	88
/ɣ/	/gɑt, ɣ ɑ t/	4	17	77
/ʂ/	/si, ʂi/	5	14	61
/ɫ/	/le, ɫ e/	6	3	7
/ʂ/	/so, ʂo/	7	2	6

Table 2. Spearman rank order correlation coefficients compar-
          ing subjects' performance in college coursework (GPA)
          IPA transcription and non-English phone production
          and self-evaluation (N=29).

Performance Compared	r_s	t
IPA Transcription and GPA	.815	5.756
		p = .01
Non-English Phone Production and Self-Perception	.502	2.905
		p = < .01
Non-English Phone Production and IPA Transcription	.320	1.755
		NS

THE TEACHING OF ENGLISH PHONETICS IN THE U.S.A.
Issues Related to Speech Pathology and Theatre

TELETÉ ZORAYDA LAWRENCE,
Emeritus Professor
Texas Christian University

The suggestion was initially made that members of this
symposium panel outline a theory of instruction procedure for
teaching phonetics to American college students. In consideration of that request, it seems appropriate to propose
that it is theoretically, as well as realistically, possible
to "hear" oral English as sounds, acoustic phenomena, which
are essential to a unique sound system recognizable as
"English." We identify such sounds as phone units belonging
to certain categories--classes--the distinctive sounds of the
language, each having definable physiological maneuverings
and so-called "articulatory positionings." It is also theoretically feasible to acknowledge that the integral sounds of
this recognized system are not produced nor perceived in
running speech as single "target sounds" per se, but are influenced by the live, dynamic acoustic context within which
each "comes to life." Still it is possible to comprehend the
relatively stable "usage-laws" of speech and to perceive and
analyze just what is occurring both acoustically and physiologically in this highly complex and equally intriguing phenomenon unique to man. In addition it is theoretically conceivable for one to be aware of the multitudinous nondistinctive
features present in English speech. Furthermore one is able
to free oneself from the confines of the written alphabet
system and represent what one perceives in symbols recognizable by those familiar with the particular transcription

system so that each who sees the symbols will relate at once
to the acoustic events perceived by the transcriber. All of
this is theoretically possible and in actuality is achieved
by those, professionals and students, trained in the phonetic
sciences.

Let us particularize relative to students pursuing professional careers in speech pathology and in theatre. At
first, one might think it a strange duo for mutual consideration; but, in reality, not so divergent. Of prime importance
however, whatever the ultimate professional goal of the student, the teacher, the professor, the one who strives to
impart knowledge, to lead, to direct, to assist, to motivate,
must have a solid background in the phonetic sciences in the
broad spectrum; and, more especially, a deep understanding of
the phonetic needs relative to the particular career discipline for which he is responsible. The one who professes
should have an enthusiasm for the course material--especially
needful--as the course is notoriously "hard-to-teach," which
may be, at times, a frustrating experience, so say those who
are not caught up in the lively interest and creativity needful for the course presentation. If it is a "chore"--perhaps
assumed because no one else was available--or because it was
needed to complete a "teaching-load"--the course is destined
to failure or, at best, to mediocrity. This discipline presents a real challenge to the instructor. Let it be met with
an equal amount of enthusiasm and, wonder-of-wonders, the
student will sense this dynamic and the course in "phonetics"
may become a "favorite course"!

It may be mundane to mention text selection and the
choice of other teaching materials; but, again, this is of
paramount import if one is not to settle into a comfortable
teaching "rut." The instructor should keep au courant with
materials available and, in the light of meaningful research
which is constantly being published, make a selection which
is in accord with the current developments in the field as
well as being compatible with the instructor. Nothing can be
deadlier than sticking with the same text year after year.
The phonetic sciences are too "live" to allow for such com-
placency. Should one use a student notebook? This is a
pregnant question, and a recognizably difficult one to answer.

It may be even more difficult than the text selection. Why
not create your own notebook? This is possible and could be
extremely helpful in the attainment of the academic knowledge
and phonetic skills required of the students in the phonetics
class.

The speech pathology major will of necessity have to have
course work in the phonetic sciences to meet ASHA (American
Speech and Hearing Association) certification of clinical
competence standards. The majority of the professionals in
this discipline are employed in elementary or secondary
schools as well as many holding positions as speech clinicians in various private clinics,hospitals and universities.[1]
They tend to work directly with the client,those in need of
their remedial skills. Without doubt one of their most valuable tools will be the skills and knowledge attained in
"that phonetics course" or if they are lucky "courses." Consequently a big responsibility rests upon that instructor to
see that this needful knowledge and those skills are imparted.
Therefore course goals should be set forth at once. What are
these course goals for the speech pathology major, what generalized knowledge is crucial for them to attain and what skills
to develop? (Even though my thrust here is expressly with the
speech pathologist-in-training in mind, the same goals relate
directly and with real import to the theatre major.)

It is necessary for the student to become aware of oral
English as _sound_ and to become comfortable with the use of
that particular oral sound system. This primary goal necessitates an acoustic orientation toward speech, rather than
the routinely learned and accepted approach by way of spelling and the written alphabet. This radically different goal-
approach to spoken language is a fundamental one which must
be acknowledged and accepted by the student if progress is
to be achieved. Therefore, the generally recognized sound
system of English must be initially presented and "learned"
by the student. At the same time, the student is beginning
to be aware of numerous additional acoustic characteristics
of the system. An aural listening stance must be taken. It
is a departure from the "usual," but in that very "difference" lies much of the challenge to learning and achievement
on the part of the well-motivated student.

   Perception skills need to be acquired and consistently
sharpened as the course proceeds. Initially, the student
becomes aware of and familiar with the so-called "target
sounds" of American English. Any approach and/or teaching
aid with which the particular instructor is effective should
be employed. Time limit prohibits a discussion of "method"--
intriguing and diverse as an individual instructor's presentation and suggestions might be. Speech is perceived as
sound (or lack of sound as that aspect relates to durational
factors). This is the essential fact to be accepted by the
student, frustrating as this approach may be to one who is
immersed in a visual, written alphabet orientation to
language.

   Likewise, skills in discrimination need to be generated
and cultivated. This implies an ability on the part of the
student to perceive and to distinguish, not only between the
distinctive sounds of the particular system, but also to discriminate and identify the nondistinctive differences of
allophonic and free variation, as well as a development of
the ability to recognize and discriminate between the various
nonsegmental contrastive features of the particular system--
those characteristics and interactions attributable to the
prosodic attributes of pitch, time, loudness, stress and
voice quality. The individual ability to discern these
acoustic factors will vary greatly with each student; some
will appear to possess keener perceptive and discriminative
skills than others. However, all will need to be given the
challenge and the opportunity to achieve a fair degree of
ability in their development. (The goals of perception and
discrimination have been set forth purposefully as separate
entities, even though they recognizably intermingle.)

   A fourth goal is necessary in which a symbol system needs
to be acquired by means of which "what is perceived" is transmitted into a generally accepted written symbolization form--
one individual symbol for each distinctive speech sound as
well as additional markings to indicate the nonsegmental
features. The various symbols and markings of the IPA
(International Phonetic Alphabet), being recognized world-
wide, appear to adequately fulfill this need. The trans-
scription system is most expeditiously presented concurrent

with the initial introduction to the sound system itself.
The student, having learned the appropriate symbols, will,
through practice, develop accuracy and speed in transcription. Weekly class oral tests in transcription prove
most helpful in assisting the student to attain expertise in
these perceptive, discriminative and transcriptive skills.
Such tests should be corrected by the instructor, or at
least by a well-qualified graduate assistant, so that areas
of difficulty and weakness on the part of each student will
be recognized early and steps taken to alleviate the problem.

The attainment of these four major course goals is
crucial for the speech pathology as well as for the theatre
major. If only a single course is available in phonetics,
their attainment presents a challenge alike to the student
as well as to the instructor. Without this basic academic
knowledge and the perceptive, discriminative skills involved,
how can the prospective speech pathologist know "what is
being heard, what is 'going-on' speechwise with the client?"
Likewise, for the theatre major to be bound continuously to
the so-called "written page" is tragic. There is no reason
why we in this country should not be as demanding of our
drama students-in-training as are our British colleagues.
In the professional training schools of Britain, the phonetic
skills are taught with exactitude. (Similarly, the British
are even more rigorous in their requirements for the development of phonetic skills for the speech pathologist-in-training.) Without these necessary phonetic skills, the theatre
major will have difficulty in truly "hearing himself"--in
knowing just what he is doing with his voice and with the
speech sounds in the script at hand. It seems needless to
emphasize the practical value of the phonetically trained
ear in both the learning and the delivery of lines when
dialect or foreign accent are involved. The same would apply
to the handling of foreign terms or place names. If this is
not to be a "hit or miss" situation, or one of routine imitation, the realization of the phonetic goals here set forth is
mandatory. The theatre student, then, by way of a trained
phonetic approach, will demonstrate assurance and be able to
devote more time and energy to the vital task at hand, which
is, expressly, to bring that particular character and life
situation into being on the stage.

A fifth goal must be stated: namely, that relative to
articulatory or physiological phonetics. It seems trite to
stress the vital significance of this aspect of the phonetic
sciences to the speech pathologist-in-training. Much of the
case-load of the speech pathologist relates to the physiological positionings and movements of the various speech organs.
If the anatomical and physiological components of the various
aspects of the sound system of English are not learned and
thoroughly familiarized, again, the clinician is grossly
hampered. So much so, in fact, that one can justly conjecture that the required certifying written examinations,
the academic clinical practicum and the clinical fellowship
year will not be negotiated and the necessary certificate
of clinical competence will not be acquired. The speech
pathologist must know how the distinctive sounds of English
are formed, how to explain all this to a prospective client,
as well as to know "how-it-feels" in dynamic production.
Of equal import is an appreciation and understanding of
the dynamics of the various sounds of English in context;
the vitally important aspects of co-articulation; the
principle of influence in which it is recognized that
speech sounds influence and, in turn, are influenced by
the sounds within a phonetic environment. Speech sounds
are dynamic and exert dynamic influences upon each other.
Rhythm and stress, the whole concept of syllabification
and vowel reduction in English are a part of these dynamic
aspects of speech which are vital to the theatre major as
well as to the speech pathology major.

These five basic goals: to learn the sound system of English per se; to be able to perceive speech as sound; to be
able to distinguish with increasingly refined acoustic skills
between the nonsegmental contrastive features perceived as
well as between those distinctive sounds which comprise the
basic sound structure of English;to be able to accurately
transcribe into IPA symbolization that which is perceived;and
to have an understanding of the physiological behavior of the
speech sounds as well as their articulatory dynamics when occurring in continuous utterance,are goals and skills indispensable to the speech pathology major as well as most desirable
for the theatre major.Without the attainment of these goals,

through academic application as well as the attainment of
practical phonetic listening and discriminatory skills, the
students in both of these disciplines are gravely penalized.
These are basic skills. How these students are motivated
and guided in their attainment is a highly individualized
matter--the privilege and perogative of the individual instructor. No one said it was easy, but it _is_ possible and
certainly should remain a challenge to both the instructor
and the student. Otherwise, the course can become a fiasco,
and, at most, a bore, a drudge. It need not be so. The
experience can and should be mutually fulfilling.

NOTE

[1]Please refer to: <u>ASHA</u> (1976), 18:435.

THE TEACHING OF ENGLISH PHONETICS IN THE U.S.A--FOREIGN DIALECTS

AUDREY O'BRIEN
Trenton State College

This paper is about the teaching of English phonetics in the U.S.A. to university students who speak English with a fairly heavy foreign accent. I can't imagine a more appropriate place than Miami to present a paper on this topic.

My most dramatic achievement in the use of phonetics with foreign students took place a number of years ago. Six Italian priests who spoke "very good, the English" were plopped down in New York. They were all very scholarly, and immediately set about learning phonetics. They had been brought to New York to teach in a seminary, but because of a shortage of priests in New York at that time, they were asked to say Mass on Sundays in various parishes. The Mass was still in Latin, so saying Mass was no problem to them, but they had to get through the reading of the Gospel in English. On the first Sunday that they tried this, the reaction in each of the churches was the same. Their English cracked up the congregations. Drastic measures were needed. So, every week, I wrote out the next Sunday's Gospel in very detailed narrow transcription, complete with intonation. And every Sunday, when it came time to read the Gospel in English, our six Italian priests read it straight from the phonetic transcription. The sudden improvement in their English was the wonder of the congregations. The phonetic transcriptions got them through their first year in New York, and by then they could manage on their own.

As you can see from this story, with a highly motivated student who speaks English with a foreign accent and who

wishes to speak English with a more nearly native pattern,
I proceed by teaching phonetics first. I start by explaining
organs of articulation and parts of the tongue. I then plunge
into consonants by explaining ways of classifying consonants,
and using that as a framework for the consonant chart. I teach
the entire consonant chart, as it applies to English. Since
this is all fairly easy, the student gains some confidence.
So, we go over the rudiments of vowel production, and I teach
a simplified version of the vowel chart for English. Later I
introduce diphthongs.

One important aspect of my teaching of the charts is
that I do not give any key words for the various sounds, not
even for the vowels or diphthongs. Instead, I provide the
student with a tape of the sounds in isolation, so he can
play it over and over to connect the sounds with the symbols.
In this way, the student avoids the danger of attaching the
wrong sound to the symbol because he mispronounces a key word.
All of this takes about three sessions. When the student can
discriminate fairly well, practical work starts. At this
point, with foreign students, I use as materials only complete sentences or phrases that might be used as sentences.
Each sentence is presented to the student in ordinary print-
ing and in narrow transcription with intonation. We stay
on one sentence until it sounds like the utterance of a
native speaker. Then we go on to the next sentence. This
is slow work. It involves watching everything: consonant
articulation, vowel quality, aspiration, exact timing, rhythm,
weak forms, melody, and often voice quality and the general
tonus of the articulators.

When the student is able to work alone between sessions,
he is supplied with Language Master cards on which sentences
are printed in ordinary script and in phonetics, and on which
the pattern is recorded. We do a lot of this before proceeding to very simple controlled conversation. Here, when
we run into difficulties, we transcribe the problem phrases
to analyze them. Almost the only way in which I deviate
from the use of whole sentences with these students is that
for substitutions that seem especially persistent I prepare
lists of paired words, contrasting the two sounds.

Throughout the practical work, the foreign students,
like the native students, are checked for efficient posture,
efficient breathing, and efficient voice production. This
approach works. It is very slow, but what sinks in, sinks
all the way in.

TEACHING PHONETICS IN THE VOICE AND DICTION COURSE

BETTY R. OWENS
University of Arizona

In considering the topic, Teaching Phonetics in the
Voice and Diction Course, we can approach the question from
a variety of viewpoints. To name a few: Are we teaching
phonetics in the voice and diction course? How are we teaching it? How should we be teaching? Indeed, should we be
teaching phonetics at all in the voice and diction course?
None of these questions can be answered in relation to all
voice and diction classes as they are taught in colleges and
universities across the country. Therefore, we must ask
some questions about the courses themselves. Who takes voice
and diction? Why do they take it? Who teaches voice and
diction? How are the courses structured? What are the instructors' objectives? And, of course, how does phonetics
relate to these questions? Speaking from my own experience
as a phonetics instructor and a voice and diction instructor,
I hope to provide some insight into these questions to those
who are concerned with the teaching of phonetics in the United
States. I shall also take a look at the subject as it relates
to the idea of minimal competencies, a notion of rapidly increasing concern to educators across the country.

First, who takes voice and diction classes? Generally,
as with most courses, those who are required to do so in order
to earn a degree in a particular field take the class. But
who is required to take voice and diction? The answer to this
question varies greatly from one university to another. The
University of Arizona, where I am presently teaching, requires
students in the following courses of study to take voice and

diction, or Development of the Speaking Voice, as it is
called: Speech Communication, Radio-Television, Human Nutri-
tion and Dietetics, Fashion Merchandising, Child Development
and Family Relations, Interior Design, Drama, Clothing and
Textiles, and Food Service Management. This list certainly
comprises an odd assortment of interests. At other universities the course may only be required of speech majors and
education majors. At still others, voice and diction is a
free elective. Instructors of voice and diction may have
their own preferences for the types of students they would
like to teach, but we are rarely asked to express them. The
importance of the above list is that somebody in the higher
education hierarchy, at one university at least, believes
that good voice quality and clear articulation are important
in a diverse number of occupations.

Regardless of the reason a student takes a course in
voice and diction, he or she has certain expectations upon
entering the course. These expectations generally fall into
two categories, improvement of skill and increased understanding. Both of these expectations can relate directly
to instruction in phonetics, as evidenced by comments from my
own students when asked to state their expectations on the
first day of class. In the skills category, into which most
comments fell, students stated such expectations as: "I hope
to be able to learn better articulation and to speak clearer";
"to be able to articulate more clearly"; "interested in
learning how to communicate with better diction"; "better
articulation and pronunciation"; and "I hope to learn to
enunciate my speech more clearly." From those students
expecting to increase their understanding come the statements:
"to get a broader understanding of the many aspects of speech";
and "to learn about my voice and how to improve it." Although
there were other course expectations stated by students, the
above comments indicate that there clearly seems to be a place
for phonetic instruction in the voice and diction course.

In addition to students' expectations, teachers' objectives should be examined as well. These will vary with the
individual, of course, but there are certain general objectives
that we should expect to find in any voice and diction course.
They are: that the student should speak with a pleasant voice

quality and sufficient volume to be understood, that the
student should gain understanding about the nature of voice
and speech and how they are produced, that the student should
speak clearly enough, with good articulation and correct
pronunciation, so that he or she may be easily understood.
The first of these objectives could be realized without instruction in phonetics, but such instruction seems to be
mandatory for accomplishing the last two. Phonetics teaches
a student how the individual sounds of speech are produced,
and therefore aids him or her in understanding the nature
of speech production as a whole. A knowledge of how the
sounds of the language are produced facilitates improvement
in producing them and thus in speaking with clear, easily
understood articulation.

     A voice and diction instructor who faces a class full
of education majors faces students with special concerns,
many of which relate directly to the subject of phonetics.
Whether the students are preparing to be elementary or
secondary level teachers, a knowledge of phonetics can be
instrumental to effective education in any subject area.
First, teachers are role models. Young students (and older
ones) are often eager to emulate their teachers in manner of
speaking and other habits. It becomes a teacher's responsibility to provide the best example possible. As stated before, a knowledge of phonetics aids one in using good
articulation. A knowledge of phonetics is also essential for
the elementary school teacher who will be teaching reading
to his or her students. Whether using phonics to teach reading or not, an understanding of the rules which govern pronunciation facilitates the teaching of reading as well as
spelling and other language arts. Instruction in phonetics
can aid the future teacher not only in speaking so as to be
understood, but also in understanding his or her students.
This last consideration may seem minor at first glance, but
it becomes more important when the following fact is taken
into account. Many teachers, especially on their first
assignments, will be placed in schools where they will have
crossed cultural, socioeconomic, or dialect boundaries.
Unless the teacher has some knowledge of dialect differences,
a subject often covered in the teaching of phonetics, there
exists the very real possibility of a communication breakdown
between teacher and student.

The decision to teach phonetics in the voice and diction
class will be governed by the composition of the class, certainly. But the structure of the course, which will vary
greatly from university to university, will also determine in
part whether or not phonetics can be taught. A class which
meets only twice a week for a ten- or eleven-week quarter
hardly leaves time for detailed instruction in phonetics,
especially transcription, if the teacher also hopes to
accomplish some degree of improvement in his or her students'
voices. Courses in which oral drill is stressed, or where
lectures are presented to large groups of students, do not
have the best structure for instruction in phonetics. Many
believe that phonetics is best learned through transcription,
and transcription requires repeated practice over a somewhat
extended period of time. If the voice and diction instructor
intends for his or her students to gain a working knowledge
of phonetics and some degree of facility in transcription,
that instructor must have the time and be willing to use the
time necessary to provide such instruction. If such time is
not available the instructor may choose not to teach phonetics
at all or to provide only a general overview of the subject,
concentrating on those aspects which are most cogent to the
particular course.

In addition to considering the needs and expectations
of the individual students who populate voice and diction
courses, we should also view these courses as they relate to
college education in a larger sense. Many school boards in
states throughout the country are deciding that students must
exhibit certain minimal competencies before they are granted
a high school diploma. While the idea of standardized testing to measure such competencies will probably never catch on
at the university level, the notion of minimal competencies
is certainly applicable. We should expect a college graduate
to exhibit certain minimum skills in a number of areas, not
the least of which is oral communication. A task force of the
Speech Communication Association reported that, "The ability
to speak and listen is essential to being an effective adult
in our society. Be it in work or social situations, the
abilities required to understand others and make oneself
understood are basic skills" (Bassett, 1977). Such abilities
may be basic, but there are many adults whose speech is

indistinct, inarticulate, or otherwise difficult to understand. Some are doctors, some are businessmen, some are
college professors. Certainly there are numerous adults who,
with little or no speech training, speak with clear, pleasant,
easily understood voices. It is the others we should be concerned about. Apart from providing students with skills and
knowledge which pertain to their specific interests or major
fields of study, voice and diction instructors, indeed, all
instructors, should be preparing students to be educated
adults, able to function well and with facility as citizens
in our society.

     Voice and diction training, including instruction in
phonetics, can contribute to the education of the whole
person. William Labov (1975) states that "there are general
features of articulation and voice quality which tend to mark
the educated speaker for us no matter what linguistic forms
he uses." Assuming that a student goes to college for an
education, we can hope that he or she would want to sound
educated upon leaving. There is more than appearance at
stake, of course. The mobility in our society today places
many persons in unfamiliar parts of the country where he or
she may discover that "the people talk funny." Some understanding of phonetics and knowledge of dialect differences
can prevent potentially funny or embarrassing communication
breakdowns from occurring. The more mobile one is, the more
opportunity for such breakdowns exists, and the more essential
training in voice and diction, including phonetics, becomes.
Even one who never ventures far from home will confront the
possibility of communicating with someone from a different
cultural background or with someone who speaks a different,
perhaps nonstandard, dialect. Knowledge of phonetics may
conceivably be vital to understanding and being understood.

     If instructors of voice and diction, and phonetics, were
asked to name those students or groups of students who should
take such a course, the answer might be a radical departure
from such fields of study as Food Service Management and
Fashion Merchandising which are now included. Many instructors
might believe, with good reason, that all students should
receive training in voice and diction. Instead of indulging
in wishful thinking, we should concentrate on our present task.

While the ability to transcribe in phonetics is not a
necessary skill for many interests and occupations, a knowledge of how speech sounds are produced and combined in connected speech can only be beneficial in learning to be an
effective adult, able to understand and to speak so as to be
understood. Whoever our students are, whatever their interests, the ability to speak clearly, to understand and be
understood, ought to be considered as skills basic to functioning as an adult. Wherever the teaching of phonetics can
facilitate the development of such skills, we should teach
phonetics. Our responsibility to our profession and to our
students demands that we employ whatever means are available
to accomplish our goals and meet our objectives.

REFERENCES

Bassett, R. E. (1977). Presented at Speech Comm. Assoc.
     Con., Washington, D. C.
Labov, W. (1975). Urbana, Ill., Nat. Coun. Teach. Eng.

THE TEACHING OF ENGLISH PHONETICS IN THE USA

SADANAND SINGH AND JEFFREY L. DANHAUER
University of Texas and Bowling Green State University

Phonetics in America is taught at various levels such as beginning introductory courses and graduate level advanced courses. It is taught in various settings such as linguistics, communication disorders, and communication arts departments. The structure of such a course depends heavily on the level as well as the setting. A course in phonetics in the areas of language and linguistics, with some exceptions, would likely emphasize the structural aspects of phonetics with ramifications to the understanding of phonetic systems of languages while placing little emphasis on speech science and the use of instrumentation. A course in phonetics in the area of communication disorders, on the other hand, would likely emphasize phonetic transcription as a tool for describing human articulation. In this instance not only is there a lack of application of instrumentation but also a lack of the linguistic approach. Obviously there exists a difference in emphasis in teaching of phonetics by the different disciplines. A course in phonetics which brings these areas together and further includes coverage of speech science is perhaps a more meaningful direction.

Science in the study of speech may be described in three segments: (1) a science of converting phonetic data to phonological and other higher order rules; (2) a correlation of physiological data to phonetic events; and (3) a manifestation of acoustic data into phonetic factors. On glancing over these three scientific approaches leading to a thorough understanding of phonetics, it appears that it would be difficult to accomplish

them all in one course. However, a beginner's understanding
as foundation for the study of phonetics is within this
scope.

     Traditionally phonetics has been taught with heavy
emphasis on production aspects of speech. More recently,
acoustic phonetics has come into being as a study of the
physical basis of phonetics. Texts of historical significance in these areas include those of Martin Joo's Acoustic
Phonetics and Potter, Kopp and Kopp's Visible Speech, and
Jakobson, Fant, and Halle's Preliminaries to Speech Analysis.
These help lay a solid foundation for the study of acoustic
phonetics. Although the methodology involved in these texts
was somewhat different, a firm scientific basis underlies all
three. Acoustic Phonetics determined a series of physical
parameters as scientific measures of speech. Visible Speech
presented versatile proportions of data delineating the
acoustic representations of both dynamic and invariant aspects
of speech. Preliminaries presented certain physical bases of
invariant cues or distinctive features as the determinants of
speech sounds of all men. Physiological aspects of phonetics
have also been part of the study of phonetics due to work by
such phonetic scientists as G. Oscar Russel, Stetson, Ladefoged, MacNeilage and others.

     Phonetic science in America has been enriched by a host
of traditions. Classical work of Scripture published during
the very beginning of the 19th Century demonstrated the success in the application of instrumental devices to the study
of phonetics as an exact science. The application of speech
science in the teachings of phonetics by such scientists as
Grant Fairbanks, John Black, James Curtis, Paul Moore, Frank
Cooper, Gordon Peterson and their disciples has been a major
direction during the last 40 years. These scientists have
influenced the actual content of the courses in American
phonetics. During the process of teaching phonetic science
they set up innovative demonstrations to make the study of
phonetics an exact science.

     In the tradition of Europe and Asia, phonetics in the
U.S. is gaining independence as a science. Due to the greater
mobility of the phoneticians and greater number of vehicles

for the promotion of their research, a great deal of interfacing is occurring among the phoneticians of different schools of thought. For example, those who believe that speech cannot be quantified (only to the extent that the quantification aids in the support of a theory) and those who believe in the process of quantification as a necessary vehicle for discovery are engaged in collaborations. Such collaborations are having a healthy impact on classroom teachings of phonetics. The works of Delattre, Lisker, Abramson, Lehiste, Wang and others have shown powerful applications of acoustic analysis techniques in the quantification of phonetic events.

One of the problems with studying and teaching phonetics relates to the complexity of speech as a signal and thus the large number of variables inherent in it. What a scientific approach does is to enable us to systematically select and isolate certain variables leading to significant data reduction. In this manner, a hierarchy of variables may be determined for the study of speech.

One of the recent advances in the teaching of phonetics involves the inclusion of perceptual correlates of articulatory and acoustic phenomena. These correlates point to a unified phonetic theory. In some instances the articulatory, acoustic, and perceptual dimensions converge to a unique solution. For example, the first and second vowel formants are described in terms of tongue height and tongue advancement dimensions. A posteriori perceptual dimensions further support these axes of the vowel diagrams.

The scientific investigation of speech production and perception has taken two directions: (1) the utilization of natural human produced utterances and (2) more recently, the use of computer produced synthetic utterances. Through the use of both physiological and acoustic data we have been able to determine a great deal of information about the speech production mechanism and how changes on it lead to changes in the output of the speech product. Through investigations involving auditory perception we are able to see what parameters of the signal are essential for communication. With the availability of computers in speech science research, we have been able to construct the physical parameters of the signal

and more tightly control and isolate certain variables and
then examine their effects on auditory processings. Studies
of this type not only help us to understand the physical
parameters having perceptual importance for a listener but
also enable us to evaluate their hierarchical structure. In
addition, rules of how the perceiver organizes acoustic input
in the linguistic domain may also be inferred. The role of
suprasegmentals such as duration and prosody can also be determined. For example, a study reported here at the ASA
meeting showed that perception of vowel duration was dependent upon the presence of all three formants in synthetically
produced vowels. When any one formant was removed, the two
dimensions of <u>tongue height</u> and <u>advancement</u> were still present, but vowel duration was lost.

For some disciplines phonetics is yet not a goal in
itself but a means to certain other goals. For example, for
a psycholinguist it may be taken as a data gathering procedure utilized for converting sound descriptions into sets
of phonological rules; for a speech pathologist it is a tool
for itemizing the exact nature of a target as well as that of
an actual production and then setting up corrective strategies
and evaluations. Science aids in the better understanding of
phonetics in all of these areas.

Due to the standardized procedure for quantification of
the speech event it has become possible to entertain a notion
of a universal phonetic theory. Cross-linguistic studies involving acoustic and perceptual analyses of different classes
of sounds have been made possible. Wide application of specto-
graphic representations of speech has made the goals of the
IPA more attainable. Real-time speech analysis devices have
proven excellent tools for examining the impact of different
phonetic variables on the acoustic properties of speech.

Finally, a question of crucial importance is whether or
not it is possible to teach phonetics at the introductory level
from a scientific point of view without having a well-equipped
speech science laboratory. While it is desirable for the
student to have some experience with the speech science
laboratory, it is quite feasible to teach about the utilization of scientific techniques and how they aid in the discovery

of new information. It is actually the teachers' responsibility to stay abreast with new developments in the phonetic sciences. This can be accomplished in part by attending
the professional meetings such as the current conference and
the Acoustical Society of America as well as remaining current
with the journals in fields of phonetics and allied sciences.

A PERCEPTION TEST AS A DIAGNOSTIC TOOL IN TEACHING GERMAN PRONUNCIATION

RUDOLF WEISS
Western Washington University

Since the perception test referred to here has already been the subject of several previous articles, it would be relatively fruitless at this point to rehash that which is already available in print.[1] What this paper will thus concentrate upon, is the implementation of a secondary characteristic of the test, i.e., its more limited use as a means of diagnosing perceptual problems related to German vowels and as a prognostic means of measuring relative success in overcoming these problems. The use as well as the relative success of this test as an integral part of an upper division phonetics course in German will be illustrated. The test has been successfully used over several years and with the aid of this test, the course has developed into a rather unique one which has met with considerable success both in actual measured results and student evaluations. The nature of this course is in part described in this paper.

The perception test was developed several years ago by the speaker at the University of Colorado Phonetics Laboratory. It was experimental-phonetic in nature and had at its purpose the determination of perceptual boundaries of length and quality in German vowels. What is particularly noteworthy for pedagogical purposes is that 100 of the 300 items contained on the test showed an agreement factor of 95-100%. This means, when only these items are considered native Germans would score an average of 98%. No native German tested to date has scored less than in the lower 90's%.

More significant is the fact that all items of the perception test are natural manipulations of various vowel
qualities and lengths in similar consonant environments.
None of the items were intended as idealized German vowels.
These hundred items thus are vowels which elicit a very
high degree of agreement in perception among native Germans
even though or perhaps in spite of the fact that they were
often intended as vowels of somewhat indistinct (i.e., in
between) quality and length characteristics. What is thus
exhibited is what the speaker believes to be more akin to
tendencies in native German perception. I do not believe
that this is something that could readily be duplicated
short of a complete remake of the entire original experiment.
This test therefore differs radically from the type of perception test which would contain nothing but theoretically
"correct" German vowels. No doubt in the latter case the
fifteen vowel distinctions could be rapidly learned by the
students and high scores could relatively quickly be realized.

However, this test measures not whether the student has
learned to classify each of fifteen vowels correctly but
measures rather the tendencies in perceiving these vowels by
the relative success in classifying 100 different vowels.
A score in the 90's would be an indicator that the student
is perceiving like a native German, or better, that he ex-
hibits tendencies in perception like that of a native German.
To date no score in the 90's has been attained bý a non-
native.[2] Even teachers of German whose association with the
German language has been at least one of six years, can
usually manage a score only in the 70's. The attaining of a
score in the 90's is thus a pedagically unrealistic, if not
impossible goal. However, the test has been administered
often enough so that indexes of "degree of nativeness in
perception" have been established for various levels of
German study.[3] In similar fashion the speaker has been able
to establish a ranking order of vowels in terms of difficulty.[4]

In its application to teaching German pronunciation the
value of the test lies primarily in the analysis of the type
of perceptual errors made. Once the nature of the errors are
determined pronunciation and listening exercises can be

developed which more specifically aid in correcting the
error. Retests can indicate the degree of progress made in
eliminating the perceptual error. Improvement is the goal
and partial success the rule since as indicated earlier
a very high perception score would seem to be a virtual
impossibility for a non-native to obtain.

It should also be pointed out that neither the test
nor the phonetics course is given solely for the sake of
improving perception. As in any other foreign language
applied phonetics course, the primary objective is the learning of the basic rudiments of the foreign language sound
system and to improve pronunciation in the foreign language.
However, perception is an obvious and normally necessary step
to production and can through the use of this test now be
measured with some degree of objectivity. Most often a close
degree of correlation exists between perceptual errors and
production errors. It would be an obvious conclusion that
if perception improves, production will also improve more or
less simultaneously. Since the test is used as an integral
part of a unique program in German phonetics, perhaps a short
description of the course as it is conducted by the speaker
would be in order.

The course in question is an upper division course in
German phonetics and has been offered for several years at
Western Washington University as well as at Southern Illinois
University.[5] This means basically that the students entering this course normally are in their third year of German
study at the college level. Often, of course, they also have
had some additional previous high school study in German.

The basic text used is Wängler's Instruction in German
Pronunciation (2nd Edition) with accompanying tapes.[6] Weithase's Sprechübungen is used as a supplementary text for
additional specific drills and exercises.[7] In designing the
course, the speaker has drawn upon his experience in teaching numerous Phonetics and Voice and Diction classes in the
Department of Speech Pathology at the University of Colorado
and has attempted to apply this to teaching German phonetics.
The students are given the perception test at the beginning of the course, usually during the second class

meeting. The test is administered again during the final
week of the quarter. During the first class meeting the
students are also given a mimeographed list of words containing a number of minimal pairs and words carefully
chosen to reflect typical German pronunciation (and orthographic) problems. Examples: (1) lügen, (2) First, (3)
Mode, (4) Stete, (5) Matte, (6) muss, etc.

In addition a reading passage of approximately one-
hundred words is given.[8] Each student is directed to
practice his pronunciation for a few days and is subsequently recorded individually. This procedure is repeated
at the end of the course. On the basis of the perception
test and recording session, each student is given an individual profile sheet which contains his/her (1) perception test
score, (2) major errors in perception as the result of interpretation of errors made on the perception test, and (3)
production errors of vowels and consonants on the basis of an
analysis of the pronunciation test. In addition orthographic
interference problems as well as those pertaining to fluency,
stress, intonation and juncture are also checked and indicated. This profile is also provided for the student at the
end of the course of study after the aforementioned tests
have been readministered.[9]

Before a more detailed discussion of the actual use of
the perception test can ensue, a brief description of the
manner in which it is taken might be in order. Before the
perception test is given, a practice sheet (which also serves
as the key to the answer sheet) is given to each student.
This sheet contains fifteen orthographically distinct variations of the utterance /bʊtən/ reflecting the 15 phonemic
vowel oppositions in German. Each is preceded by the letters
A through O. After the student is confident that he can
associate a different pronunciation with each of the fifteen
utterances, he/she is then requested to listen to 300 items
and is asked to indicate on a separate answer sheet which
one of the fifteen orthographic choices it most sounded like
by writing the letter preceding the item on the answer sheet.
When the test is completed only the significant one-hundred
high correlation items are graded.

The errors made on these items are subsequently analyzed. The letters A → O are of course first translated into phonetic symbols: A = /iː/, B = /ɪ/, C = /eː/, D = /ɛ/, etc. An individual interpretation of the substitutions made yields an interesting insight into the perceptual problems of the students and gives a prognosis about the production problems that can be expected.

Some of the more typical problems include the following: (1) Vowel length--A survey of the errors made could indicate that the student is consistently substituting long vowels for short ones and vice versa. This is often especially true for low vowels. For example /ɑː/ is often substituted for /a/ and vice versa. A quick tabulation of errors can reveal whether or not the student is basically aware of length distinctions. If, for example, /eː/ or /yː/ were substituted for /iː/ then the perceptual problem would be one primarily of a qualitative nature, not one of length confusion. If on the other hand /ɪ/ or /ɛ/ were substituted, this would indicate not only difficulty in perception of quality but more primarily real confusion as to the significance of vowel length. Tallying up the length errors will yield on indication of the difficulty a student is having with length perception in general. A closer look at the errors will give an indication as to the degree of that problem in relationship to specific vowels.

(2) Vowel quality--As pointed out in the examples above, even when a student does not exhibit a clear perceptual differentiation of long/short vowels, real problems with vowel quality may also exist. A substitution of /ɪ/ for /iː/ would indicate a primary length perception problem as well as some confusion of quality. A substitution of /eː/ for /iː/ would indicate a primary quality perception problem. A substitution of /ɛ/ for /iː/, however, would indicate not only a problem in length perception, but also a very real problem in quality perception as well. Whereas the severity of the problem of length can be measured by counting the long/short vowel substitutions, the severity of the quality problem can be measured by the distance in articulation of the vowel perceived as compared to the vowel that should have been perceived. In general, substitutions of vowels other than directly neighboring vowels would indicate severe perception problems in regard to vowel quality.

(3) <u>Umlauting</u>--(Problem of lip-rounded front vowels)--
The umlauted vowels are a special source of confusion for
American students, primarily because no real counterparts
exist for them in English. Even though students are usually
made aware of their existence already early in their course
of study, problems related to them often follow students even
into the most advanced stages. The problems seem to be two-
fold in perception: either umlauted vowels are confused with
non-umlauted counterparts and/or they are confused with other
umlauted vowels. Examples of the former would include substitutions of /i:/⟷ /y:/, /I/⟷ /Y/, etc. Whereas examples
of the latter would include /y:/⟷ /ø:/, /Y/⟷ /œ/, etc.
Both types of perception problems could, of course, also be
present along with a basic length perception difficulty
(Ex. substitutions of /I/⟷ /y:/ or /y:/⟷ /œ/). In
general, both types of perception problems are commonly found
at this level. Even though more or less firm perceptual
categories may have been established for other front vowels,
the lip-rounded counterparts may still be totally confused as
the second type of substitution would indicate. If considerable confusion in regard to the normal front vowels already
exists one can rest assured that even greater confusion will
exist in regard to their lip-rounded counterparts.

(4) <u>Orthographic problems</u>--The responses to the perception test can also indicate orthographic problems.These exist
even at this level but are fortunately easier to correct,since
correction relies primarily upon learning the correct sound-
symbol correspondence. The most typical orthographic problems
would include consistent substitution of (F) <u>baten</u> or (G)
<u>batten</u> for (C) <u>beten</u>, (D) <u>betten</u>, or (E) <u>bäten</u>. Also highly
suspected as an orthographic problem would be substitution of
back vowels for lip-rounded front vowels and vice-versa.
Examples would include (N) böten ⟷ (J) boten, (L) büten⟷
(H) buten, etc.

Although a number of other types of perception errors
could be pointed out, it might be more meaningful to take a
look at a specific case. In this instance,perception test results for a student (J.N.) recently enrolled in the German
Phonetics course are analyzed; the materials to follow are
based on the actual substitutions made by the student.

On Chart II these errors have been transformed to
phonetic symbols. Length errors as well as primary quality
errors are indicated. The relative difficulty of each vowel
is reflected by the percentage score of misclassifications.
(Ex. /i:/ was misclassified 17% of the time.) The substitution in perception is given at the far right.

On the basis of this chart some specific observations
can be made in regard to this individual's perception:
(1) The total number of errors made was 67 of 100 yielding
a perception test score of 33%. This score is somewhat low
as compared to the mean average of all students tested at
this level which was 58%. (2) The most difficult vowels for
this student with errors of 100% were: /e:/, /ɛ/, /a/, /u/.
Those missed more than 80% of the time also include:[10] /ø:/,
/ɑ:/, /ɛ:/. (3) The single major error in this case is incorrect length perception. By counting the number of incorrect
length substitutions made, we find that 57 of the 67 (or 85%
of all errors) involved at least in part incorrect length perception. The LAF (length agreement factor) for this student
was thus a scant 15% in comparison to the norm which was for
this level 35.7%.[11] (4) When errors are made in perception of
quality they tend to be made towards vowels lower in articulation /i:/ > /e:/ /u:/ > /ʊ/ etc. This is consistent with typical perception patterns of students at this level. (5) This
student also had some tendency to classify umlauted as non-
umlauted vowels but more often (83% of the time) the umlauted
vowels were simply confused for each other. There was almost
no tendency to classify non-umlauted vowels as umlauted vowels,
however. (6) There is also some evidence of minor orthographic
interference problems. For example there was a considerable
tendency to classify (F) baten or (G) batten as (E) bäten,
suggesting some interference from English.

A vowel chart such as indicated in Chart III can be very
helpful in visually clarifying major perception errors. On
this chart the student's major errors (vowels missed more
than 50%) and perceptual tendencies as indicated by arrows
pointing to the most common substitutions made are shown.
In reality, this individual's errors in producing the vowels
reflected most of the errors indicated in perception. Once
the individual errors have been determined, steps can be taken

to simultaneously correct production and rechannel perception through specific listening-speaking drills. For
example, if length is a major problem, production drills
can be undertaken which stress long-short minimal pairs.
In all drills, it is insisted that a consistent even
exaggerated difference be made in vowel length. If, on
the other hand, confusion in quality is the primary
problem, more drills stressing quality differences can be
undertaken. (Ex. Lehne - Lohne, Biene - Bohne). If
lip-rounded front vowels are a major problem, more time
can be spent drilling umlaut differences (Ex. Sehne -
Söhne, Sohne - Söhne) or if confusion among umlauts
exists drills such as Höhle - Hölle, Hüte - Hütte, etc.,
are emphasized. If a problem exists with ·orthographic
interference, minimal pairs stressing the suspected
orthographic problems and conflicts should be used.
(Ex. baten - beten, baten - bäten, etc.). In general,
wherever possible, extensive use is made of minimal pair
drills. These drills are goal-directed to minimize
particular individual problems. Once the problem has been
made clear to the student and the difference demonstrated
and practiced, further practice in other situations
(new words and sentence context) is then undertaken.

    The program described above has been highly successful.
With few exceptions, almost everyone has shown marked improvement in perception (i.e., more native-like perception)
as demonstrated by retest at the end of the course. The
average improvement has been 12.5 percentile points (from
an average 63% to 75.5%). The relative improvement has
been approximately 20%. In fact, the students who have
taken this phonetics course improved their perception on
the average to a level surpassing those of the graduate
students of German tested in the past who did not have the
benefit of the phonetics course. Their average score
proved to be approximately 73%.

    The test itself has been the invaluable focus and de-
parture point of the phonetics course and lies at the basis
of the success of the program. Continued use and refinement
of the test is planned. The test also has potential for
automation and could serve as the basis of a programmed

individualized phonetics course. The speaker plans to explore this possibility at some future date.

NOTES

[1]See R. Weiss, (1974), _Ling_. 123:59-70, and R. Weiss
and H. H. Wängler, (1975), _Phonet_. 23:180-199.

[2]A retest of one student did show a remarkable 96% score
after having taken the phonetics course described in the
paper. It was discovered, however, that the student did have
a bilingual background (French/English) at an early age which
would not be typical of other students tested.

[3]See R. Weiss, (1976), _Proc. Fourth Inter. Cong. Appl._
Ling., Stuttgart, Hochschul Verlag: 513-524.

[4]Ibid., p. 514.

[5]The course has been taught by the speaker at Western
Washington University as German 320 and 314 during 1970-1977
and at Southern Illinois University as German 412 in 1974-1975.

[6]H. H. Wängler, (1972), St. Paul, EMC Corporation.

[7]I. Weithase, (1970), Köln, Böhlau Verlag.

[8]The reading passage is taken from Ernst Jünger (1960),
Stuttgart, Ernst Klett Verlag.

[9]Save for the perception test, the manner in which these
profiles are made is actually very similar to what I have done
in Voice and Diction courses for American students.

[10]The ranking order of vowels from most difficult to least
difficult for all students at this level is: /oe, ε:, υ,
$\emptyset$:, u:, y:, a, $\mathfrak{o}$, e:, $\mathfrak{a}$:, o:, ε , I, i:/.

[11]LAF is a term coined by the speaker (see Weiss, R. (1976),
AILA Proceed., Stuttgart, Hochschul Verlag.) The term LAF
refers to the factor of length agreement in classifying vowels
by substituting vowels agreeing in length (long for long, short
for short).

Chart I

A.	bieten	A.	[i:]
B.	bitten	B.	[ɪ]
C.	beten	C.	[e:]
D.	betten	D.	[ɛ]
E.	bäten	E.	[ɛ:]
F.	baten	F.	[ɑ:]
G.	batten	G.	[a]
H.	buten	H.	[u:]
I.	butten	I.	[ʊ]
J.	boten	J.	[o:]
K.	botten	K.	[ɔ]
L.	büten	L.	[y:]
M.	bütten	M.	[ʏ]
N.	böten	N.	[ø:]
O.	bötten	O.	[œ]

Chart II

J.N.	Errors		Substitutions*		
	Length	Overall%			
A. [i:]	(0%)	17%	[e:]		
B. [ɪ]	(33%)	33%	[ɛ:]		
C. [e:]	(100%)	100%	[ɛ]		
D. [ɛ]	(100%)	100%	[ɛ:]		
E. [ɛ:]	(54%)	82%	[a]	[ɑ:]	[ɛ]
F. [ɑ:]	(87%)	87%	[a]	[ɔ]	
G. [a]	(100%)	100%	[ɑ:]		
H. [u:]	(67%)	67%	[ʊ]		
I. [ʊ]	(100%)	100%	[o:]	[ø:]	[u:]
J. [o:]	(33%)	33%	[ɔ]		
K. [ɔ]	(67%)	67%	[u:]		
L. [y:]	(20%)	20%	[ʏ]		
N. [ø:]	(56%)	88%	[œ]	[y:]	[ʊ]
			[u:]	[ʏ]	
O. [œ]	(50%)	75%	[y:]	[u:]	

Total Errors: 67

Score: 33%

Length Errors: 57/67

LAF: 15%

*In descending order - most frequent to least frequent

916   RUDOLF WEISS

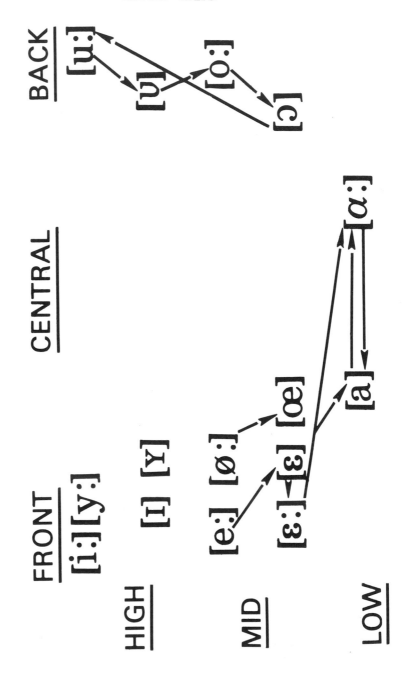

K. CHILDREN'S SPEECH AND LANGUAGE ACQUISITION

DEVELOPMENT OF "NUCLEAR ACCENT" MARKING
IN CHILDREN'S PHRASES

GEORGE D. ALLEN, SARAH HAWKINS, AND MARGARET R. MORRIS
University of North Carolina

Our studies of children's developing phonology center
on development of rhythm. By rhythm we do not mean poetic
meter, as in "Hickory, dickory, dock," nor do we mean simply
the ordering of a sequence of events, nor the precise timing
with which such events occur, though each of these may enter
into our total notion of rhythm. Instead we mean by rhythm
the structure of a sequence in time, this structure being a
higher level construct which has as its partial determinants
order, time, and various substructures (such as sequential
units). Rhythm as we define it cannot be understood without
knowing both the nature of the units and their sequential
structure. Thus we are attempting to investigate both the
sequential units themselves, such as segments and syllables,
and the organization of these units into rhythmic sequences.

A majority of past experimental studies have focused on
the properties and timing of the units with less attention
directed at their sequential organization. For example, we
know a great deal about intrinsic segment duration, and recently we have seen an increase in interest in how these
durations change as a function of speaking rate, degree of
syllabic stress, position in word or utterance, or sequential
phonetic context. Segments and syllables have been investigated from nearly every conceivable point of view, from the
physiological to the acoustical to the perceptual, and in the
best of these studies the rhythmic and prosodic contours are
carefully controlled. Far less often are the tables turned,

however, with prosody being the object of study. Fry (1958) has examined the relative importance of the various cues underlying stress accent, Lehiste (1960) has investigated the ways in which the junctural contrasts are conveyed, and a number of studies have looked into the relationships among fundamental frequency, pitch, and intonation; there is a need, however, for a great deal more research into these processes in English.

Some of our recent studies have concerned three aspects of sequential structure which we believe to be important in defining the rhythm of spoken English phrases, namely the structure of the syllable margin and the (two) prosodic features termed ± HEAVY AND ± INTONATION by Vanderslice and Ladefoged (1972). Their features are outlined in Table 1. Since rhythmic phenomena are often very difficult to study in speech produced by adults, we have chosen to look at these aspects in children's phonology, with the expectation that although they will be more simply structured, they should nevertheless show a pattern of development toward adult norms. The present paper discusses the development of one of these three aspects, the prosodic feature ± INTONATION.

As noted in Table 1, Vanderslice and Ladefoged follow tradition in designating one syllable of each phrase or sense group as the "nuclear accented syllable." That sylla-ble, and only that syllable, is marked +INTONATION; like other accented syllables, it is marked phonetically by greater duration and intensity and by a "pitch obtrusion." The re-mainder of the phrase is characterized, usually by means of a change in pitch, as one of three intonation contours, falling $\begin{bmatrix} +\text{CADENCE} \\ -\text{ENDGLIDE} \end{bmatrix}$, rising $\begin{bmatrix} -\text{CADENCE} \\ +\text{ENDGLIDE} \end{bmatrix}$, falling-rising $\begin{bmatrix} +\text{CADENCE} \\ -\text{ENDGLIDE} \end{bmatrix}$. This compression of a multitude of possible English pitch contours into just three categories they admit to be an oversimplification, but they argue that major dis-tinctions in meaning are in fact captured. Without intending in any way to prejudge the validity of their argument, we sought to discover by what phonetic means (such as for exam-ple pitch, duration, or intensity) children marked the +INTONATION syllables of their utterances.

The subjects were five children, ranging in age from two years two months to three years nine months; their names and ages are shown at the left-hand side of Table 3. Eric and Johnny are brothers, Julie is the daughter of the third author, and the others are Julie's friends. Eric I and II are the same child at different times. Each child was tape recorded while conversing with his mother and/or father at home. The first 50 usable utterances of each conversation served as the corpus to be analyzed.

We should note at the outset a bias in our procedure: in order to determine the phonetic correlate or correlates of the feature +INTONATION, we had to determine the "nuclear accented syllable," the location of which depended upon our interpretation of the meaning of the sense group, which in turn depended substantially upon the relative phonetic properties of the syllables in the phrase. Thus, even though the meaning of a phrase was partially determined by its context, all of the syllables recognized by us as +INTONATION were chosen because they had some phonetic property which distinguished them from the other syllables in the phrase. In only four out of 300 phrases was no syllable so recognized; how often we selected the correct syllable as the nucleus, however, cannot be decided with certainty, since one cannot ask children this young what they mean in each case.

The phonetic characteristics of these nuclear accented syllables are grouped into the seven categories shown in Table 2. These categories were originally defined perceptually, as we transcribed the children's utterances, but we have since verified our perceptions substantially with acoustic measurements, as will be discussed later. Some of these categories are rather straightforward, such as 'pitch only' or 'length.' The categories 'doubling,' 'diphthongization,' and 'syllable accretion' require some explanation, however.

Basically, these three phenomena represent a range of possible ways to lengthen the vocalic nucleus of the syllable in question. Doubling is thus just extra length, as in Eric's pronunciation of the word <u>red</u> in <u>It is gonna be red</u> as /ˌɪt ˌɪz ˌgɔ̃ə ˌbi ˈɹɛ̃d/ or Julie's <u>Erik</u> as /ˈeeˌɹɪk/. The pitch falls smoothly throughout the monosyllable /ɹɛ̃d/ and holds steady in the extra long first syllable /ˈeeˌɹɪk/.

'Diphthongization' is like 'doubling,' except that the vowel quality changes throughout the nucleus. An example is Julie's production of the word lightning as /ˈɭaɪːˌdɛn/ Finally, 'syllable accretion' is the most extreme of the three forms of lengthening, in that the pitch, and often the quality as well, change in the middle of the vocalic nucleus. Thus we hear Julie say <u>because it's a little bit too gone</u> as / ˌkʌz ˈɪts ə ˌlɪdl ˌbɪt ˌtu ˈgɔ̃n/ and Elly says /ˈeksˌwaɪɪn ˈzili/.

    One could argue that the only difference between 'doubling' and 'diphthongization' is the underlying vowel, but that would miss an important pattern in the data, namely that although there were many underlying and surface diph-thongs in the children's words, there are very few instances of 'diphthongization,' as we have defined it. Instead, the diphthongs tend more often to be categorized as 'syllable accretions,' that is, they are accompanied by a large pitch break. We thus observe a difference in the way these children tend to lengthen pure vowels <u>vs</u> diphthongs: the pure vowels get lengthened or doubled, and the diphthongs get broken in half to form two syllables. We hasten to note that this is just a tendency, however, since many pure vowels, even lax ones, are found in the 'syllable accretion' category.

    Along with our impressionistic transcriptions, we have also measured relevant acoustic properties of many nuclear accented, non-nuclear accented, and unaccented syllables. Fundamental frequencies, durations, and relative intensities were measured from standard oscillographic tracings, except when some extraneous noise interfered, in which case spectro-grams were also prepared. These measurements verify our per-ceptions of greater pitch and length, and in addition they often show a double intensity peak for both the 'doubling' and 'syllable accretion' categories. The physiological origin of this double peak is however, unknown.

What to us is the most interesting result of this study concerns the children's pattern of nuclear accent marking as a function of the relevant syllable's position in the phrase. As may be noted in Table 3, we have counted the number of nuclear accented syllables of each phonetic accent type occurring in phrase-final vs non-final position. An example of this difference in position, from Elly's tapes, would be the final accented monosyllable dog in He's a dog, vs the non-final first syllable of the word pirate in the sentence A 'pirate dog. Although there is variability among the children, there is also a substantial agreement that 'syllable accretion' is used only for phrase-final syllables, whereas 'pitch only' and 'length' are used primarily for syllables in non-final position. The only substantial exception to this pattern is Eric, who often used long or extra long vowels in final position without an accompanying abrupt change in pitch.

Looking more closely at the difference between final and non-final position, we note that the two phonetic correlates which show the least overlap are "syllable accretion" (almost always final) and "pitch only" (almost always non-final). This difference represents some support for the hypothesis that although accentuation in English is often redundantly signaled by simultaneously greater duration, pitch, and amplitude, greater duration is virtually required in phrase final position, with pitch and amplitude redundant, whereas in non-final position it is a change in pitch that is required, with duration and again amplitude redundant. This hypothesis correlates nicely with universal principles of rhythmic perception, in which relatively longer events tend to terminate rhythmic groupings while events differing in pitch tend to initiate groupings (Woodrow, 1965).

This frequent doubling and syllable accretion in phrase-final syllables may help explain why a relatively large number of languages have penultimate lexical stress. If a change in pitch is used to signal stress accent, then sufficient time must be given for the pitch to change. If there is a syllable following the accented one, as in penultimate stress, then the pitch change may be distributed over the two syllables, either smoothly, or with an

abrupt change at the margin. Occasionally our children
did produce post nuclear contours on unlengthened syllables in final position (5 of 113 cases), but most of the
time substantial lengthening was observed, more than the
amount required in adult English.

Our work on the development of rhythm and prosody in
children's speech is just beginning, but already we have seen
something of what we had hoped to see, namely the use by
children of phonetic structures that lie intermediate, in
a number of different ways, between their very earliest
utterance forms and the much more complex phrasing of adult
English. Of course there are presumably a wide variety of
articulatory, perceptual, and cognitive constraints on
children's speech behavior that influence the relationship
between these forms and that therefore obscure our understanding of the overall developmental process; we describe
what we believe to be just such a constraint on the rhythmic
form of the young child's speech in Allen and Hawkins (1978).
Nevertheless, by listening to the rhythm of English through
our children's ears, as it were, we can hope to learn more
of what the most salient features are of that important but
as yet poorly understood level of our language.

REFERENCES

Allen, G. D., and Hawkins, S. (1978).In Current Issues in the
    Phonetic Sciences, Amsterdam, John Benjamin B.V.
Fry, D. B. (1958). Lang. Speech, 1:126-152.
Lehiste, I. (1960). Phonet., 5:1-54.
Vanderslice, R., and Ladefoged, P. (1972). Lang., 48:819-
    838.
Woodrow, H. (1951). In S. S. Stevens (ed.) Handbook Exper.
    Psych. New York: Wiley and Sons, 1224-1236.

Table 1. Principal grammar-expounding prosodic features
          of English

Feature Name	Comments	Phonetic Correlates
± heavy	A light syllable is "un-stressed" and of briefer duration (cet. par.) than a heavy one	Full articulations vs reduced timing
± accent	An accented syllable corresponds roughly to IPA primary stress	Presence vs absence of increased respiratory energy and laryngeal adjustment, causing a pitch obtrusion
± intonation	Abstract feature assigned to nuclear accented syllable, implying a plus value of one or both of the following features	None
± cadence	Affects the post-nuclear portion of a sense group	Presence vs absence of a low (usually falling) pitch pattern
± end glide	Affects either the whole post-nuclear portion of a sense group, or (with ⌐+ cadence⌐) only the terminal portion	Presence vs absence of rising pitch pattern
± emphasis	Subsumes Trager-Smith's pitch 4	Extra large pitch obstrusion on an accented heavy syllable

From: Vanderslice, R. and Ladefoged, P. (1972). Language,
       48:819-838.

Table 2.   Categories of the phonetic corelates of +INTONA-
           TION, used to describe the utterances of five
           children

Pitch only	– Syllable marked by pitch changes relative to adjacent syllables, usually upward, with no unusual lengthening.
Length	– Longer than adjacent syllables, usually accompanied by higher pitch and greater force or amplitude.
Doubling	– Extra long vowel, accompanied by unchanging or smoothly changing pitch; usually in syllables showing contrast or emphasis.
Diphthongization	– Vowel quality changes smoothly; pitch changes smoothly, if at all.
Syllable accretion	– Pitch changes abruptly, over a large range, usually from high to low, in the middle of a vowel.
Not marked	– Utterance appears to be complete but has no syllable distinguished by any of the above.
Incomplete	– Utterance appears to have been interrupted before the +INTONATION syllable.

From: Vanderslice, R. and Ladefoged, P.   (1972).   Language,
        48:819-838.

TROCHAIC RHYTHM IN CHILDREN'S SPEECH

George D. Allen and Sarah Hawkins
University of North Carolina

Since rhythmic phenomena are often very difficult to
study in speech produced by adults, we have chosen to look at
these aspects in children's phonology, with the expectation
that although the child's rhythm will be more simply structured, it should nevertheless show a pattern of development
toward adult norms. There must be, however, a wide variety
of articulatory, perceptual, and cognitive constraints on
children's behavior, that will influence the relationship
between the child's earliest speech forms and the more complex phrases of adult English, and thereby tend to obscure
our understanding of the overall developmental process. In
this paper we would like to describe what we suspect may be
one such constraint, namely that trochaic rhythm may in
some sense be more basic to or compatible with children's
speech than other rhythmic forms.

In classical prosodics, whose principal domain of application is Latin and Greek poetry, metrical feet are defined
in terms of syllable durations; thus a trochee is a foot type
consisting of one long syllable followed by one short syllable.
It has long been known, however, that durational metrics does
not serve very well as a descriptive medium for the rhythm of
the tonic stress languages like English; the accentual foot
serves much better, and so in this paper we shall use the
term 'trochaic' to refer to falling accent, that is, an
accented syllable followed by an unaccented syllable. Words
like rhythm, data, and garbage are trochaic by either definition; words like sunshine, rainfall, or even the word trochee

itself, are classical spondees, but trochaic in our terms.
Very young children's reduplicated disyllables generally have
this second form, at least for the child learning English;
that is, the child produces a second syllable which is both
longer in duration and more precisely articulated than would
an adult. Thus he says /'ma͵ma:/ instead of /'mamə/,
/'dæ͵di:/ instead of /'dædɨ/. However, the stress contour,
marked by intonation, is clearly perceived by the adult listener as falling, that is, first syllable stressed.

What other evidence is there for a trochaic constraint
on children's rhythm, other than this prevalent accentuation
of the reduplicated disyllable? One source of data is the
young child's lexicon. Looking just at the polysyllabic
items, there is a huge preponderance of words with falling
accent, at least for English speaking children. Among Amahl
Smith's 223 stage 1 words, for example, 92 are polysyllabic
in their adult form, and 85 of those, over 90%, have falling
accent (Smith, 1973). Three exceptions have rising accent,
namely the words away, escape, and come out, and four others,
banana, outside, lie down, and rubberband, have some other
accent contour. This preponderance of falling accents in
early polysyllables is no doubt partly the result of there
being greater numbers of nouns and adjectives than verbs in
the early lexicon; the observed selectional bias goes far
beyond the statistics of English, however.

Another source of evidence is children's productions of
trisyllabic words which, in their adult form, contain one
light syllable on each side of the stressed middle syllable,
for example banana. Such words are often produced with the
correct number of syllables and accentual pattern; if they
are simplified to disyllabic form, however, it is always to
trochees rather than iambs. Thus, for example, we get
/'nænə/ or / ˈbænə /, for banana, but never /bə ˈnæn /,
/'teto/ or /'peto/ for potato, but never /pə'tet/, /ˈ|ɛktʊk/
or / wɛktʊk/ for electric, but never /ə ˈ|ɛk/. This con-
straint against word initial light syllables has been noted
by other developmental phonologists, such as Ingram and is
widely attested both for English and crosslinguistically.

A third kind of evidence for a trochaic constraint on
children's speech concerns the meter of English nursery

rhymes and children's counting-out rhymes. There is a
distinction between these two, in that nursery rhymes are
generally composed for children and taught to them by adults,
whereas counting-out rhymes are composed and transmitted
independently of adults within the subculture of rather
older children (say, five to eleven year olds). In his
collection of 873 counting-out rhymes from 19 languages
(about half of the rhymes being in American or British
English), Bolton noted that "The prevailing rhythm is trochaic and dactylic, with occasional departures from a consistent metre" (1888, p. 45). The same can be said for
English nursery rhymes. Furthermore, if we restrict our
focus to rhymes in the Oxford Dictionary of Nursery Rhymes
(Opie and Opie, 1951) that have nonsense words in the first
line, presumably composed to fit the meter ideally, we obtain 14 trochaic forms, such as 'Humpty Dumpty,' 11 dactylic
('Doodledy, Doodledy, Doodledy, Dan') but only one with an
initial weak syllable ('A dillar, a dollar'); in addition,
there are 18 'mixed' forms, having extra beats somewhere in
the first line, all of which however begin with a strongly
accented syllable ('Lavender's blue, diddle diddle'). Thus
we see that the words young English-speaking children choose
to say (that is, their lexicon), the way they choose to say
their words (that is, by dropping initial light syllables),
and the words that are specially composed for or by children
(their nursery rhymes and counting-out rhymes), all suggest
very strongly a falling accent contour. There are further
data to suggest that the trochee is more basic to this rhythm than the dactyl, but for reasons of time we shall not
explore that issue any further here.

Instead we shall turn now to cross-linguistic support for
the trochaic constraint proposed for English. As you can
imagine, there has been little discussion of such matters in
cross-linguistic literature on developmental phonology;
nevertheless, there are a few hints here and there. First,
regarding the lexicon, the German-English bilingual child,
Hildegard Leopold, at age two had a vocabulary numbering
about 200 items, of which 75 are polysyllabic in their adult
form (Leopold, 1939). Of these 75 polysyllables, 61 have
falling accent, 9 have rising accent, 4 have some other more
complex contour, and the contour on <u>hello</u> is unknown. Sixty-
one out of 75, just over 80%, is not as great a bias toward

falling accent as Amahl Smith showed, but it is still substantial and involves both German and English items.

English and German both have predominantly falling
lexical accent, especially on nouns; Zuni also shares this
stress constraint, and Kroeber (1916) has noted that one
Zuni child's first dozen or so words were reduplicated
forms with falling accent. What happens, however, in
languages with lexical stress located predominantly in
other than the first syllable? Our observations of French
children's reduplicated syllables are that they have rising
accent, in agreement with the general pattern of French and
against the trochaic hypothesis. Yet more interesting,
perhaps, Stoel-Gammon (1976) reports that baby-talk words in
Brazilian Portuguese also have final stress, again contrary
to the trochee, but here contrary as well to the general
pattern of the adult language, which has penultimate stress.
Even worse is Comanche, which, according to Casagrande (1948)
has rising accent on children's reduplications, but for which
Hyman (1975) claims the adult language has initial stress.
It would appear from this brief enumeration that the trochaic
constraint does not show up strongly as any universal accentual pattern on reduplicated disyllables. Let us leave this
point for the moment unresolved and return to it after we
have discussed some other data.

The second kind of evidence discussed earlier for
English concerned the deletion of word initial weak syllables. As noted there, Ingram (1976) has discussed this
phenomenon, and his examples include some from French.
Additional examples come from the bilingual Hildegard, from
Ferguson (1964) for Spanish, and from Stoel-Gammon (1976)
for Brazilian Portuguese. There are exceptions in each
child's data, however, and without a fairly complete synchronic lexicon it is difficult to estimate the relative
frequency with which initial weak syllables are deleted.
Furthermore, without trisyllables of the form weak-strong-
weak, such as banana, we cannot determine whether a weak
syllable in initial position is in fact more likely to drop
than one in final position. We must conclude, therefore,
that the cross-linguistic evidence for initial weak syllable
deletion is too sparse to serve as strong support for the
trochaic hypothesis.

The evidence from nursery rhymes is a little stronger. Burling (1966) collected nursery rhymes from adult native speakers of English, Peking Chinese, Bengkulu, Cairo Arabic, Yoruba, Serrano, Trukese and Ponapean, and he summarized the data in the formula 'Four accents to a line; four lines to a stanza.' Furthermore, most of the examples he cites have falling accent. We have been following on Burling's lead by recording similar material from native speakers of a wide variety of languages, 33 so far, with similar results. The only major exception is once again French, with predominantly rising accent in every type of material.

The total weight of this cross-linguistic evidence for the trochee as a universal constraint on children's speech rhythm is probably adequately described as 'unimpressive,' and in the absence of any other kinds of data we should probably turn our attention elsewhere. There is other evidence, however, from within the general area of segmental phonology, which although not conclusive is quite suggestive of the sort of constraint we are proposing.

Suppose that one rhythmic shape is in fact more natural than another for a word or a phrase. Then such a shape should be an easier framework within which to learn something else, since less mental time and energy would have to be devoted to keeping track of the rhythm. In this sense, Handel's (1974) data on listeners' relatively better performance in perceiving four- and eight-beat patterns could serve as a partial explanation for the theoretical four-beat nursery rhyme shape proposed by Burling. In this same sense, if the trochee is a more natural rhythmic pattern for children's words, then we should see earlier or better learning of segmental phonemic processes in trochaic words than in words with rising accent. One attested example for Italian comes from Von Raffer-Engel's son, who acquired totally correct articulation of two nearly identical segmental sequences four months apart. /ˈpapːa/ meaning <u>food</u>, was articulated correctly at nine months; /paːˈpa/ which means <u>father</u>, was not correct until 13 months; the earlier form was the one with falling accent (1973). Such an interaction between two levels of phonology, with segmental constraints being acquired first in a trochaic context, would be additional evidence for our hypothesis.

Another example of this kind of interaction, we suggest, is children's acquisition of fricatives. As Ferguson (1972) notes, "Production of fricatives is easiest to acquire in post-vocalic, final position or intervocalically." Examples abound, such as the fact that Hildegard Leopold used / ʃ / in a total of 24 words, 21 of which were monosyllables with the / ʃ / in final position. Waterson (1971) cites similar evidence from her son's speech.

The reason for this preference for fricatives, especially voiceless sibilants, to appear in final position may be that such segments are treated by the young child as weak syllables. These sounds are acoustically similar in both duration and intensity to weak syllables, and they demand relatively high air flow for their production as well. In his paper on respiratory activity during speech, Ladefoged (1968) noted two of his eleven adult subjects had consistently higher subglottal pressures for voiceless fricatives than for other consonants, suggesting that these speakers used a "comparatively large increase in muscular activity at these moments." The relatively slower rate of young children's articulation may therefore cause this extra air flow requirement to stand out for them, making the fricatives seem nearly syllabic. If weak syllables are preferred in final position, under the trochaic constraint, then the observed forms should result. Such a process could also explain why the initial /s/ in s-clusters is occasionally metathesized to word final position, as in Hildegard's production of the word stone as /doʊʃ/. The separation of the initial sibilant away from the vocalic nucleus by the intervening stop (or other consonant) may make it seem especially syllabic and therefore relatively more susceptible to the trochaic constraint.

Finally we suggest that a trochaic constraint may be seen in syntactic development as well. Slobin (1973) observes that children acquire syntactic markers more readily as suffixes or infixes than as prefixes, and he characterizes this tendency as the general perceptual strategy "pay attention to the ends of words." Our rhythmic explanation would predict this same difficulty with producing light syllable prefixes, though it would not necessarily extend to perceiving them. The relative validity of our hypothesis, as opposed to a constraint on children's perception (such as the one Slobin suggests), should therefore be relatively easy to test by observing whether or not children understood these forms (words with initial light syllables, sibilants, or grammatical markers) considerably before they produce them.

In summary, although the accentual form of young children's speech, when viewed cross-linguistically, does not show an obvious trochaic form, the evidence we have presented here suggests that such a constraint may in fact exist and may make itself felt in a variety of more subtle ways throughout the child's developing language. We do not have any idea as yet why the trochaic form should be preferred, though it is quite sensible, in the light of more general psycho-biological knowledge, that some rhythmic constraint should exist. Our task for the immediate future is thus to explore in a direct and coherent fashion the validity of our hypothesis; perhaps as a result of that research the outlines of some underlying mechanism may emerge.

REFERENCES

Bolton, H. C.   (1888).   New York: Appleton and Company.
Burling, R.   (1966).   Amer. Anthro. 68:1418-1441.
Casagrande, J. B.   (1948).   Internat. J. Amer. Ling.14:11-14.
Ferguson, C. A.   (1964).   Amer. Anthro. 66:103-114.
Ferguson, C. A.   (1972).   Proceed. Internat. Cong. Ling.,
     647-664.
Handel, S. (1974). J. Exper. Psych. 103:922-933.
Hyman, L. M. (1975). On the Nature of Linguistic Stress.
     Unpub. manuscript.
Ingram, D.   (1976).   London: Edward Arnold.
Kroeber, A. L.   (1916).   Amer. Anthro. 18:529-534.
Ladefoged, P. (1968).   Annals N.Y. Acad. Scien. 155:141-151.
Leopold, W. F. (1939).   Evanston, Northwestern Univ. Press.
Opie, I., and Opie, P. (1951). Oxford University Press.
Raffler-Engel, W. von (1973). New York, Holt, Rhinehart and
     Winston.
Slobin, D. I. (1973). Holt, Rhinehart and Winston.
Smith, N. V.   (1973). Cambridge, England, The Univer. Press.
Stoel-Gammon, C. (1976). Stanford University.
Waterson, N. (1971). J. Ling. 7:179-211.

SUPRAGLOTTAL AIR PRESSURE VARIATIONS ASSOCIATED
WITH CONSONANT PRODUCTIONS BY CHILDREN

W. S. BROWN, JR.
University of Florida

The production of most consonant sounds in American
English is characterized by a build-up of air pressure in the
oral cavity. This pressure build-up is a result of articulatory resistance (either partial or complete) to the outgoing
respiratory air stream. Over the past three decades a considerable amount of information regarding consonant sound
production has been generated by observing (and quantifying)
the associated variations of supraglottal air pressure. This
information has primarily described the voice-voiceless distinction between consonant cognate pairs, variations in the
syllabic position of consonants, the effect of utterance rate
and vocal intensity on consonant production, and durational
characteristics of consonant production.

The supraglottal air pressure variations to date have
been confined to describing consonant productions in adult
speech (with the exception of data reported by Subtelny,
Worth and Sakuda in 1966, including only ten children from six
to ten years of age). The lack of supraglottal pressure data
associated with children's speech is somewhat surprising since
the air pressure data for adult speakers has been shown to be
extremely useful in understanding the physiological production
of consonant sounds. This becomes even more behooving when
developmental and maturational information associated with the
patterns of consonant production in children's speech may be
generated through the use of supraglottal air pressure measurement.

In this regard, the purpose of the present study was to
provide developmental information concerning consonant articulation in children's speech through the recording of supraglottal air pressure variations. Such a study is ideal when
considering that the air pressure data associated with adult
consonant productions can serve as a compatible "model" of
maturated sound production.

Figure 1 is a summary of the supraglottal air pressure
data associated with several parameters of articulatory and
phonatory characteristics of consonant production for adult
speech; these data will serve as the model of which the air
pressure values from children's speech will be compared.
First, note that for consonant class, adult speakers exhibit
greater air pressure values for voiceless consonants as
compared to their voiced cognates. Furthermore, stop consonants exhibit greater air pressures than continuants, with
nasal consonants exhibiting the least overall pressures. As
for the syllabic position of the consonant, initial and medial
consonants exhibit greater air pressure values when compared
to final consonants. Regarding utterance rate, air pressure
increases with faster utterance rates (at least up to five
utterances per second). For consonant duration, air pressure
pulse durations are found to be longer for voiceless consonants
as compared to their voiced counterparts. And finally, supraglottal air pressure is found to increase as vocal intensity is
increased.

All of these characteristics of supraglottal air pressure
variations associated with adult consonant production are pre-
dicated and predictable based on the rules of articulatory behavior and aerodynamic principles of speech production, and
are typical of mature speech patterns of American English.
Consequently, we now have an excellent model of consonant
production by which to make comparisons of any population of
speakers. Based on this model then, which assumes that normal
adult speakers are representative users of their language system, the present study was designed to investigate the patterns
of consonant production in young children, especially in regards to maturation and consonant sound development characteristics of the formative years of a youngster's speech.

PROCEDURES

A total of 50 children, 25 males and 25 females, served as the subjects for this study. This subject group represented children from kindergarten through fourth grade, specifically five through nine years of age. All in all, each grade or age group consisted of ten children (five males and five females). All the children were selected on the basis of having normal hearing and whose language usage and speech patterns were representative of their respective grade or age level.

Each child was asked to repeat a series of CVC and VCV syllables in the carrier phrase, "Say _____ again." The syllables contained the consonant cognate pairs, /p,b/, /t,d/ and /s,z/ with the vocalic element being the vowel /a/. These consonants represent stop plosives and continuants and appeared in the initial, medial and final syllabic position. The subjects were instructed to repeat the syllables in a normal and comfortable manner.

To obtain the recordings of supraglottal air pressure, a method similar to that used for adults was incorporated. A polyethelene tube.110 inches in diameter served as the air pressure sensing tube. Normally, for adults, this sensing tube is constructed to fit around the buccogingival sulcus, around the last molar and into the posterior portion of the oral cavity (or in some cases through the nares and down into the oral pharyx). However, neither of these procedures could be used with young children. The nasal intrusion procedure is too traumatic for children. The custom fitted tube around the buccogingival sulcus and into the oral cavity was found to either gag the children or the tube was continuously clogged by excessive salivation by the children. Consequently, the investigator protruded a slightly curved tube into the corner of the mouth, which extended in an upward position toward the palatal vault and well behind the point of articulatory contact in the front of the mouth for the experimental consonants /p/, /b/, /t/, /d/, /s/ and /z/. This procedure was found not to interfere with the normal articulatory process of these consonants and was comfortable for the young children.

The air pressure sensing tube was connected to a differential pressure transducer, the signal amplified and the
resultant pressure pulse displayed on an oscillographic writer.
From the oscillographic record, peak supraglottal air pressure
measures were made for each of the experimental consonants.

RESULTS

The results of the experiment can best be shown in the
following series of figures. Figure 2 indicates that little
difference in peak air pressure exists between male and female
speakers between the ages of five through nine years of age.
A trend appears to develop for the third grade group as a
substantial difference occurred between males and females.
However, the fourth grade speakers again exhibited no substantial difference, with the males demonstrating slightly
higher overall peak air pressures. The data for adults indicates that female speakers usually demonstrate slightly
higher overall air pressures when compared to males. It has
been reasoned that this difference results from the fact that
females, on the average, have smaller vocal tracts than males,
thus generating higher pressures. In the case of the age
group used in this study at least, it appears that the
children as yet differ physiologically regarding vocal tract
size.

In Figure 3, two observations can be made. First, the
overall air pressure values for voiceless consonants are from
approximately seven and one-half to eight cm H_2O and for their
voiced counterparts approximately five and one-half to six and
one-half cm H_2O. These values are substantially larger than
those reported for adult speakers by two to four cm H_2O. The
reasoning, here again, is that the larger pressure values
associated with the children's productions are attributable
to the smaller vocal tract size of the child compared to the
mature adult.

The second observation is concerned directly with the
comparison of the phonological characteristics of children's
consonant articulation with that of the adult model. It can
be observed in this figure that the voice/voiceless air
pressure distinction between consonant cognate pairs characteristic of adult speech, is also characteristic of kindergarten through fourth grade aged children.

Similarly, it can be observed in Figure 4 that, like adults, the peak air pressure values for initial and medial placed consonants were substantially greater when compared to final consonants throughout the five through nine year age group.

Finally, as demonstrated in Figure 5, similar to their adult counterpart, the children speakers produced bilabial stop consonants with greater peak air pressures than continuants. The data for the lingua-alveolar stop consonants (t,d) are somewhat misleading. In actuality, the initial and medial air pressure values for /t/ and /d/ were greater than for the sibilants /s/ and /z/. However, when the final position air pressure values are averaged in, they pull the overall pressure values considerably downward since final lingua-alveolar stops are most usually produced with only a lingual "tap" and the air pressure values are often below one cm H_2O.

The primary purpose of this investigation was to compare consonant articulation of children with an adult model. This model was appropriately provided by the supraglottal air pressure data associated with adult speakers. Figure 6 compares the supraglottal air pressure trends associated with the children's consonant productions with the adult model (for the two phonological experimental conditions utilized in this study: consonant class and syllabic position). As can be observed, although the overall peak air pressures are greater for the children, the phological system used for the production of consonants by children speakers five through nine years of age is nearly identical to the adult phonological system.

It can be concluded that the phonological characteristics of consonant articulation in American English appear to be well established by at least five years of age. Similar studies are presently in progress at the Institute for Advanced study of the Communication Processes utilizing subject populations extending back to at least preschool age children three years of age. From these studies we hope to gain knowledge as to when the phonological characteristics of

consonant production first appear and/or are established
by children speakers, and indeed if certain features may
be inherent as some investigators have postulated.

REFERENCES

Subtelny, J. D., Worth, J. H. and Sakuda, M.   (1966).
    J. Speech Hear. Res. 9:498-518.

FIGURE 1

SUMMARY OF SUPRAGLOTTAL AIR PRESSURE (P_{10}) RESEARCH

Consonant Class
Voiceless consonants exhibit greater P_{10} than voiced.
Stop consonants exhibit greater P_{10} than continuants.
Nasal consonants exhibit least P_{10}.

Syllabic Position
Initial/medial consonants exhibit greater P_{10} than final consonants.
No difference in P_{10} between initial and medial consonants (this conclusion is controversial; some experimenters report medial consonants
exhibit greater P_{10}, others report that initial consonants are greater).

Utterance Rate
P_{10} increases with faster utterance rates (up to about 5 utterances
per/second at which point P_{10} declines as the rate continues to
increase).

Consonant Duration
P_{10} pulse durations are longer for voiceless consonants than voiced.

Vocal Intensity
P_{10} increases as vocal intensity increases.

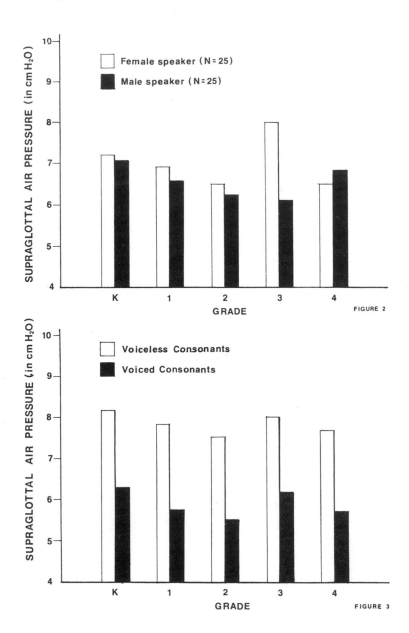

FIGURE 2

FIGURE 3

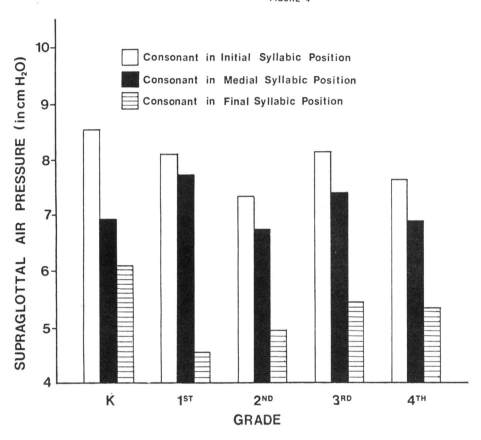

FIGURE 4

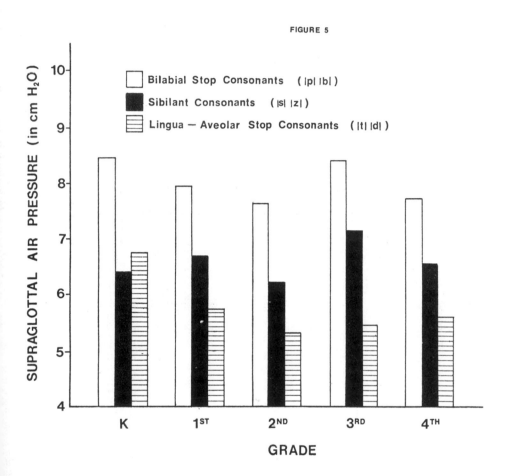

FIGURE 5

FIGURE 6

Summary of supraglottal air pressure (P_{10}) data associated with consonant productions for children speakers (ages 5-9) compared to adults.

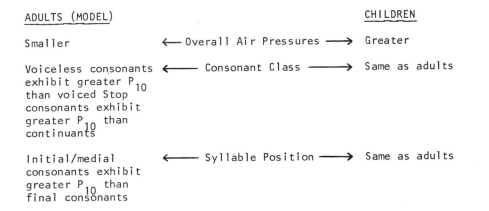

ADULTS (MODEL)   CHILDREN

Smaller   ← Overall Air Pressures →   Greater

Voiceless consonants ←—— Consonant Class ——→   Same as adults
exhibit greater P_{10}
than voiced Stop
consonants exhibit
greater P_{10} than
continuants

Initial/medial   ←—— Syllable Position ——→   Same as adults
consonants exhibit
greater P_{10} than
final consonants

AN INDICATOR OF THE ONSET OF PUBERTY IN MALES

E. THOMAS DOHERTY AND HARRY HOLLIEN
University of Florida

In the past, a number of studies have been carried out examining the vocal characteristics of males from early childhood through old age (see, for example, Curry, 1940; Fairbanks et al., 1949; Mysak, 1959; Hollien and Malcik, 1962; Hollien and Shipp, 1972). In these studies, the speaking fundamental frequency level (SFF) and its variability, pitch sigma (PS), were reported primarily as a function of chronological age. Of those investigations that were directed explicitly at adolescent voice change, few reported values for other variables (for example, height and weight) which could provide additional information regarding the degree of maturation of the speaker. Thus, it usually is not possible to determine whether or not any particular individual included in a given investigation has reached adolescence. We attempted to remedy this problem in the present study; here a large number of parameters, all relating to growth and development (age, vocal characteristics and body dimensions were included), are examined in order to more precisely view the process of pubescence in males. Naturally, the primary focus of this project is on adolescent voice change. However, our approach demands that some indication of the approximate level of maturity also be obtained--either directly or as contained in some implicit form in the measured parameters.

We also attempted to meet a second problem inherent in most investigations of adolescent voice change. The basis for this difficulty has been described by Tanner (1962) who, when examining the growth process during adolescence, observed that there is substantial variability in chronological age as it relates to the onset of puberty. Apparently, each "stage" of development begins when a previous stage has been completed and progresses at a rate unique to the individual. In other words, the process of adolescent development would appear to begin as a unified activity for a given subject and all of the component structures mature in a parallel manner. Indeed, Tanner noted that all of the structures he studied showed their maximum growth rate simultaneously. In any case, in order to examine the rates of voice chance, most investigators employed cross-sectional studies. Unfortunately, this approach often masks the maturation levels of individual subjects and provides only "average" estimates of development and/or behavior. Thus, in order to estimate stages of development for both the total group and individual subjects, we selected a longitudinal approach. For this purpose, each subject participated in the experiment for a period of over four years and was examined at regular intervals. We hypothesized that, even though the onset and duration of a particular developmental process might differ from individual to individual, the pattern should be similar across subjects. Thus, it was expected that the curves representing the observed changes could be aligned independently of chronological age. Since several measures of a subject's growth were obtained, and each was expected to show some variability, an overall visual pattern matching approach seemed impractical. Therefore, a computational method was employed in data analysis--specifically the statistical technique of cluster analysis. Finally, if these groupings correlated with our intuitive estimates of the growth process, we expected that the data could be used to provide an estimate of the point of development at which puberty occurs in males.

METHOD

Subjects. Sixty-five males were selected from the Wichita Kansas public schools. These subjects were selected randomly except that those chosen were judged to possess an average speaking ability and to be free of any clinically significant speech or hearing disorder. Of this original group, measures were obtained bi-monthly for over forty months for a subgroup of forty-eight subjects.

Measurement Procedures. As noted, measurements were obtained on each subject at bi-monthly intervals. On each occasion, data were collected for each of 14 variables relating to age, vocal characteristics and body dimensions. All subjects read a standard selection, "The Rainbow Passage," at a moderate rate, producing every word, articulating clearly and "speaking loudly enough to be heard throughout the room." Occasionally, additional readings were elicited in order to obtain satisfactory samples. Using this sample of speech, the IASCP Fundamental Frequency Indicator (FFI) was utilized to extract the speaking fundamental frequency (SFF) and its variation, pitch sigma (PS). Each subject also was required to provide phonational frequency range (PFR) data by a stimulus matching procedure. The stimuli were presented at semitone intervals, and the lowest and highest frequencies an individual could sustain were considered to constitute the limits of his range. From these data, his PFR, also in semitones, was calculated. Finally, at each of the bi-monthly sessions, each subject's physical development was noted. To do so, several body dimensions were recorded, i.e., weight, height, head circumference, chest circumference (inspired and expired), waist size, and arm and leg length--in kilograms or centimeters as appropriate.

Statistical Analysis. Since the primary purpose of this study was to examine the vocal development of males through adolescence, and determine the onset, duration and completion of puberty, it was necessary to identify the various stages of development for each subject. Therefore, the three classes of variables--age, vocal characteristics and body dimensions--were subjected to a cluster analysis technique. The basic clustering method is a form of correlational analysis which groups variables into common factors--i.e., it constitutes a form of factor analysis which assigns a variable totally to a factor rather than distribute it across several factors (Fouchter, 1954). The particular clustering technique employed in this study, however, is sensitive to groupings of cases (observations). That is, when the total set of observations is split into a specific number of groups, the partitioning of the data set is performed in such a manner that a maximum reduction in the variance is observed--thus assigning homogeneous sets of observations to each group. While it often is difficult to

provide descriptive labels for the groups that are formed,
it was expected that, for the present study, the clusters
would be composed of observations which could readily be
associated with the developmental process. Moreover, it
should be pointed out that the particular basis for the clustering technique is related to the form of the groups. Techniques are available to establish groups where the distribution of members may have somewhat irregular boundaries.
However, in the present study, it was assumed that the
clusters would be best delimited by convex surfaces,
i.e., hyperspheres about a central point would define the
cluster (Sokal and Sneath, 1963). A case is admitted to a
cluster if its Eucilidian distance from the center of that
hypersphere is less than the distance to the center of any
other cluster.

Obviously, most of the 14 parameters measured were expected to display steadily developing patterns. That is,
except for unusual cases, the body dimensions should increase
systematically with only weight and the vocal characteristics
showing an occasional reversal during the growth process. A
reasonable expectation, then, concerning the composition of
the clusters may be one paralleling the time continuum, i.e.,
in successive observations, a subject proceeds from one group
to the next. Although the age at which a subject advances to
the next group may change, he should progress steadily toward
the clusters that define the more developed individuals. It
also was expected that increasing the number of clusters would
lead to similar divisions of the age continuum.

Since there was no a priori justification which would
permit us to consider any one parameter in the present vector
to be more critical to the establishment of than clusters than
any other, weighting factors were employed in order to insure
that each variable was treated equally. The weighting factor
selected for each parameter was the reciprocal of the variance,
i.e., each value was multiplied by 1/v. This approach provides
a "spread" of values for each variable that is approximately
the same, i.e., differences between the maximum and the minimum
are almost equal for all variables (Sokal and Sneath, 1963).

RESULTS

The obtained data set was divided into two-to-six clusters as the classification of all observations into a single group is, in a sense, trivial for this research. While, as expected, our major interest relates to the development of three clusters corresponding to "pre-," "neo-," and "post-" adolescence, it is of interest also to describe the formation of additional clusters as the number of groups was increased. When two clusters were generated, the post-adolescent group was essentially separated from the pre- and neo-adolescent groups indicating that the post-adolescent group is more distant from either of the other two than they are from each other. Further, the post-adolescent group contained only about 38%--rather than 50%--of the observations suggesting that some homogeneous patterns may exist within the data. When the cases were divided into the three clusters that were expected to correspond to the pre-, neo-, and post-adolescent groupings, an F-ratio was computed for each variable in order to examine if there was a significant reduction in the variability of that parameter as a result of the clustering. Table 1 demonstrates that the variance of each was significantly reduced--a finding which indicates that there is statistical justification for grouping the subjects into three clusters.

Table 2 presents the means for each variable in each of the three clusters. For most variables, there is a rather predictable change across groups. The age and body dimensions all increase consistently from the pre- to neo- to post-adolescent clusters. While the voice quality variables generally show a consistent change across clusters, some of them (i.e., Pitch Sigma and range) do not do so but rather follow more-or-less expected patterns. With respect to the other parameters, the variability in the frequency of voice and the range increase; the SFF and minimum sustainable tones decrease. Only the maximum producible frequency increases for the middle group while decreasing for the oldest set.

As the number of groups was increased in successive clusterings, it is interesting to note that the neo-adolescent group remained virtually unchanged. For four groups, the

youngest group "split" into what descriptively may be labeled
"small" and "large" sized subjects. Similarly, when the data
was organized into five clusters, the oldest group also was
split more or less by body dimensions. However, even in the
six group approach, the neo-adolescent population remained
essentially unchanged and still contained approximately one-
third of the observations (subjects). Thus, it may be seen
that the use of various numbers of categories (or clusters)
simply demonstrated the effectiveness and stability of this
approach--and that the three chosen categories can be justified as functional when the pubesent process is studied.

DISCUSSION AND CONCLUSIONS

When the analyses of the present data are compared to
those previously carried out on the same subjects by Hollien
(1978), several differences can be noted. Basically, he
utilized the SFF measures to generate a neo-adolescent category by specifying that members of this group should exhibit
SFF levels between 145 and 190 Hz. By doing so, he obtained
a mean SFF level of approximately 185 Hz and a mean age of
just over 14 years (these estimates essentially agreed with
the Hollien and Malcik, 1967, results). As may be seen, the
clustering technique specifies a higher SFF (217 Hz) for this
group on the one hand, and a mean age which is several months
younger on the other. The clustering approach produces a
mean SFF that is not too unlike Curry's (1940) but specifies
a mean neo-adolescent group that is much younger than his.

In the previous studies of adolescent voice change, no
clear pattern of changes in pitch sigma were observed. Curry
(1940) found that pitch variability increased with age while
Hollien and Malcik (1967) found a decrease in variability for
the fourteen-year-olds. Although these differences are not
significant, the pitch sigmas for the population in this study
follow the pattern described by Hollien and Malcik; that is,
there is a slight decrease in PS at approximately fourteen
years-of-age.

The pattern of change for the maximum sustainable frequency displayed a different shape than did those for the other
variables. However, the increase from the pre-to the

neo-adolescent group was not significant. Statistically, they continued to maintain a constant f_0 level for the upper limits of their range. Moreover, it is interesting to note that, while these subjects were capable of producing a wider range of frequencies as neo-adolescents than pre-adolescents, they actually reduced their f_0 variability when reading.

Based on the results of the cluster analysis technique, it is obvious that the neo-adolescent group is extremely robust, i.e., the subjects placed in that group appear to be extremely homogeneous. While the age range for individuals classified in this group extended from 159 to 169 months (or thirteen years and three months to fourteen years and one month), each underwent a period of accelerated growth during this period. Further, when these values are compared to the data presented by Tanner (1962), it would appear that his estimates of the onset of puberty in males corresponds reasonably well with the average age of the members of our neo-adolescent cluster.

Further analyses of these data are planned. Obviously, the growth and vocal change patterns of these subjects will be reported as a function of chronological age in order to provide more complete information concerning the vocal changes that can occur in males. In addition, patterns of growth and development will be studied with respect to their relationship to the onset of puberty. From the results of the cluster analyses, the individual patterns of vocal and physical maturation will be aligned on a statistically determined common point. It then may be possible to more precisely describe the process of adolescent development-- especially for voice and speech.

REFERENCES AND ACKNOWLEDGEMENT

Curry, E. T. (1940). Sp. Mono., 7:48-62.
Fairbanks, G., Wiley, J. M. and Lassman, F. M. (1949).
    Child Devel., 20:63-69.
Fouchter, B. (1954). Princeton, New Jersey, D. Van Nostrand
    Company, Inc.
Hollien, H. and Malcik, E. (1962). Sp. Mono., 29:53-58.
Hollien, H. and Malcik, E. (1967). Sp. Mono., 34:80-84.

Hollien, H. and Shipp, T.   (1972).   J. Speech Hear. Res.,
    15:155-159.
Hollien, H.   (1978).   Proceed. 1978 Symp. on Care of the
    Prof. Voice (in press).
Mysak, E. D.   (1959).   J. Speech Hear. Res., 2:46-51.
Sokal, R. R. and Sneath, P. A. A.   (1963).   San Francisco,
    W. H. Freeman and Company.
Tanner, J. M.   (1962).   Oxford, Blockwell Scientific
    Publications.

This research was supported by grants from NINCDS.

Table 1.   F-ratios for three clusters. These F-ratios are
          indicative of the degree by which variance was
          reduced.

Age	53.0
SFF	203.3
Pitch Sigma	16.7
Min. Frequency	182.1
Max. Frequency	90.2
Frequency Range	6.3
Weight	545.2
Height	369.6
Head Circumference	82.8
Chest (Inspired)	433.7
Chest (Expired)	364.1
Waist	312.9
Arm Length	312.8
Leg Length	190.5

$F_{.01}$, 3, 956 = 3.78

Table 2.   "Center"--or means--for each variable in each
            cluster.

Variables	Pre-Adolescent	Neo-Adolescent	Post-Adolescent
Age (mo.)	155.8	161.9	173.5
SFF (Hz)	245.5	217.0	141.5
Pitch Sigma (S.T.)	2.9	2.7	2.9
Min. Frequency (S.T.)	38.7	37.4	28.7
Max. Frequency (S.T.)	82.7	83.5	75.1
Frequency Range (S.T.)	44.1	46.1	46.4
Weight (kg)	38.2	50.0	60.8
Height (cm)	148.1	159.0	171.4
Head Circumference (cm)	54.6	55.6	56.6
Chest (Inspired) (cm)	75.4	83.1	88.9
Chest (Expired) (cm)	70.1	77.2	82.8
Waist (cm)	62.7	69.3	72.1
Arm Length (cm)	61.0	65.5	72.1
Leg Length (cm)	69.6	75.2	81.8
N	339	353	268

SOME COMPETENCIES INFLUENCING PHONEME ACQUISITION IN CHILDREN

RAPHAEL M. HALLER
Illinois State University, Normal

The development of a child's language may be measured by describing the phonologic, syntactic, semantic and pragmatic rules that he has learned, as evidenced in his speech comprehension and expression. While many competencies associated with language acquisition have been described, their measurement and interrelationship are open to question. This paper attempts to identify some of these competencies as they presumably influence normal phoneme acquisition and to provide some hypothetical examples of how these emerging competencies might influence phoneme production.

Phoneme acquisition data on Caucasian children speaking Midland dialect have been reported by Templin (20) among others. However, different points of view have been expressed regarding the definition of acquisition. For example, Sander (17) has suggested that a phoneme is acquired when it is "customarily" produced, that is, when a phoneme is used in at least two phonetic contexts. By this definition, the age at which we would expect a child to produce a phoneme would be based on the youngest age at which most children have been found to use this phoneme. Sander concluded his review of the phoneme acquisition literature by listing the following ages by which consonant phonemes should be acquired:

> Before 2 years /h, m, n, w, p, b/
> 2 years /t, d, k, g/

$$3 \text{ years} \quad /j, f, s, r, l/$$
$$4 \text{ years} \quad /d, z, v, \int, t\int/$$
$$5 \text{ years} \quad /\theta, \eth/$$
$$6 \text{ years} \quad /ʒ/$$

In general, Sander asserts that nasals, stops and glides are
acquired by age three years, sibilants essentially by age four
years and flat fricatives by age five years. Implicit in these
norms is the notion that phonemes are acquired gradually, so
that a three-year-old child might produce the /s/ phoneme in
the word initial and word final positions when occurring singly
but not <u>within</u> a word or as part of a cluster. The property of
phonemic inconsistency seems to be related to the emergence and
maturation of a number of competencies.

It seems axiomatic that maturing sensory and perceptual
competency would explain many normal articulatory inconsistencies in preschool children. While auditory sensation is well
developed by age one year, auditory perception continues to
mature during the phoneme learning period. For example, auditory memory span may correlate with the rate of phoneme
acquisition. Locke (5) found that children with high scores
on an auditory memory task were better able to imitate non-
English phones than were children with low scores on the same
auditory memory task. Oral proprioceptive competency may also
influence phoneme acquisition. In several studies of phoneme
imitation, Locke (3, 5) found that children with defective oral
stereognostic performance were poorer phoneme imitators than
children with normal oral stereognostic performance, as defined
by the ability of children to recall the shape of a three-
dimensional object placed in the mouth without visual cues.
Finally, attentiveness, or vigilence, may be a competency per-
meating <u>all</u> sensory and perceptual tasks. In yet another study
Locke (11) observed that four-year-old children with relatively
well developed articulation were more vigilent and were better
able to imitate a Swedish disyllable than were children with
relatively poor articulation. In that study vigilence was
defined as the subject's performance in signaling the occurrence
of a suprathreshold auditory signal.

A child's emerging motor integrity may also influence
phoneme acquisition. Gallaher <u>et al</u>. (2) suggested that if a

child's articulatory inconsistencies are a function of phonetic
context, these inconsistencies may be explained by emerging
motor competence. Miner (15) suggested that the major contextual variables are a phoneme's syllable position, stress,
frequency of occurrence and phonetic environment. On the
other hand Gallagher et al. hypothesized that if a child's
phonemic inconsistencies are not context-oriented, the child
may have a motor deficit. Locke (10) attributed typical nonstandard articulatory productions to their relative ease of
articulation. In fact, studies of phoneme discrimination
(e.g., 8) have consistently concluded that children differentiate between many phonemes spoken by others which the
children themselves do not produce, further suggesting that
phoneme perception integrity before the age of five years
surpasses oromotor integrity.

Frequently observations of communicatively impaired persons help generate hypotheses about normal development. For
example, the high prevalence of articulation defects among the
mentally retarded has been amply documented. In evaluating
the speech of many of these individuals, the writer has observed a generalized hypotonicity in all voluntary behavior.
One symptom of this behavior seems to be articulatory undershoot, or incomplete articulatory valving, resulting in our
perception of phoneme omission. This perception is often
changed when the clinician notices that the "missing" phoneme
is produced intrusively in phrase or sentence context. For
example, the client first omits the final consonant in naming
a picture of a cup but then produces the sound in repeating
the sentence, "Put the cup on the table." The point is that
motor integrity may influence normal developmental articulatory productions in children as well as in the retarded population.

Another maturing competency is motor planning. Again,
observations of communication impaired persons may be helpful
in explaining normal articulatory maturation. Yoss and Darley
(23) have observed that some children with deviant articulation
are also deficient in carrying out a series of non-vocalized
orofacial gestures, typically omitting or reversing the order
of a gesture. An Analogous phenomenon among normal children
is metathesis, or phoneme inversion, such as the pronunciation

of "magazine" as "mazagine." In a serial recall experiment,
Locke (6) observed that subjects engaged in subvocal rehearsal in their attempts to recall words. This rehearsal was
recorded electromyographically, even though it could not be
observed unaided. Whether subvocal rehearsal is an integral
part of phoneme acquisition is a question meriting future
research.

Linguistic competence has been the focus of much recent
research in normal phoneme acquisition. Underlying the research in this area has been the assumption that sensorimotor
integrity alone is insufficient to insure central language
processing integrity. Several studies (13, 21) have indicated
that articulation impaired children are also defective in
general language skills, particularly in syntax (18) and in
phoneme discrimination (13). Postvocalic consonant omissions
have been singled out as correlating highly with language
disorders (13, 16). This relationship is perhaps dramatically represented in some unpublished data (19) on articulation test results with 16 retarded adults. While 55 per cent
of their total articulation errors were rated as substitutions,
51 per cent of their word final errors were rated as omissions.
It is apparent from the results of these studies that normal
phoneme acquisition is influenced by--or is indeed a component
of--general language development. In fact, Menyuk (14) has
asserted that children acquire distinctive features and not
phonemes, per se. While Foley and Locke (1) found that their
subjects' knowledge of phonologic rules did not correlate
with their articulatory status, it is still possible that
phonologic rule acquisition may explain some inconsistent
and transient articulatory productions of young children. For
example, the writer has observed that many three-year-old
children aspirate voiceless stops in prevocalic clusters, e.g.,
pronouncing spell as /sp^{h}ɛl/.

Another linguistic competency investigated by Locke (9)
is acoustic imagery, defined as the child's ability to identify
rhyming words. Whether this ability relates to the rate of
phoneme acquisition is open to question.

Perhaps the most elusive competency which may relate to
phoneme acquisition involves psychosocial variables. What is

the effect on articulatory production of such factors as emerging ego-strength, independence, self-care, parental nurturing and peer experience? These relationships have received relatively scant attention. Winitz (22) has suggested that parental speech models are crucial in children's phoneme acquisition and has indicated that children often develop articulation defects as a result of lax parental speech expectancies. The writer has frequently encountered parents whose children are fully intelligible to them but virtually unintelligible to others. Many parents have confessed to the writer that they considered their children's articulation defects to be "cute." The effects of these parental standards and reactions on their children's subsequent phoneme development without speech therapy remain to be studied.

REFERENCES

1. Foley, H. M., and Locke, J. L.   (1971).   J. Commun. Dis. 4:259-262.
2. Gallagher, T. and Shriner, T.   (1975).   J. Speech Hear. Res. 18:168-175.
3. Locke, J. L.   (1968).   Percept. Motor Skills 26:1259-1264.
4. Locke, J. L.   (1968).   J. Speech Hear. Res. 11:428-434.
5. Locke, J. L.   (1969).   J. Speech Hear. Res. 12:185-192.
6. Locke, J. L.   (1970).   J. Verbal Learn. Verbal Behav. 9:495-498.
7. Locke, J. L.   (1970).   Asha 12:7-14.
8. Locke, J. L.   (1971).   Percept. Motor Skills 32:215-217.
9. Locke, J. L.   (1971).   Percept. Motor Skills 32:1000-1002.
10. Locke, J. L.   (1972).   J. Speech Hear. Res. 15:194-200.
11. Locke, J. L.   (1973).   Lang. Speech 16:156-168.
12. Locke, J. L.   (1975).   J. Speech Hear. Res. 18:176-191.
13. Marquardt, T. P., and Saxman, J. H.   (1972).   J. Speech Hear. Res. 15:382-385.
14. Menyuk, P.   (1971).   Englewood Cliffs, N. J., Prentice-Hall.
15. Miner, L. E.   (1976).   Proceed. XIV Internat. Cong. Logo. Phoniat., Basel, S. Karger, 330-333.
16. Panagos, J. M.   (1974).   J. Speech Hear. Dis. 39:23-31.
17. Sander, E.   (1972).   J. Speech Hear. Dis. 37:55-63.
18. Shriner, T. M., Holloway, M. S., and Daniloff, R. G. (1969).   J. Speech Hear. Res. 12:319-325.

19. Steward, P. R.   (1977).   Unpublished Research, Illinois
        State University, Normal, IL.
20. Templin, M. C.   (1957).   Minneapolis, University of
        Minnesota Press.
21. Whitacre, J. D., Luper, H. L., and Pollio, H. R.   (1970).
        Lang. Speech, 13:231-239.
22. Winitz, H.   (1975).   Baltimore, University Park Press.
23. Yoss, K. A. and Darley, F. L.   (1974).   J. Speech Hear.
        Res.   17:399-416.

TIMING RELATIONSHIPS AND STRATEGIES USED BY NORMAL SPEAKING CHILDREN IN THE SELF-REGULATION OF SPEAKING RATE

E. CHARLES HEALEY
University of Nebraska

Until recently, researchers have essentially ignored the temporal patterns that speakers spontaneously adopt in an effort to reduce their habitual speaking rate. Past research has shown that decreases in the speech rate can be achieved in either of the following ways: (1) increase the frequency and duration of pauses that are taken between words being uttered (e.g., "I. . .am. . .a. . .man"); (2) prolong the sounds contained within an utterance (e.g., "III aaammm aaa mmmaaannn" since prolonging the vocalic portion of a syllable, in effect, would produce a dramatic increase in the length of time that a speaker continues vocalizations within word or syllable boundaries); or (3) a combination of prolonging the vocalic portion of a syllable and an increase in the frequency and duration of the pauses taken between words (e.g., "III. . .aaammm...aaa...mmmaaann).

A strong measure of support for a speaker using a pause-time strategy to reduce the speaking rate was obtained in the studies by Goldman-Eisler (1961a, b,c); Lass and Noll (1970) and Lass and Deem (1971, 1972). These studies demonstrated that a set of temporal patterns, in the form of pause time relationships, existed during speech produced at a slow rate.

There is some evidence to suggest that not all normal speakers control their speaking rates in this manner. Kozhevnikov and Chistovich (1965) found that the two adult

962 E. CHARLES HEALEY

speakers they tested slowed their speaking rate by prolonging
the duration of the vowels in an utterance. Changes in the
speaking rate by this method produces an increase in the segment duration and in turn, an extension in the time it takes
to say the utterance.

To date, there have not been any systematic attempts to
explore the timing relationships and rate reduction strategies utilized by a group of normal children. The present
study was conducted to evaluate the manner in which children
voluntarily reduce their speaking rate and compare their
temporal patterns with that which is known about the adult
speaker. An investigation of this type should make it possible to determine if there are maturational differences between
the rate reduction of a child and that of an adult.

METHOD

Subjects: The sample of subjects included ten male children
between the ages of seven and twelve years with a mean age of
nine years, four months. Prior to the experiment each subject was evaluated and found to have normal articulation and
hearing acuity.

Procedures: All recordings of each individual involved in
the study were made in an elementary school room having low
ambient noise levels. All testing was individualized and
completed in a single session. The subjects' responses were
recorded on a high quality tape-recorder (Nagra IV-D).

Once the subject was comfortably seated, he was instructed to repeat two sentences after hearing a tape-recorded
sample of each through a loud-speaker. The recordings consisted of a model of each test utterance repeated three times
by an adult male with normal speech. The two experimental
sentences were: "Pass the sauce to me" and "Sis took the
case out." All subjects produced these two sentences ten
consecutive times in two conditions. In one condition, the
Basal Rate Condition (BRC), subjects were instructed to speak
in their normal conversational rate and manner. The Modified
Rate Condition (MRC) required that the subjects produce the
sentences at a speech rate which they considered to be approxi
mately one-half as fast as the rate they used in the BRC.

Before the subject responded in the MRC, the experimenter replayed the first set of repetitions. This was done so that the subject could approximate a level of "half the speaking rate." Following that, he was asked to repeat the sentence ten consecutive times at the slow rate. The extent to which the subject did or did not reach the level of "one-half the speaking rate" was not at issue in this experiment.

Data Analysis: For each sentence in each condition, the child's first and last repetitions were discarded to control for starting and finishing effects. Then five of each subject's remaining eight repetitions of each test sentence in each of the two conditions were randomly selected for study. From these five repetitions of each sentence, the experimenter extracted four temporal measures of speech. The four temporal measures were: (1) consonant duration; (2) vowel duration; (3) duration of inter-word silent-intervals; and (4) utterance duration.

These dependent variables were obtained and measured from wide-band spectrograms produced by a Voice Print (Series 700) sound spectrograph. All measurements were first made in millimeters and then converted to a millisecond value. Separate spectrograms were produced for subjects' (1) five repetitions of sentence #1 in the BRC; (2) five repetitions of sentence #1 in the MRC; (3) five repetitions of sentence #2 in the BRC; and (4) five repetitions of sentence #2 in the MRC. Subjects' mean, median, and standard deviation scores were obtained for each of the four dependent measures.

RESULTS

One aspect of this study was an investigation of the extent to which subjects reduced their speaking rate from the Basal Rate Condition (BRC) to the experimental or Modified Rate Condition (MRC). Changes in the rate of speech were expected to be reflected primarily in the utterance duration dependent measure. When the utterance duration raw scores in each condition were examined, it became apparent that the longest utterance duration raw score for any subject in the BRC was less than the same subject's smallest utterance duration score in the MRC. Since this finding was characteristic of all subjects, it can be conclusively stated that all

subjects had significantly slower speaking rates in the MRC
than in the BRC. Thus, it can be stated that each subject
responded appropriately to the task, that is, followed the
instructions to "talk more slowly." Also of interest was
the rate reduction strategy employed by subjects.

In order to provide an objective account of the rate
reduction strategies preferred by the group as well as by
the individuals themselves, the investigator decided to determine all rate reduction strategies in the following way:
First, the median duration of inter-word silent interval
score (i.e., pause duration) was calculated for each subject on sentences #1 and #2 in the BRC. These scores were
divided by the median utterance duration values associated
with the same two sentences in the BRC. The same procedure
was followed in the MRC. This type of mathematical manipu-
lation resulted in a percentage of time (i.e., utterance
duration minus pause duration) was then completely attributable to consonant and vowel productions within the
sentence. Thus, both pause duration and consonant-plus-
vowel duration percentage values were computed for the BRC
and MRC. What was of interest, though, was the amount of
change that occurred in the above percentage scores as the
subject went from the first to the second of these conditions.
The percent difference scores (i.e., the MRC percentage scores
minus the BRC percentage scores) were utilized to ascertain
the rate reduction strategy employed by each subject. If a
subject had a slight perference for a "pausing" rate reduction strategy there would have been a positive change in the
direction of the pause duration score in the MRC. That is
to say, the subject spent proportionately more time pausing
in the MRC as compared to the BRC and devoted proportionately
less time to consonant and vowel productions in the MRC as
compared to BRC. If the positive change had occurred with
the consonant-plus-vowel duration percentage scores, then
the subject would have used a prolongation rate reduction
strategy. It should be noted that this computational procedure also allows for no change in the percentage scores
from the BRC·to MRC. If the subject had performed in this
manner he would have shown "no preference" for either the
pausing or prolongation rate reduction.

An inspection of the data indicated that six of the ten subject (60%) used the pause strategy on both sentences. By contrast, none of the subjects used a prolongation strategy across the two test sentences. Another issue of importance relates to the strategies employed by the remaining four subjects. Their rate reduction patterns were as follows: First, two of the four subjects started on sentence #1 by prolonging and finished on sentence #2 by pausing. Second, one child utilized a pause strategy at the beginning of the experiment and then changed to a prolongation strategy on sentence #2 by pausing. Finally, one other subject was found to have a slight preference (i.e., 2% change from the BRC to MRC) for pausing on the first sentence but then did not adopt any preference for a strategy on sentence #2. The lack of any preference on sentence #2 for this last subject meant that the proportions of total utterance duration devoted to pauses and to consonant-plus-vowel productions remained the same from the BRC to the MRC.

The investigator noted that none of the subjects started and finished the study with "no preference" for one of the two rate reduction strategies. It can be said, therefore, that all subjects showed at least some preference for one of the two strategies on one of the two experimental test sentences. Even though the majority of subjects preferred the pause strategy, it was quite obvious that there were other individual strategies used to reduce the speaking rate.

DISCUSSION

In discussing my findings, I would first like to restate the purpose of the study. It will be recalled that this experiment sought to determine how a group of normal speaking children fit the trends established by adults when they are instructed to slow their speaking rate.

It is worth noting that the majority of speakers' preference for the pause rate reduction strategy in this study is consistent with the results of the Goldman-Eisler, Lass and Noll, and Lass and Deem studies. These researchers reported that the major reductions in an adult's speaking rate were accomplished by means of increasing the duration and number of pauses taken between words. The present study may be the first to demonstrate that children adopt the same rate reduction speech behavior as adults.

This investigator can only speculate as to why the majority of subjects adopted the pausing strategy. Like the adults, a child strives to communicate the spoken message in an intelligible and meaningful way. It may be that pausing between words decreases the speaking rate but has little effect on the intelligibility or meaning of the words themselves. By contrast, the prolongation strategy, while effective in diminishing speech rate, also disturbs various durational characteristics of words.

This latter effect carries with it the possibility of a reduction in word intelligibility or meaning. Further research in this area with larger sample sizes will serve to support or refute these findings and suppositions.

REFERENCES

Goldman-Eisler, F. (1961a). Lang. Speech 4:171-174.
Goldman-Eisler, F. (1961b). Lang. Speech 4:220-231.
Goldman-Eisler, F. (1961c). Lang. Speech 4:232-237.
Kozhevnikov, V. A. and Chistovich, L. A. (1965). Washington, D. C.: Joint Pub. Research Service.
Lass, N. J. and Noll, J. D. (1970). Cleft Palate J. &;275-283.
Lass, N. H. and Deem, J. F. (1971). Acta Symbol. 2:54-63.
Lass, N. J. and Deem, J. F. (1972). Proc. 7th Inter. Phonet. Sciences, The Hague: Mouton.

WHAT THE CHILD'S PERCEPTION OF WORD-FINAL OBSTRUENT
COGNATES TELLS US ABOUT HIS PERCEPTUAL MASTERY
OF ENGLISH PHONOLOGY

JO ANN WILLIAMSON HIGGS AND BARBARA WILLIAMS HODSON
University of Edinburgh and
University of Illinois

When the child achieves perceptual mastery of the
phonology of his language is an important unresolved question
in child language. Some linguists have assumed this occurs
in infancy, while others believe the learning process takes
considerably longer. We believe that our recent study on
the phonological perception of word-final obstruent cognates
provides data relevant to this theoretical issue, and we
would therefore like the opportunity to discuss that work and
its implications with you now.

Given the great interest in child language in recent
years, remarkably little research has been done on the child's
perception of the phonological system of language. Ferguson
and Garnica (1975) give a full account of our knowledge to
date. Very briefly, some linguists such as Stampe (1969) and
Smith (1973) believe that the child perceives speech in terms
of the adult phonological distinctions very early on indeed;
the child has full perceptual competence very early and has
only production "incompetence." Whereas the work of other
linguists such as Garnica (1973), Edwards (1975) and Waterson
(1971) indicates that the learning of phonologically significant features of the language is a slow learning process
spanning more than the earliest years of childhood.

Our purpose in this investigation was to provide experimental evidence relevant to this important theoretical issue.

Briefly, we asked whether four-year-old children were able to decode sets of familiar minimal pairs as well as adults. We intentionally chose minimal pairs exemplifying a sub-system of English which is characterized by a complex relationship between the phonetic cues and the phonological contrasts of word-final obstruents. The phonological contrast between /p/-/b/, /t/-/d/, /k/-/g/, and /s/-/z/ is normally said to be one of voicing; i.e., in the realizations of the first of each cognate pair, the vocal folds are <u>not</u> vibrating, but in the second of each pair they are. However, for most accents of English (and certainly for General American and for Received Pronunciation) voicing is optional at word-final. That is not to say that the phonological contrast which exists in other environments is neutralized in this context; rather, that the linguistic contrast is realized through phonetic features other than presence or absence of vocal fold vibration. Almost certainly the salient feature is the comparative duration of the preceding vowel. It is a general rule of English that the vowels before /p, t, k, s/ in the same syllable are shorter than vowels before /b, d, g, z/.

So the difference between <u>heat</u> /hit/ and <u>heed</u> /hid/, to use Daniel Jones' example, is not primarily one of voicing. Vocal fold vibration ceases immediately after or even before the stop closure phase of /d/. The perceptual clue upon which English listeners depend when the context does not disambiguate <u>heat</u> and <u>heed</u> is almost certainly a durational one. It is a general rule of English that vowels before voiceless consonants in the same syllable are shorter than vowels before their voiced cognates; so /hit/ will have a relatively shorter /i/ than would have /hid/. This rule holds for vowels before all the obstruent cognates of English.

This differential influence of final consonants upon the duration of preceding vowels in English, which was described by British and European linguists long before the development of modern instrumental laboratory techniques, was verified in the laboratory by the acoustic phonetic research of House and Fairbanks (1953) and later by Peterson and Lehiste (1960). Meanwhile, Denes (1955) with the use of synthetic speech demonstrated that "the perception of voicing of the final consonant to preceding vowel decreases," this despite his use of a <u>voiceless</u> consonant throughout. More recently, Malécot

(1970) has found that "the duration of vowels before final
consonants is both a powerful and sufficient acoustic cue"
for differentiating between the classes of cognate pairs
which he tested. Raphael (1972) found that regardless of
the voicing of voicelessness of the final consonant,
"listeners perceived the final segments as voiceless when
they were preceded by vowels of short duration and as voiced
when they were preceded by vowels of long duration."

Since similar durational phenomena have been observed in
other languages, Chen (1970) asked whether this kind of vowel
durational differential is characteristic of the phonological
system of English; i.e., is learned and language-specific, or
whether it might be conditioned by an inherent physiological
feature of articulation; i.e., a language-universal. His
study of four languages substantiated the findings of Zimmerman and Sapon (1958) and led him to conclude that although
it is a language universal that vowel duration varies as a
function of the voicing of the following consonant, the
dramatic durational difference to be found in English is a
learned language-specific speech habit characteristic of the
phonological system of English.

Now let me describe our experiment. The four sets of
minimal pairs used in this study were rope/robe, seat/seed,
pick/pig, and ice/eyes. The minimal pairs were embedded in
the carrier phrase. "Which one is _____." The pairs were
presented under two test conditions--a normal spoken presentation and a whispered presentation. During whisper, instead
of altering between vibration and an open state as the vocal
folds do during normal conversational speech, the vocal folds
alter between the stretched whisper state and open. So in
this presentation the correct identification of an item must
be based upon the utilization of cues other than presence or
absence of vocal fold vibration. The audio tape was made
from tape recorded randomized questions read in normal voice
and in whisper by a trained General American male speaker.

The 20 child subjects were ten boys and ten girls who
had had their fourth birthday, but not their fifth, and who
attended the University of Illinois Institute for Child Behavior and Development Preschool. They are more accurately
thought of as "advantaged four-and-a-half-year-olds" rather

than "normal four-year-olds."   The 20 adults, ten men and ten
women, were all students in an introductory linguistics class
at the University of Illinois.

All subjects were native English speakers and all had
normal hearing. Although the children were required to pass
a 25 decibel pure tone audiometric sweep test (500, 1000,
2000, 4000 Hz) to ascertain that their hearing acuity was
normal, the adult subjects were simply asked whether or not
their hearing was to their knowledge, within normal limits.

The visual stimuli from which the subjects had to choose
their answers were mounted on a large poster board 12 x 24
inches, which was placed immediately in front of each subject.
The eight objects or pictures were glued to the board in the
following randomized order: top row--a sunflower seed, a
picture of a bathrobe, a toothpick, a picture of a car seat;
bottom row--a picture of eyes, a picture of a pig, a drawing
of an ice cube, and a small piece of rope.

Now a word about the experimental procedure. For the
children, a training session preceded the experiment. Each
child pointed to non-test pictures on a small poster board
when so instructed.Then each child named the pictures on the
experimental poster board to insure recognition familiarity.
The test itself was not initiated until the child demonstrated
the ability to say the appropriate labels for all eight items.
For the adult subjects, no pretest training was given; rather
each item on the experimental poster board was simply named
by one of the experimenters.

Each subject was tested individually by the same
two experimenters. The subjects were told that they
would hear a man say or whisper, "Which one is . . ." and
that they were to point to what it was. The words were presented free-field via a high quality audio tape recorder with
twin speakers. Errors were recorded on a test form which
listed the words in the randomized order in which they were
presented.

Finally, the experimental results: a split-plot two-
factor mixed model analysis of variance was utilized to

determine whether children perceived phonological differences
of word-final obstruent minimal pairs as well as adults did.
This design also allowed for comparisons under two conditions:
normal speaking voice and whispering. The responses by the
children were significantly different from those of the adults
(p < .001), but differences between the spoken and whispered
variables were not statistically significant, nor was there
significant interaction.   The obtained means for each
variable (i.e., for a possible total correct score of 16)
were: children, 13.85; adults, 15.93; spoken, 14.9; and
whispered, 14.88. The mean number of errors for the children
for both conditions (i.e., possible total correct score of
32) was 3.9; the median was 4; and the mode was 8. Two of
the children responded correctly to all 32 stimuli. Three
adults and one child missed only one item.

It should be noted that none of the erroneous identifications were outside of the pair to which the stimulus word
belonged. For the 80 total presentations or seat, for
example, the children pointed to seed 33 times, but never to
a member of any of the other three pairs (See Table 1). Two
of the adults pointed to seat for seed and one pointed to
pick for pig.

Because there is so much variation in the number of
errors produced by the different cognate pairs--ice/eyes
produced only one error, whereas seat/seed produced 38, let
us consider the acoustic characteristics of the test stimuli
which might account for these differences. There are many
phonetic features embedded in the speech continuum of the
test utterance which could serve to signal the phonological
contrast between a pair. I shall describe each of these
potential contrastive phonetic features in turn.

First let us consider differences of vowel duration.
All measurements were made from broad band spectograms produced by a Kay Sonograph 6061-A. Since the very nature of
the acoustical display of speech often defies the segmental
analysis which the phonetician wishes to impose upon it, we
will discuss briefly some of the criteria for the segmentation procedures which we followed. These are substantially
those established by Fant (1960) and Peterson and Lehiste
(1960).

The beginning of the vowel was taken to be that point at which there was energy present in all formants. In the case of the utterances in normal voice, this acoustic energy was displayed as periodic striation; however, in the case of whisper, the aperiodic sound source produced aperiodic striations in formant bands.

The aspiratory interval preceding the vowels in normal voice pick and pig, were regarded as part of the preceding stop. However, unfortunately, in whisper, the "aspiratory period" is not visually discernable from the following vowel; immediately upon the release of the plosive there is a formant structure which does not alter significantly throughout the duration of the vowel. To impose an arbitrary "vowel beginning" in the middle of the continuum seemed unjustified. Therefore, in the cases of two items, whispered pick and whispered pig, the vowel lengths are measured from the release of the preceding stop. This means, in effect, that those two vowel durations although comparable with one another, are not directly comparable to normal voice pick and pig or to any of the other vowel durations.

Segmentation of liquid/vowel sequences are notoriously difficult. However, in our speaker's utterances of rope/robe, the transition from /r/ to vowel was in each case marked by a sudden change from the presence of lower formants only to the presence of all formants, thus easing our segmentation task.

The vowel durations are given in Table 2. The ratios between the cognate pairs vary between .46 and .67 with the mean ratio being .59. These vowel differentials are within the range found by other researchers. These differences do not, however, seem to explain the difference in numbers of errors between the various cognate pairs.

Secondly, let us consider the durational differences between the cognates. It is frequently said that "it is a general rule of English (and of most if not all other languages) that, after a given vowel, syllable-final voiceless consonants are longer than the corresponding voiced consonants" (Ladefoged, 1975, p. 45). If this is so, then the durational differences of the cognate itself might serve as perceptual clues to the linguistic identity of an utterance. The durations of the 12 stop closures and the four fricative durations are given in Table 3.

Apparently our trained General American speaker did not follow the general rule suggested by Ladefoged and others. The durational difference between each of the six pairs of stop closures was never more than 19 msec.; three of these differences were in the direction predicted and three were in the opposite direction. The stop closure durations, therefore, do not appear to be ordered by the linguistic considerations suggested. The fricative durations, on the other hand, might well be rule governed, although there are only four examples upon which to base this supposition. Certainly the significant difference between ice and eyes might explain the low error rate produced by this pair relative to the others.

Although the explosion of word-final stops which are also utterance-final is optional in English, our speaker exploded all stops in this context. Hence it is possible that qualitative differences between the releases of a pair served as additional clues to the linguistic contrast involved. Since both releases of a pair were voiceless and both were produced through similar articulatory movements resulting in similar acoustic loci, one might reasonably ask what might be the basis for any qualitative difference? Differences in muscular tension and differences in intraoral air pressure are both candidates. Murry and Brown (1976) have found that although voiceless stops generally have greater supraglottal air pressure than the voiced cognates, that these differences are not found for whispered speech samples. However, rather than enter into the time-honored controversy concerning the features tense/lax, or fortis/lenis, and their physiological bases, or the lack of them, we simply record the possibility of there being qualitative differences between the releases of a pair. We made no further phonetic or acoustic analyses of the twelve final stop releases. If information obtained from the stop release aids in the perception of the linguistic contrast, then by including the releases in our test tape, we made the task relatively easier than it would otherwise have been.

Finally, we consider differences in voicing. In our introductory section, we described the tendency in English and, indeed, many other languages, to neutralize the voicing feature between obstruent cognates in the context relevant to our discussion. It is critical, therefore, to determine not just by auditory means, but by instrumental analysis, precisely when vocal fold vibration ceased in each of the test stimuli normal voice utterances of robe, seed, pig, and eyes. (The issue is, of course, irrelevant to the whispered utterances of the same four words.)

The realization of robe was exceptional; vocal fold vibration continued approximately 108 msec. after the stop closure, or for almost three-fourths of the total closure duration. The realizations of the other three were entirely voiceless. In the cases of both seed and pig, voicing ceased with the onset of the stop closure, and in the case of eyes, voicing stopped approximately 53 msec. before the onset of the alveolar friction. This period of "voiceless vowel" was attributed to the vowel and as such was included in the measurement of the vowel. Thus there is no phonetic contrast in voicing between 15 of the 16 cognate pairs. There is, however, a significant difference in this respect between the normal voice rope/robe stimuli and this difference should have aided in the perception of the linguistic contrast. In fact, of course, rope/robe had the second highest number of errors, 28 for both whisper and normal voice.

We are now ready to answer the question posed by the title of this paper. What does the child's perception of word-final obstruent cognates tells us about his perceptual mastery of English phonology? The results clearly indicate that the four-year-old's learning of the phonology of English is incomplete. Admittedly, the sub-system exemplified by the minimal pairs used in this study is characterized by a complex relationship between the phonetic cues and the phonological contrast; so, in a very real sense, the child has more to learn in order to correctly decode the speech continuum in this context than in many others. Only three of the twenty-four year-olds missed from two to eight of the 32 items, indicating that even in their cases considerable learning had already occurred. The fact that the response for each and

every error was the cognate pair for the correct item seems
to suggest that the error was due to incorrect perceptual
decoding rather than any other difficulty with the experimental task.

These results are consistent with those of Garnica (1973)
and Edwards (1975) and substantiate the notion of Waterson
(1971) and others that the learning of the phonologically
significant features of the language is a slow learning process spanning more than just the earliest years of childhood.
Indeed, it is difficult to find any justification whatsoever
for the notion that the child has full perceptual competence
very early and has only production "incompetence."

REFERENCES

Chen, M.   (1970).   Phonet., 22:129-159.
Denes, P.   (1955).   J. Acoust. Soc. Am., 27:761-764.
Edwards, M. L.   (1974).   J. Child Lang., 1:205-219.
Fant, G.   (1960).   s-Gravenhage.
Ferguson, C. and Garnica, O.   (1975).   New York, Academic
     Press, 153-180.
Garnica, O. I. (1973).   New York, Academic Press, 215-222.
House, A. S. and Fairbanks, G. (1953).   J. Acoust. Soc. Am.,
     25:105-113.
Ladefoged, P.   (1975).   New York: Harcourt Brace Jovanovich.
Malecot, A.   (1970).   J. Acoust. Soc. Am., 47:1588-1592.
Murry, T. and Brown, W. S., Jr.   (1976).   J. Phon., 4:183-187.
Peterson, G. and Lehiste, I.   (1960).   J. Acoust. Soc. Am.,
     32:693-703.
Raphael, L.   (1972).   J. Acoust. Soc. Am., 51:1296-1303.
Smith, N. V.   (1973).   Cambridge Univ. Press.
Stampe, D.   (1969).   Fifth Reg. Mtg. Chicago Ling. Soc.,
     Chicago.
Waterson, N.   (1971).   J. Ling., 7:179-211.
Zimmerman, S. A. and Sapon, S. M.   (1958).   J. Acoust. Soc.
     Am., 30:152-153.

Table 1. Analysis of children's erroneous responses.

Stimulus	Response	Errors	Stimulus	Response	Errors	Pair Total
rope	robe	17	robe	rope	11	28
seat	seed	33	seed	seat	5	38
pick	pig	18	pig	pick	1	19
ice	eyes	1	eyes	ice	0	1
	TOTALS	69			17	86

Table 2. Vowel durations before word-final obstruent cognates
in msec. (a. utterances in normal speaking voice;
b. utterances in whisper).

				Ratio
rope	a. 136 b. 132	robe	a. 204 b. 261	a. .67 b. .51
seat	a. 104 b. 144	seed	a. 173 b. 260	a. .60 b. .55
pick	a. 72 b. 126	pig	a. 112 b. 224	a. .64 b. .61
ice	a. 195 b. 293	eyes	a. 421 b. 448	a. .46 b. .65

Table 3. Durational differences between the cognates; duration in msec. of the stop closure of the friction.
(a. utterances in normal speaking voice; b. utterances in whisper).

rope	a. 142 b. 160	robe	a. 152 b. 176
seat	a. 125 b. 131	seed	a. 115 b. 112
pick	a. 147 b. 152	pig	a. 128 b. 171
ice	a. 356 b. 412	eyes	a. 165 b. 196

A RIGHT EAR EFFECT FOR AUDITORY FEEDBACK CONTROL
OF CHILDREN'S NEWLY-ACQUIRED PHONEMES

WALTER H. MANNING AND LINDA L. LOUKO
Memphis State University and University of Nebraska

During the last 20 years many investigators have employed dichotic listening tasks to indicate superior right
ear performance for adult subjects (Berlin and McNeil,1976).
Utilizing unique variations of the typical dichotic procedure
Abbs and Smith in 1970 and Sussman et al. in 1971 and 1973
generated data suggesting that adults tend to rely primarily
on the right ear channel of their auditory feedback system
to monitor the accuracy of their own articulatory production.
While several other investigators have also reported superior
right ear performance in children by using dichotically presented stimuli, the possibility of a right ear effect for the
auditory feedback control of articulatory production in children has not been investigated.

Recently, Manning et al. (1976, 1977a, 1977b, 1977c)
and Campbell et al. (1976) have suggested a procedure for
estimating the motor stability of newly learned articulatory
patterns in children. Briefly, these investigations have
employed binaural auditory masking in order to temporarily
disrupt a child's ability to auditorially monitor his or her
articulatory production. The results indicate that a child's
articulatory performance under auditory masking appears to
provide an indication of the child's reliance on his or her
auditory feedback channel for monitoring correct production.
This procedure also appears to provide an estimate of the
stability or automatization of the child's newly acquired
articulatory pattern. Hence, it was the purpose of the pre-

sent investigation to utilize this procedure, by presenting
auditory masking in a binaural, a monaural-right ear, and
a monaural-left ear fashion, to investigate the possibility
of an ear effect in the auditory feedback control of
children's newly-acquired phonemes.

METHOD

Subjects. The subjects in this study were 40 elementary school children enrolled in articulation therapy.
These children had an average age of 7 years, 11 months and
ranged in age from 6 years, 5 months to 10 years, 4 months.
All children had normal hearing as indicated by an audiometric screening. All of the children were enrolled in
articulation therapy for an interdental /s/ or /r/ misarticulation at the time of the study. In order to control for
severity of misarticulation, children with more than two
additional misarticulated phonemes did not participate in
the study.

Preparation of the Stimuli. The auditory masking consisted of a tape recording of competing speech. The competing speech was constructed by having two adult males and
two adult females simultaneously read four different phonetically balanced passages. This competing speech masking had
been used in four previous investigations of a similar nature.
The Deep Test of Articulation was used to elicit articulatory
responses from the children because it provided a visual,
rather than an auditory stimulus. In addition, it enabled
the examiners to sample each child's production in a variety
of phonetic contexts. Because the design of the present
study required that each child be tested with the Deep Test
a total of four times, the Test was shortened for use in this
study to a total of 30 test contexts rather than the possible
total of 46.

Experimental Procedures. During the initial(no masking)
condition, each child was administered the shortened Deep Test
for his or her particular phoneme (either /s/ or /r/). The
test was administered by the experimenter in a quiet room
with only the child and the experimenter present. In order
to insure a relatively high level of correct acquisition of
the newly-acquired phoneme, only children who scored at

least 80% correct on this initial condition were used. The
experimental masking conditions took place during the same
session and required readministration of the shortened Deep
Test. Competing speech masking was presented through earphones under three conditions: (1) masking presented to both
ears, (2) masking presented to the right ear only, and (3)
masking presented to the left ear only. These three masking
conditions were presented in a counterbalanced order to control for possible learning and fatigue effects. In each instance, the auditory masking was presented at 80 dB SPL.
Intra- and interjudge agreement for item by item scoring of
the children's responses on the Deep Test were 95% and 98%,
respectively.

Data Analysis. The number and percentage of children
who showed a decrease, an increase, or no change in their percent correct scores from the initial (no masking) condition
to each of the three masking conditions were tabulated. In
addition, the children's percent correct scores for the unmasked and each of the three masking conditions were analyzed
via a one-way analysis of variance for repeated measures.
Post hoc tests were also computed to compare each of three
masking conditions with the initial (no masking) condition.

RESULTS

Analysis of the children's percent correct scores from
the initial condition to each of the three masking conditions
indicated that the disruptive effect of the masking was
greater for those children who received the masking in both
ears or in the right ear only than when the masking was presented to the left ear only. This relatively greater disruption resulting from binaural or monaural-right ear presentation of the masking was indicated both by the number of
children who decreased in their percent correct scores under
masking as well as by the decrease in the children's actual
percent correct scores across the unmasked and the three
masking conditions.

As indicated in Table 1, the largest percentage of children who showed a decrease in their percent correct scores
took place when the masking was presented to the right ear

only (40%). The smallest percentage of children who showed
a decrease in their percent correct scores occurred when the
masking was presented to the left ear only (25%). Use of a
Cochren Q Test (Siegel, 1956) indicated a significant difference in the number of children who decreased in their percent
correct performance across the three masking conditions. This
was significant at the p < .05 level. Also, it may be seen
in Table 1 that the smallest percentage of children who showed
an increase or no change in their percent correct scores occurred when the masking was presented to the right ear only
(7.5% and 52.5%, respectively). Lastly, the largest percentage of children who showed an increase or no change in their
percent correct scores occurred when the masking was presented
to the left ear only (12.5% and 62.5%, respectively). These
same findings are also graphically presented in Figure 1.

The children's mean percent correct scores during the
initial (no masking) condition and each of the three masking
conditions were 96.60% for the no masking condition, 91.20%
for the binaural masking condition, 91.78% for the monaural-
right ear masking condition, and 92.50% for the monaural-left
ear masking condition. Use of a one-way analysis of variance
for repeated measures indicated a significant difference in
the children's percent correct scores across the four adminis-
trations of the Deep Test. Bonferroni t tests for correlated
means were used for post hoc testing. The difference between
the means of the no masking condition and the monaural-right
ear binaural masking conditions were 4.82% and 5.40%, respectively. Both of these difference scores were greater
than the calculated Bonferroni critical difference ratio of
4.73 and thus, were statistically significant at the p < .05
level. The difference between the mean of the no masking
condition and the monaural-left ear masking condition was
4.10%. Since this difference score was smaller than the calculated Bonferroni critical difference ratio of nonsignificant
difference was found between the children's percent correct
scores on the no masking condition and the monaural-left ear
masking condition.

DISCUSSION

In several respects, the outcome of the present investigation has much in common with previous attempts to study ear

preference in both adults and children. There was, for example, a good deal of variation across the performance of the individual subjects. Not all of the children demonstrated a right ear effect for the auditory masking. In addition, while the overall performance of the children under the monaural-right ear masking was significantly poorer than the children's performance under monaural-left ear masking, the actual difference between ears for the percent correct scores of most children was slight. Such variation in individual subject performance as well as minimal quantitative differences between ears is typical of investigations of this nature.

Furthermore, the outcome of the present investigation of mildly misarticulating children is consistent with the findings of several previous investigations with adult subjects. Abbs and Smith (1970) disrupted the articulatory production of adult female subjects by altering their auditory feedback system via application of delayed auditory feedback. The present study, on the other hand, disrupted the newly learned articulatory production of misarticulating children by altering their auditory feedback system with competing speech masking. However, the results of both investigations suggest that distortion of an individual's auditory feedback in the right ear results in significantly more disruption of correct articulation than distortion of the subject's feedback to the left ear.

The results of the present study are also similar to the findings of Sussman (1971) and Sussman et al. (1973). While Sussman investigated the articulatory ability of adult male subjects as they learned to perform a new non-speech (tone tracking) task, the present study investigated the articulatory ability of children as they performed a newly learned speech task. In both investigations a significant right ear effect was associated with the auditory feedback channel of the subjects. Thus, the results of the present study extend the feelings of Abbs and Smith (1970) with normal-speaking adult females, as well as the findings of Sussman (1971) and Sussman et al. (1973) with normal-speaking adult male subjects by also suggesting a bias toward right ear control for the auditory feedback system of mildly misarticulating children.

Results of the present study also provide some support for the findings of Sommers et al. in 1976. As part of a larger investigation, Sommers et al. studied the relationships between the severity of articulatory defectiveness and dichotic ear preference. These investigators found a high linear relationship between articulation errors and ear preference; the greater the number of articulation errors, the greater the tendency for words to be recognized from the left ear. Furthermore, while severely misarticulating children had a greater tendency to recognize and report words from the left ear, mildly misarticulating children showed a greater right ear ability, but to a lesser degree than a group of normal speaking children. The mildly misarticulating children studied by Sommers et al. were similar to the children employed in the present study both in terms of age and number of misarticulated phonemes.

Although different tasks were employed in these two investigations, a right ear effect was noted in both cases. Thus, while a bias in favor of the right ear has been noted in several previous studies of young children where dichotic presentation methods were used, the results of the present investigation provide the first indication that there may also be a right ear bias for children's monitoring of their own speech output--at least for mildly misarticulating children.

Lastly, several studies have suggested that the more severely misarticulating child tends to perform less well than his normal speaking or mildly misarticulating counterparts on a variety of perceptual and linguistic measures. Yoss and Darley (1974) have suggested that this differential performance by severely misarticulating children may be the result of central nervous system immaturity. If this is the case, perhaps poorer performance by severely misarticulating children would be observed on a task similar to the one employed in the present study. Differential performance by severely misarticulating children of normal intelligence (or perhaps misarticulating children of below normal intelligence) may provide further support for Sommer et al.'s suggestion of a lack of right ear processing in such individuals.

REFERENCES AND ACKNOWLEDGEMENTS

The authors would like to thank Ms. Adaline Reis and the speech-language pathologists of the Millard Public Schools, Millard, Nebraska, for their assistance in selecting the children for this study.

Abbs, J. J. and Smith, J. U. (1970). J. Speech Hear. Res.,
    13:298-303.
Berlin, C. and McNeil, M. (1976). Springfield, Ill., Charles
    C. Thomas, 327-387.
Campbell, T., Manning, W., Robertson, P. and DiSalvo, V.
    (1976). Hum. Comm., 1:37-45.
Manning, W., Keappock, N. and Stick, S. J. Speech Hear. Dis.,
    41:143-149.
Manning, W., Wittstruck, M., Loyd, R. and Campbell, T.
    (1977a). J. Speech Hear. Dis., 42:358-363.
Manning, W. and Scheer, B. (1977b). J. Comm. Dis. (in press).
Manning, W., Ortman, K. and Scheer, R. (1977c). Conven.
    Amer. Speech Hear. Assoc., Chicago..
Siegel, S. (1956). New York, McGraw-Hill.
Sommers, R., Meyer, W., Brady, W. and Jackson, P. (1976).
    J. Spec. Ed., 10:5-14.
Sussman, H. (1971). J. Acoust. Soc. Am., 49:1874-1980.
Sussman, H., MacNeilage, P. and Lumbley, J. (1973). Conven.
    Amer. Speech Hear. Assoc., Detroit.
Wike, E. (1971). Chicago, Aldine-Atherton Pub.
Yoss, A. and Darley, F. (1974). J. Speech Hear. Res., 17:
    399-417.

Table 1. Performance of children during each of the three
          masking conditions.

Masking Conditions	Performance of Children					
	Decrease		Increase		No Change	
	N	%	N	%	N	%
Binaural	13	32.5	4	10.0	23	57.5
Monaural-Right	16	40.0	3	7.5	21	52.5
Monaural-Left	10	25.0	5	12.5	25	62.5

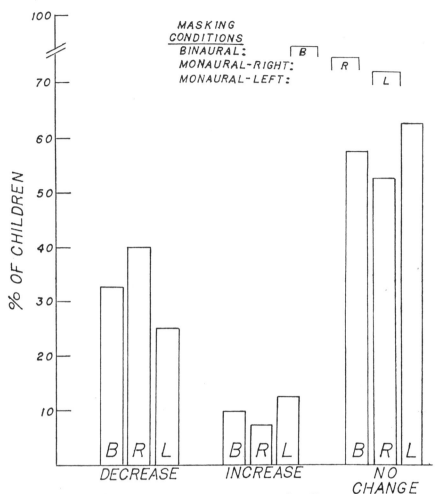

FIGURE 1. PERFORMANCE OF THE CHILDREN DURING THE 3 MASKING CONDITIONS

AN EXAMINATION OF THE ARTICULATORY
ACQUISITION OF SWEDISH PHONEMES

STUART I. RITTERMAN AND ULLA E. M. RICHTNÉR
University of South Florida and University of Florida

In 1973, Fritzell observed that there was no study of
the acquisition of Swedish phonemes based upon a standardized
test of articulation. To date, in the absence of such a test,
norms have yet to be established. The use of informal, non-
standardized tests, have been employed to that end. Stenborg
and Bengtson (1970) examined the phonetic proficiency of 739
four-year-old Swedish children. They constructed a 39-item
picture test, employing all Swedish phonemes except supra-
dentals. They found that 34% of the children tested lisped.
The three most frequently misarticulated phonemes were /ç/,
/ʃ/, and /r/. Stenborg and Bengtson (1970) also concluded
that normal Swedish children, for the most part, complete
their mastery of the Swedish phoneme system by four years of
age. They observed that it is uncommon for Swedish children
to receive speech therapy prior to age six. Inasmuch as
Swedish children begin their formal education at age seven,
they concluded that, for therapy to have sufficient time to
be effective, earlier detection was indicated.

In 1963, Westerlund, in a study of six-year-old articulatory defective Swedish children, found /r/ to be the most
frequently misarticulated phoneme. The most frequent substitutions for /r/ were /j/ and /l/. Significant substitutions involving voiced for unvoiced stops /b/p, d/t, g/k/ were also observed. In addition, substitutions were made for /s/, /ʃ/,
and /ç/. Place substitutions (dorso-velar for apico-dental
/g/d, k/t, ŋ/n/ were frequently observed. Of the vowels

examined, the most frequently occurring substitution was
u/y. In his review of these studies Fritzell concluded:
". . .initially in the phonemic acquisition of Swedish,
there are gross distinctions like vowel versus consonant as
in "mamma"; nasal versus oral as in "mamma" versus "pappa."
In the next stage the child learns to distinguish between
open versus closed vowels as in "pappa" and "pippi" and between labial versus lingua-dental articulation as in "pippi"
and "titta." Thus the phoneme acquisition develops according
to universal rules; it has been found that Swedish children
learn last the fine distinctions between the voiceless
fricatives s-, tj-, and sj-." (Author's translation of
Fritzell, 1973, p. 28)

The purpose of the present study was to develop a
standardized test of articulation, along the Templin (1957)
model, for use with Swedish children. Following Stenborg
and Bengtson's (1970) suggestion, a pre-school standardiza-
tion population was employed. As a necessary consequence
of developing such a standardized instrument, "developmental"
norms are generated. These norms should not, however, be
interpreted to infer that the authors suggest an orderly
sequential development of phonemes that is invariable for
each child. The norms obtained as a function on any test,
the Swedish Articulation Test (SWAT) included, must be
interpreted within the constraints and limitations inherent
in that test.

METHOD

The Swedish Articulation Test (SWAT) was administered
to 150 children selected from public nurseries and pre-schools
in the Stockholm area. The subjects consisted of 25 males
and 25 females from each of three age groups. The age groups
represented were 4, 5, and 6 years of age. The children selected demonstrated no evidence of hearing loss, were from
monolingual homes, were not placed in special education
classes and demonstrated no anomolies which would present a
hazard to the acquisition of normal articulation. The test
instrument employed was the 109 item Swedish Articulation
Test (Richtner and Ritterman, 1975). Employing Elert's (1970)
classification of consonants and vowels having phonemic value

in Swedish, the SWAT was designed to examine consonants,
vowels, and consonant clusters in varying phonetic environments . The test employs the spontaneous elicitation mode.
Each child was examined individually by a female graduate
student of speech pathology. Inter.- and intra-examiner
reliability was determined prior to the onset of testing
and exceeded 90% in both instances.

RESULTS

Age. On both the complete 109 item Swedish Articulation
Test, as well as on each of its constituent components, a
consistent pattern was noted for performance by age. The
results of 3x2 two way analyses of variances of subject
errors as a function of age and sex indicated in each case
that while the 4 year age group committed significantly more
errors than either the 5 or 6 year age groups ($p < .05$),
there were no significant performance differences between
the 5 and 6 year olds ($p > .05$).

Sex. No significant differences in performance as a
function of sex group membership were observed on either the
complete 109-item SWAT or any of its component sub-tests
($p > .05$). In addition, no significant age by sex interactions were observed ($p > .05$).

The means and standard deviations of errors committed
on the SWAT and its constituent components are presented by
age and sex in Tables 1 through 14.

DISCUSSION

Age and Sex. The findings of the present study are not
consistent with those of Templin (1957) with respect to
performance by age. While both this and Templin's study
indicated that the 4 year olds were significantly different
from 5 and 6 year olds, unlike the Templin study, we observed
no differences in performance between the 5 and 6 year old
groups. These differences may be attributable, in part to
differences in the instruments employed and the populations
sampled. The finding of no between-sex differences coincides
with those of Poole (1934), Wellman et al. (1931) and Templin

(1957). Although between-sex differences were not statistically significant, unlike previous studies which noted a trend in which females committed less errors than males, the reverse trend was noted. That is, males tended to commit fewer errors than their female counterparts at each age level examined. This may well be a function of differences in the populations sampled, testing instruments and the from 28 to 44 years separating the studies cited and the present study.

Vowels. Of all the phoneme groups tested, the vowels were the only phonemes for which there were no differences as a function of either age or sex. The most frequently erred vowel was /œ/; this was found to be defective in 16% of the children tested. The most frequently substituted sound for /œ/ was /ø/. This phoneme accounted for 79% of the total substitutions for /œ/; the o/œ accounted for the remaining 21%. Westerlund (1963) found that /y/ was the most frequently misarticulated vowel. In the present study /y/ errors accounted for only 1.69% of the total vowel errors. It is not clear if Westerlund included both /y/ and /Y/ in his computations, or if they were separated as in the present study. In the present study, when /y/ and /Y/ are combined, they account for 10.17% of the total vowel errors. The second most frequently misarticulated vowel in this study was /ö/. This vowel accounted for 16.95% of the total vowel errors and was misarticulated by 6.67% of the subjects.

Consonant Singles. Of the 21 consonant singles tested, the four most frequently misarticulated were /s/, /ʂ/, /ʃ/ and /ç/. The most frequent substitutions for these sounds were / θ/s, θ/s, θ/ʃ/, and /c/. It may be observed that in each of these substitutions, place, rather than manner of articulation was involved. In comparing the results of this study to those of Luchsinger and Arnold (1959), in which the distribution of errors of American English and German speaking children were compared, striking similarities are observed. Abstracting the German figures from a study by Mohring (1938), Luchsinger and Arnold found that the five most frequently misarticulated consonants were /s/, /ts/, /z/, /ʃ/, and /ç/. The three of these phonemes appearing in Swedish were also among the most frequently misarticulated

on the SWAT. The findings of the present study also agree
with those of Stenborg and Bengtson (1970), but not with
those of Westerlund (1963). Westerlund found /r/ to be the
most frequently erred phoneme. This phoneme was the third
most frequently misarticulated phoneme in the Stenborg and
Bengtson study and the eighth most frequently erred phoneme
on the SWAT.

A factor which may account for these observed differences might lie in the populations utilized. Both the
Stenborg and Bengtson (1970) and the present study employed
a normal population of children with a wide range of articulatory proficiency. Westerlund (1963) utilized a population
of diagnosed articulatory defectives. The extent to which
organic defects contributed to the composition of Westerlund's
population was not reported. The differences between the
Stenborg and Bengtson (1970) study and the present investigation may also be attributable, in part, to the differences
in the test instruments employed. In the former study, a
39 item screening test was used, while in the present study
a more extensive 109-item test was employed.

Retroflex. In general, when errors occurred on retroflex sounds they were for the most part, dentalizations.
The only retroflex that did not follow this general rule was
/s/. The most frequent substitution for /s/ was the interdental /θ/. In all, 33.33% of all children tested failed
at least one retroflex item.

Word Position. Templin (1957) reported a higher mean
number of correct responses for single consonant items in
word initial and medial positions than in word final position.
In the present study, it was found that word initial consonants were misarticulated more frequently than either word
medial or word final consonants. These differences may
simply be attributable to differences in the distribution
of Swedish and English phonemes.

Clusters. The most frequently misarticulated consonant
clusters were those which contained the /s/ phoneme; /s/-
clusters accounted for 75% of all cluster errors among the 4
year olds, 89.5% of all 5 year old cluster errors, and 95% of
the cluster errors committed by the 6 year olds.

CONCLUSIONS

The results of this study would seem to indicate that the SWAT is a useful instrument for the examination of the articulatory performance of the Swedish pre-school population. The test was designed to provide a standardized test instrument by means of which the speech sounds of Swedish may be examined spontaneously by means of easily recognizable pictures. The scores given for the SWAT and each of its constituent parts are not intended to be used as cutoff scores in the determination of whether or not a child should be placed in therapy. Rather, they are intended to serve as a reference for performance by age and sex to the distribution of errors in a pre-school population. These norms may be used as a guide for counseling parents as to the articulatory status of their child in comparison to his/her peers.

REFERENCES

Fritzell, B. (1973). Stockholm; Almqvist and Wiksell.

Luchsinger, R. and Arnold, G. E. (1959). Sprachheilkunde. Wein, Springer-Verlag.

Poole, I. (1934). Ele. Eng. Rev., 11:159-161.

Richtnér, U. and Ritterman, S. I. (1975). Depart. Comm., Univ. So. Fla.

Stenborg, R. and Bengtson, I. (1970). Nord Tidskr Tale Stem., 30:71-76.

Templin, M. C. (1957). Minn., Univ. Minn. Press, #26.

Wellman, B. L., Case, I. M., Mengert, I. G., and Bradbury, D. E. (1931). Univ. Iowa Stud. Child Wel., 5(2).

Westerlund, J. (1963). Nord Tidskr Tale Stem., 23:77-89.

Table 1.   Mean number of errors on the 91 item consonant test
           by age, for girls, boys, and both sexes combined.

	Girls (n=25)		Boys (n-25)		Both Sexes (n=50)	
CA	Mean	S.D.	Mean	S.D.	Mean	S.D.
4	16.56	14.72	14.92	11.17	15.74	12.96
5	7.32	8.42	7.68	9.13	7.50	8.78
6	8.52	8.07	5.44	6.49	6.98	7.28

Table 2.   Mean number of errors on the 57 consonant singles.

	Girls		Boys		Both Sexes	
CA	Mean	S.D.	Mean	S.D.	Mean	S.D.
4	5.48	6.04	4.90	4.51	5.19	5.28
5	2.20	2.50	2.44	2.93	2.32	2.77
6	2.00	2.33	1.42	1.68	1.71	2.01

Table 3.- Mean number of errors on the 33 blends.

	Girls		Boys		Both Sexes	
CA	Mean	S.D.	Mean	S.D.	Mean	S.D.
4	10.46	9.26	9.89	7.51	10.27	8.38
5	5.12	6.38	5.24	6.75	5.18	6.57
6	6.52	6.22	4.00	5.19	5.26	5.71

Table 4.   Mean number of errors on the 9 /r/-blends.

	Girls		Boys		Both Sexes	
CA	Mean	S.D.	Mean	S.D.	Mean	S.D.
4	1.44	2.72	1.12	2.40	1.28	2.56
5	.40	1.60	.36	1.80	.38	1.70
6	.08	.28	.40	1.80	.24	1.04

Table 5. Mean number of errors on the 14 /s/-clusters.

CA	Girls		Boys		Both Sexes	
	Mean	S.D.	Mean	S.D.	Mean	S.D.
4	7.44	5.81	7.96	5.92	7.70	5.87
5	4.52	5.87	5.76	5.91	4.64	5.89
6	6.36	6.20	3.60	4.88	4.98	5.54

Table 6. Mean number of errors on the 5 /l/-blends.

CA	Girls		Boys		Both Sexes	
	Mean	S.D.	Mean	S.D.	Mean	S.D.
4	.64	1.38	.16	.80	.40	1.09
5	.04	.20	.00	.00	.02	.10
6	.04	.20	.00	.00	.02	.10

Table 7. Mean number of errors on the 6 miscellaneous
          clusters.

CA	Girls		Boys		Both Sexes	
	Mean	S.D.	Mean	S.D.	Mean	S.D.
4	1.00	1.53	.60	1.08	.80	1.36
5	.20	.41	.16	.37	.18	.39
6	.00	.00	.08	.28	.04	.15

Table 8. Mean number of errors on the 18 single plosives.

CA	Girls		Boys		Both Sexes	
	Mean	S.D.	Mean	S.D.	Mean	S.D.
4	.40	.87	.16	.47	.28	.64
5	.16	.37	.00	.00	.08	.19
6	.00	.00	.04	.20	.02	.10

Table 9. Mean number of errors on the 69 pressure consonants.

CA	Girls		Boys		Both Sexes	
	Mean	S.D.	Mean	S.D.	Mean	S.D.
4	15.36	13.31	13.92	10.08	14.64	11.70
5	7.12	8.13	7.32	8.47	7.22	8.30
6	8.40	7.96	5.28	6.21	6.84	7.09

Table 10. Mean number of errors on the 18-single fricatives.

CA	Girls		Boys		Both Sexes	
	Mean	S.D.	Mean	S.D.	Mean	S.D.
4	3.08	2.86	2.80	2.18	2.94	2.52
5	1.60	1.78	1.64	1.68	1.62	1.73
6	1.64	1.73	1.08	1.35	1.36	1.54

Table 11. Mean number of errors on the 7 retroflexes.

CA	Girl		Boys		Both Sexes	
	Mean	S.D.	Mean	S.D.	Mean	S.D.
4	1.92	2.40	1.60	2.00	1.76	2.20
5	.36	.91	.68	1.55	.52	1.23
6	.32	.85	.20	.50	.26	.68

Table 12. Mean number of errors on the 17 initial consonant singles.

CA	Girls		Boys		Both Sexes	
	Mean	S.D.	Mean	S.D.	Mean	S.D.
4	1.88	2.32	1.48	1.23	1.68	1.78
5	.88	.97	.64	.64	.76	.81
6	.68	.69	.68	.69	.66	.69

Table 13. Mean number of errors on the 15 final consonant singles.

CA	Girls Mean	Girls S.D.	Boys Mean	Boys S.D.	Both Sexes Mean	Both Sexes S.D.
4	.96	1.37	.84	.90	.90	1.14
5	.48	.59	.60	.76	.54	.68
6	.48	.71	.28	.54	.38	.63

Table 14. Mean number of errors on the 18 vowels.

CA	Girls Mean	Girls S.D.	Boys Mean	Boys S.D.	Both Sexes Mean	Both Sexes S.D.
4	.72	1.02	.44	.82	.58	.92
5	.26	.52	.32	.75	.29	.64
6	.48	.96	.16	.37	.32	.67

Table 15. The ten most frequently misarticulated phonemes.

Phoneme	Total Errors	Number of Items Testing Phoneme	Percent of Total Errors
/s/	177	3	39.33
/ʂ/	24	1	16.00
/ʃ/	71	3	15.78
/ç/	22	1	14.67
/ɖ/	40	2	13.33
/ɳ/	36	2	12.00
/ʈ/	28	2	9.33
/r/	25	3	5.56
/j/	12	3	2.67
/v/	7	3	1.55

Consonant Singles   The Swedish Test of Articulation
(Konsonanter)

Initial			Medial			Final	
1. pil	[p-]	18. apa	[-p-]	35. tupp	[-p]
2. boll	[b-]	19. gubbe	[-b-]	36. näbb	[-b]
3. tomte	[t-]	20. råtta	[-t-]	37. get	[-t]
4. docka	[d-]	21. skidor	[-d-]	38. hund	[-d]
5. katt	[k-]	22. pojke	[-k-]	39. tak	[-k]
6. gungar	[g-]	23. flygplan	[-g-]	40. tåg	[-g]
7. fisk	[f-]	24. soffa	[-f-]	41. tuff	[-f]
8. sol	[s-]	25. rosett	[-s-]	42. hus	[-s]
9. sked	[ʃ-]	26. borstar	[-ʃ-]	43. garage	[-ʃ]
10. kjol	[ç-]	27. strykjärn	[-j-]	44. berg	[-j]
11. ljus	[j-]	28. huvud	[-v-]	45. brev	[-v]
12. vas	[v-]	29. hoppar hage	[-h-]	46. lamm	[-m]
13. häst	[h-]	30. kammar	[-m-]	47. mun	[-n]
14. morot	[m-]	31. banan	[-n-]	48. säng	[-ŋ]
15. nål	[n-]	32. tunga	[-ŋ-]	49. bil	[-l]
16. lås	[l-]	33. Kalle Anka	[-l-]	50. bur	[-r]
17. räv	[r-]	34. hare	[-r-]		

Supra-dentals   Initial Clusters   Vowels
(Supradentaler)   (Continued)   (Vokaler)

51. tårta	[-ʈ-]	74. spindel	[sp-]	92. isbjörn	[i]
52. gardin	[-ɖ-]	75. stor	[st-]	93. indian	[I]
53. barnvagn	[-ɳ-]	76. sko	[sk-]	94. segelbåt	[e]
54. stjärt	[-ʈ]	77. smörgås	[sm-]	95. äpple	[ɛ]
55. bord	[-ɖ]	78. snögubbe	[sn-]	96. "bää"	[æ]
56. björn	[-ɳ]	79. svamp	[sv-]	97. byxor	[Y]
57. kors	[-ʂ]	80. slips	[sl-]	98. syr	[y]
		81. springer	[spr-]	99. öga	[ø]
Consonant Clusters		82. strumpa	[str-]	100. öra	[œ]
(Konsonantförbindelser)		83. skruv	[skr-]	101. "muu"	[ʉ]
Initial		84. mjölk	[mj-]	102. uggla	[ö]
58. plokar	[pl-]			103. pojke	[ɑ]
59. prinsessa	[pr-]	Medial Clusters		104. hatt	[a]
60. blad	[bl-]	85. anka	[-ŋk-]	105. bada	[ɑ]
61. bröd	[br-]	86. flaska	[-sk-]	106. orm	[ɔ]
62. träd	[tr-]			107. bat	[o]
63. tvättar	[tv-]	Final Clusters		108. ding-dang	[ɔ]
64. droppe	[dr-]	87. burk	[-rk]	109. stol	[u]
65. klocka	[kl-]	88. korv	[-rv]		
66. kniv	[kn-]	89. ost	[-st]		
67. krona	[kr-]	90. mask	[-sk]		
68. kvarn	[kv-]	91. svans	[-ns]		
69. glas	[gl-]				
70. gris	[gr-]				
71. fjäril	[fj-]				
72. flagga	[fl-]				
73. fram	[fr-]				

CONSONANT PHONEMES IN SWEDISH STANDARD LANGUAGE AND THEIR MOST USUAL ALLOPHONES (Elert, 1970, p.80)[*]

Phoneme	Allophones	Phoneme	Allophones
/p/	[p'] [p]	/k/	[k'] [k]
/t/	[t'] [t] [ʈ]	/b/	[b]
/d/	[d] [ɖ]	/j/	[j]
/g/	[g]	/r/	[r] [ẓ] [R] [ɼ]
/f/	[f]	/l/	[l] [ɭ]
/s/	[s] [ʂ]	/h/	[h] [ɦ]
/ç/	[ç] [cç]	/m/	[m] [m̥] [ɱ]
/ʃ/	[ʃ] [s]	/n/	[n] [ɳ] [ṇ] [ɲ]
/v/	[v] [v̥]	/ŋ/	[ŋ]
/a:/	[a:]	/y/	[Y]
/a/	[a]	/ɔ:/	[o']
/e:/	[e:]	/ɔ/	[ɔ]
/i:/	[i:] [ij]	/ɛ:/	[ɛ:]
/i/	[I]	/ɛ/	[ɛ]
/ɷ/	[ɷ:] [β]	/ɛ:/	[æ:]
/ɷ/	[ɷ] [U]	/ɛ/	[æ]
/ɯ:/	[ɯ:] [ɷβ]	/ø̇/	[øT]
/ɯ/	[e]	/ø:/	[ø:]
/y/	[y:] [yy]	/ø:/	[œ']
/e/	[e]	/ø/	[œ]

*Elert, C.C., Ljud och ord i svenskan. Stockholm: Almqvist and Wiksell, 1973.

OBSERVER RELIABILITY IN MAKING IMPRESSIONISTIC
JUDGMENTS OF EARLY VOCALIZATIONS

IDA STOCKMAN, DAVID WOODS AND ABRAHAN TISHMAN
Howard University

Typically, prelanguage noncry vocalizations have been
described in terms of specific phonetic qualities which the
listener believes he hears (e.g., Irwin, 1948; Irwin, 1951;
Cruttenden, 1970). Observer reliability in making such impressionistic judgments has not been systematically studied.
Yet, such data are relevant to evaluating the validity of
claims made about early vocal behavior based solely on
listener judgments, particularly in view of arguments that
prelanguage vocalizations may be inappropriately represented
by segments characteristic of a language and reflective of
adults' language experience bias. However, the recently held
position, that no strict discontinuity exists between prelanguage and language behavior (e.g., Kaplon and Kaplon, 1970
and Oller et al., 1976), encourages speculation that the
validity and reliability of listener judgments may be differentially related to the child's age and certain types of
vocal qualities. The purpose of this study was to examine
listener agreement in the phonetic transcription of children's
nonlanguage vocalizations at early ages.

METHODS

The vocalizations were sampled from four female babies
in the age range 7-21 months. All babies had uneventful
birth and medical histories and were within normal limits of
functioning and development according to mothers' case history
reports. The vocalizations of one baby, designated as the

primary subject, were sampled weekly at 7-12 months, and subsequently at 15, 16, 20, and 21 months. To permit study of the consistency of agreement trends for different children, three additional babies were sampled in each of two to four consecutive months at ages 9 through 15 months. The vocalizations were recorded in the home by the mother using a Panasonic-Technics model tape recorder. Mothers were instructed to tape spontaneous vocalizations during play with minimal verbal interaction. The raw data were edited to yield noncry, nonvegetative vocalizations of reasonably clear audio quality. From these edited samples, 60 vocalizations were randomly selected from each month of sampled data of the primary subject and 30 from each month of each of the other three babies. About 15% of these samples in each month were randomly selected for repeated judgments to permit study of listener self-agreement. For listener presentation, the 1032 vocalizations, ranging from 1 to 4 seconds in duration, were randomly ordered by child, and for each child, by month and week. Repeated presentations were interspersed among nonrepeated samples.

Three phonetically trained listeners of English speaking background provided written transcriptions of each vocalization under binaural earphone conditions in a sound-proof booth. Each vocalization was presented three times. Five seconds separated successive presentations of the same vocalization and 10 seconds separated different vocalizations. The transcriptions (in IPA notation) were compared among the judges for number, type, and order of segments in each vocalization using procedures to optimize a segment-by-segment match. This matching procedure was also applied to each judge's repeated transcriptions of identical vocalizations. To illustrate, Figure 1 shows the three judges' transcriptions of two vocalizations produced in months 8 and 15.

Inspecting the original transcriptions in the left-hand portion of the figure, one is struck immediately by the amount of variation among the judges. They differed in respect to the number of segments transcribed, the choice of particular segments, and the choice of diacritical modification of the segments. For example, vocalization number 162 was perceived as having either two, three, or seven segments. Furthermore, two judges recorded a vowel in the first position, while the

remaining judge recorded a glottal fricative /h/. But the
transcriptions are not at all as random as they may at first
seem to be. A matching technique was used to align the
transcriptions so that, where possible, phonetically similar
segments appeared in the same segment-column, as is seen in
the right-hand portion of Figure 1. In the discussion of
the inter- and intrajudge agreement below, the term segment-
column refers to the set of three (interjudge) or two
(intrajudge) matched positions of the three or two transcriptions (respectively) being compared. Every segment-
column had at least one segment.

To maximize comparability among judges, we took some
liberties with certain glide-diacritics like /y/ and /w/ and
with long or repeated vowels. For example, in the matched
transcription of vocalization number 504, judge two's glottal
stop /ʔ/ stands alone in segment-column one because we assumed
that the three vowel segments in column two represented responses to similar aspects of the acoustic signal. This is
further supported by the phonetic similarity of the three
stops in segment-column three. The fourth segment-column has
the identical glide segment /w/ for all three judges in the
matched transcription. This identity was achieved at the
expense of segmentalizing the originally transcribed glide-
diacritics of judges one and two. Similarly, judge three's
originally transcribed /ɑ/ vowel, which is extended by an
arrow over three segments, is matched as a single /ɑ/ segment
with diacritic length /:/ against judge two's lengthened schwa
/ə:/ and judge one's /ɑ:/. Thus, the matching technique always maintained the segment order of the original transcription
but modified the segmental value of certain diacritics.

RESULTS

The matching technique outlined above appeared to greatly
increase the comparability of transcriptions although a good
deal of interjudge variability still existed. The judges
varied systematically from each other in at least three ways:
(1) segment bias, (2) threshold of transcribability, and (3)
narrowness of transcription. Segment bias was exemplified by
higher frequency of transcription of certain symbols. Judge
two usually transcribed a glottal stop in initial position

before a vowel as, for example, in vocalization 504 of month 15. In fact, judge two transcribed 45 glottal stops in that month (for child FS) compared to a total of seven for the other two judges. Judge one, on the other hand, was the only judge to use /I/ (15 in month 15). The second systematic bias was the threshold of transcribability. Many vocalizations varied considerably in their intensity. There was not always clear demarcation between babbling and silence. The judges varied in their tolerance of weak signals. Judge two had the lowest threshold of transcribability and took pains to transcribe even very weak, breathy vowels. Observe, for example, the sequence /əhəh+/ at the end of judge two's transcription of vocalization 162, which was apparently below the threshold of transcribability of the other two judges. In month seven, the earliest month of data collection, judge two transcribed 36 voiceless barred i's /ɨ̥/ compared to none for the other judges. The third systematic bias was the traditional narrowness of transcription. Judges one and two both used narrower transcription than judge three. This was most evident in the frequent use of diacritics on vowels to indicate raising, lowering, backing, or fronting. It is interesting to note that, in general, the diacritics marked a decrease in the variability among judges. So, for example, in vocalization 162, judges one and two transcribed back /ɑ/ vowels in segment-column two but indicated diacritically that they were fronted /</. This increased their comparability with judge three's front /æ/. Similarly, in vocalization 504, judge one's fronted and raised /ʌʔ/ in segment column 2 moved it in the direction of judge two's mid-central schwa /ə/.

The systematic analysis of the data was based on two sets of matched transcriptions: (1) the <u>interjudge</u> set, in which every vocalization was transcribed by each of the three judges, and (2) the <u>intrajudge</u> set, in which approximately every seventh vocalization was repeated and transcribed by each of the three judges. For the interjudge set, the frequency with which all three, or just two of three, judges agreed on segments or a selected feature of segments in segment-columns was tallied for each month and child. Similarly, for the intrajudge set, the frequency with which each judge agreed with himself was tallied for each month and child The analysis focused on four questions as discussed below.

Segment Agreement (Interjudge). The first question
asked to what extent identical segments were transcribed by
the three judges after application of the above-described
matching procedure. Figure 2 gives an overview of the results of this analysis. Each bar represents the percentage
of segment-columns for a given child and month in which all
three judges (hatched portion) or two of three judges (un-
hatched portion) had identical segments (disregarding diacritics). The "floating" bars will be discussed below. The
percentage of three-way agreements on transcribed segments
ranged from as low as 2% on SW-10 (i.e., on child SW, month
10) to 25% on FS-20. Except for FS-20 and FS-21, agreement
varied around 10% without any obvious pattern for child or
month. When the percentage of agreement was based on two
of three judges, agreement, ranged from 36% (SW-9) to 60%
(FS-20 and FS-21) and averaged around 50%. Except perhaps
for the greater three-way agreement in FS-20 and FS-21, no
clear trends appeared either across children or across months.

Segment Agreement (Intrajudge). The second question
addressed was the extent to which each judge transcribed
identical segments in repeated presentation of a vocalization
after the matching procedure had been applied. The "floating"
bars in Figure 2 represent the percentage of segment-columns
(for each child-month) in which a judge had identical segments
(disregarding diacritics) averaged across the three judges.
Mean intrajudge agreement varied from 30% (SW-9) to 92%
(SW-10) with a mean for all children and months of 59%. In
all but three child-months (SW-9, NH-13, and NH-14), the
average intrajudge agreement exceeded interjudge agreement.
The average intrajudge agreement shown in Figure 2 masks
individual differences in self-agreement among the judges.
For example, for CA-14, the individual percentages of self-
agreement were 74%, 61%, and 46% (mean 60% in Figure 2).
However, no judge yielded systematically higher self-agreement
than the other judges for all child-months nor did any judge
show a clear trend of higher self-agreement as the age of the
children increased.

Segment Agreement by Phonetic Type (Interjudge). The
third question asked whether agreement among judges was higher
on some phonetic types than on others. Table 1 summarizes

1002 IDA STOCKMAN, DAVID WOODS AND ABRAHAN TISHMAN

this analysis for just three months of the primary subject
(FS-7, FS-12, and FS-21). The percentage of agreement for
each phonetic type represents the proportion of all agreements (two-way and three-way combined) on segments of that
phonetic type. The percentages are given both for consonants and vowels and for several subclasses of each. The
percentages of segments transcribed (all judges combined) of
each phonetic type are also shown. Two trends were apparent
from this analysis. First, the percentage of agreement varied
according to phonetic type and month, but second, the percentage of agreement for a given phonetic type correlated closely
with its relative frequency of transcription. In other words,
agreement was higher on segments which were more frequently
transcribed. For example, the amount of agreement on stops
was 19% in FS-7 in which the relative frequency of stops was
17%. In FS-21, agreement and relative frequency coincide
at 25%.

In the earliest month (FS-7), the percentage of agreement was higher on vowels than consonants. As age increased,
the proportion of consonants agreed upon and transcribed increased whereas that of vowels decreased. Although the rank
order of consonant and vowel subtypes was not constant across
ages, stops were the most frequently agreed upon and transcribed segments among consonants at each age, while front
segments predominated among vowels. The analysis of agreement
by phonetic classes obscured some noteworthy differences among
the individual segments of these classes. For example, in
FS-7, 87% of all fricatives were /h/ and 89% of all stops
were /ʔ/. Or, perhaps of greater import, the three vowels
/i ɑ u/, often noted in early language utterances, increased
from 7% to 20% of all transcribed vowels between FS-7 and
FS-12.

Feature Agreement (Inter- and Intrajudge). The analysis
of interjudge agreement on segments leads to the conclusion
that it is relatively infrequent for all three judges to have
exact agreement on a particular segment. This basic conclusion did not vary with child or age, except for the two
later months of FS (FS-20 and FS-21). Closer inspection of
the data revealed, however, that when the judges failed to
agree on particular segments, they often transcribed segments
with significant phonetic similarity.

The fourth question was thus the extent to which interjudge and intrajudge agreement improved when agreement was
based on a phonetic feature rather than on segment identity.
Table 2 presents a preliminary analysis along these lines for
FS-7, FS-12, and FS-21. Using just those segment-columns in
which all three judges transcribed a segment, at least one of
which was a stop, a comparison was made between the percentage
of segment-columns in which all judges had the identical segment and the percentage of segment-columns in which all judges
had stop segments (whether or not they were identical). The
preliminary results showed a dramatic increase in the agreement when it was based on stop feature identity rather than
on stop segment identity. The differences were greatest in
FS-12 and FS-21. Table 2 also shows the relative increase
in self-agreement for each judge when the percentage of
agreement was based on the stop feature instead of the exact
stop segment.

In conclusion, it appears that listeners agree less often
on the presence of specific segments than one might expect.
It is questionable, therefore, whether an impressionistic
approach permits strong claims to be made about the phonetic
content of early nonlanguage vocalization in terms of the
specific types of segments produced. However, the systematic
increase in agreement which was observed across ages using a
'feature identity' criterion suggests that disagreements among
judges were not random. This encourages speculation that
listeners responded in similar ways to what may have been
dominant or broad characteristics of the acoustic signal.
That is, the symbols used differed among judges although
they represented (in the case of stops) a sound quality
typical of sudden disruption and release of air flow. To
the extent that these judgments are corroborated by acoustic
records, inferences might be reasonably drawn about the actual
phonetic content of early vocalizations. We would not expect
stoplike characteristics or any other feature which may be
present in the early vocal repertoire to necessarily have the
same productive and acoustic shape as those used later in
speech. One would suspect a shift in the actual acoustic
characteristics over time prior to language onset although
all shifts may not be easily represented by a traditional
IPA system or even discerned by the listener.

Our investigation continues in the direction of (1)
exploring agreement on other vocal features across age in
the same manner as stops were explored and (2) analyzing
the acoustic correlations of the judges' transcriptions in
an attempt to show more precisely what aspects of the signal
they were attending to both in their choice of particular
segments as well as in the number of segments transcribed.

REFERENCES

Cruttenden, M. A.   (1970).   Brit. J. Dis. Comm., 5:110-117.
Irwin, O. C.   (1948).   J. Sp. Hear. Dis., 13:31-34.
Irwin, O. C.   (1951).   J. Sp. Hear. Dis., 16:159-161.
Kaplon, E. L. and Kaplon, G. A.   (1970).   New York, Holt,
    Rinehart and Winston.
Oller, D. K., Wieman, L. A., Doyle, W. J., and Ross, C.
    (1975).   J. Child Lang., 3:1-11.

Table 1. Distribution of Interjudge Agreement and transcribed segments by phonetic type and age for child FS (N = number of segment-columns with two- or three-way agreements; X = total number of segments transcribed).

Phonetic Type	Age (Months)					
	% Agreemt N=247	% Transcr X=1055	% Agreemt N=170	% Transcr X=992	% Agreemt N=264	% Transcr X=1123
Consonants	37%	38%	54%	48%	55%	54%
Stops	19	17	31	25	25	25
Fricatives*	14	15	8	12	9	10
Glides	4	6	15	12	8	9
Nasals	0	0	0	0	13	10
Vowels	63%	62%	46%	52%	45%	46%
Front	46	32	19	19	21	18
Central	16	25	16	18	11	14
Back	1	5	10	14	13	13

Table 2.   Percentages of interjudge and intrajudge segment
and feature agreement on stops at 7, 12, and 21
months for child Fs.   (N = number of segment
columns in which all three transcriptions (interjudge) or both transcriptions (intrajudge) included
at least one stop).

Type Age (Months) Agreement	7	(N)	12	(N)	21	(N)
Interjudge Agreement						
Segment	40%		14%		24%	
		(35)		(78)		(78)
Feature	49		44		73	
Intrajudge Agreement						
Judge 1 Segment	60		67		88	
		(10)		(19)		(17)
Judge 1 Feature	90		79		100	
Judge 2 Segment	79		90		89	
		(19)		(20)		(27)
Judge 2 Feature	95		95		96	
Judge 3 Segment	73		37		67	
		(11)		(16)		(18)
Judge 3 Feature	82		62		89	

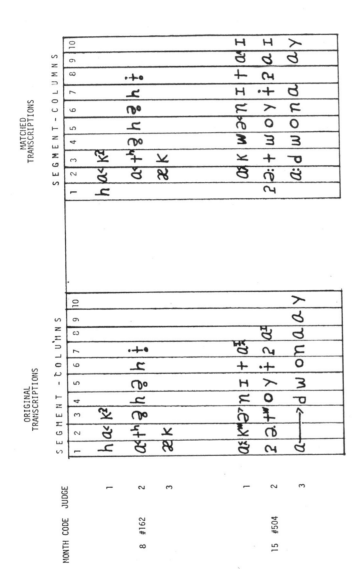

FIGURE 1.   EXAMPLES OF ORIGINAL AND MATCHED TRANSCRIPTIONS.

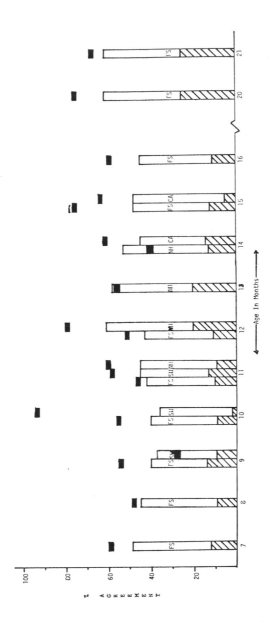

FIGURE 2.   PERCENTAGES OF INTERJUDGE SEGMENT AGREEMENT FOR EACH
AGE AND SUBJECT.

INTERFERENCE AND THE PERSISTENCE OF ARTICULATORY RESPONSES

HARRIS WINITZ AND BETTY BELLEROSE
University of Missouri-Kansas City

Interference applies to acquired knowledge or behavior which prevents or reduces learning and recall. In the classical investigations on long-term memory, interference is generated when similar material is learned closely in time (Hall, 1971). The learning of target material, usually a list of words, is either preceded by (proaction) or followed by (retroaction) linguistically related material. After some predetermined interval of time the target material is tested for recall. That is, subjects learn two lists, but recall only one list. The employment of the two lists during learning results in a reduction in recall of the target list relative to recall under appropriate control conditions.

In 1960 Underwood and Postman coined the term extra-experimental interference to refer to interference stemming from non-laboratory acquired material. In general, the theory proposed that linguistic material (letter sequences and words) could be identified which would be subject to interference. It was hypothesized that letter sequences for which the transitional probabilities are of low frequency (such as WYE) would be subject to proactive interference from letter sequences for which the transitional probabilities are high (such as, WHI). Also they proposed that high frequency words would be subject to greater proactive inter-ference than low frequency words because frequent words would evoke a greater number of other word associations. Lists were developed by Underwood and Postman for which prior interfering constraints, according to their theory, were maximized for experimental lists and minimized for control lists. In contrast to the classical investigations on interference, only a single list (experimental or control) was learned and recalled. To date, satisfactory demonstration of extraexperimental interference in retention has not been produced (Hall, 1971).

The present study is an experimental attempt to produce phonological interference in short-term memory from extraexperimental sources. According to the letter sequence hypothesis, non-English sequences should be subject to interference from English sequences. Presumably, the same hypothesis would apply to phonetic sequences presented auditorily. Differences in perception and/or production were ruled out by selecting sounds for which the acquisition rate for control sounds was equivalent to that for experimental sounds, or those which violate English phonological constraints.

Although it is well recognized that one's native phonological system will interfere with the discrimination and articulation of non-native sound elements (Brown and Hildum, 1956; Lotz, Abramson, Gerstman, Ingemann and Nemser, 1960; Winitz and Bellerose, 1965, 1972), it is not known whether phonological knowledge can cause a reduction in recall for sound items which have been correctly encoded. Of clinical interest is the observation that articulatory errors recur well beyond the clinical sessions in which correction has taken place (Van Riper and Irwin, 1968; Winitz, 1975). Possibly, articulatory errors can be regarded as an extraexperimental source of interference.

METHOD

Subjects: Children were selected from three third-grade classrooms in a school drawing from a white middle-class neighborhood. All subjects had normal hearing and speech, were monolingual speakers and were of normal intelligence, as defined by school records. The mean age of the 48 children was 106.77 (S.D. 4.05) months. Twelve boys and twelve girls (N = 24 in each group) were assigned at random to control and experimental groups.

Materials: Two lists, each consisting of three items,
were developed. The experimental list contained three non-
English sequences: / 3a , úmÎ , vɛ /. In initial word
position the /3/ is not allowable. The vowels /I/ and /ɛ/
cannot be realized in the terminal position of stressed open
syllables. The corresponding control items were permissible
English sequences: [dʒa],[úmî], [veI]. Both the control and
experimental items are non-English words. For each list
there are six possible orders of presentation. Two children
within each sex group were assigned by rotation to one of the
six presentation orders.

It would have been ideal to develop more than one list,
but unfortunately, extensive pretesting indicated that most
items require many trials before they are acquired (Winitz
and Bellerose, 1972). In tests of extraexperimental sources
of interference the number of original learning trials should
be comparable for control and experimental lists (Underwood
and Postman, 1960), because the rate of original learning
will influence recall (Underwood, 1964).

Procedure: Each child was tested individually in a
room not far from his classroom, and given preliminary
practice with the learning and recall of colors. The training lists were presented by the examiner live and then by tape
recorder. Each child was asked to repeat each item immediately after presentation. If the child failed to produce the
list correctly on the first live trial, he was given a second
trial. Immediately following the live presentation, all
children were administered one tape recorded trial. The live
trial was initially used so that the presentation rate would
accommodate individual children. The inter-item interval for
the taped presentation was 5 sec. and the live presentation
was approximately at this rate. Correct responding was
acknowledged for the live trials only. The subjects were not
informed that they would be asked to recall the list following the retention interval. The total retention interval was
30 sec. during which each subject was instructed to count
backward from 30. Each subject was instructed to stop counting after 25 sec. In the five remaining seconds each child
was given the recall instructions. Timing of the retention
interval was controlled by signals placed on the tape and

letting the tape recorder run for the full 30 seconds. Following the 30 sec. retention interval, subjects were tested
by free recall, that is, each subject was "asked to say"
the three items of the list. In the free recall period each
child was given further opportunity to recall each item of
the list if he initially failed to do so, until he indicated
he could no longer recall an item (usually 15 sec. for each
item).

Each response was scored according to standard (non-
narrow) phonetic transcription. The phonetic units used in
this study were sufficiently distinctive to make reliable
assessments. Unusual productions or approximations of these
standard phonetic "targets" were not observed. Eight experimental subjects were given two live trials (a second adminis-
tration of the list), because of errors on the [úmî] sequence
(N=7), and the [ʒa] syllable (N=1). Two control subjects
were given two live trials because of errors on [úmî] . Five
experimental subjects were initially eliminated from the study
for failure to respond correctly on the second live trial
(N=3) or to respond correctly to the tape recorded list (N=2).
These five subjects were replaced by children from the subject pool. This elimination would tend to bias the experimental group with students of increased learning skills, and
therefore work in opposition to the hypothesis under examination.

RESULTS AND DISCUSSION

Retention: The experimental and control sequences were
scored without regard to the correctness of the remaining unit
in the sequence, that is, a response was scored as correct as
long as the test sound (/ʒ dʒ I i ɛ ei/) was recalled correctl
In Table 1 the summary statistics are given. The total number
of correct responses (total correct possible = 71) is greater
for the control than the experimental group. The difference i
is significant (z = 2.70, p < .01), using the Mann-Whitney U
test for large numbers. It may also be observed from Table 1
that each control item is recalled correctly more often than
its respective experimental item, although the difference is
small for the [vɛ] - [veI] pair.

As indicated above, 10 children, 8 experimental and 2 control, failed to receive perfect scores in the first trial of original learning. Conceivably, their initial difficulty may have produced differences in retention. Accordingly, it was of interest to examine the scores for this group of subjects. Of the 8 experimental subjects, 7 had initial difficulty on /úmî/ and one on /ʒa/. Following the retention interval, six of the seven retained their error on /úmî/. The subject who initially erred on /ʒa/ correctly produced this sound following retention. The results for /úmî / are well within chance expectation (See Table 1), as only 5 correct responses were obtained for the total group, one from the 7 subjects who initially failed, and 4 from the 17 who correctly responded on the first live trial.

We do not regard failure on the first live trial as an error in learning, but rather a false expectation on the part of the subjects. Because English phonological rules were violated, it is possible that some subjects merely thought the item was mispronounced (Brown and Hildum, 1956). Because this point cannot be resolved easily, a second z score, using the Mann-Whitney U test, was calculated for only those subjects who responded correctly to the first live trial (N = 16 for experimental group; N = 22 for control group). The resultant z was 10.71 (p < .001). As a group, the 8 experimental subjects who were excluded from this analysis performed as well or better than the experimental group as a whole when all three sequences were taken into consideration, which accounts for the marked increase in the significance level.

Errors: A summary of the errors is presented in Table 2. Errors were consonantal or vowel changes, and omissions (no responses). The errors of the experimental group were in the expected direction. For /ʒa/ the phonologically permissible /s/, /ʃ/ and /tʃ/ were anticipated. However, /dʒ/ was also anticipated, but did not occur. For some reason, place, but not voicing was preserved. Generally, the vowel errors observed for /úmî/ and /vɛ/ were anticipated in that phonetic similarity was preserved. Of interest is the fact that five of the errors for /úmî/ preserved the feature of laxness (/ɛ/ and /ə/). The /ɛ/ errors may have reflected the fact that the "feature" of non-allowability had been coded, and

perhaps manifested as an intra-list intrusion. Evidence for
an interference hypothesis cannot be easily made from a comparison of the errors for the control and experimental
groups, as the error types are similar. Further, the experimental errors were not easily predictable. The two lists
were phonetically similar and, therefore, resulted in phonetically similar errors.

CONCLUSION

The aim of this experiment was to examine extraexperimental phonological interference by utilizing non-English
sequences. Miniature phonological lists were briefly repeated and then recalled 30 seconds following original learning. Phonologically inadmissible sequences were recalled
less well than phonologically permissible sequences. The
source of interference appears to be the phonological system
of English.

The present findings cannot identify the sources of proactive interference, such as coding, availability and access-
ability (Postman and Underwood, 1973). For example, it is
unknown as to whether the experimental items were initially
coded correctly or incorrectly, were of minimal strength
relative to the control items, and/or were recalled in a way
which led to retrieval errors. Additionally, the present
experiment did not examine phonological interference over
long intervals of time. A parametric study in which time is
varied should be conducted. Using tests of recognition, as
well as varying temporal intervals, would seem to be important
in disambiguating the sources of interference.

An interesting implication of these findings for articulation training pertains to the relative ordering of the several
teaching stages when more than one sound is in error. A serial
order of training would involve a start to finish program
(acquisition-generalization-recall, beginning with syllables
and terminating with conversational speech) for each defective
sound. Training on a second defective sound would not begin
until the first defective sound had been corrected well beyond
the acquisition stage. A parallel order of training would
restrict training for all defective sounds to the same stage

of articulatory proficiency. According to this procedure,
the defective sounds as a group would be retrained to each
pre-established level of proficiency although not necessarily trained simultaneously within each level of proficiency.

    Parallel training would appear to be a preferred routine
in clinical practice when the evidence suggests that multiple
sound errors are governed by underlying phonological rules
(Compton, 1970; Ingram, 1976). Conceivably, phonological
patterns will not be significantly altered by the correction
of one sound which is a part of a network of sound errors.
The interfering effects of a deviant phonological system may
reduce the recall of a corrected sound, even though the
corrected sound can be imitated correctly. It would appear,
then, to be disadvantageous to select a single sound from a
set of defective sounds and emphasize only this sound until
conversational capability is achieved (Van Riper, 1972;
Weston and Leonard, 1976). Serial training, then, ignores
the phonological framework of the error sounds. Alternatively,
parallel training considers the phonology of the sound errors
and stresses phonological change as well as production training.

REFERENCES

Brown, R. & Hildum, D. C. (1956). Lang., 32:411-419.
Compton, A. J. (1970). J. Speech Hear. Res., 35:315-339.
Hall, J. F. (1971). N.Y., Lippincott.
Ingram, D. (1976). N.Y., Elsevier.
Lotz, J., Abramson, A. S., Gerstman, L. J., Ingemann, F.,
    and Nemser, W. J. (1960). Lang. Speech, 3:71-77.
Postman, L. & Underwood, B. J. (1973). Mem. Cognit., 1:19-40.
Underwood, B. J. (1964). J. Verb. Learn. Verb. Behav.,
    3:112-129.
Underwood, B. J. and Postman, L. (1960). Psych. Rev.,
    67:73-95.
Weston, A. J. and Leonard, L. B. (1976). Lincoln, Nebraska,
    Cliff Notes, Inc.
Winitz, H. (1969). N.Y., Prentice-Hall.
Winitz, H. & Bellerose, B. (1972). J. Speech Hear. Res.,
    15:677-689.

Winitz, H. and Bellerose, B.   (1965).   J. Verb. Learn. Verb.
    Behav., 4:78-102.
Winitz, H.   (1975).   University Park Press.
Van Riper, C.   (1972).   Englewood Cliff, N.J., Prentice-Hall.
Van Riper, C. and Irwin, J. W.   (1972).   Englewood Cliffs,
    N.J., Preintice-Hall.

Table 1. Number correct for control and experimental groups.

Experimental Group		Control Group	
Total Score	24	Total Score	47
/ʒa/	8	/dʒa/	17
/úm Î /	5	/úmi/	17
/vɛ/	11	/veɪ/	13

Table 2. Summary of errors for Control and Experimental
          Groups

Unit	Experimental Groups	Unit	Control Group
/ʒa/	/ʃ/(5) * /s/ (1) /tʃ/(1) Om**(9)	/dʒa/	/j/ (2) /g/ (2) Om (3)
/úmÎ/	/eɪ/(5) /ə/(3) /ɛ/ (2)/i/ (1) Om (8)	/úmî/	/eɪ/ (2) Om (5)
/vɛ/	/eɪ/(3)/a/ (3) /u/(1) /i/(1) Om (5)	/veɪ/	E***(3)/u/ (2) /i/(1)/ɛ/(1) Om (4)

*   Number of tokens
**   Om = omissions
*** E = other errors:/ʒ, ou, ɛr/

L. SPECIAL ISSUES IN PHONETICS

TRANSCRIPTION OF THE AMERICAN r

GEORGE D. ALLEN
University of North Carolina

The primary goal of phonetic, as opposed to phonemic, transcription is commonly held, at least by American phoneticians, to be to represent speech as it is spoken by some speaker or class of speakers. Thus, one recent phonetics text states that "Phonetic transcription is defined as the representation of the sounds of spoken language with corresponding graphic symbols. Underlying any phonetic transcription (is the) simple principle (that) 'Each distinct sound of a language is represented by one and only one graphic symbol.'" A more correct picture of phonetic transcription, however, is offered by Abercrombie, and again I quote, "Strictly speaking, phonetic transcription records not an utterance but an analysis of an utterance ... If the analysis is in general phonetic terms, the transcriber will identify segments as the representatives of general phonetic taxonomic categories." The difference between these two attitudes, and I might add here parenthetically, "Vive la difference," is often difficult to transmit to beginning students who would rather not have to listen carefully and think about what they hear; yet one often _must_ listen and analyze in preparing even rather broad phonemic transcriptions. I believe that the American r represents just this sort of more complex transcription situation, and my goal here is to present and support a strategy that will be suitable for narrow systematic phonetic transcriptions of 4-sounds by students in a first course in articulatory phonetics.

Let me begin by reminding you _very_ briefly of some of the basic phonetic facts about the American r, on which I

hasten to add that I am not at all an authority. The technical term 'rhoticization' comprises two articulatory types
of r, namely the retroflex r, involving an upward retraction
of the tongue tip, and the bunched or molar r, which Uldall
describes as "articulated by contracting the tongue in a
fore-and-aft direction and bunching it up toward the upper
back molars." Both gestures are accompanied by sulculization,
whereby the midline of the back of the tongue is grooved and
the sides raised, and Ladefoged states further that there is
often retraction of the tongue root. The acoustic result of
these gestures is a substantial lowering of the third formant,
and some lowering of the second as well.

    Phonologically, r plays a dual role in American English,
sometimes as an approximant consonant, distributed similarly
to the other approximants w, j, and l, and sometimes as a
vowel. Its vocalic role may furthermore be subdivided into
two cases, namely the pure vowel / ɝ /, as in the word her,
and the so-called 'post-vocalic' r, as in the words here or
hair. These different phonological roles, and the fact that
most phonetics textbooks present systems within which it is
impossible to distinguish them adequately, are the principal
motivation for this paper.
    I feel that a variety of symbols can and should be used
to transcribe r in its various roles. Like w and j, r can
occur as a prevocalic consonant, either alone, as in the
word red, or clustered with obstruents, as in bread or spread.
(See Table 1, item 1) In these environments, the articulation
is truly approximant, so that the consonant r-symbol, upside
down in IPA and rightside up in American systems, is warranted.
In the first syllable of the word rural, for example (See
Item 2), the consonantal / ɹ / stands in the same relation to
the vocalic / ɝ / as /w / does to the vowel /u / in a word like
woo, and as / j / does to /i / in the word ye. In the word
rural, the closely articulated r-approximant opens slightly
into the following ɝ -vowel.

    This approximant / ɹ / also occurs occasionally in inter-
vocalic position, though not as often as the literature would
lead one to believe. For example, such a pair of words as
marl and moral (Item 3) might be contrastively differentiated,
in a dialect which does not distinguish cot from caught, by

pronouncing them /mɒɜɾ/ and /'mɒɹəɾ/; that is the disyllabic
nature of <u>moral</u> is made explicit by inserting a consonantal
/ ɹ / intervocalically. Analogous distinctions involve w and
j (Item 4), as for example in contrasting <u>lore</u> from <u>lower</u>
and <u>lyre</u> from <u>liar</u>.

As noted earlier, the vocalic r is of two phonetically
and phonologically distinct types. As a pure vowel, its
quality does not change, except as a function of neighboring
consonants, and it should be transcribed with a single symbol.
Thus, in item 5, words like <u>err</u>, <u>her</u>, <u>herd</u>, <u>'pervert</u>,
<u>per'vert</u>, and <u>murderer</u> may all be transcribed with a single
/ ɝ / vowel. As you may note in my transcriptions, however,
I prefer to use two ɝ -symbols, the / ɝ / and the schwar,
so as to be able to represent syllable weight; let us stay
with just the one symbol for now, however, and return to the
issue of syllable weight later.

The post-vocalic r appears in syllabic nuclei which
change in quality through time. Such vowels are commonly referred to as either glides or diphthongs, depending upon the
presence or absence of a relatively steady state portion of
the vowel. Glides, which possess such a steady state portion,
may furthermore be of two types, namely off-glides or on-
glides, depending upon whether the steady state portion comes
at the beginning or at the end of the vowel. If we use a full-
sized symbol to represent the steady state portion and a
small superscript symbol for the off- or on-glide, we can
thus transcribe words like <u>here</u> and <u>hair</u> as in item 6. Such
pronunciations often occur in strongly accented productions
of these words. Although these words are not pronounced as
on-glides /hⁱɝ/ or /hᵉɝ/ in standard dialects (see Item 7),
I can point out for purposes of illustration that many Americans pronounce words like <u>herd</u> and <u>bird</u> (No. 8) with schwa
or / ʌ / on-glides, giving /hᵊɝd / or /hᴧɝd /, /bᵊɝd / or
/ bᴧɝd /.

Diphthongs have a steadily changing vowel quality
throughout the syllable nucleus, and so should be transcribed
with the two vowel symbols, full-sized, that represent the
beginning and ending qualities. Thus an alternate pronunciation of words like <u>here</u> and <u>hair</u> is as in No. 9 /hɪɝ / and
/ heɝ/, in contrast to the glides /hiɝ / and /heɝ / discussed a

moment ago. Note that I use a ligature, or tie, to join the
two symbols, in recognition of their composing a single
syllabic nucleus. I feel that it is very important in any
phonologically relevant transcription to represent the correct number of syllables; thus, the transcription of lore
and lower, as in Item 10 on the handout, even though they
may be exact homophones, correctly represents the fact that
a /w / may appear in alternative pronunciations of the
second but not the first.

Having introduced what I believe to be a good system for
transcribing the American r in systematic phonetics, at least
to a decent first approximation, I would now like to discuss
some other alternatives and reasons for accepting or reject-
ing them. I shall start with the very common but very misleading transcription of the pure   ɝ-vowel as a diphthong or
other composite, beginning with either a schwa or an /ʌ /
vowel and ending with a schwar, an / ɝ /, or a consonant symbol. As I noted earlier, there are dialects in which words
like heard are pronounced /hᵊɝd/ or /hʌɝd /, or even diph-
thongally as /hə̯ɝd / or /hʌ̯ɝd /. These pronunciations are
as distinct, however, both socially and phonetically, as is
/ bɝd / from / bɜd /. We thus must keep the pure   ɝ-vowel
separate, with its own symbol or symbols. This decision then
has the additional advantage of permitting us to use the
ɝ   symbol instead of the consonant r symbol in diphthongs
involving post-vocalic r. Since the rhoticization is not so
closely articulated there as in pre-vocalic position, we can
represent the phonetic facts more accurately in this position
using the vowel symbol.

I would now like to discuss reasons for the use of both
/ɝ / and schwar to represent the pure   ɝ-quality, /ɝ / in
stressed or heavy syllables, schwar in light ones. Since in
many standard dialects, my own included,   ɝ-vowels in these
two environments have identical qualities, the use of two
symbols must be justified on some other grounds. We could
appeal, for example, to substantial phonetic differences in
duration or intensity; that is not really necessary, however,
especially in the phonologically motivated atmosphere of my
remarks here today. American English transcriptions often
use two special symbols, the schwa and the barred i, to represent the vowels of light unstressed syllables. These vowels

are said to be used, for example, in the word the (see No.
11), the schwa when the is followed by a consonant, as in
the man, the barred i when it is followed by a vowel, as in
the apple. Without going into the phonetic and phonological
motivation for these special symbols, I shall simply note
that by adding the schwar to schwa and barred i not only will
we then have a symbol to represent fairly accurately the
quality of any light syllable, we will also have no need
for a special mark to denote heavy vs light syllables. Thus
the distinction between 'pervert and per'vert can be represented in the segmentals alone. For many transcription purposes, a phonemically motivated three-level syllable stress
system such as that proposed by Vanderslice and Ladefoged is
adequate. If the two lower levels, heavy unaccented vs
light, are distinguished in the transcription on the basis
of the symbol used for the nuclear vowel, then only heavy
accented syllables need be distinguished by some special
stress mark. Thus No. 12 shows the words impersonator and
impersonation transcribed first with both primary and
secondary stress marks, as Kenyon and Knott would do, and
then just with the primaries, as the special use of schwa,
schwar, and barred i permits.

Finally, let me discuss very briefly the American English post-vocalic l. This is the only one of the four
approximants to appear as a consonant in word final position,
as in several of the words on the handout. Because of, the
strong velarization or pharyngealization with which these
final l's are pronounced, however, many speakers of standard
dialect omit the apico-alveolar contact altogether, thus
producing a back unrounded vowel instead of a lateral approximant. I therefore suggest that, just as post-vocalic r
should be transcribed with an ɚ-vowel, so should this commonly occurring post-vocalic l be transcribed with either of
the two back unrounded vowel symbols / ɯ / or / ɤ /, depending
on which of velarization or pharyngealization the speaker
uses. Thus my pronunciation of the word hole would be transcribed as either of the two strings shown in No. 13 on the
table, depending on whether or not I employ apico-alveolar
contact.

The American r presents many problems in transcription,
because of the variety of phonological roles it plays and the

corresponding diversity of·phonetic forms it takes.   In
spite of these problems, phonetics texts generally offer
oversimplified strategies for transcribing r, so that the
beginning student, faced with the task of narrow systematic
phonetic representation, has no way to resolve the resulting
ambiguities.   In this paper I have proposed a slightly more
complex strategy, which I hope will help to solve that problem.   This proposed system, shown in No. 14, may be summarized
as follows: for r in its consonantal, or prevocalic, role,
use lower case r, upside down for IPA and rightside up if
the standard American dialect context is understood; in its
role as a pure vowel, use / ɝ / and perhaps also schwar if a
weak variant is desired; in its post-vocalic role, where it
colors another vowel, use either a glide or a diphthong symbol, depending upon how the total syllabic nucleus is produced.   I hope that you will find this system useful and
that you will tell me how to improve it.

See examples on the following page.

EXAMPLES

1. red [ɹɛd]; bread [bɹɛd]; spread [spɹɛd].

2. rural [ɹɝəɫ]; woo [wu]; ye [ji].

3. marl [mɒɹɫ]; moral [ˈmɒɹəɫ].

4. lore [lɔɝ]; lower [ˈlowɚ];
   lyre [laɪɝ]; liar [ˈlaɪjɚ].

5. err [ʔɝ]; her [hɝ]; herd [hɝd];
   pervért [pɚˈvɝt]; pérvert [ˈpɝvɚt]; murderer [ˈmɝdɚɚ].

6. here [hiˠ]; hair [heˠ].

7. (Do not occur) here [hⁱɝ]; hair [heɝ].

8. herd [hᵊɝd] or [hʌɝd].
   bird [bᵊɝd] or [bʌɝd].

9. here [hɪɝ]; hair [hɛɝ].

10. lore [lɔɝ]; lower [lɔɝ].

11. the man [ðəˈmæ̃n]; the apple [ðɨˈæpɫ].

12. impersonator [ĩmˈpʰɝsəˌneˈɾɚ], [ĩmˈpʰɝsəneˈɾɚ];
    impersonation [ĩmɪpɝsəˈneˈʃən], [ĩmpɝsəˈneˈʃən].

13. hole [hoɫ], [hoɤ].

14. A basic system for transcribing the American r:

    a. As a pre- or intervocalic consonant, use [ɹ] (IPA) or
       [r] (American).
       example: red [ɹɛd], moral [ˈmɒɹəɫ].

    b. As a pure vowel, use [ɝ] and perhaps also [ɚ] (schwar)
       example: her [hɝ], pérvert [ˈpɝvɚt].

    c. For post-vocalic r, use [Vˠ] or [Vɝ] (V = vowel).
       example: here [hiˠ] or [hɪɝ].

ALPHABETS, ORTHOGRAPHIES AND THE INFLUENCE OF SOCIAL-HISTORICAL FACTORS

UZBEK BAITCHURA
Leningrad

Problems of alphabets and orthographies have been much discussed during two last centuries and up to now, certain principles (phonetic/phonemic, morphological, etymological, historical) have been established. With the progress of culture and the development of languages, different innovations use to appear in the existing rules of writing although the changes in the language justifying these innovations do not take place every three or even 30 years, as some Soviet philologists assume, but they require many centuries, as can be seen from the example of the Turkic languages. Of the most importance however, are social-political factors, not scientific ones. Thus, if a people is exterminated (e.g., after a war), its language disappears together with the alphabets and the orthographies for nobody will be left to speak or write it.

As it is known, the adoption of this or that alphabet is, in the first place, connected with the religion of the people, e.g., the Latin, Arabian and Cyrillic alphabets. The struggle of religions and of peoples lie at the bottom of all more or less important debates concerning merits and drawbacks of any alphabet because disputes in arms are accompanied by disputes in ideologies. Thus, in the vast territory of the Russia of today, two great forces opposed each other in a deadly struggle during the last millenium. These were Christian Russians waging an offensive war against

Moslim Turks, which were in defense. Although the Turks
by far surpassed Russians both in culture and in number,
they were defeated because of the lack of unity. Millions
of men, young and old, and especially of women and children
have been massacred during many centuries, as not only historical documents but even Frederic Engels (in his Anti-
During) retell us. But the Turks were too many to totally
eliminate, and the rest were allowed to live--although under
hundreds of restrictions. Among them, besides the serfdom
for the majority, was the prohibition to live in many places
(e.g., near big rivers), the prohibition of many trades, of
secular education, of the periodic press, etc.

     The aim of the Russian imperialism was to crush the
Turkic peoples not only physically but also morally by
annihilating their national culture. Thus, the czarist
Minister Miljutin has said: "The Russian alphabet must
finish what was begun by the sword" (See Kultura i Pis'men-
nost' Vostoka, Vol. VI, Baku, 1930, pp. 5, 8). With the
help of replacing of the Arabian alphabet of the Turks by
the Russian Cyrillic script, the czarism intended to
separate them from their inherited culture and to erase
from the memory of the people the remembrance of its past
because it was an obstacle in the way of forced Russifica-
tion. This is the background.

     From the linguistic point of view, an alphabet is only
a system of signs and one such system is neither better nor
worse than any other, provided they answer the social-
political aims and technical requirements. Thus, the
Chinese hieroglyphs are very well adapted for their
literary language to be used also by other peoples (Japanese,
Koreans, etc.) as their common coine uniting them. The
syllabic principle of writing is good for languages with
many dialects. And the Latin and Greek alphabets intended
basically for phonetic writing are totally unsuitable for
these purposes. But none of these principles has ever been
carried out consistently in any language.

     In the course of many centuries, the Turkic peoples
have developed their common literary language called
"Chagatai" or "Turki," which was a coine based on the

Arabian alphabet and partly on its orthography (in which
the syllabic principle was predominant). That is, the
plural affix lar/ler was rendered by three or two letters:
لر or لر although in some dialects (as Baškir), the number of the phonetic variants of this affix can be over
twenty, namely, lar/lär/lor/lör/nar/när/nor/nör/tar/tär/tor/
tör/dar/där/dor/dör/zar/zär/zor/zör, etc.--whereas in Tatar
and some others there are only four or eight variants.

In the present orthographies, all these variants are
designated. However, this is unnecessary for understanding
as it separates the languages from one another, whereas the
Turkic coine served to unite the Turkic peoples into one
nation. Moreover, this "nation" enjoyed a common literary
language because its orthography was based on the principle
of differentiation of words and not on differentiation of
sounds. Thus, although in different dialects some words
were pronounced differently, the written form was comprehensible for all and, under the influence of the common
literary language Turki (Chagatai), the Turkic dialects
were approaching each other. However, such development
would thwart the plans of Russian imperialism whose aim was
to separate the Turkic peoples from each other--only the
unity with Russians being allowed (See I. Levin, "Materialy
k politike tsarizma v oblasti pis'mennosti inorodcev," KPV,
VI, pp. 3-19).

Accordingly, in the 1920's a campaign was organized in
the Soviet press and at the First All-Union Turkologic Congress (1926) in order to induce the national minorities of
Russia, and the Turkic peoples, to replace their alphabets
with the Latin. The motivation was to bring these peoples
nearer to the "higher" culture of Europe, due to the alleged
unfitness of their former alphabets (Arabian, Uighur, etc.)
for the phonetic structure of their languages and because of
the supposed insufficiency of all their culture. Thus, the
First Minister of Education of the USSR, A. V. Lunačarskij,
wrote in 1926 that the Arabic alphabet had been separating
the peoples of the Orient from the European culture and that
"the literature existing in the Arabian language ... has no
big practical value" (See KPV, VI, pp. 20-21).

At the Congress, different questions of history, ethnography, philology and pedagogy were discussed but its basic problem and principal aim was to induce the Turkic peoples to replace the Arabian alphabet with Latin (cf. Proceedings, p. 176). Although several scholars such as academicians V. V. Bartold, S. F. Oldenbourg, and L. V. Ščerba had been invited, the majority of the participants consisted of little educated non-specialists and some of them even acknowledged this themselves (See Proceedings, p. 293, etc.). The main parties were represented; on the one side, by Russian professors N. F. Jakovlev, L. I. Žirkov, and by some other participants who tried to demonstrate that the Arabian alphabet was totally unfit for rendering the phonetic structure of the Turkic languages and, on the other side, by the Tatar delegation, among which were Professors G. Sharaf and G. Alpar, who were against latinization and supported the Arabian alphabet (suggesting that only some improvements of the orthographic rules might be required). The position of scholars such as Bartold was expressed by Akad. Ščerba who said: "In the problem which occupies the Congress in the first place, namely, in the problem of the alphabet ... I consider myself utterly incompetent to express any opinion because this is a national question, it is settled on the basis of cultural-political considerations, and ... I should simply believe myself to have no right, as a representative of another nation, to interfere in any way into this matter" (Proceedings, p. 176). The tendentiousness of the Russian organizers of the Congress may be seen clearly from the fact that only the reports and contributions delivered in the Russian language were published in the Proceedings of this, a Turkological Congress, whereas the addresses in the Turkic languages were omitted--even a particularly valuable report by Professor G. Alpar. The result was that the Proceedings primarily reflected the speeches which had a Russian orientation.

All arguments in favor of replacing the Arabian alphabet by the Latin can be reduced to the following:

1. It was argued that the number of Arabian letters was insufficient to designate the speech sounds existing in the Turkic languages. This argument is not substantiated. First, it is always possible to add the

necessary signs, as is usually done. Second, the
Arabian letters far outnumber the Turkic speech sounds
(phonemes). Third, there is no need to designate all
ten or twelve vowels even if we had adopted the phonetic writing because, according to W. Radloff's acoustical perception and my experimental investigations of
over a dozen Turkic languages and dialects, the reduced
and short narrow vowels mostly fall out in connected
speech, and it is enough to have letters for six long
vowels in Tatar and the corresponding vowels of the
other Turkic languages. Fourth, it is not the vowels
but the consonants which confer the meaning in the
Turkic languages. And last, the phonetic principle is
not applicable to all languages except in scientific
transcription. This is why Arabic orthography was
mainly based on the syllabic principle and the requirements to render the speech sounds are totally out of
place here.
     2. The second argument against the Arabic script
was contradicting the first because it stated that the
Arabic alphabet has too many signs! In the Arabian
alphabet used by Tatars, 19 letters have four forms
and the remaining 13 letters have two variants each
depending on the position of the letter at the beginning,
in the middle, or at the end of the word--or if written
separately,which was regarded as an unnecessary complication. However, this argument does not stand up to
criticism. First, it is always possible to drop unnecessary signs--as is usually done. Second, all European
alphabets have the same "complication" for every letter
in them also has at least four variants, namely, (1)
block letters; (2) cursive letters; (3) capital letters;
and (4) small letters. For example, in German there
are eight variants because it has, besides the Latin,
also the Gothic script. However, in this regard there
is a difference. In the Latin and the Cyrillic alphabets, the four forms of one letter often have nothing in
common with each other (cf. the letter A) because they
only reflect the historical fact that letters of these
alphabets are of heterogenious origin. Some of them
descend from writing by carving on a hard material
(direct lines) and others were invented for writing on

paper (circular lines). On the other hand, in the
Arabian alphabet, the four (or two) variants of one
letter usually retain the resemblance in the main and
differences are usually limited to the additional
joining of lines at the beginning and/or the end of
the letter. This system is of the convenience to the
writer and greatly facilitates writing. Hence comes
the greater speed of writing in Arabian script because
of its better adaptation for writing, to which the
omission of many vowels (without injuring the sense)
also greatly contributes. Thus, the writing of an
experienced and well educated person approaches, in
its speed, that of stenography, without loosing in
distinctiveness and intelligibility. Finally, as to
distinctiveness, the Arabian characters (and especially
words) possess this quality to a much greater degree in
comparison with the Latin and Cyrillic.

   3. It was stated that the speed of type-setting
was a little less in the Arabian script; viz., 5500-
6000 letters a day instead of the 7500-8000 letters
for Latin and Cyrillic (Proceedings, p. 265). These
data are doubtful as was stated by G. Sharaf. However,
it is of greatest importance that Arabian orthography
requires approximately twice as few letters to express
the same number of words and ideas as do the Latin and
the Cyrillic alphabets. For this reason, one page of
the Arabian script contains nearly twice as many words
as does Latin or Cyrillic writing.

   4. It was argued that Arabian writing is more
difficult to teach than the Latin or Cyrillic. However,
the percentage of literate Tatars before the Revolu-
tion surpassed by several times that of literate Russians
in the Kazan province (according to V. I. Lenin's data).
And nowadays, the percentage of illiterates in Turkey is
no less than in Iran although in the former the Latin
alphabet is used whereas in the latter it is the Arabic.
Moreover, the following point must be taken into consideration. Although it may appear easier for pupils
to learn the individual letters of the Latin or
Cyrillic alphabets, the same is not true for adults.
For them, this situation constitutes an obstacle hampering writing because words are perceived not as groups

of letters but as hieroglyphs and adults do not read
words by letters but as a whole. Thus, the Arabic would
appear superior to the Latin as the Arabian orthography
renders only those features of words which are important
for the understanding of the text by natives and those
who know the language. Hence, the Russians argued that
the Latin and the Cyrillic alphabets are more comprehensible for them and easier to learn than the Arabic
script. It is true that the Arabian writing is intended for those who know the language and not for
foreign beginners. However, no nation would be expected to change their alphabet in order to make it
more comprehensible to foreigners (e.g., the English
would not adopt Chinese hieroglyphs in order to
facilitate studies of English for the Chinese). This
is why G. Sharaf replied (to this argument) that it is
good when the cap suits Van'ka (or Tom) but Van'ka
(or Tom) should not be picked up to be suited for the
cap.

        5. The problem of economy was avoided by the
adherents of latinization, and no wonder for, in comparison to the Greek, Latin and Cyrillic scripts, the
old alphabets of semitic origins are much more compressed and compact, having become, during their much
longer course of development, better adapted for rendering human speech.

I have reviewed nearly all of the arguments against
Arabian writing and they appear inconsistent from the
scientific point of view. No wonder that the Tatars, the
descendants of Bulgers and one of the Turkic nations
of the highest culture, rejected the idea of latinization
and preferred their inherited Arabian alphabet--which had
served them for a millenium. Not only the Tatar delegation
at the Congress, but also 96% of all Tatar intellectuals
who had taken part at the discussions, voted for the Arabian
alphabet (Cf., e.g., Proceedings, pp. 242, 283, 321, et
passim; G. Ibrahimov, Tatar mädänijäty nindi jul belän
baračaq, Qazan, 1927, p. 4, and others). However, as expected, the Congress (organized by governmental autorities
in support of latinization) passed the resolution and after

the Congress, the Arabian alphabet was replaced by Latin
in all Turkic republics.

The adherents of latinization also intended to replace
the Russian Cyrillic writing with Latin--which would have
been a progressive measure. Thus, Lunačarskij wrote:
"The idea of latinization of the Russian alphabet received
a powerful incentive from the success of the latinization
of the writing of the peoples which had used the Arabian
alphabet. Henceforth, our Russian alphabet has estranged
us not only from the West but also from the East..." (KPV,
VI, p. 23). "This (latinization) gives us maximum of
internationality connecting us not only with the West but
also with the East, it especially facilitates teaching
diminishing the number of letters, it renders a greater
closeness to the typographical print ... almost to 20%,
which presents an enormous economy" (p. 25). The eminent
Russian linguist N. F.Jakovlev added to these the following arguments: "The existence of the Russian alphabet in
the USSR presents an indisputable anachronism, a kind of
graphical barrier." "The national masses of the Soviet
Union have not yet forgotten its russificatory role. The
curse of the autocratic oppression by the Great-Russian
national-chauvinism is still weighing upon the very graphic
form of this alphabet." "In the period of building socialism,
a new alphabet ... an international graphic form must be
adopted which would be in keeping with the international
content of the socialist culture." According to Jakovlev,
latinization of Russian would increase the speed of writing
by 15%, the distinctiveness would increase by four times,
the time of teaching would, accordingly, be reduced, etc.
(KPV, VI, pp. 35-41). Moreover, the latinization of the
Russian alphabet has been supported, in principle, by V. I.
Lenin (KPV, VI, p. 22).

Accordingly, a "Subcommission on Latinization of the
Russian Alphabet at the Department of Science" of the
Ministry of Education of the RSFSR has been organized and it
passed the resolution (of January 14, 1930) which supports
such latinization (See KPV, VI, pp. 209-221). The project
was well substantiated and showed the good will of Russians
to elevate international collaboration to a new and a higher
scale. However, this project was not carried out after

Lenin's death in (1924). Moreover, in the late thirties, the Latin alphabet (which had been adopted for the Turkic and other languages) was replaced by the Cyrillic writing of Russians--and without any discussions, conferences or explanations. The replacement of the adopted Latin script by Cyrillic writing overturns all argumentation in favor of replacement of the Arabic script by the Latin and proves that latinization was only an intermediate stage facilitating transmission from the Arabic to the Russian script, as was correctly forseen by the adherents of the Arabic alphabet. Thus, the political forces again ignored the scientific and supposedly scientific argumentation in this issue.

The Cyrillic writing was introduced into the Turkic languages at the period when many linguists and turkologists who had taken part in the discussions on latinization existed no longer or were neglected. Many who had opposed the replacement of the Arabic alphabet by Latin were already dead (as G. Alpar) or in prison (as G. Sharaf). That appears to be why the orthographic rules were conceived by persons of little knowledge.

Many conferences and books have been devoted to the problems of orthography of the Turkic languages. Among them are two symposiums recommended by the Institute of Linguistics of the USSR Academy of Sciences, namely, (1) Voprosy soveršenstvovanija alfavitov tjurkskix jazykov (1972), edited by N. A. Baskakov and Orfografii tjurkskix literaturnyx jazykov SSSR (1973), edited by K. M. Musaev. (The latter title implies that orthographies of non-literary languages are also possible!) According to Baskakov, the total sum of the signs of the Latin alphabet used in all Turkic languages is 39, whereas the same figure for the Turkic alphabets based on the Cyrillic script is equal to 74. As the total number of phomemes of the Turkic languages is the lesser, this author concludes that the Cyrillic script has served to separate and estrange the Turkic languages from each other (p. 7). Secondly, both he and Musaev admit that the Cyrillic alphabet has been transferred to the Turkic languages together with all defects of the Russian orthography (including the letters denoting two sounds, etc.). In order to improve this situation both Baskakov and Musaev recommend that such pairs of sounds

as p/b, t/d, k/g, $č/š$, $š/s$, $ž/š$, etc. be designated by one
letter each. Moreover, Musaev writes: "The existing
orthographic rules have already a thirty-years' history,
during which they have been incessently improved" (p. 8).
One can only agree with his further statement that "at the
present time retardation of the theory of writing in comparison to the practical work in this area is more striking
than 30-40 years ago" (p. 12), and that "Now it is most
important to give the people a scientifically substantiated
writing" (p. 27) because such writing surely does not exist.
Moreover, in addition to the basic drawbacks of Russian
orthography, many new defects have been added in the course
of these "improvements."

According to Musaev, "the principle cause of the
adoption of the Russian alphabet was a strive to approach
the Russian people, the progressive Russian culture, a
strive to study and master the Russian language" (p. 46),
whereas Baskakov, to the contrary, writes that the adoption
of the Russian orthography only hampered the teaching of
both the Russian and of the native tongue (pp. 9-10)--and
he is quite right. Baskakov, as a Russian by nationality,
could allow himself such a conclusion, whereas Musaev, being
a Kazakh, could not.

The process of constant adaptation of the orthography
and the literary languages of the Turkic peoples to the level
of the youngest generation and to the level of the least
educated common person is destructive because any literary
language presents a product created by innumerable writers,
poets, scientists and scholars as well as by other intellectuals. Thus, the task must be to elevate the common people
to the higher level of the literary language by teaching and
not to degrade the literary language to the level of the
uneducated. This latter course can only lead to annihila-
tion of the literary language. In short, the Cyrillic
orthography was unfit for the Turkic languages at the moment
of its adoption and remained unfit after all further "improvements." The only result was that these changes rendered
illiterate all those who had been literate before.

It is true that the tendencies of language development can be taken into consideration when establishing or improving the norms of a literary language. However, these tendencies must be considered not within the narrow limits of one state, but on a wide international scale if we agree that it is international collaboration that must be promoted and not confrontation or assimilation of one language by another. It is here that the general trend toward latinization clearly manifests itself all over the World from Europe to both Americas and Australia as well as in Africa and Asia, as the Latin script has become the main international means of communication. Thus, if we want to elevate international collaboration to a still higher level, we must adopt the Latin alphabet as the principal alphabet for the Russian language and for all other languages in the USSR (some of them using it already), whereas the Cyrillic alphabet, as well as the Arabian and other national alphabets, can remain a secondary subject to be taught at school like the Gothic script is in Germany. These measures would be consistent with the requirements of progress and with the spirit of our time, which consists of a general trend toward mutual understanding and international collaboration for the benefit of man and human welfare rather than in national or governmental isolation and confrontation.

VISIBLE SPEECH CUES AND SANDHI VARIATION
RULES IN FRENCH

SIMON BELASCO
The Pennsylvania State University

Some thirty years ago Pierre Delattre began his important investigations in acoustic spectrography, which led to his numerous findings and publications on the acoustic cues of vowels and consonants. With respect to the acoustic aspects of the current study, we have drawn from two of the 1968 articles of Delattre entitled "La radiographie des voyelles francaises et sa corrélation acoustique," published in The French Review (1968a) and "From acoustic cues to distinctive features," published in Phonetica (1968b). Our discussion of articulatory phenomena is based on the treatment found in the Delattre articles, and The Sound Pattern of English (1968) by Chomsky and Halle (hereafter referred to as SPE). The distinctive feature concept used in the treatment of the phonological rules is basically that of SPE as interpreted by F. Dell (1970).

Figure 1 represents sagittal profiles of eleven French oral vowels (upper portion) and four French nasal vowels (lower portion) obtained by Delattre (1968a) from tracings of x-ray films projected on opaque glass. For oral sounds, the vocal tract may be constricted in three ways: (1) by narrowing the glottis, (2) by narrowing the lips, or (3) by moving some part of the tongue near some point on the buccal or pharyngeal walls. Figure 1 also shows that constriction of the lips and/or tongue obtain for every vowel except the oral vowels /ɛ/ and /œ/.

Figure 2 shows the height of formant 2 relative to the
height of formant 1 for each vowel, positioned according to
the sagittal profiles in Figure 1. The vowels themselves
are actually positioned according to the relative height of
their formant 1--with the lowest formant 1 at the top
(vowels /i/, /y/, /u/) and the highest formant 1 at the
bottom (vowels /a/, /ɑ/). It will be noted that formants 1
and 2 for vowel /œ/, 550 Hz and 1400 Hz, respectively, are
closest to the first and second resonances of the ideal tube
of uniform length, 500 Hz and 1500 Hz, respectively. The
next closest vowel is /ɛ/ with a formant 1 frequency of 550
Hz and a formant 2 frequency of 1800 Hz. It is this vowel
that is usually designated as the neutral vowel (Chomsky
and Halle, 1968). Acoustic phoneticians generally agree
that the ideal resonances reflect the neutral position of
the speech organs of the vocal tract. Among other things,
the neutral position serves as a reference point for identifying articulatory features such as anterior, coronal, high,
back, low, round, tense, etc. For French, the neutral position of the low mid lax vowel /œ/ coincides with schwa /ə/
(as in regarde).

The position of formants 1 and 2--relative to some
fundamental frequency---is enough to identify the oral vowels
on a spectrogram. This is also true of nasal vowels--with
the added feature that formant 1 for these vowels is reduced
in intensity. Excluding the "neutral" vowels /œ/ and /ɛ/,
all the other vowels are produced by constrictions occurring
at the lips, glottis, and in the buccal-pharyngeal passage
due to tongue movements. The frequency of formant 2 depends
on the front cavity formed by lip and tongue constriction.
The frequency of formant 1 depends on the back cavity formed
by tongue and glottis constriction. Theoretically, both
cavities communicate, and any articulatory change in one
affects the resonant characteristics of the other. However,
what has been stated concerning the front and back cavities
is more or less true from a practical standpoint. The relation of vocal tract constriction and cavity size to the
height of formants 1 and 2 may be stated as follows: (1)
the size of the opening of a cavity is directly proportional
to the height of a formant, (2) the overall size of a cavity
is inversely proportional to the height of a formant, (3)

the length of the opening of a cavity is inversely proportional to the height of a formant.

Delattre accounts for the relative heights of formants
1 and 2 by taking the "size" of the "cavity" and the "size"
of the "opening" into consideration but not the "length" of
the "opening." We shall chart his relations with the
"corner vowels" /i/, /u/, /a/--although Delattre constructed
no such chart nor did he attempt to relate his data to distinctive feature cues of vowels. For the time being we shall
disregard the statement concerning the length of the opening
of a cavity. On the left side of Figure 3, each of the
vowels /i/, /u/, /a/ has two rows labeled Front-Back and
two columns labeled (size of) opening and (size of) cavity.
The entries l and s correspond to the values large and
small. In the center of the chart the two columns labeled
high high list entries with different values of + and -.
The value + or - in the left column correlates with the
size of the opening of a cavity. The + or - in the right
column correlates with the overall size of a cavity. The
relative height of each formant is indicated by a double
entry (++, --, +-, -+). High formants are correlative with
large openings and small cavities and conversely.

It will be noted that the traditional articulatory
vowel triangle plots the vowels in terms of "tongue elevation" (high-mid-low) and "tongue backing" (front-central-
back), whereas the acoustic vowel triangle plots them according to formant frequency (high-mid-low) for both formant 1
and formant 2. Thus for formant 1, the vowels /i/, /y/, /u/
are "high" on the articulatory triangle and "low" on the
acoustic triangle. Conversely, the vowels /a/, /ɑ/ are "low"
on the articulatory triangle and "high" on the acoustic
triangle. Acoustically then for formant 1, vowels /i/, /y/,
/u/ are "low," /e/ /ø/ /o/ are "low mid" (-mid), /ɛ/, /œ/,
/ɔ/ are "high mid" (+mid), and /a/, /ɑ/ are "high." By the
same token for formant 2, vowels /i/, /e/ are "high"
(2500-2200 Hz), /ɛ/, /y/, /ø/, /œ/, /a/ are "mid" (1800-1350
Hz)--with /œ/, /a/ specified as "low mid" or "-mid" (1400-
1350 Hz)--and /ɑ/, /ɔ/, /o/, /u/ as "low" (1200-750 Hz).

Since it is easier to judge the relative "length"
rather than the "size" of the constrictions at the lips
and tongue from Delattre's sagittal profiles in Figure 1,
Figure 4 assigns acoustic distinctive feature values to
each of the 11 vowels according to the relative size of the
front and back cavities and the relative lengths of their
points of constriction. The letters l and s stand for
"large" and "small," respectively, when referring to cavity
size but stand for "long" and "short" when referring to the
length of a constriction. The letter n stands for "neutral"
and m for "medium." Thus, large (cavity) and long (opening)
= low frequency, and small (cavity) and short (opening) =
high frequency. The unrounded non-back vowels /i/, /e/, /ɛ/,
/a/ have a relative length of opening at the lips of "non-
long," or--more precisely--"short" for /i/, /e/, "neutral"
for /ɛ/, and "medium" for /a/. The lip constriction is
relatively "long" for the remaining vowels /y/, /ø/, /œ/,
/ɔ/, /o/, /u/, /ɑ/--primarily due to lip rounding. The
overall size of the front cavity for /a/ appears to be
larger than for /ɑ/, which would make formant 2 lower for
/a/--were it not for the relatively greater length (and
smaller size) of the lip constriction for /ɑ/.

Synthetic playback experiments have shown that it is
possible to identify each vowel from the relative heights of
their formants 1 and 2 alone. Except for /i/, which has a
formant 3 frequency of 3000 Hz, all vowels tend to have a
formant 3 frequency stabilized at 2500 Hz. In addition to
the fact that vowels are relatively longer, this feature
helps to distinguish vowels from subclasses of resonant or
sonorant consonants which show different frequency values
for formant 3. In short, longer duration and a stable
formant 3 frequency is correlative with the distinctive
feature value +syllabic. Conversely, shorter duration and
an unstable formant 3 frequency is correlative with the
distinctive feature value -syllabic.

From an acoustic-articulatory-auditory standpoint, it
is more accurate to correlate the height of a formant with
the relative distance of constrictions of nodes and anti-
nodes in the vocal tract. Nodes and anti-nodes also occur
at different points in the buccal-pharyngeal passage. The

<u>frequency</u> <u>of</u> a <u>formant</u> <u>rises</u> <u>as</u> <u>a</u> <u>constriction</u> <u>approaches</u>
<u>a</u> <u>node</u> <u>and</u> <u>falls</u> <u>as</u> <u>a</u> <u>constriction</u> <u>approaches</u> <u>an</u> <u>anti-node</u>.
In a tube of ideal length, a node is located at the closed
end (the glottis), and an anti-node at the open end (the
lips) for formants 1, 2, and 3. Nodes and anti-nodes follow
each other at time intervals of 1/4 wave length. The frequency of formants 1, 2, 3 will rise or fall as the constrictions formed by the lips, tongue, and glottis, respectively, approach a node or an anti-node in the vocal
tract--not only for vowels but for all consonants. The
transitions of consonants before and after vowels either
implicitly or explicitly point toward three loci. Each locus
represents the resonant point of formant 1, formant 2, and
formant 3. For any given formant, one consonant will show a
higher or lower locus than another consonant according as
the points of constriction in the vocal tract approach nodes
or anti-nodes. As a result, the consonants with similar
place or manner features show similar configurations on spectrograms in transit to and from their loci as they precede
or follow other speech sounds.

Figure 5 illustrates according to Delattre the acoustic
cues sufficient and necessary for the perception of French
consonants. They total 11 place cues in 3 categories: (1)
frequency of formant 2 transitions, (2) frequency of formant
3 transitions, (3) relative frequency of turbulence; and 17
manner cues in 6 categories: (1) direct-fast transitions,
(2) frequency of formant 1 transitions, (3) turbulence or
low periodic link, (4) short turbulence, (5) discontinuous
links, (6) voice bar or long preceding vowel, etc. Many
of the manner cues overlap and many are mutually exclusive
for each set of consonants. No doubt all of these "cues"
are present in real speech, and Delattre suspected that there
were others which he had not discovered. It is also true
that in the presence of noise, it is possible to understand
speech even though many of the cues are not perceived. It
is even possible to use certain cues to infer other cues that
may not be present in the speech continuum. For example, it
is possible to identify the final /t/ and /d/ in <u>pat</u> and <u>pad</u>
from the relative length of the preceding vowels pronounced
with no "hold" or "release" phase. This indicates that

redundancy of acoustic and articulatory cues is necessary
to insure perception of speech under non-normal conditions.
Just as traditional distinctive feature theory relies on a
minimum number of cues to describe linguistic phenomena, so
may acoustic distinctive feature theory work with a minimum
number of cues to describe the same phenomena. The missing
features can be supplied by proper redundancy rules. In
this study we will not treat redundancy rules to any extent.
Our object is to describe those cues isolated by synthesis
which can serve as acoustic distinctive features. We will
cite representative samples of phonological and sandhi
variation rules to illustrate when acoustic distinctive
features can or cannot be used in place of traditional distinctive features.

     Figure 6 represents the Delattre chart of synthetic
spectrographic patterns of French consonants based on
acoustic features. Consonant transitions displayed verti-
cally in columns, and horizontally in rows, are preceded
and followed by the near neutral French vowel /ɛ/. Formants
3, 2, 1 of the vowel /ɛ/ are distinctively visible in each
block, as are the consonant transitions going to and from the
vowel. All transitions related to the perception of the
same consonantal distinctive feature converge toward their
characteristic loci regardless of the vowel that may precede
or follow. Formant 3 and 2 transitions correlate with place
features and formant 1 with manner features.

     "Locus theory"--as claimed by Delattre (1968b)--"des-
cribes the direction which a given formant transition
must take in order to contribute to the perception of a
given consonantal distinctive feature." The concept of
formant loci has been questioned by various acousticians,
among others, G. Fant (1968), K. Johansson (1969), and E.
Emérit (1974, 1975, 1976). The latter especially has maintained that except for perhaps dentals and alveolars, there
is no absolute frequency toward which the vowel formant
transitions "point" in going to and from consonants. Accordingly, what is universally characteristic about formant
transitions is their "qualitative" direction--not their
"quantitative" locus or point. For example, Figure 7 shows

that the F2 transition of a <u>charniere</u> <u>formantique</u> <u>initiale</u>,
i.e., initial consonant plus vowel sequence, always rises
for labials and descends for velars, no matter what the
color of the following vowel is. On the other hand, the F2
transition for dentals and alveolars point to a locus of
1750 Hz, which rises for a following /i/, /e/, is level or
"straight" for the neutral vowel /ɛ/ and descends for
following /a/, /ɔ/, /o/, /u/.

For the purpose of this paper, we are more concerned
with the direction the formants take rather than with their
precise loci or points. However, we should like to add that
the concept of locus as maintained by Delattre may not be
entirely out of the question. Instead of a point or dot, a
locus might be represented by a relatively larger area such
as a circle, or a parabola, or even a sphere containing
parallel multiple bands of continuous points--toward which a
formant transition might direct itself. The diameter of
each "formant-locus-sphere" would vary for different individuals, but the positions on the sphere toward which the
transitions pointed would be relatively the same for a given
consonant or consonant sub-class--with respect to the color
of preceding or following vowels. Be this as it may, instead
of citing the frequency points for each formant, we will draw
attention to the configurations in each column or row in
order to grasp <u>visibly</u> the relation between formant height,
and place and manner features.

In Figure 6, column 1 contains labials. Formants 3 and
2 point downward in each block forming two "v-like" shapes
for each consonant. Column 2 contains dentals. Formant 3
points up and formant 2 points down, forming a "diamond-
like" or "oval-like" shape. Column 3 contains /ɥ/, which
is similar to the formant 3/formant 2 configuration of the
labials in column 1. Column 4 contains the fricatives /ʃ/
and /ʒ/. Formant 3 points down and formant 2 points up
forming the configuration of a "pincer" or "claw." Column 5
contains the palatals /ɲ/ and /j/. Both formant 3 and
formant 2 point up in the form of two inverted "v's." The
velars /k/ and /g/ in column 6 show pincer or claw-like
configurations like those in column 4. If /k/ and /g/ occur

before /o/ and /u/, they are labialized by these vowels,
and the F2 locus is assumed to be in the neighborhood of
700 Hz. Emérit maintains that the locus is more like 3000
Hz for all following vowels (Emérit, 1974, 1975, 1976). In
any event, the claw-like configuration still obtains. Velars
are distinguished from other obstruents by short mid turbulence. Column 6 contains the pharyngeal /R/. Formants 3 and
2 form an oval-like configuration like that of the dental
/l/ in column 2. They differ, however, in the direction
taken by their formant 1 transition.

     Of course, such configurations are valid only if we
adopt neutral /ɛ/ as the ideal transitional vowel by con-
vention. For example, in Figure 7, the direction of the F2
transition for the dentals changes--proceeding from /di/
to /du/. Thus, the configuration of /dɔ/ looks more like
/gɔ/ than like /dɛ/. Instead of using such terms as double-
v, oval-like, claw-like, double-inverted-v-like, we can
specify the direction of the transitions as either high, mid,
or low. Thus, the labials have the formant 3 and formant 2
acoustic "place" feature specification +low +low, respectively. The dentals have the acoustic place feature +mid
-mid. Pharyngeal /R/ has +mid +low, the palato-aleolar
-mid +mid, and the palatals +high +high. The velars have
-mid +high plus short mid turbulence if we wish to specify
the distinction for preceding or following rounded vowels.

     Although Delattre uses the formant 1 transition as a
"manner" cue, it is possible to use formant 1 height to
specify more precisely the "place" feature. For example,
the formant 1 transition for /R/ points up. The formant 1
transition for every other consonant points down. Calling
this feature "low," we can more completely specify /R/ as
+mid +low -low, or as blank blank -low if we wish to incor-
porate redundancy rules. Labials may be more fully identified as +low +low +low, dentals as +mid -mid +low, palato-
alveolars as -mid +mid +low, palatals as +high +high +low,
and velars as -mid +high +low. The rounded glide /w/ +low
+low +low is readily distinguishable from the "close"
rounded glide /ɥ/ -mid -mid +low.

Delattre finds four degrees of formant 1 height having loci at zero Hz for stops; 250 Hz for fricatives, nasals, and glides; 400 Hz for the lateral /l/; and 700 Hz for /R/. In addition to -low for /R/, we have 3 degrees of +low for the other consonants: +low at 0 Hz, +low₁ at 250 Hz, and +low₂ at 400 Hz. Using the three subclasses of +low for formant 1, we can further distinguish labial stops (+low) from other labials (+low₁) dental stops (+low) from /l/ (+low₂), and these from other dentals (+low₁). Palato-alveolars and palatals may be further specified as +low₁. Consonants may be further distinguished from each other by manner cues--but using only a relatively small part of those suggested by Delattre. Sonorants have a low periodic link for formant 1 (+low link). Obstruents have no such low periodic link (-low link). Nasals are differentiated from other sonorants by the feature specification +discontinuous link. Fricatives are marked by +long turbulence, and stops by -long turbulence (short). Voiced consonants have the feature -fundamental (voice bar). Voiceless consonants have the feature -fundamental. This system permits the various acoustic features to be grouped in all the necessary "natural classes" so that phonological rules may effectively operate on them in derivations.

To recapitulate: the transitional characteristics of formants 1, 2, 3 identify the so-called "place" acoustic cues for every non-vowel. Only four acoustic cues of manner: low link, discontinuous link, long turbulence, and fundamental are necessary to distinguish subclasses such as sonorant vs. obstruent, nasal vs. sonorant, fricative vs. stop, and voiceless vs. voiced.

The acoustic features high, mid, low for vowel formants are not equivalent to the features high, low for consonant formants nor are they equivalent to the articulatory move-- ments of the features high, low, back, etc. in traditional distinctive feature theory. Acoustic theory is purely a phonetic theory. Except in certain specific contexts, it cannot take grammatical features into consideration; it cannot account for morpheme or word boundaries; it can only

consider those acoustic "cues" that can be observed in a
relatively uninterrupted continuous flow of speech.   In
French, changes in form occur for pronominal modifiers that
do not take place where these modifiers are in postnominal
position.   In some environments, the feminine forms are
sometimes phonetically different from corresponding mascu-
line forms, and both may differ from the plural forms.
In other environments, there are no phonetically realized
differences for any of these forms.

Except for indicating boundary features, it appears
that by restricting the number of acoustic cues suggested
by Pierre Delattre, it is possible to use acoustic spectrographic features as acoustic correlates of traditional
distinctive features to state sandhi variation rules.

REFERENCES

Chomsky, N. and Halle, M.   (1968).   New York, Harper and
      Row.
Delattre, P.   (1951).   Middlebury.
Delattre, P.   (1948).   French Rev., 21:477-484.
Delattre, P.   (1968a).   French Rev., 48:48-65.
Delattre, P.   (1968b).   Phonet., 18:198-230.
Dell, F.   (1970).   Unpub. Doctoral Diss., MIT.
Dell, F.   (1973).   Paris, Hermann.
Emérit, E.   (1974, 1975, 1976).   Phonet., 30:1-30; 31:6-37;
      32:425-466.
Fant, G.   (1968).   Amsterdam, Holland, 173-277.
Johansson, K.   (1969).   Stud. Ling., 23:69-82.

This research was made possible by the PSU LA College Fund
for Research; Grant 1976a.

FIG. 1

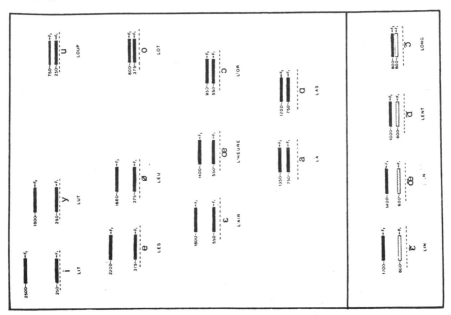

FIG. 2

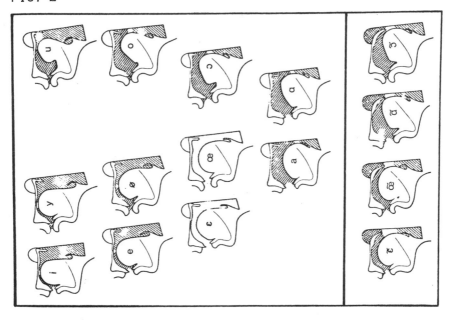

	Formant 1			Formant 2		
		opening length	cavity size		opening length	cavity size
[i]	+ low	l	l	+ high	s	s
[y]	+ low	l	l	+ mid	s	s
[u]	+ low	l	l	+ low	l	l
[e]	– mid	s	l	+ high	s	s
[ø]	– mid	s	l	+ mid	l	s
[o]	– mid	l	s	+ low	l	l
[ɛ]	+ mid	n	n	+ mid	n	n
[œ]	+ mid	n	n	– mid	l	n
[ɔ]	+ mid	m	m	+ low	l	l
[a]	+ high	m	s	– mid	m	l
[ɑ]	+ high	m	s	+ low	l	l

FIG. 4

FIG. 3

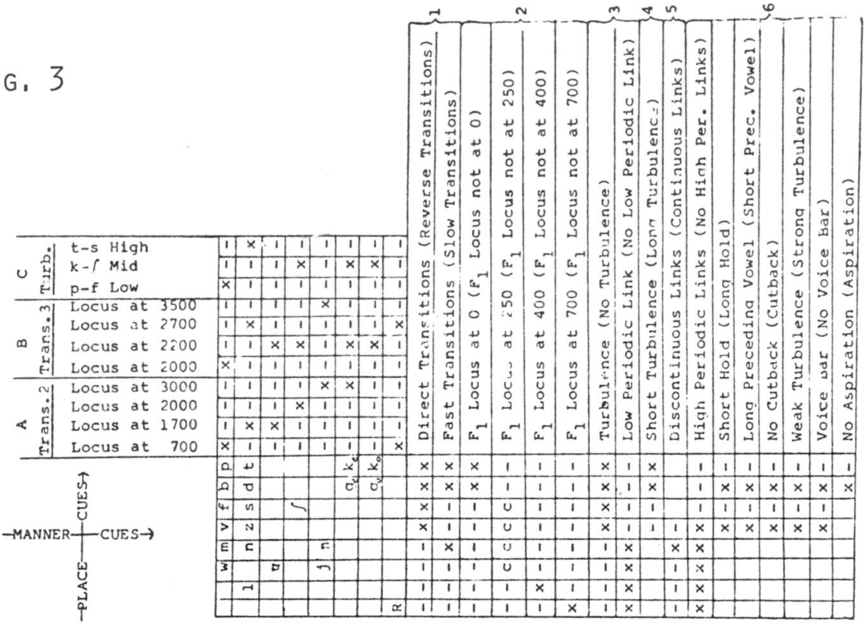

			Direct Transitions (Reverse Transitions)	Fast Transitions (Slow Transitions)	F_1 Locus at 0 (F_1 Locus not at 0)	F_1 Locus at 250 (F_1 Locus not at 250)	F_1 Locus at 400 (F_1 Locus not at 400)	F_1 Locus at 700 (F_1 Locus not at 700)	Turbulence (No Turbulence)	Low Periodic Link (No Low Periodic Link)	Short Turbulence (Long Turbulence)	Discontinuous Links (Continuous Links)	High Periodic Links (No High Per. Links)	Short Hold (Long Hold)	Long Preceding Vowel (Short Prec. Vowel)	No Cutback (Cutback)	Weak Turbulence (Strong Turbulence)	Voice Bar (No Voice Bar)	No Aspiration (Aspiration)
C Turb.		t–s High	I	×	I	I	I	I	I	I										
		k–ʃ Mid	I	I	I	×	I	×	×	I										
		p–f Low	×	I	I	I	I	I	I	I										
B Trans.3		Locus at 3500	I	I	I	I	×	I	I	I										
		Locus at 2700	I	×	I	I	I	I	I	×										
		Locus at 2200	I	I	×	×	I	×	×	I										
		Locus at 2000	×	I	I	I	I	I	I	I										
A Trans.2		Locus at 3000	I	I	I	×	×	I	I	I										
		Locus at 2000	I	I	I	×	I	I	I	I										
		Locus at 1700	I	×	×	I	I	I	I	I										
		Locus at 700	×	I	I	I	I	I	I	×										
PLACE CUES	MANNER CUES	p / t / c̆ k̆ / c̬ k̬	×	×	×	I	I	I	×	I	×	I	I	I	I	I	I	I	I
		b d /	×	×	×	I	I	I	×	I	×	I	×	×	×	×	×	×	×
		f s / v z	×	I	I	∪	I	I	×	I	I	I	I	I	×	×	×	I	
		m n / ɲ	I	×	I	∪	I	I	I	×	×	×	×	×	×	×	I	
		w ɥ / ɹ	I	I	I	∪	I	I	I	×	I	×							
		l	I	I	I	I	×	I	×	×	I	×							
		R	I	I	I	I	I	×	I	×	I	×							

FIG. 5

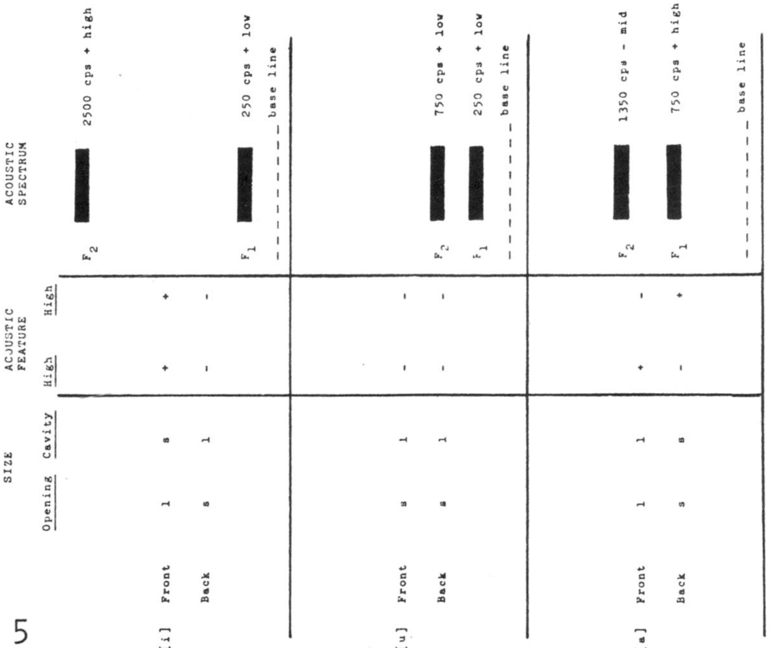 SIZE		ACOUSTIC FEATURE		ACOUSTIC SPECTRUM
Opening	Cavity	High	High	
[i] Front	l	s	+	+	F_2 2500 cps + high
Back	s	l	–	–	F_1 250 cps + low / base line
[u] Front	l	l	–	–	F_2 750 cps + low
Back	s	s	–	–	F_1 250 cps + low / base line
[a] Front	l	l	–	+	F_2 1350 cps – mid
Back	s	s	–	–	F_1 750 cps + high / base line

FIG. 6

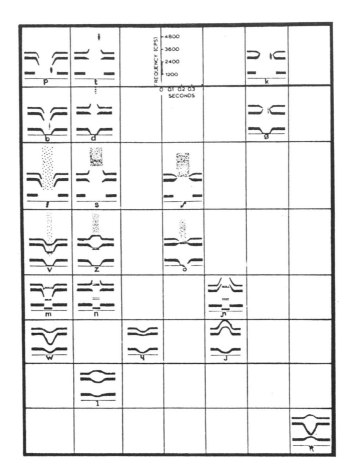

FIG. 7

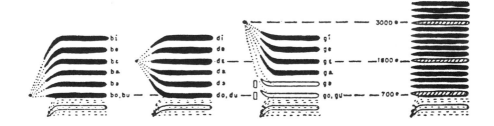

EFFECTS OF MASKING ON SUBVOCAL SPEECH
AND SHORT-TERM MEMORY

CURT HAMRE AND WILLIAM HARN
Northern Michigan University

In this exploratory study we were interested in relationships among three influences on recall of monosyllabic word
strings: Latency of response, subvocal speech, and high-
intensity noise.

Latency of Response. Romans and Milisen (1954) discovered that imposing delays between stimulus and response
seemed to have a beneficial effect on children's imitative
phoneme production. They reported improved accuracy of
phoneme reproduction with delays up to nine seconds, and
accuracy deteriorated with delays longer than nine seconds.
The question addressed in this study was: Do imposed delays
of zero, four, eight, and twelve seconds have an impact on the
accuracy with which subjects recall word strings?

Subvocal Speech. Locke (1970) suggested that the ability
to retain linguistic units in short-term memory may be a function of the motor coding of acoustic stimuli through subvocal
speech. He defined subvocal speech as "the articulatory
aspects of language related behavior which are covert but
measurable." The question addressed in the present study was:
Does subvocal speech have an impact on ability to recall word
strings?

It is not obvious how one might best induce or inhibit
subvocal speech. Subjects could be asked to rehearse silently,
or not to; or, during a delay, subjects could be presented with

stimuli which compete with the verbal stimuli of interest.
We attempted to influence the amount of subvocalization
through the agency of high-intensity noise, hypothesizing
that if high-intensity noise increases vocal loudness
(Lombard effect), so will it increase subvocal activity.

High-Intensity Noise. Does high-intensity noise, presented during a post-stimulus delay, have a detrimental or
beneficial effect on ability to recall word strings? If noise
interferes with processing it should impair recall, but if
noise induces or increases subvocal rehearsal it could improve
recall.

PROCEDURE

Subjects were five female college students with normal
hearing and speech. At the beginning of the experimental
session, each subject had surface electrodes placed over the
thyroid cartilage for electromyographic observation of laryngeal activity. Subjects were tested individually within one
afternoon in an IAC suite. Each subject listened to eight
series of monosyllabic words taken from PB-50 word lists.
Each series was comprised of six words presented at two
second intervals. Overall, then, each subject was asked to
recall eight series of words with six words in each series, a
total of forty-eight words.

Each series of six words was followed by a pure tone which
served as the signal to begin saying the words just heard. Two
series were followed immediately by the pure tone signal; for
the remaining six series there was a delay imposed between the
last word and the pure tone signal. For two series each the
delay was four seconds, eight seconds, and twelve seconds. All
stimulus words were tape recorded and presented via TDH-49
headphones through a Maico 24 dual channel audiometer.

For half of the series subjects were presented with 85dB
(re: HL) white noise during the intervals between the last
word in the series and the pure tone signal. For the other
half of the series no noise was presented, and the four no-
noise series were presented first.

RESULTS AND DISCUSSION

With respect to latency of response, subjects were
asked to recall two series (twelve words) in each of four
trials: zero, four, eight, and twelve seconds delay. Grouping the five subjects together, and combining the noise and
no-noise conditions, a score of sixty was possible for each
trial (twelve words x five subjects). When asked to repeat
the words immediately, the five subjects recalled forty-four
of the sixty words. With a delay of four seconds they recalled fifty-three, at eight seconds they recalled firty-four,
and at twelve seconds delay they recalled forty-nine of the
sixty words.

While these findings are compatible with Romans and
Milisen's (1954), that accuracy of production is best when
delays of eight or nine seconds are imposed, a limitation of
the present procedure was a failure to tax short-term memory
more than we did. Requiring that subjects retain only six
words is probably too easy, and it may be that the effects of
imposing a delay will be more dramatically evident if subjects are asked to recall eight--ten words in a series.

With respect to the effects of noise on recall, half of
the eight series comprised a noise condition and half a no-
noise condition. With four series in each condition and six
words in each series, a score of twenty-four was possible for
each subject; a score of 120 for five subjects grouped was
possible for each condition. In the no-noise condition, subjects obtained a score of 97/120 (80 percent), and with noise
present subjects recalled 107/120 words accurately (90 percent)
Although this result would also appear to be influenced by the
simplicity of the task, it is important to point out that all
subjects demonstrated this increase in accuracy of recall in
the noise condition. This finding at least permits the conservative conclusion that the introduction of noise did not
impair recall, a finding which is difficult to square with a
noise-impedes processing model.

Finally, with respect to the potential influence of subvocal speech on recall, we obtained data from surface electrode
recordings of laryngeal activity with noise present and with

noise absent. Only the highest point reached by the EMG
needle was noted by the experimenter, and a substantial increase in laryngeal activity during noise conditions was
observed in this way for every subject. This increased
laryngeal activity may or may not be a reflection of an
aspect of subvocal speech. It is tempting to suggest that
subvocal speech was enhanced during noise conditions, and
that this provides partial explanation for the marginally
improved recall of all subjects when noise was present. It
would be useful to introduce other electrode placements in
order to determine whether the presentation of high-intensity
noise produces a more general (not laryngeal-specific) arousal.
If such arousal is found to attend improved recall during
noise on verbal and nonverbal tasks, then noise-induced en-
hancement of attention (rather than increased subvocal
speech) may offer the simplest explanation for findings of
the present study.

    In conclusion, it would seem that further research on
the effects of delays and noise on recall will contribute to
an understanding of the role of speech production mechanisms
in short-term memory.

REFERENCES

Locke, J. (1970). Asha 12:7-14.
Romans, E., and Milisen, R. (1954). J. Speech Hear. Dis.
    Monog. Suppl. 4:71-78.

THE EFFECTS OF MASKING ON APRAXIA: EVIDENCE
FROM SPECTROGRAPHIC DATA

CURT HAMRE AND WILLIAM HARN
Northern Michigan University

The spectrograph affords the investigator an opportunity
to examine phonetic transition effects in continuous speech,
and it has been particularly useful for studying phone to
phone discrepancies in stuttered speech (Agnello, 1975). No
attempt has been made to utilize this instrument to similarly
describe apraxia of speech, although casual suggestions that
stuttering and apraxia are alike can be found in the literature
(Hamre, 1972; Luchsinger and Arnold, 1965, p. 703; Orton, 1937,
pp. 193-199; Saunders, 1962, pp. 35-44). Since no catalogue
of commonalities between stuttering and apraxia has been published, overlapping phenomenology (gleaned from the literature
and clinical evidence) are summarized in Table 1.

Hamre (1976) has described a Language Systems and Processing (LSP) model of stuttering; a modified version of LSP
is included here (Figure 1) to formally illustrate the predicted functional similarity between stuttering and apraxia.
The present investigation tests a prediction derived from the
LSP model: if masking noise facilitates fluency in stuttering,
then it should also facilitate fluency in apraxia of speech.
There are essentially three major assumptions contained in the
LSP model; this view proposes that both stuttering and apraxia:
(1) represent restricted phonological and prosodic language
"systems," and impaired formulation/execution with respect to
language "processing" parameters; (2) may be context-sensitive
(Jakobson, 1972) disorders. That is, stuttering and apractic
errors may be predictable if phonetic transitions are examined
rather than, for example, certain phonemes. Also, there seem

to be nonlinguistic (situational) regularities which influence frequency and severity (if not loci) of errors in
stuttering and apraxia; (3) vary from "simple" to "complex"
depending on (a) contextual constraints which operate for a
given patient, (b) the number of language systems involved,
and (c) the extent of language processing impairment. Because
of the apparent similarities between stuttering and apraxia,
it is logical to predict that the well-known effects on
stuttering of masking noise should also operate on apraxia
of speech. Deal (1970) found that masking had no significant
effect on phonemic accuracy in apractics. However, since
masking promotes fluency in stuttering, it would seem to be
more productive to examine phonetic transitions (rather than
phonemic accuracy) of apractic speech under masking.

PROCEDURE

Subjects were four males with neurological impairments
of vascular origin, aged 47, 56, 61, and 76 years. Diagnosis
of apraxia of speech was made by a speech pathologist after
comprehensive examination including the Porch Index of Communicative Ability (Porch, 1967). Subjects passed pure-tone
audiometric screening (20dB intensity level) at 1K, 2K, 4K,
and 6K (ISO, 1964).

Tasks were adapted from the Mayo Clinic Test of Apraxia,
and included (a) sustained phonation of vowels, (b) dia-
dochokinesis--syllables, (c) word and sentence repetition,
(d) picture description, and (e) a reading passage. Each
subject performed the tasks twice, once without and once with
binaural white-noise masking of 85-90dB (SPL). Subjects were
instructed not to increase vocal loudness during the masking
condition and, subjectively, the examiners judged loudness
to be approximately equal for both conditions. Two subjects
completed the masking condition on day 1 and the non-masking
condition on day 2, the other two subjects vice versa. All
sessions were recorded on audio-tape and complete transcripts
were made. Comparative tasks (with and without masking) were
analyzed spectrographically.

RESULTS

Analyses of sonagrams, tape recordings, and transcripts provided evidence pertinent to (a) specific phonetic transition effects and (b) general continuity effects of masking noise. First, findings specific to ease of phonetic transitions in the masking condition are as follows: (1) Comparative sona- grams revealed that, in the masking condition, formant transi- tions from and toward consonant targets more closely approxi- mated patterns seen on sonagrams for normal speakers for: (a) CVC syllable production tasks and (b) segments of connected speech. (2) Second-formant hubs appeared to be more "clearly defined" in the masking condition. (3) Response latencies were audibly shorter in the masking condition. (4) Transcripts and audio-recordings showed that there were fewer false-starts while initiating an utterance in the masking condition.

Second, several changes were observed in the masking condition which seem more germane to prosodic effects (melody, general continuity) than to specific phonetic transition effects: (1) In the masking condition, multi-syllabic words more closely approximated correct phonetic structure, stress pattern, and number of syllables. (2) On listening to com- parative word-strings with and without masking, sentence prosody more closely approximated that of normal speech in the masking condition. (3) All subjects produced more words and more different words for picture descriptions in the mask- ing condition (Table 2), suggesting that masking seemed to enhance ease of productive language diversity.

DISCUSSION

Preliminary findings should be regarded with caution, and the results reported here should be considered as hypotheses which may or may not be verified by more extensive research. To the extent that further research supports these results, however, this study seems to lend some credence to a model which describes stuttering and apraxia as disturbances of similar speech and language operations. If masking has a favorable influence on fluency in apraxia of speech, how might this effect be explained? Does alteration of <u>feedback</u> offer a cogent explanation? Upon finding that masking had no significant impact on accuracy of phoneme production in appractics, Deal (1970) suggested that ". . . in apraxia of speech the motor system is not capable of proper functioning regardless of the effects of auditory feedback."

It may be more fruitful to examine the possibility of a feed-forward operation. Wingate's (1970) analysis suggests that neither feedback nor "distraction" offer tenable explanations for the improved fluency of stutterers under masking. He suggested that masking may promote fluency because it "induces certain changes in vocalization." It is reasonable to consider that masking may have a similar forward-flowing effect on the production efforts of apractics. Theoretically, at least two neural operations could account for fluency facilitation under masking: (1) Masking may provide an activation (above threshold) of neuronal patterns feeding into motor speech outlets. (2) Masking may occupy neuronal patterns which otherwise disrupt the integrity of motor speech outlets. The phrase "neuronal pattern" here refers to a functional neural assemblage serving language production--for example, engram, cell-assembly, or hologram (Pribram, 1971).

Finally, the authors would like to suggest that if it is found that a large number of stuttering and apractic errors occur on similar phonetic strings--if they are "context-sensitive" disorders--this may shed some light on a core question facing speech scientists: What is the most difficult phonetic string to say? There would appear to be two feasible, but contradictory answers to this question: (1) Maximal Distance: extreme excursions of the articulators are the hardest to say. This is the principle underlying the common use of "pa-ta-ka" to test the functional integrity of the speech mechanism. (2) Minimal Distinctiveness: slight excursions of the articulators are the hardest to say. This is the principle underlying "tongue twister" construction. It should be instructive to investigate the extent to which one or the other of these principles accounts for the bulk of (a) stutterings, (b) apractic errors, and (c) errors in normal speech.

REFERENCES

Agnello, J. (1975). New York, NY: Speech Hear. Inst.
Deal, J. (1970). Paper, Amer. Speech Hear. Assn.
Jakobson, R. (1972). Scient. Amer., 227:72-80.
Hamre, C. (1972). Brit. J. Dis. of Comm., 148-150.
Hamre, C. (1976). Paper Amer. Speech Hear. Assn.
Orton, S. (1937). New York, Norton.
Porch, B. (1967). Palo Alto, Consult. Psycho.
Pribram, K. (1971). Englewood Cliffs: Prentice-Hall.
Saunders, K. (1962). Baltimore: Johns Hopkins.
Wingate, M. (1970). J. Speech Hear. Res., 13:861-873.

Table 1. Overlapping phenomenology: stuttering and apraxia
of speech.

A. Core feature: Transcient phonetic transition disability
B. Lexical integrity, but motor pattern of word momentarily
    unavailable
C. Neuromuscular integrity, although dysarthric disturbances
    may be present in addition to the stuttering of apraxia
D. Inconsistent phonemic errors
E. Greatest production difficulty:
    1. language of high propositionality
    2. initiating an utterance
    3. nouns, adjectives, adverbs, verbs
    4. positively correlated with word length
    5. when "anxious"
    6. stressed syllables (not experimentally verified for
        apraxia, but predicted based on clinical observation)
F. Least production difficulty:
    1. "Automatic" utterances
    2. Repetitions of an utterance (some individual and
        situational variability reported)
    3. Singing
G. Individual variability on ability to predict loci of
    errors ("expectancy")
H. Effective treatment strategies:
    1. Facilitating ability to initiate utterances easily
    2. Improving effectiveness of "groping" for phonetic
        transitions
    3. Utilizing linguistic and situational hierarchies

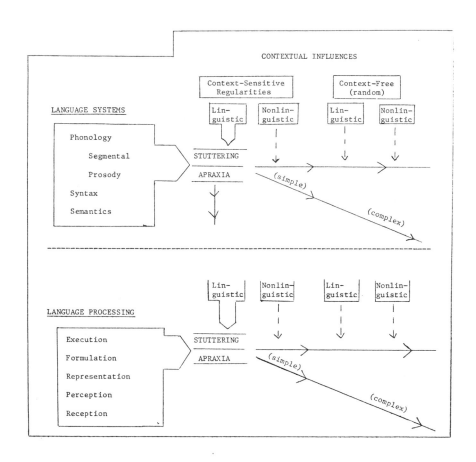

FIGURE 1:   A Language Systems and Processing (LSP)

Model of Stuttering and Apraxia

Table 2. Type/token ratios for picture descriptions of four apractic speakers with and without masking noise.

	With Masking				Without Masking		
Subjects	Number of Words	Number Different Words	Type/Token Ratio	Subjects	Number of Words	Number Different Words	Type/Token Ratio
1	94	57	60.6	1	80	39	48.7
2	133	60	45.1	2	127	38	29.9
3	70	43	61.4	3	58	25	43.1
4	82	44	53.6	4	65	28	43.0
Mean:	94.8	51	55.2		82.5	32.5	41.2

EXPERIMENTS AND OBSERVATIONS MADE USING A REAL-TIME SPECTRUM ANALYZER (RTA): ONE FORMANT VOWELS AND FORMANT MERGER

ANTTI IIVONEN
University of Helsinki

In this paper the following issues are treated: (1) a real-time spectrum analysis for phonetic applications is described, (2) vowel spectra which consist of only one formant peak or in which several formant peaks are observed, but in which two close formants have been merged into each other, are discussed and (3) consequences of these observations for a perceptual theory are treated in connection with preliminary synthesis experiments using one formant vowel stimuli.

On the Properties of a RTA

The real-time spectrum analysis equipment available at the University of Oulu is described in Figure 1. Several alternative regulations concerning the time and frequency resolution make adequate selections for spectral studies possible. This means that successive spectra can be displayed and measured e.g. in 5 or 10 msec. time intervals. Satisfactory time resolution is achieved by means of a sweep limit control which limits a cut off frequency (e.g. 4000 Hz for vowel analysis) from a selectable total frequency range (e.g. 50 or 20 kHz). The analyzer applies 500 filter channels. If all channels are used, a new spectrum can be resolved in 50 msec. The sweep limit technique makes it possible that a lower channel number can be selected. Because every channel

needs 100 microseconds for analysis, the time interval
between successive spectra depends on the total amount of
the channels below the cut off frequency. If the total
frequency range is 20 kHz and the sweeping upper limit is
set at 4000 Hz, the time interval between successive spectra
is 10 msec, because only 100 channels are involved. For
varying problems varying selections concerning the time
resolution and the frequency upper limit can be made (see
also Iivonen, 1975). So far three different subroutines
are available. They can be outputted numerically and
graphically. The graphical outputs are presented in Figure 2.
The graphical registration of single spectra needs about 3
seconds. A numerical representation of a spectrum (i.e.,
teletype output) containing ca. 30 data points (i.e. Hz and
dB values, see e.g. Figure 3) takes ca. 20 seconds.

One Peak Vowels Observed Using Sound Sonagraph and RTA

Several one peak back vowels (i.e. vowels consisting
of one observable spectral peak) are observed earlier by
means of the sound sonagraph (e.g. Iivonen, 1970, concerning
the German /u:/ and /U/ p. 63, practically also /o:/ and
/ɔ/ p. 61, and in some cases also /a:/ p. 82-83). One peak
vowels are more frequent in female than in male voices because of the lower density of partial tones (see the examples
in Figure 4). In several cases the acoustic output of the
Finnish /uu/ as in suu 'mouth' shows only one single peak
(see Figure 4). Only in a part of these cases the RTA is
able to show the second formant in one or two of the successive spectra during the steady state of u. The higher formant
peaks are often totally lacking. Some speakers produce u
spectra containing clear formants F1 and F2.

Merger of Two Close Formants

In several cases realizations of front vowels of the
type ø, y, or e show the merger of the formants F2 and F3.
It also happens frequently that all the higher formants of a
i type vowel (i.e. formants F2, F3, and F4) form one single
broad "peak" (see the example of Figure 5 and Iivonen 1970
concerning the German /y:/ and /e:/ p. 57 as well as /ɛ:/

p. 86). See also Ladefoged's suggestion for measurement of
formants with peak coincidence 1967, p. 87. It seems that
the merger of formant peaks is an individual property or is
due to the sound environment. It is also more frequent in
female than in male voices. It is, however, true that the
merger is possible also in male voices. Inspite of the
merger this kind of vowels are recognized correctly and they
sound quite natural. They must therefore be explainable also
in our perceptual vowel theory.

Experiments with Synthetic One
Formant Back Vowels

In natural vowels which show only one spectral peak
actually two formants (poles) can be assumed to exist on the
production level (i.e., resonatory). In speech synthesis,
however, such stimuli can be produced from which one or more
formants are removed. Very preliminary experiments with
the formant generator OVE Ic the responses of five listeners
to one formant stimuli simulating mainly the back vowels were
compared with responses to two formant stimuli. Fifty-eight
stimuli with constant 300 msec. duration and 100 Hz fundamental frequency were classified by five listeners (forced
choice including Finnish a, e, i, o, u, y, ä=ae, or ö=∅).
Fifteen from the stimuli were one formant vowels (see Figure
6).

Before the perception tests the stimuli were analyzed
with RTA. The analysis showed in some cases deviations from
the selected values and besides some distortions appeared
(e.g. some spurious higher spectral peaks when F1 was high).
Special attention was paid on these cases. They also explain
some of the exceptional responses in Figure 7 which shows
the responses with curves connecting identical responses (the
lowest area contains the responses a, ä, i, and e. The
listeners could also indicate, if a response was "sure,"
"preferred," or if the stimulus sounded as "unnatural"
(i.e. totally inhuman). Following results were obtained:
(1) The synthesized one formant vowels can be identified as
vowels (majority in our test as back vowels). (2) From the
6 x 15 one formant vowel responses 11 were classified as
"unnatural," and 22 from them as "sure." (3) Individual

differences were observed in the responses (see Figure 7).
(4) The same listener showed different responses when the
test was repeated (see Figure 7, subject TN). (5) The one
formant vowels were identified seemingly without influence
of the lacking F2, i.e., the cue for the listeners was the
same frequency level of Fl as in the two formant stimuli.

Further experiments with modified arrangements are in
progress. The results with analysis and synthesis seem to
indicate that we should pay special attention on the formant
merger and on its special case, one peak vowels. We should
also explain them within our perceptual vowel theory. It
might be reasonable to suggest that although the vowels can
be described and distinguished on a Fl/F2 plane, the Fl/F2
plane contains redundancy considering the back vowels.

REFERENCES

Iivonen, A.   (1970).   Comment. Hum. Lit. 45.
Iivonen, A.   (1975).   8th Int. Cong. Phon. Sci., Leeds.
Ladefoged, P.   (1967).   London.

ACKNOWLEDGEMENTS

Support was provided by the University of Oulu, the Finnish
Academy, and Mr. Urpo Kasurinen.

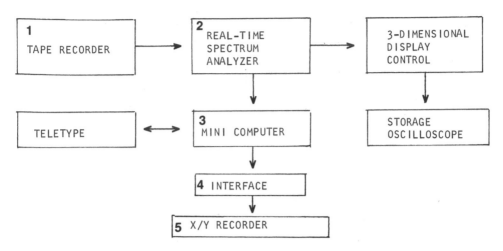

FIGURE 1.   Combination of the devices used in real-time
            speech analysis for phonetic applications.

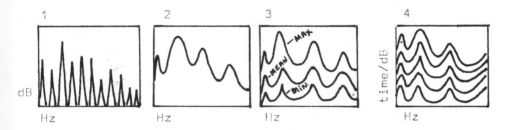

FIGURE 2.   Subroutines in the spectral processing.   (1) short
            time spectrum of a single spectrum (narrow band up
            till 150 Hz), (2) envelope with variable smooth-
            ness, (3) variability within an unlimited number
            of spectra (= min/max/mean representation), (4)
            temporally successive spectra with changeable
            time interval.

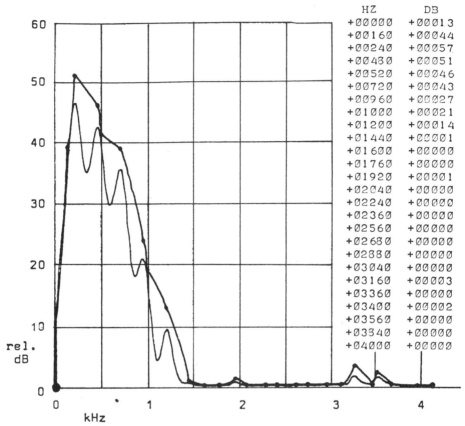

FIGURE 3. A German vowel /o:/ in Monden produced by a female speaker 80. Upper curve: envelope of the
spectrum. Lower curve: narrow band short time
spectrum. On the right: numerical representation (= teletype output) of the envelope, i.e.,
"turning points" indicating the Hz and dB values.
Practically only one formant peak is observable.
Please note also that there is no total fit with
numbers and figure because of the difficulties
in calibrating the x/y recorder. The dB value
13 in the first channel is due to a distortion
caused by the basic frequency of the electric
current.

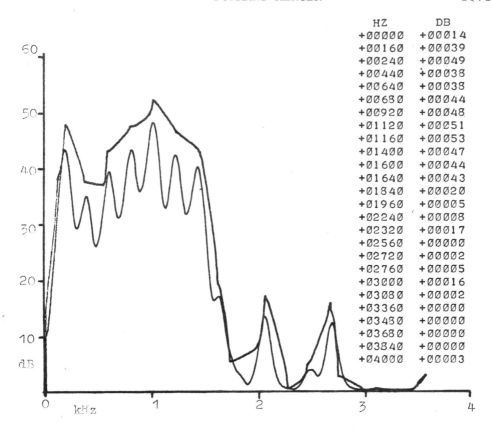

HZ	DB
+00000	+00014
+00160	+00039
+00240	+00049
+00440	+00038
+00640	+00038
+00680	+00044
+00920	+00048
+01120	+00051
+01160	+00053
+01400	+00047
+01600	+00044
+01640	+00043
+01840	+00020
+01960	+00005
+02240	+00008
+02320	+00017
+02560	+00000
+02720	+00002
+02760	+00005
+03000	+00016
+03080	+00002
+03360	+00000
+03480	+00000
+03680	+00000
+03840	+00000
+04000	+00003

FIGURE 4.   A German vowel /a/ in <u>machen</u> produced by a female
            speaker BD. Note that the strong maximum of F$_0$,
            which usually occurs in mid and open back vowels
            is not treated as formant. Note also that the
            formants F1 and F2 practically form one single
            maximum. In the example also the formants F3 and
            F4 are observable.

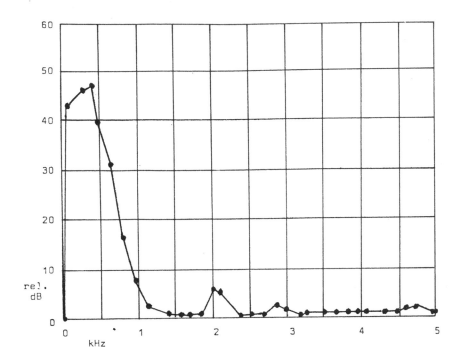

FIGURE 5.

Envelope of a sustained isolated vowel u̱ produced
by the author (Finnish, male). The spectrum shows
no separate F1 and F2. Similar cases can be observed in natural Finnish utterances.

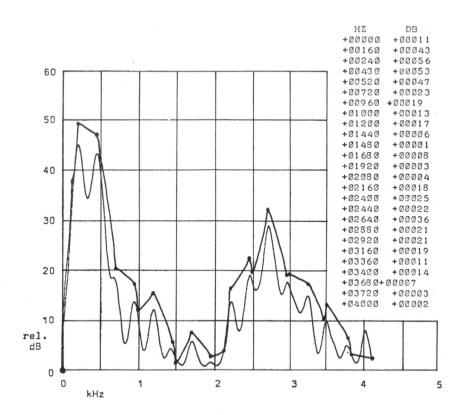

HZ	DB
+00000	+00011
+00160	+00043
+00240	+00056
+00430	+00053
+00520	+00047
+00720	+00023
+00960	+00019
+01000	+00013
+01200	+00017
+01440	+00006
+01480	+00001
+01680	+00008
+01920	+00003
+02080	+00004
+02160	+00018
+02400	+00025
+02440	+00022
+02640	+00036
+02880	+00021
+02920	+00021
+03160	+00019
+03360	+00011
+03400	+00014
+03680	+00007
+03720	+00003
+04000	+00002

FIGURE 6.

A German vowel /e:/ in <u>Wesen</u> produced by a female
speaker BD. Note that the formants F2 and F3
have a common spectral peak.

one formant (F1) vowels

two formant vowels

Hz					
300	u	ö ö y ö ö u u u	o	ö ö u u u u u u	y	y y y y u u u u
350	ö		u		u	
400	ö	ö ö ö ö o o u u	o	ö o u a o o o o	u	ö ö u ö u o u o
450	ö		o		o	
500	a	ö e a o o a ä	a	ä a a a a o a	o	ö ä ö o o o o
550	a		a		a	
600	a	a a a a a a	a	a a a a a ä	a	a a a a a y
650	a		a		a	
700	ä	a a a a a	a	a a a a a	ä	a a a a a
750	ä		a		ä	
800	ä	a a o a	a	a a ä a	a	a a ä a
850	ä		a		ä	
900	ä	a o ä EL, female	a	a a a HK, male	a	e a a SL, male
950	a		a		a	
1000	a	a ö	a	a -	a	a ä

Hz					
300	u	a y y - a u u u	u	ö y y u u u u	u	y y y u u u u u
350	ö		ö		u	
400	ö	ö ö u ö o o u o	u	ö ö u ö u o o o	o	ö ö o ö o o o o
450	e		ö		o	
500	ö	ö ö a a o o o	ö	ö ä ö o o o o	o	ö ö a a a o o
550	a		ä		a	
600	a	ö ä a a a a	a	ä ä a a a o	o	a a a a a a
650	a		a		a	
700	ä	ä ö a a ä	ä	ä ä a a a	a	a a a a a
750	a		ä		a	
800	-	a a ä a	ä	ä a e ä	a	a a a a
850	ä		ä		a	
900	ä	ä ä i TN1, female	ö	i ä ä TN2	a	a - - AI, male
950	a		ä		a	(author)
1000	a	a i	ä	ä i	-	a -

Hz 1300 1200 1100 1000 900 800 700 600   1300 1200 1100 1000 900 800 700 600   1300 1200 1100 1000 900 800 700 600

F2   F2   F2

FIGURE 7.

Responses of five listeners to synthetic one formant and two
formant stimuli produced by an Ove Ic synthesizer. Note that
the one formant vowels were produced with 50 Hz, the others
with 100 Hz intervals. The lines connect identical responses.
The lowest area includes - however - the responses /a, ä, i,
and e/. The circle indicates an exceptional response. Note
that /ä/ corresponds roughly to an /æ/; /ö/ corresponds to
/œ/ and /ø/. "-" means: decision impossible.

SPEECH SYNTHESIS BY RULE USING THE FOVE PROGRAM

FRANCES INGEMANN
University of Kansas and Haskins Laboratories

A program for speech synthesis which uses the OVE III synthesizer (Liljencrants, 1968) to generate the acoustic output signal has been developed at Haskins Laboratories. This program called FOVE has been designed to allow the user who is not a computer programmer to test various acoustic-phonetic rules for speech synthesis. FOVE is based on the OVEBORD program designed by Kuhn (1973), which in its turn was developed from a modified Holmes-Mattingly algorithm (Holmes et al., 1964; Mattingly, 1968). Because speech can be synthesized without delay as soon as a set of rules is available and a phonetic text has been typed in, a researcher can work on the rules interactively by making a minor modification, listening to the output to determine the effect of the change, and deciding whether to retain the modification or to make other changes.

Table 1 shows the components used to synthesize speech. The input for a text consists of phonetic symbols for English phonemes, two stress marks and three kinds of intonation marks. Acoustic values for the phonetic symbols are assigned by a set of tables (one or more for each phonetic symbol), allophone rules, and invariant internal rules not accessible to the user for processing these user-specified variables.

Each table provides values for all the parameters on OVE III except the fundamental frequency. OVE III parameters with their ranges and steps are listed in Table 2. The phoneme table also provides values for durations (numbers 4-8 in Table 1) and transitions (numbers 23-78). In addition, the

phoneme table assigns each phoneme a so-called distinctive
feature number, whereby sounds can be grouped into traditional phonetic classifications for use in allophone rules
and to determine which of two adjacent phonemes will provide
weighting and durational values for transitions. Mattingly
(1968) has described the assignment and use of these distinctive feature numbers in the program from which OVEBORD and
FOVE are both derived.

Allophone rules allow any of the values of the phoneme
tables to be changed in specified environments. The set of
environments available is basically the same as that given
in Mattingly (1968). Prosodic information is provided by
the stress and intonation markers. Durational differences are
specified by allophone rules. Fundamental frequencies are
determined by 12 pitch specifications. Three of these provide an initial frequency and the range within which the frequency may vary. The remaining 9 are associated in a complex
way with the major stress mark (the minor stress mark has no
effect on fundamental frequency) and intonation markers. Six
of the pitch specifications determine the steps by which the
frequency may rise or fall in relation to the presence or
absence of major stress marks. The remaining three specify
the final frequency contour starting at the last major stress.
There are, in addition, rules which the user may not vary that
do such things as determine syllable boundaries, location of
tonic syllable, and dominance of one phoneme table over another
for purposes of deciding transition values.

To see how well speech could be synthesized using this
program and to determine which values are most suitable for
the phoneme tables and which allophone rules are needed, I
have been working as time has permitted since 1974 on a set of
rules. Periodically, the rules have been tested on listeners
unfamiliar with synthetic speech to find out what progress was
being made and to see what specific sounds remained in need of
improvement. The overall results of these tests are given in
Table 3. An example of the kind of speech synthesized by rule
in early 1977 is the following passage which contains the instructions for the CMU sentences whose intelligibility scores
are reported at the top of Table 3. (A recording of the synthetic speech was played at this point.)

The CMU sentences are based (with minor modifications
to split very long sentences into two shorter ones) on those
devised by Shockey (1974) at Carnegie-Mellon University.
They contain all the phonemes of English in at least two
environments. The sentences are meaningful but frequently
odd so that correct responses are more dependent on correct
phoneme identification than they might be in more predictable
sentences. Listeners unfamiliar with synthetic speech were
asked to write down the sentences after hearing each sentence
spoken twice. By 1977, listeners to FOVE-generated synthetic
speech were able to get 84% of the words correct and, when
intended phonemes were matched with responses, 91% of the
phonemes correct, with vowels scoring slightly better than
consonants.

Somewhat lower scores were obtained on the Mitchell test
(Mitchell, 1974) for words in isolation which were heard only
once. The Mitchell test consists of 4 lists of 50 monosyllabic
words each, designed to test 22 consonants in initial position,
13 consonants in final position, and 15 vowels and diphthongs.
The listener is presented with a choice of five words differing
only in one or two distinctive features. Because the test was
originally devised to be used with natural speech to assess
hearing impairments or transmission systems, the choices did
not always make provision for the kind of errors listeners
make with synthetic speech. For this reason, listeners were
allowed to write down another answer if none of the words on
the answer sheet corresponded to what they heard. Only the
specific sound being tested in each word was scored. Under
these conditions, phonemes were only 86% correct in contrast
to 91% in sentences.

Because the CMU sentences contained very few examples
of some sounds and some are omitted entirely from the Mitchell
lists, for the 1976 rules a new set of 24 phonetically diverse
(PD) sentences was devised to contain additional tokens of
sounds poorly represented in the CMU sentences and new contexts for all sounds. Although not so intended, these sentences turned out to be considerably easier as a set than the
CMU sentences, scoring 88% word intelligibility with 92%
phonemes correct. When scores are that high, it is difficult
to detect improvement and so the set as a whole was not used
for further testing. However, a subset of the PD sentences

was formed by eliminating all but one of the sentences which had had fewer than two errors in the 1976 test. In addition, a few long sentences were shortened to delete clauses or phrases on which no errors had been made. The number of sentences constituting the new subset PD sentences (labeled SPD in Table 2) was thirteen. These sentences scored about the same on the 1977 rules as did the CMU sentences, with a slightly higher word correct score and a slightly lower phoneme score.

The last set of sentences reported in Table 3 are 50 syntactically normal nonsense sentences taken from Nye and Gaitenby (1974). These sentences consist of four mono-syllabic English words in the frame 'The _____ _____ _____ the _____'; for example, 'The short arm sent the cow.' These sentences reduce the ability to predict the test words on a semantic basis. It should be noted, however, that a semantic effect could not be avoided entirely: a number of listener errors were in the direction of making the sentences meaning-ful. In this test the listeners were presented with the sentence frame on the answer sheet and asked to fill in the four blanks after hearing each sentence only once.

Two scores are given for these sentences. The first scores were obtained when the listeners heard these sentences at the beginning of the test session. The second scores are for the same sentences when they were preceded by 10 similar sentences used to test natural versus rule durations (Ingemann, 1977). Comparison of the two scores reveals an obvious learn-ing effect. A second point to be noted is that although the word scores are somewhat lower than the meaningful sentences (77% and 82% in contrast to 84% for CMU sentences and 85% for SPD sentences), the phonemes were correctly identified at approximately the same rate in all three sets of sentences.

Another test involved extended listening to find out how well listeners could understand and obtain information from synthetic speech. A test comparing the 1974 rules with other synthesis versions and natural speech has been reported in Nye et al. (1975). Only the results for 1974 rules, which scored the highest of the synthesis versions tested, will be summarized here.

Two texts from a published reading test for college-bound and college students were synthesized. One text was approximately 2000 words in length and the other 1700. Natural speech recordings of a male speaker were used as a control. Each listener heard one text synthesized and the other text in natural speech. After hearing a text played through once without interruption, the listeners were required to answer fourteen multiple choice questions. Listeners were allowed to selectively replay passages and check off answers until they were confident that all the questions had been answered correctly. The time the listeners took to answer the questions (including the replay time) was recorded. The results in Table 4 show that there is little difference between natural speech and the 1974 rules. The apparent superiority of synthetic speech is not significant because the variance of the data is so large (only 6 listeners heard the 1974 rule version of the synthetic speech). This kind of test has not been repeated for more recent versions of the rules but there is no reason to believe that the quality of speech generated by FOVE would be any poorer.

It would appear then that FOVE is capable of producing speech which is fairly intelligible, especially after a short period of adaptation. There is, however, still room for improvement.

Certainly some of this improvement can be achieved through better specification of the variable available in the FOVE program. But progress will be slow and totally acceptable speech will not be achieved because of limitations of both the hardware synthesizer and the program. A few of these limitations are mentioned below.

Although OVE III produces remarkably good vowels, it does not provide parameters for making nasals and fricatives which closely match real speech. Voiced fricatives are especially poor. There is also the problem of clicks which occur when the periodic (voicing) source is turned off in the middle of a cycle. Within the program, the major source of frustration is the limited number of environments for which allophone rules can be written. It is simply not possible to specify certain allophonic variants. For others, it becomes necessary to resort to labyrinthine solutions. For example, it may be

necessary to specify a minor allophone in the phoneme table
and then have a series of rules to change values to the major
allophone in a variety of other environments which are provided by the program. Even worse is the situation in which,
in order to produce a modification in a limited environment,
there must first be a change in a larger context and then one
or more rules to change values back to their original specifications in all but the desired context. Not only are such
contorted manipulations undesirable on general principles,
but because there is a limit on the total number of allophone
rules, once the space is used up no further allophone rules
may be written.

Related to the difficulties with the allophone rules is
the assignment of distinctive feature numbers which determine
which transition values will be used between phonemes. Since
the distinctive feature numbers are part of the phoneme table,
it is easy to change the number originally assigned to a
phoneme by the programmer. However, in so doing, the allophone rule environments also change since the environments
have been specified internally in the program by distinctive
feature numbers. Thus, advantages achieved in dominance are
offset by the loss of certain environments for allophone rules.

There are also problems related to the automatic syllable
division of FOVE. These can be overcome by inserting word
boundaries wherever necessary and writing allophone rules for
word final and word initial allophones, but then any other
rules related to word boundary will also apply. Further
problems arise with pitch assignment. Pitch automatically
rises on syllables with a major stress, making English sound
like a pitch accent language in which pitch rises on accented
syllables. Furthermore, there are problems with final contours because the same pitch specification is used as a component of more than one contour. There is also difficulty in
finding single values which are acceptable for both sentences
in which a major stress is on the last syllable and sentences
in which the last major stress is followed by a number of
syllables.

Given a working program which already produces relatively
good speech, it might be worthwhile modifying FOVE to give

the user access to the component of the program which determines allophone environments. For the production of more
natural pitch changes, the user also needs greater control
over the fundamental frequency as well. With these kinds of
modifications, I believe significant improvements could be
made rather quickly in FOVE synthesis by rule. However, some
problems would still remain. The decision was reached at
Haskins Laboratories that rather than spend time modifying the
existing system, the point had been reached to take what had
been learned from FOVE and to design a new program. Accordingly, a new program operating on different principles from
its predecessor is now under development (Cooper et al.
1978). This program is based on user defined and internal
rules that give greater weight to the integrity of the
syllable as a unit of speech production. When this new program is available, further work will be necessary to assess
its speech quality in relation to FOVE and other synthesis
systems.

REFERENCES

Cooper, F. S., Gaitenby, J. H., Ingemann, F. et al. (1977).
    Bull. Pros. Res. BPR 10-27:185-187.
Cooper, F. S., Gaitenby, J. H., Ingemann, F. et al. (1978).
    Bull. Pros. Res. BPR 10-28 (in press).
Holmes, J. N., Mattingly, I. G., and Shearme, J. N. (1964).
    Lang. Speech, 7:127-143.
Ingemann, F. (1977). J. Acoust. Soc. Am., 62:S62.
Kuhn, G. M. (1973). J. Acoust. Soc. Am., 54:339.
Liljencrants, J. C. W. A. (1968). IEEE Trans. Audio Electro-
    coust., AU-16:137-140.
Mattingly, I. G. (1968). Supp. Haskins Lab. SR 33.
Mitchell, P. D. (1974). J. Acoust. Soc. Am., 55.S55.
Nye, P. W. and Gaitenby, J. H. (1974). Haskins Lab. SR
    37/38:169-190.
Nye, P. W., Ingemann, F. and Donald, L. (1975). Haskins
    Lab. SR 41:117-126.
Shockey, L. (1974). ARPA Network Info. Cen., SUR Note 128.

Table 1.   FOVE program for synthesizing speech using an OVE
            III synthesizer.

   I.   Input: phonemic transcription consisting of English
        phonemes plus two stress marks and three types of
        intonation marks.

  II.   User specified values.

        A.   Phoneme tables

             1.   Name
             2.   Second name
             3.   Distinctive feature number
             4.   Duration (in time frames, usually 6 msec. each)
             5.   Initial voicing
             6.   Final hiss
             7.   Final friction
             8.   Hiss for initial portion of following segment

                  Values for OVE III Control Parameters
             9.   Amplitude of hiss
            10.   Amplitude of formant buzz
            11.   F1 frequency
            12.   F2 frequency
            13.   F3 frequency
            14.   F1 bandwidth
            15.   F2 bandwidth
            16.   F3 bandwidth
            17.   Amplitude of nasal buzz
            18.   Frequency of nasal buzz
            19.   Amplitude of friction
            20.   Pole/zero ratio
            21.   Fricative pole 1 frequency
            22.   Fricative pole 2 frequency

                  Weighting of adjacent values to determine
                  boundary values
            23-36. Weight of present phoneme values (9-22)
            37-50. Weight of adjacent phoneme values (9-22)

                  (Table 1. continued on next page)

Table 1 (continued)

Transition durations
    51-64. Duration of transitions for parameters 9-22
            in the present phoneme
    65-78. Duration of transitions for parameters 9-22
            in the adjacent phoneme

B. User specified values

C. Internal rules which include

    1. Dominance of one phoneme over another
    2. Syllabification
    3. Location of tonic syllable and resultant pitch
        assignments.

Table 2. Summary of OVE III synthesis parameters

Parameter	Range	Step
Fundamental frequency	50-315 Hz	.8%
Amplitude of Hiss formants	0-30 db	2 db
Amplitude of periodic source	0-31.5 db	.5 db
First formant	200-1260 Hz	.8%
Second formant	500-3200 Hz	.8%
Third formant	1000-6300 Hz	.8%
F1 bandwidth increment	63-188 Hz	12 Hz
F2 bandwidth increment	66-470 Hz	31 Hz
F3 bandwidth increment	76-750 Hz	250 Hz
Nasal amplitude	0-30 db	2 db
Nasal formant	200-1230 Hz	3%
Fricative amplitude	0-30 db	2 db
Pole/zero ratio	0-31.5 db	.5 db
Fricative formant 1	1000-6200 Hz	3%
Fricative formant 2	2500-15700 Hz	3%

Table 3.   Percent correct for three sets of rules on various
           intelligibility tests.

	1974 Rules	1976 Rules	1977 Rules
CMU Sentences			
Words	75%	81%	84%
Phonemes	83%	86%	91%
Consonants	81%	86%	90%
Vowels	85%	88%	93%
Mitchell Lists			
22 Initial Cons.	78%	79%	79%
13 Final Cons.	77%	79%	84%
15 Vowels and			
Diphthongs	97%	96%	99%
Total	84%	84%	86%
PD Sentences			
Words		88%	
Phonemes		92%	
SPD Sentences			
Words			85%
Phonemes			89%
Syntactically Normal			
Nonsense Sentences			
Words			77, 82%
Phonemes			89, 91%

Table 4.   Average time spent answering questions and number of
           errors in a listening comprehension test.

	Time	Errors
1974 Rules (N = 6)	4.30 min.	2.0
Natural Speech (N = 24)	4.52 min.	2.29

ON THE HISTORY OF QUANTITY IN GERMANIC

ANATOLY LIBERMAN
University of Minnesota

This paper is a synopsis of a much longer work. It aims
at gathering up the broadest facts of the complex history of
quantity in Germanic and dispenses with references to previous scholarship only due to lack of space. As regards the
Scandinavian background of my exposition, the reader may
consult: Liberman, 1976 and 1977.

There can be little doubt that at the earliest recon-
structible stages Germanic dialects were mora-counting. The
fact that, by Sievers's law, Gothic <u>mikiljan</u> is prosodically
equal to <u>domjan/wandjan</u> (<u>mikileiþ</u> and <u>domeiþ</u>/<u>wandeiþ</u> are both
opposed to <u>wasjiþ</u>) proves that two short syllables in Gothic
were tantamount to one long, which is the best indication of
mora-counting. The same numerical rule (resolution of a long
syllable) prevailed in skaldic poetry. In West Germanic, two
short syllables were also equal to a long one: cf. the results of prehistoric apocope (traditionally, but erroneously,
called syncope), by which a word like Old English <u>feld</u> dropped
its final syllable, while <u>sŭnŭ</u> remained disyllabic.

Mora-counting is especially well known from ancient Greek
and Latin. Both are dead languages and cannot be heard today,
so that mora-counting presents itself to a twentieth-century
scholar merely as a mechanism regulating the distribution of
"tones" or "dynamic stress." Similarly, in Germanic studies
mora-counting (if recognized) is at best viewed as a rule
which allowed skalds to resolve a long syllable, determined
the shape of Gothic endings, or truncated the final syllable

of feld while sparing /u/ in sunu. It is not clearly
realized that if a long syllable is phonologically divisible
into two moras, there must also be a phonetic tool whereby
to carry out this division. Ideally, a bimoric vowel is
actually cut into two parts. In one modern Germanic language
a tool endowed with the function of splitting a vowel is
still extant. The language is Danish, and the tool is stød.

Modern Danish is no longer a classic mora-counting
language; however, the stød brings out the equation: a long
vowel = a short vowel + a resonant (or a short vowel + any
voiced consonant), for only they can serve the stød's basis.
The antiquity of the stød is a debatable problem, but, if my
reconstruction of Scandinavian accents (1976) is correct and
if the geminates by Holtzmann's law are really cases of the
oralized stød, then the stød goes back to Proto-Scandinavian,
and the "tones" of Swedish and Norwegian are a late development. It is easy to prove that all Germanic languages preserved mora-counting till their "middle" periods, for apocope
which started everywhere approximately between the 13th and
15th centuries originally depended on the length of the root
syllable, exactly as in ancient West Germanic. Some additional facts from Scandinavian dialects with level stress
testify to the same (Liberman, 1977).

The end of mora-counting is the main event in the history
of Germanic quantity. It was brought about by apocope and
must have progressed in a similar way in all "middle" Germanic
languages. The picture is comparatively easy to reconstruct
only for Scandinavian. Scandinavian apocope began in disyllabic
words whose root contained a long sonorous sound. These were
also words with the stød. As a natural result of this process,
the stød was largely banished into monosyllables and due to
this incident became their marker. This function was alien to
the stød, and the stød could not cope with the new role and
perished altogether (it became an unmarked accent 1, while
no-stød was elevated to a marked accent 2), but in Danish it
survived, though weakened by the necessity to do two things
at once: to be a peripheral mora-counting device in monosyllables and an indicator of monosyllables, whose monosylla-
bicity, once apocope had come to an end, needed no indication.
The stød might also get oralized (as in some Danish dialects)

or turn into juncture (as in the dialects of West Jutland and probably Icelandic, Faroese, and several Swedish and Norwegian dialects, where the counterpart of the West Jutland stød is preaspiration). After the disappearance of the stød, or, better to say, after the completion of apocope, Germanic languages, with a partial exception of Danish, began to count syllables, not moras.

Prior to apocope, Germanic length was the reverse side of moras. Old Germanic did not know long and short vowel phonemes (that contrary to a widespread belief): "long" vowels were bimoric and had stød, while short vowels consisted of one mora. Apocope destroyed mora-counting, and length became a syllabic feature. If we go by Scandinavian data, apocope started in the syllables of the TĀTE or TARE type (see above: T, A, R, E designate any consonant, any long vowel, any sonorous consonant, and an unstressed vowel, respectively), and for TĀTE it resulted in TÃ:T , i.e., TÃT with a circumflex. Later, apocope extended to hundreds of other words, TĂTE among them, but every time it occurred it caused the same process, sc., an apocopated word acquired the same shape as TA:T   (i.e., it lengthened its root vowel and obtained the circumflex). The circumflex could stay on the word for centuries but could vanish as a prosodic entity,and the lengthened vowel in an old open syllable would be the only trace of the change. That open-syllable lengthening was caused by prosodic rather than phonemic forces also follows from English where /e/ could become merged with /ẹ:/ or /ę:/ but could yield a third sound different from both (I prefer to leave out of discussion the problem of /i/›/ē/,/u/›/ō/).

In old monosyllables of the   TA:T   type, with old bimoric vocalics, vowels remained long, though not bimoric. The types TAT:, TA:T: also remained intact. To sum up, right after apocope, Germanic languages must have possessed the following types: (1) TĂT ‹TÃT,   (2) TĀTT ‹TÃTT and TAT₁T₂,   (3) TĀT TÃT,   (4) TĀT ‹TÃTE, TĂTE,   (5) TĂTT TĂTT. There were few words of type (2) and not too many of type (1), so that most syllables at that epoch were long (it must be remembered that a TĂT noun would become disyllabic in declension). This purely statistical fact caused a great upheaval, at least in Scandinavian, viz. lengthening of short-syllable words

represented by (1), though this change must have started
after open-syllable lengthening when all TATE words had become
TÃ:T.   The old TĂT words could join type (3) or type (5).
Type (2) also followed suit and shortened its vowel.   The
changes left Scandinavian languages with three types under
the main stress: TA:T, TAT: (or TAT₁T₂) and TÃT.

   In mora-counting languages ties between "long" and
"short" vowels are likely to be very strong for a "short"
vowel is simply a mora, a unit of length, a phonological
(not, of course, an arithmetical) half of a "long" vowel
(the question whether Germanic had trimoric vowels will not
concern us here). This may explain why in the early history
of Germanic vowels there is so much symmetry between short
and long. It is, for instance, hard to account for the
phonologization of the products of Gothic and Old English
breaking, because their environment changed insignificantly
or not at all. For both languages it has been suggested that
phonologization happened under the influence of the long
counterparts of /ɛ/, /ɔ/ (in Gothic) and /ɛa/, /eo/ (in Old
English). This is, to my mind, a plausible hypothesis, given
mora-counting. But when mora-counting had collapsed, the
traditional ties between long and short broke, and it was then
that new-long and new-short vowels (new in the sense that they
were no longer "moric") began to drift in different directions.
From then on short vowels have changed very little and let
long vowels play their own game.

   This game is known as vowel shifts. In a language with
the main type of prosodic opposition /V:C/ vs. / VC:/ a vowel
is either free or checked, not just long or short. The best
manifestation of vocalic freedom is diphthongization. The
Swedish-Norwegian change of ā>ō, ō>ū, ū>ü does not very well
fit this description, but even this abortive shift only became
possible after long vowels had been liberated of their bimoric
value. However, in Scandinavian we find "great" vowel shifts
too, viz., in some dialects of northern Sweden and in literary
Icelandic and Faroese. A vowel is free at the moment when
apocope ousts the stød and destroys mora-counting. It is a
characteristic fact that the only Scandinavian language which
has not undergone even a weak vowel shift is literary Danish,
i.e., the only one which preserved mora-counting and its tool

(the st∅d). Apocope, as pointed out above, begins in words
of a definite phonetic structure and later expands its sphere
of influence. Its universal weapon is the generalization of
the circumflex accompanied by the lengthening of the originally
short-syllable roots. On the other hand, we have seen that
apocope and the end of mora-counting gives a mighty impulse
to vowel shifts. If in the early history of Germanic quantity the major event was apocope and transition from mora-
counting to syllable-counting, in the later epoch (from
middle periods onwards) everything depended upon which
change happened first: the spread of apocope to all or most
of the words of the TATE type and, consequently, vowel-
lengthening in open syllables or a vowel shift. The order
was probably unpredictable. In Scandinavian languages the
vowel shift took place earlier than open-syllable lengthening.
In West Germanic, notably in English, the shift lost the race
to the lengthening (among English scholars who do not usually
compare their data with Scandinavian this fact has created an
illusion that the Great vowel shift was prepared by the open-
syllable lengthening).

But before turning to English we must ascertain whether
the model for the history of Scandinavian quantity outlined
above is at all applicable to West Germanic. At present it
is only possible to offer a tentative solution. Several facts
point to important similarities between Scandinavian and
West Germanic. The main of them are as follows: (1) West
Germanic languages were originally mora-counting and are now
syllable-counting, so somewhere along the way the same
transition must have taken place as in Scandinavian; (2) In
German there exists a large group of dialects with the st∅d
(rheinische Schärfung); (3) In English too we find a degraded
st∅d, sc. the glottal stop.

I believe that,by and large, West Germanic quantity developed along the same lines as Scandinavian and that apocope
and vowel shifts in English and German are processes of the
same nature as in Scandinavian. The main difference lies in
the circumstance that, e.g., in English, where there was a
very strong vowel shift (but comparable with that in Ice-
landic), it occurred later than the emergence of the $\bar{V}\breve{C}:\breve{V}\bar{C}$
opposition (in English, the latter is well represented

by the dialect of "Ormulum"), and the new diphthongs were not drawn into it. The English vowel shift left the language with two types: $V\bar{C}$ vs. $D\check{C}$ (D stands for a diphthong) and thus made nonsense of the $V\bar{C}:V\bar{C}$ opposition. From a historical point of view, the West Germanic correlation of syllable cut (Silbenschnitt) is the correlation of syllable quantity ($\bar{V}\check{C}$ vs. $\check{V}\bar{C}$) destroyed by a late vowel shift. The fall of English geminates was, without doubt, also caused by the vowel shift (not by apocope): a syllable-counting language which had lost the correlation of syllable quantity did no longer need final geminates.

A last remark is in order. All the processes launched by apocope are a possibility, not a necessity. Apocope allowed them to happen, but none of them HAD to take place. For this reason, we still find a whole spectrum of Germanic dialects: some have preserved the $T\check{A}T$ type, in others $T\check{A}T$ has become $T\bar{A}T$, but $T\check{A}TE$ is possible; still others have vowel shifts in the most rudimentary form (or do not know them at all) and permit $T\bar{A}TT$ words as a thousand years ago, etc., etc., so that a student of Germanic can, though in a jerky way, traverse the span of about a millenium remaining in the twentieth century.

REFERENCES

Liberman, A. S. (1976). Arkiv för Nord. Fil., 91:1-32.
Liberman, A. S. (1977). Scand. Stud., 49:1-12.

AUTOMATIC LOCATION OF STRESSED SYLLABLES IN FRENCH

PHILIPPE MARTIN
University of Toronto

Pitch visualizers used as teaching devices could be more effective if the fundamental frequency curves displayed were segmented into syllabic portions. Furthermore, the automatic location of stressed syllables in the sequence would allow to relate the information presented to a theory of intonation which links the melodic contours of stressed syllables to the (surface) syntactic structure of the sentence (Martin, 1975). This paper examines the possibility of such an operation by evaluating the performance, on French material, of algorithms similar to those used for English data. Stress, as any other phonological entity, is difficult to characterize by definite acoustic features. Perceived stress, whose auditory location depends heavily on the particular experiment used to determine it, has been known to be correlated with primary acoustical factors such as intensity, syllabic duration, variation of fundamental frequency, vowel quality, and with some secondary factors such as glottal stop, disjuncture, aspiration and the like, all of which can interact with each other.

Nevertheless, a pilot study was undertaken on a corpus of some 90 French sentences read by two speakers, whose stressed syllables were located by a panel of trained listeners. The sentences used contain most of the possible combinations of V+C in French, and present all the possible arrangements of syntactic structures of up to four stressed syntactic units. The analysed material was processed by an U.V. recorder in order to get a better understanding of the simulated algorithms by visual inspection.

The stressed syllable location problem can be divided
into two parts: (a) segmentation of the speech wave into
syllabic-like units; (b) location of the stressed elements
in the sequences of these pseudo-syllables. Algorithms presented for English usually follow the same path. In its
automatic division into pseudo-syllabic units, Mermelstein
(1975) for instance, proceeds from "convex hulls" given by
a "loudness function" (which is the intensity of a bandwidth
filtered 500-4000 Hz speech wave). Lea (1974) used a peak
tracking algorithm working on the intensity curve of speech
bandpass filtered between 60 and 3000 Hz. The segmentation
of French material into syllabic-like segments uses a closely
related approach; pseudo-syllabic centers were determined
from the intensity peaks (above a certain threshold) of the
bandpass filtered speech wave, and syllable-nuclei were
defined as the regions of intensity lying no more than 4 dB
below the peaks. With the elimination of the very short
nuclei mostly due to the presence of /k/ or /g/ consonants,
the results obtained were quite good with the higher limit of
the "loudness function" being equal to 2500 Hz, and the lower
limit to 400 Hz. The high limit allows the three first formants of all the French vowels to be taken into account by
the loudness function, with a good rejection of fricatives
like /s/ or /ʃ/. With the lower limit equal to 400 Hz
voiced consonants with a high amplitude fundamental and second
harmonic are adequately rejected, except for the case of the
liquid sounds /l/ and /r/, which could be better eliminated
with a higher limit, if this wouldn't produce the complete
attenuation of low first formant vowels such as /u/ and /i/.
A variable limit of approximately 2.5 F_0 would not improve
the performance of the algorithm for female voices.

Besides the wrong segmentation of sequences VlV or VrV,
there is the problem of vocalic linking, where two or even
three consecutive vowels can be syllabic nuclei (ex. "en juin
et en juillet"). In these cases, only a procedure using the
formant data could eventually perform the segmentation, if
the vowels are different. A further pseudo-syllabic division
is realized from the syllabic nuclei according to the CV
pattern, which is the most frequent in French. Once the
syllabic frontiers have been located, an energy integral
algorithm has been used to rank the syllables into decreasing

integrated intensity. This has been shown to be effective in 81% of the cases, and in 87.5% of the cases (217/258 stressed syllables), if the last syllable was always taken as stressed (muphis syntactic constraint). The use of fundamental frequency variations as an extra cue did not seem to bring any improvement for the particular data used.

The analysis of the errors (i.e., number of syllables erroneously taken as stressed) showed that most were caused by the intrinsic low intensity of the /i/ vowel (compared to high intrinsic intensity of a, ã and e) and by the presence of vocalic linking, one of two or three consecutive vowels being stressed. These results are comparable with the rate of correct location of stressed syllables obtained by Lea (1974) for English data. They come close to the optimum auditory results which are about 95%. Nevertheless, it seems that for automatic melodic contour applications such as for teaching purposes, the percentage of correct location should be much better. Since the addition of some other acoustical parameters correlative with stress does not seem worthwhile, a simpler solution would be to give separate information to the algorithm, such as the number of stressed syllables of each sentence, or better, the nature of the vowels in the syllabic sentence as well as the eventual presence of stress on them. The problem of multiple consecutive vowels could be treated in the same way.

The principle of operations for such a teaching machine would involve a 2 channel input: the first of which will provide the speech signal, and the second, digitally coded information about the length of the sentence, the nature and the number of syllables, as well as the location of the units which have to be stressed. The recognition task will then be limited to ensure that the energy integral of the syllables to be stressed, eventually multiplied by a correction factor depending on the intrinsic intensity of some vowels (Lehiste, 1970; Rossi, 1967), is large enough if compared to the average of the energy integral taken for all of the syllables. This approach would provide a relatively simple way to ensure a close to 100% correct recognition, since the only source of error could come from the segmentation algorithm, whose weaknesses could again be corrected by the information fed directly to the program.

REFERENCES

Lea, W. N.   (1974).   Unival Report No P x 10791, St. Paul,
     Sperry Univac.
Lehiste, I.   (1970).   Cambridge, MIT Press.
Martin, Ph.   (1975).   Ling., 146:35-67.
Martin, Ph.   (1978).   Montreal, Didier (In press).
Mermelstein, P.   (1975).   J. Acoust. Soc. Am., 58:880-883.
Rossi, M.   (1967).   Actes Cong. Sci. Phon., Prague, 779-786.

ACOUSTIC CUES AND CONSONANT CLUSTERS

FRANK PARKER
University of British Columbia

Descriptions of phonological change within generative
grammar specify segments in terms of distinctive features
(DF's). Such segments are then said to be inserted, deleted,
or modified in a given environment. For example, devoicing
of a stop in final position would be characterized as:
+ obstruent, - continuant, + voice -------→ (-voice)
/_____#. Such descriptions alone, however, rarely provide
explanations of <u>how</u> and <u>why</u> phonology changes. Thus, it is
not surprising that generative analyses have been the subject
of criticism recently. For example, Chen and Wang state,
"... while the application of the generative model to historical phonology has stimulated remarkable advances in our
ability to state 'diachronic correspondences,' it has shed
precious little light on the mechanism of phonetic change"
(1975:265). The reason that generative descriptions do not
explain change is fairly clear. First, phonological change is
typically context-dependent, but the specification of segments
in terms of DF's is not. For example, in English /b/ in certain positions has been lost: <u>comb</u> < OE <u>camb</u> /kamb/. In
other positions, /b/ has been devoiced: <u>unkempt</u> < OE <u>cemban</u>.
In still other positions, /b/ has remained unchanged: <u>stub</u>
< OE <u>stybb</u>. A DF analysis of the segment /b/ in all of
these words, however, would be the same, namely: (+ obstruent,
- continuant, - coronal, + anterior, + voice). Second, change
must to some extent be considered a function of the physical
speech signal, since it is the one facet of language that the
language learner has direct access to. After exposure to the

signal, the listener apparently internalizes a phonology
based on the inferences he makes about its structure
(Anderson, 1973:776-78). Yet DF's are not part of that
signal. It has been shown repeatedly that "... the formal
properties of phones considered as perceptual entities
(that is, in terms of DF's) are very different from the
formal properties of phones considered as acoustic events
(Fodor, Bever, and Garrett, 1974:299). Moreover, this finding has been shown to hold for infants as well as adults.
Eilers concludes from her study of speech perception in
infants "... that a model of infant speech perception which
assumes innate detectors for abstract linguistic features
fails to account for the infants' differential treatment of
the abstract features in a variety of concrete acoustic
phonetic contexts" (1977:1335). In other words, since
infants can discriminate between two segments in one phonetic
context but not in another, they apparently are not responding
directly to DF's.

Let us consider a specific example of phonological change
which an abstract analysis in terms of DF's can describe but
not explain. In German, voiced stops after nasals have been
devoiced and/or deleted. In particular compare the development of /ŋg/ clusters in Northern German (NG) and in Standard
German (SG) to the relative stability of /ŋk/ clusters in
these dialects.

	/ŋg/ (NG)		/ŋg/ (SG)	
Ding	sing.	pl.	sing.	pl.
'thing'	/dIŋg/	/dIŋgə/	/dIŋg/	/dIŋgə/
	/dIŋk/	/dIŋ ə/	/dIŋk/	/dIŋə /
			/dIŋ/	

	/ŋk/ (NG and SG)	
Fink	sing.	pl.
'finch'	/fIŋk/	/fIŋkən/

The /ŋg/ sequences have undergone three changes:

(1) /g/ --→ /k/ / /ŋ/ ___#

(2) /k/ --→ ∅ / /ŋ/ ___# in SG, wherever /k/ ‹

(3) /g/ --→ ∅ / /ŋ/ /ə/   /g/

These phenomena have been discussed by a number of investigators, most notably Kiparsky (1972), Hooper (1976), and
Vennemann (1970, 1974). Kiparsky claims that the dialects in

question question have an underlying post-nasal /g/, but
that through time German has added two ordered rules to its
grammar: (1) a rule that devoices all final and preconsonantal obstruents and (2) a rule that deletes /g/ after a
nasal. He accounts for the difference between NG and SG by
hypothesizing that the rules were reordered in SG so that /g/
-deletion applies before devoicing (1972:209-210). Although
this is a clear characterization of German phonology at
different points in space and time, Hooper notes that "Rule
reordering is a <u>description</u> of a particular linguistic change
but, in itself, not an explanation" (1976:92). Hooper, I
think, is correct; it is not at all clear what would motivate
a speaker to spontaneously reorder two rules in his grammar.
Hooper, however, does not attempt to explain the changes that
have occurred; rather, she argues against Kiparsky's claim
that there is an underlying /g/ in both dialects of German.
Hooper, who takes her analysis from Vennemann (1974), proposes
that NG has an underlying /k/ inserted by an 'arbitrary'
morphophonemic rule but that SG has neither a /g/ nor a /k/
in its underlying representation (1976:95,97). Although her
analysis is preferable to Kiparsky's in that she assumes
that a speaker would be constrained from internalizing an
underlying form that contains a segment which never appears
phonetically (Vennemann's Strong Naturalness Condition), she
still avoids the question of what caused the change in the
first place. She claims that the two rules, devoicing and /g/
-deletion, were simply 'added' to the grammar of German
(1976:97). Vennemann, on the other hand, does 'attempt an
explanation' of the 'g' -deletion phenomenon; he notes that
/g/ is deleted after a nasal when the /g/ occurs before zero
stress (1970:74). This solution, however, is incomplete in
two respects. First, it does not deal with the devoicing of
/g/ to /k/, and, second, it is simply a statement of the conditioning environment for /g/ -deletion; it does not explain
the relationship between /g/ -deletion and zero stress.

    Since the generative analyses do not seem to shed much
light on the actual mechanism of phonological change, it
might be worthwhile to examine the German data in terms of
AC's. The AC's relevant here are those for final post-vocalic
stops (as in <u>cat</u> - <u>cad</u>), post-nasal stops (as in <u>can't</u> -
<u>canned</u>), and post-vocalic nasals (as in <u>can</u>). It is known

that stop release in final position is sufficient to discriminate between voiced and voiceless stops (Malécot, 1958:
379; Wang, 1967:343). However, stops in final position may
be unreleased (Francis, 1958:73; Chen and Wang, 1975:270).
In the case of unreleased post-vocalic stops, the voice value
is signalled by the manner in which the preceding vowel is
terminated. That is, a post-vocalic stop is cued by abrupt
termination of the preceding vowel and a post-vocalic voiced
stop is signalled by gradual termination of the preceding
vowel. 'Termination' here is defined in terms of the period
of vocal cord vibration during the transition from vowel to
stop. Before a voiced stop the period gradually lengthens;
no such change occurs before a voiceless stop (Parker, 1974:
218). Moreover, gradual vowel termination is an ambiguous
AC. Both a vowel in final position and a vowel preceding a
voiced stop exhibit period lengthening. If a post-vocalic
voiced stop is unreleased as in cued /kjud/, it is often
confused with a vowel final utterance such as cue /kju/
(Parker, 1974:217).

The situation is even more complex with AC's for post-
nasal stops. If a nasal is followed by a voiceless stop,
the vowel becomes nasalized and the nasal segment drops out.
That is, can't /kænt/, for example, becomes /kæt/ phonetically.
Thus, a post-nasal voiceless stop has the same AC as a post-
vocalic voiceless stop--abrupt termination of the preceding
vowel; the only difference between such utterances is in the
nasalization of the preceding vowel. On the other hand, the
nasal preceding a voiced stop does not drop out phonetically;
that is, canned /kænd/ becomes /kæ̃nd/ phonetically (Malécot,
1960; Parker, 1977a). The AC for a post-nasal voiced stop,
then, cannot be gradual vowel termination, since such a stop
is not directly preceded by a vowel. Instead, a post-nasal
voiced stop is cued only by its release; if it is not released, it is acoustically similar to an utterance without a
stop. That is, canned /kænd^j/ is acoustically the same as
can /kæ̃n^j/ (Parker, 1977a:102).

Two significant facts emerge from this discussion of
AC's. Not only are AC's (especially those for stops) highly
context-dependent, but also they vary in their relative
strength and ambiguity. If we restrict our discussion to the

AC's for final, unreleased stops and nasals, we can rank
these cues as follows. (Let V=vowel, N=nasal, and C=stop.)

Strongest - VN   - (can /kæn$^\lrcorner$/) - AC's present throughout
                                                    vowel and closure

          VC   - (cat /kæt$^\lrcorner$/)   - one unambiguous cue,
          /-vce/   abrupt vowel termination

          VNC   - (can't /kæ̃t$^\lrcorner$/) - same as above
          /-vce/

          VC   - (cad /kæd$^\lrcorner$/)   - one ambiguous cue, grad-
          /+vce/   ual vowel termination

Weakest - VNC   - (canned /kæ̃nd$^\lrcorner$/) -no AC
          /+vce/

The cues for final voiced stops, then, are weaker than those
for final voiceless stops, which are in turn weaker than
those for final nasals. (Here an ambiguous cue is assumed
to be weaker than an unambiguous cue.)

The directionality of change is, however, only part of
the picture. It is also necessary to determine what causes
the appearance of acoustically unstable segments in the first
place. For the purposes of illustration, let's assume the
simplest, most 'natural' type of syllable structure--
$C_1V_1C_2V_2C_3V_3$ (See Schane 1973:52-53). When stress becomes
fixed on the first syllable (as has occurred in all the
Germanic languages), the unstressed vowels are reduced and
eventually lost; that is, $C_1V_1C_2V_2C_3V_3$ --→ $C_1V_1C_2 \vartheta C_3 \vartheta$--→
$C_1V_1C_2 \vartheta C_3$ --→ $C_1V_1C_2C_3$. Since, as we have seen, the AC's
for stops are carried by neighboring vowels, then loss of
the final /ə/ removes half of the potential cues for C_3 and
loss of the preceding /ə/ obliterates the remaining cues of
C_3 as well as half the cues for C_2. Thus, after the unstressed
vowels are reduced and deleted, the ranking of C_1 - C_3 in
terms of the relative strength of their AC's is C_1-strongest,
C_2 - weaker, and C_3 - weakest. This provides us with a complete (if somewhat oversimplified) model of phonological change:
fixed stress causes vowel reduction and deletion, which in turn
causes weakening of AC's for the neighboring consonants. Those
consonants with weak AC's are replaced by segments with
stronger AC's.

Let us now return to the problem of explaining the three
changes that have occurred in German. The first change is the

devoicing of post-nasal stops in final position, specifically
/g/ --→ /k/ /ŋ/ ___#. We must begin by putting this
phenomenon into its historical context. First, the proto-
forms for members of the Ding-Dinge and Fink-Finken paradigms
originally had a full vowel following the nasal+stop clusters; we may assume this, because in Indo-European, nouns
typically ended in a nonreduced vowel or carried an inflectional suffix beginning with such a vowel (Misra, 1968:52-60).
The reconstructed forms then are /dIŋgV/-/dIŋgV/ and /fIŋkV/-
/fIŋkVn/. (The exact quality of the vowel is unimportant.)
Second, these vowels eventually reduced to /ə/, due to the
fixed stress on the first syllable of native words (See
MacCarthy, 1975:10). Thus, the proto-forms reduced to
/dIŋgə/-/dIŋgə/ and /fIŋkə/-/fIŋkən/, respectively. Third,
the AC for the /g/ in the Ding paradigm, but not that for
the /k/ in the Fink paradigm, is carried by the /ə/. Stop
release in final position constitutes an incipient centra-
lized vowel; that is, /Cˉ/=/Cə/ (Parker, 1977a:103). Therefore, since the AC for a post-nasal voiced stop is release,
and since release =/ə/, then the AC for the /g/ in /dIŋgə/
must be /ə/. Fourth, eventually the final /ə/ in the singular was lost. This created an acoustically unstable situation, since it in essence deprived all final post-nasal
voiced stops of their AC.

   Three possibilities existed to compensate for this unstable situation. (1) The stop could simply have been released. However, this apparently was not a viable alternative
since release would contradict the general loss of final /ə/.
That is, since /Cə/=/Cˉ/, loss of final /ə/ necessitates
nonrelease of the stop. Moreover, releasing the stop would
cause the singular and plural forms to fall together. That is,
since /dIŋgˉ/ and /dIŋgə/ are similar acoustically, the
singular/plural distinction would have been obliterated for
all nouns of the Ding-Dinge paradigm. (2) The stop could have
been lost. That is, /dIŋg / might have become /dIŋ/. Why it
did not is somewhat unclear. However, we have to assume that
although simple loss of /g/ was a viable alternative, it simply
did not occur. It is worth noting that in English, where the
same phonetic conditions obtained, voiced velar and labial
stops were lost after nasals. For example, in Mod. E. we
have climb /klaim/ < ME climbe /klImbə/<OE climban /klImban/

(Parker, 1977a). (3) The stop could be preserved without
being released. This alternative involves substituting a
segment with a relatively strong AC /k^{J}/ for one with a weak
AC /g^{J}/. 'Substitution,' however, may be a misleading term.
It might be more accurate to say that this change involves
shifting dependence from one AC to another. Before the loss
of the /ə/, the /ə/ itself provided the AC for the preceding
/g/ in Ding. Loss of /ə/ forced the cue to be shifted from a
position following /g/ to a position preceding it, that is,
to the preceding vowel. However, in the V+N+C series, the
only type of stop that is directly preceded by a vowel is a
voiceless one. Thus, in order to preserve the final stop
in the singular Ding paradigm, speakers had to depend on the
preceding vowel to carry the AC; this, however, necessitated
devoicing the stop. The steps in this process can be reconstructed as follows:

/dɪŋ g ə/   - AC for /g/ carried by following vowel
/dɪŋ g^{J}/   - no AC
*/dĩg^{J}/   - impossible sequence
/dĩk^{J}/   - AC for /k/ carried by preceding vowel

    This analysis accounts not only for the devoicing of
final post-nasal /g/ in German but also for final devoicing
phenomena in general. First, devoicing of a final stop
following a homorganic sonorant consonant (for example, nasals
and laterals) is common. In English, for instance, we have
dialect variants such as burned-burnt, learned-learnt,
spilled-spilt, and smelled-smelt. Moreover, pronunciations
such as killed /kɪlt/ are common in some varieties of nonstandard English. Historically there was a /ə/ between the
sonorant and /d/. The /ə/ was deleted in time, bringing the
sonorant and /d/ together. Since English was in the process
of losing all final /ə/'s, this pressured speakers into producing unreleased /nd/ and /ld/ clusters in final position.
One method of accommodating this pressure without deleting
the final stop was to shift the cue from the stop itself to
the preceding vowel, which in turn motivated the devoicing
of /d/ to /t/. (Note that /spɪl^{J}/ and /spɪld^{J}/ are acoustically equivalent, whereas /spɪl^{J}/ and /spɪlt^{J}/ are quite
distinct.)

A more general example of final devoicing associated with loss of release is provided by speakers of languages which lack morpheme-final consonants. Stampe states that in such languages loan words with final voiced consonants are pronounced with a final vowel or a final voiceless consonant. For example, /dɔg/ tends to be reproduced as /dɔgə/ and /dɔk/ variably by speakers of languages such as Tamil, Japanese, and Italian (personal communication). The explanation for this phenomenon is similar to that for the German data. Post-vocalic voiced stops have two cues: release and gradual termination of the preceding vowel. The pronunciation /dɔgə/ represents dependence on the release cue. When unreleased, however, a post-vocalic voiced stop is not only reduced to a single cue, gradual vowel termination, but an ambiguous cue at that. Thus, for a speaker to preserve the stop without having to release it and without having to depend on an ambiguous cue, he may signal it unambiguously by abrupt termination of the preceding vowel. This, of course, entails devoicing the stop.

Let us now consider the second phonological change illustrated by the German data--the loss of post-nasal voiceless stops in final position in SG. In particular, post-nasal /k/ was deleted in final position sometime after the Middle High German period, changing Ding from /dɪŋk/ to /dɪŋ/. The primary force effecting the loss of /k/ is the relative weakness of abrupt vowel termination as the AC for post-vocalic stops. (Recall that /dɪŋk/ reduces to /dĩk/ phonetically.) We know that unreleased stops are harder to perceive than nasals in the same articulatory position (Chen and Wang, 1975:270-271). Thus, the AC for the final segment in /dĩk˩/ is weaker than that for the final segment in /dĩŋ˩/. We may hypothesize that even though the listener was exposed to /dĩk˩/, he assigned the utterance the structure /dĩŋ˩/ because the cue for the nasal is stronger than that for the stop. The speaker then internalized the underlying form /dɪŋ/.

Still it remains to be shown why the /k/ was lost in the Ding paradigm but not in the Fink paradigm. That is, /k/ was lost in final position after a nasal, but only where /k/ was historically derived from /g/. Even though we have to assume

that both /k/'s were acoustically identical, the cause for
such 'selective' change may be found in paradigm pressure.
That is, a /k/ occurred in the plural of the Fink paradigm
(/fIŋkən/) but apparently not in that of the Ding paradigm
(/dIŋə/). Although the AC's for both /k/'s were weak, the
/k/ in Fink could be reconstructed on the basis of the /k/
in Finken; whereas the /k/ in Ding was lost since there was
no stop in Dinge to serve as a model. German provides other
examples of similar phenomena. For example, hintbere in Old
High German shows up as Himbere in SG. The /t/ is unreleased because it is followed by another obstruent (See
Wang, 1967:343). Therefore, the only AC for /tʲ/ is abrupt
vowel termination. Because of the weakness of the cue, the
/tʲ/ was apparently not perceived by new speakers and thus
was not internalized as part of the base form of hintbere.
In the absence of the /t/, the nasal was free to assimilate
to the point of articulation of the /g/. Moreover, the loss
of final, unreleased voiceless stops is not restricted to
German. This phenomenon is, in fact, fairly widespread.
For instance, Chen and Wang discuss the different stages of
the loss of such stops in different dialects of Chinese.
This can be explained as a function of the relative weakness of abrupt vowel termination as an AC. Final voiceless
stops were unreleased in Chinese, and because of the relative weakness of the single cue, the stops were no longer
perceived and were eventually lost.

In summary, the analysis presented here is more than
simply an attempt to account for three changes in German
phonology. It is rather an effort to show, first, that
phonological change cannot be fully understood without reference to AC's. Such cues are context-dependent just as
phonological change is, and AC's are the elements of the
signal by means of which speakers recover phonological segments. Second, AC's form part of a general paradigm of
phonological change. Fixed stress causes vowel reduction and
eventual deletion. Vowel loss in turn introduces consonants
(in particular stops) into acoustically unstable positions by
eliminating the environments that carry their cues. Third,
the direction of phonological change is a function of the
relative strength of the AC's for the segment involved. Segments with relatively weak AC's tend to change into segments

with stronger Ac's. In particular, the cues for final voiced
stops are weaker than those for final voiceless stops, which
in turn are weaker than those for final nasals. The German
data discussed here exemplify this general progression:
/dɪŋg/ ‑‑> ·/dɪŋk/   ‑‑> /dɪŋ/.

REFERENCES

Anderson, H. (1973). Lang., 49:765-793.

Chen, M. Y. and Wang, S-Y. (1975). Lang., 51:255-281.

Cole, R. and Scott, B. (1974). Psych. Rev., 81:348-374.

Eilers, R. E. (1977). J. Acoust. Soc. Am., 61:1321-1336.

Fodor, J., Bever, T., and Garrett, M. (1974). New York,
      McGraw-Hill.

Francis, W. N. (1958). New York, Ronald Press.

Hooper, J. (1976). New York, Academic Press.

Kiparsky, P. (1968). New York, Holt, Rinehart, Winston,
      171-202.

Kiparsky, P. (1972). Englewood Cliffs, Prentice-Hall,
      189-227.

Liberman, A. M., Cooper, F. S., Shankweiler, D. P., and
      Studdert-Kennedy, M. (1967). Psych. Rev., 74:431-461.

Macari, N. (forthcoming). J. Phon.

MacCarthy, P. (1975). London, Oxford Univ. Press.

Malécot, A. (1958). Lang., 34:370-380.

Malécot, A. (1960). Lang., 36:222-229.

Misra, S. S. (1968). Calcutta, World Press.

Parker, F. (1974). J. Phon., 2:211-221.

Parker, F. (1977a). J. Phon., 5:97-105.

Parker, F. (1977b). J. Acoust. Soc. Am., 62:1051-1054.

Schane, S. (1973). Englewood Cliffs, Prentice-Hall.

Stampe, D. (1969). Chicago Ling. Soc., 5:443-354.

Vennemann, T. (1970). Phonet., 22:65-81.

Vennemann, T. (1974). Washington, Georgetown Univ. Press.,
      202-219.

Wang, S-Y. (1967). Cambridge, MIT Press, 343-350.

PHONETIC AND INTERDISCIPLINARY NEW PERSPECTIVES
IN PARALINGUISTIC STUDIES

FERNANDO POYATOS
University of New Brunswick

The linguisticness of paralanguage and the lexicality
of the Basic Triple Structure. Although the space limitations
logically imposed by the Editor do not allow for the much more
elaborate discussion contained in the complete version of this
paper, I will attempt to outline the more important aspects of
my work in paralanguage to date.

Verbal language, although the most elaborate and advan-
tageous transactional tool and the backbone of human communication, is certainly not an autonomous system, as it is semantically, morphologically and syntactically shaped by elements
other than those traditionally regarded as linguistic. This
is confirmed by the very nature of the Basic Triple Structure
of human communication, language--paralanguage--kinesics, which
I consider the indispensable framework through which verbal
and nonverbal systems must be viewed, whether analyzing the
mechanism of personal interaction or trying to hypothesize
about the phylogenetic and ontogenetic development of
language, paralanguage or kinesics (Poyatos, 1977a). In
fact, from the point of view of communication in whatever
discipline, the study of verbal language in isolation is
scientifically unrealistic, and this is easily demonstrated
by: (a) a semantic progression where a 'naked' verbal sentence is successively endowed with paralinguistic and kinesic
features, but above all by (b) a triple transcription which
shows beyond doubt the unique co-structuration of the three
systems as we record, in a musical-score type of presentation:

phonemic transcription, the four paralinguistic ones, the
orthographic transcript, and a three-level kinesic notation
(head, arms and hands, and trunk and legs), plus a description of the setting and other pertinent contextual elements;
and (c) a revision of the very concept of language (differing among disciplines at any rate) through the application
of Hockett's design-feature scheme to paralanguage and
kinesics as well, modifying three of his features (the vocal-
auditory channel is identified as kinetically based, 'imitative' should be added to arbitrariness and conventionality,
since we produce echoic sounds and iconic gestures, and
semanticity should be applied to the Triple Structure) and
adding seven more (inheritance, shared or idiosyncratic nature
interactionality, graphic representability, verbalization vs
nonverbalization, co-structuration with preceding or succeeding silence and stillness, and intraespecific encoding and
decoding and interspecific decoding). Furthermore, these
approaches prove the lexicality of the three systems--and
their possible mutual substitution within a preserved syntactical order even within a sentence--whose kinetic base
suggest in turn a protolinguistic double structure (vocal/
nareal phonetic movements plus external kinesics) from the
early stages of anatomical and cognitive development, although
kinesics could have lost status as the vocal-tract repertoire
increased. They also suggest a common historical and adaptive
development and cognitive sofistication affecting language,
paralanguage and kinesics, i.e., from rougher, broader constructs in either system to more subtle ones. Finally, the
obvious co-structuration of the three systems, which should
not be foreign to phonetics, prompts the revision of two
concepts. First fluency, as it must be understood as verbal
and nonverbal and as developing from childhood, seeking therefore interactive fluency and also as regards the perceptual
capabilities of our co-interactants, perhaps socioeconomically
and educationally inferior, or impaired. Secondly, redundancy
since the various behaviors can be either redundant or complementary (supporting, emphasizing, contradicting) to each
other, and because even while being redundant they may produce
a personal or cultural style.

  Segmentality vs nonsegmentality in relation to
paralanguage. Even if we limit our analysis to the vocal-
auditory channel, encompassing language and paralanguage, we

recognize two levels of production, i.e., two distinct types
of activities: (a) some which precede or follow each other
as discrete portions of a non-continuous whole: words
(phonemes), vocal nonverbal constructs ('Uh,' 'Tz-tz'), and
silences or breaks in that audible chain of segmentable
events (to which kinesic activities must be added) and (b)
some others which clearly change throughout that communicative stretch, with not so clear boundaries and which, besides,
seem to override the former, from syllables to much longer
portions, and varying slightly but with a cumulative impression never given by the clearly discrete parts of speech,
therefore not being segmentable: intonation, paralinguistic
primary qualities, qualifiers and differentiators (to which
still positions must be added).

The fact that many non-vocalic, non-consonantal, closed-
lip or open-lip utterances are regarded by some as intonation
('intonation without words') leads to the equivocation that
intonation can be isolated, that is, separated from a segmental stretch of speech and uttered alone, when in reality
we are again producing the two levels just referred to, the
segmental one (in this case a paralinguistic construct) and
the nonsegmental or intonational one. Although intonation
can be both grammatical and attitudinal it does not mean that
it can carry any more meaning than nasality or whispering
would by themselves, unless they occur with words or with
paralinguistic alternants (regarded as segmental) like
'Eeugh!,' 'Hmm!.' One cannot speak with intonation only.
We can modulate a long stretch like 'Mmmmmmmm!,' but then
we are simply evoking an established and perfectly coded
verbal or paralinguistic utterance, to both of which either
a person or a domesticated animal will easily react.

Another neglected fact in communication and as regards
segmentality is the importance of silence and stillness, as
opposed but complementary to sound and movement and as meaningful systems in themselves which enhance the importance of
the Basic Triple Structure and its ontogenetic and phylogenetic superiority over other systems. Silence can be
defined as the message-conveying non-activity which limits
segments of audible utterances travelling over the vocal/
nareal-auditory channel, marking their beginning, duration
and end, and linking them or putting a stop to them. But

'linguistic' silence overrides only audible-visual (a finger
snap) silent-visual kinesic constructs (a head nod), and it
is not a void, but has meaning, and it can be regarded as
paralinguistic, its kinesic counterpart and semantic complement being 'segmental' stillness. Elsewhere (Poyatos,
1978a) I have elaborated somewhat on the semiotics of silence
and stillness, a much needed perspective even within phonetics
and general linguistics, but here I will just indicate: (a)
that silences, as truly noncommunicative 'unfilled' pauses
occur only before, between and after interactive encounters
between speaker and listener, that is, as noninteractive
periods unrelated to the so-called interactive turns; (b)
that other than true noninteractive silences, breaks are
always linguistic, paralinguistic or kinesic true pauses
within or between turns, because when one of the activities
is interrupted the other two, or at least one of them, will
certainly fill that gap, hence the important semantic and
structural interrelationships of the three systems among
themselves and with silence and stillness; (c) that, unlike
communicative linguistic-paralinguistic and kinesic pauses,
noncommunicative silence and stillness cannot be said to be
limited at both ends by predictable behaviors, nor support,
emphasize or contradict the verbal and nonverbal messages,
nor show any specific structure or functions, since they
happen outside communicative encounters; and (d) that referring to 'filled' or 'unfilled' pauses in relation to
verbal language only is utterly misleading, since verbal
silences are not necessarily vocal silences (i.e., paralinguistic), and because a complete silence just cannot be
'unfilled,' for kinesic, proxemic, dermal, thermal, and
chemical signs may convey certain messages as efficiently
or more than words on occasions, performing important interactive (even syntactical) functions within different types
of pauses. Furthermore, one must recognize that silence and
stillness are always qualified and, therefore, granted a
measurable dimension, by: their co-structuration with preceding, simultaneous or succeeding activities; the intensity
of the co-occurring activities, whether sensible or just
mental, during silence or stillness; and their duration, which
is ultimately related to both co-structuration and intensity.

Further to these schematic comments on segmentality, it
would be appropriate to add that, while segmental communicatio

is mostly controlled and conscious on the part of the emitter,
the same cannot be said of the nonsegmental behaviors, which
seem to belong to two categories: natural, biological, either
normal or pathological (e.g., a breath-intake pause, a spastic
movement), and controlled, whether personal and idiosyncratic
or culture-specific, according to status, occupation (e.g.,
the auctioneer, the preacher), and situational context (e.g.,
reading to children).

    Paralanguage in relation to Total Body Communication
and interaction. Two or more human bodies engaged in natural
conversation can transmit information to each other through
kinetic (both for vocal language and kinesics), chemical,
dermal, or thermal messages, which impinge on the visual,
acoustic, dermal, olfactory, thermal, and kinesthetic
receptors, either individually or simultaneously, whether as
a primary system (e.g., kinesics - visual perception) or a
secondary system (e.g., perspiration - visually assumed odor
(Poyatos, 1977a, 1978a). Since paralanguage combines with
all the other nonverbal systems one cannot overlook its
interactive dimension, which involves, first of all, natural
conversation--a spontaneous communicative exchange of verbal
and nonverbal signs between at least two human beings--and
the contrived conversation best exemplified by the theatrical
performance, in which verbal language and nonverbal activities are not properly co-structured: intonation patterns do
not always correspond to the memorized verbal constructs,
paralinguistic features such as volume, rhythm, glottalic
control, specific types of laughter, etc., do not seem to
agree with the type being portrayed, the situational context,
and the cultural background.

    It must also be born in mind that paralanguage, like any
other systems, performs always one of these two functions in
the course of interaction: as modifier of one's own behavior
or our co-interactants, by modifying the meaning (supporting,
emphasizing, or contradicting the basic message, or changing
the form of the signs to be emitted, or the type of behavior
altogether), or simply as contextual element; while both
modifiers and contextual elements perform either a self-
regulatory function (among one's own behaviors) or an interactional one (among those of the different participants).

It follows, therefore, that in order to progress through
a gradually deeper analysis of oral language we must investigate how verbal expression and the other message-conveying
systems relate to each other and regulate the smooth or
irregular flow of the exchange between the speaker (sender)
and the listener (receiver), by analyzing: certain turn
rules and counterrules (turn claiming, -yielding, -taking,
-suppressing, and -holding), simultaneous behaviors (turns,
conclusion, turn claiming, and -yielding), interactional
pauses (failed turn taking and -claiming, turn opening,
hesitation, feedback-seeking, and turn ending), sender's
within-turn behaviors (counterfeedback, turn opening, -pre-
closing, -closing, and -suppressing), and receiver's within-
turn behaviors (feedback, clarification request, higher-
volume request, verbatim repetition of the speaker's last
statement, re-statement, simultaneous conclusion, and prompt-
ing signals).

In addition, this realistic perspective of verbal and
nonverbal communication prompts the revision of two traditional concepts. First, fluency, understood as nonverbal
as well as verbal (essentially the Basic Triple Structure)
and developing from childhood, seeking therefore interactive
fluency--and even more, cultural fluency when in a foreign
country (i.e., verbal and nonverbal)--, but also as regards
the perceptual capabilities of our co-interactants, perhaps
socioeconomically and educationally inferior, or impaired.
Secondly, redundancy, as the various behaviors can be either
redundant or complementary (supporting, emphasizing, contradicting) to each other, and because even while being redundant
it may produce a personal or cultural style. On the other
hand we must carefully differentiate between primary and
secondary systems among the behaviors, understood in this case
as determined by the intensity and location of the various
systems in the behavioral stream.

The morphological and functional classifications of
paralanguage. The morphological classification of paralinguistic features I proposed before (Poyatos, 1975 and earlier,
1976) was originally based on Trager's (1958) pioneering
paper and some incomplete but inspiring early applications
(Pittinger, 1957; Pittinger, Hockett and Danehy, 1960;

McQuown, 1957; Austin, 1965), upon which I attempted to
enlarge according to phonetic (i.e., phonological), semantic,
and functional criteria (in part as advocated by Crystal,
1974, the best state-of-the-art paper to date), which ack-
nowledges four well differentiated categories.

        Primary qualities are fundamental constituents
of human speech which differentiate, first of all, a person
from the others. Crystal (1971:198) defines 'voice quality'
as "the idiosyncratic, relatively permanent, vocal background
of an individual, which allows us to recognize him . . .it may
be both segmental and nonsegmental in character, but the
latter is usually the dominant factor. It is a physiologically determined activity, over which most individuals have
little or no measure of control." (Others call it 'voice
set,' 'speaker identity,' etc.) I have classified as primary qualities: timbre, resonance, volume, tempo, pitch
register, pitch interval, pitch range, syllabic duration,
intonation range, and rhythm, recognizing four basic factors:
biological, that is, purely somatic (such as sex and age,
conditioning, for instance, timbre), physiological, thus
variable, whether due to temporary malfunctions or to traumatized states (nasal resonance due to cattharr, improper
timing in aphasias), cultural (e.g., higher volume of Latins
and Arabs, certain dialectal peculiarities), and social,
such as status (the slow tempo of superiority), occupation
(the orality of a preacher), or certain functions, like baby
talk, story-telling, etc. In other words, primary qualities
can also be based on non-permanent factors that produce a
sort of secondary or temporary voice set in a person, just
as some qualifiers (next category) can become basic characteristics of a given individual, either as a permanent profile
or in certain situations. I will comment only on volume,
that is, loudness due to the respiratory and articulatory muscular effort, referred both to utterance or speech and to
single syllables (beyond stressed or unstressed ones, e.g.,
'It was awful'). Like pitch or speed, it possesses syntactical and cognitive value, as in a speeded-up low-volume (and
pitch) parenthetical observation, and its parameter can go
very high (fortisimo) to very low (pianisimo), either rising
(crescendo) or falling (diminuendo). Volume has an important
culture-identifying value, as Arabs and Latin, for instance,

are louder in streets and public places than the average
Anglo-Saxon. Elaborating elsewhere on punctuation (Poyatos,
1978b), I have discussed how there is no logical reason not
to indicate with precision that a sentence is uttered with
high volume, or very high, from beginning to end, or only
part of it. While Spanish makes it clear by using ¡ -----! ,
both English and Spanish could specify instances such as:
¡___, -----! , ¡¡------! , -----!! . The reader, for one
thing, would be able to mentally synchronize himself with
the text much better instead of finding an un-anticipated
high volume at the very end of a long sentence, or being
obliged to qualify a whole sentence with high volume when
only part of it carries it.

        Modifiers, encompassing qualifiers and differen-
tiators, are a series of vocal effects produced by factors
like the direction and characteristics of respiratory air,
by the way it is controlled in the vocal bands and how they
vibrate, by certain changes in the pharynge, by the soft
palate position, by how articulation is produced in terms of
muscular tension and position of the organs, and by the
anatomical configuration and shaping of the lips and the
lower mandible. Some, of course, may appear as permanent
traits of a person's voice, in which case they qualify words,
differentiators and alternants as true primary qualities,
while others may be due only to temporary states or contextual
circumstances, such as the labializing effect of baby talk,
the ingressive utterance of verbal expressions of terror, or
the traumatized nasality of certain malfunctions. Some are
reported as being phonologically used in certain languages,
and others only paraphonologically, and most of them modify
from syllables to long portions of speech, while a few others
modify the verbal utterance occasionally (e.g., laughter),
or appear isolated from it, in which case they must be regarded as alternants, the next major category of paralinguistic phenomena.

        It is within qualifiers (respiratory--, glottis--
laryngeal--, velar--, pharyngeal--, articulatory--, labial--,
and maxillary control, and articulatory tension) that we first
encounter the typical ambiguity, from a phonetic point of view
of most of the descriptive or definitory labels employed, the
utter lack of accurate physiological descriptions to refer to

those effects, and the complete absence of orthographic forms
to indicate, at least impressionistically, some important
attitudinal features, just as we utilize exclamation marks
or repetition of letters to symbolize drawling. Although
they can also appear as primary qualities, they do not show
clear parameters in which to identify different degrees of a
continuum, as they usually involve more than one anatomical
and/or physiological change in the laryngeal or pharyngeal
areas, for instance. Ideally, each one ought to be analyzed
in terms of: anatomical and/or physiological configuration
(e.g., relaxed vocal band vibration, weak arytenoid closure);
auditory effect (e.g., nasal twang); voice type it produces
(e.g., nasopharyngeal, creaky, breathy); co-occurrent verbal
and nonverbal behaviors, as some qualifiers may be part of a
whole established construct (e.g., pursed lips + lowered brows
with irritated 'Oh, let me alone!'); phonological use (e.g.,
glottal stop in some West African languages); paralinguistic
use (e.g., glottal stop for scorn, 'Terrible!'); abnormal
occurrences (e.g., hoarse voice of trachyphonia); and notation for phonetic purposes and because the core of the message
may sometimes be carried by a qualifier.

Differentiators (laughing, crying, coughing,
sneezing, belching, yawning, hiccoughing, snorting) characterize psychological and physiological states, and are
closely co-structured with kinesic behavior while being
modified by primary qualities and qualifiers, since even reflexes like sneezes, belches and hiccoughs condition specific
accompanying kinesic hand behaviors, for instance, according
to cultural norms. Among them, laughter deserves further
research as regards: its biological foundation (age, sex,
some sexual deviances); the influence of the psychological
configuration on its frequency of occurrence, duration,
acoustic characteristics, and eliciting factors, as well as
temporary emotional states and their relations to cultural
norms about them; pathological varieties; social implications
of laughter display with respect to the same or different
states and their contextual situation; the hidden or explicit
etiquette norms about laughter; the phonetic variants of
laughter according to the socioeconomic and cultural characteristics of the person; laughter in non-interactive situations, that is, when the person is alone; its simultaneous or
alternating co-structuration with verbal language and with

kinesics (as in smiling) and the basic cross-cultural
differences; its co-structuration with proxemics, as well as
with chemical (e.g., tears), dermal (e.g., blushing) systems;
and the study of definitory references and descriptions of
laughter in the narrative literature of the various cultures.

Alternants, which I have discussed before (1975,
1976), constitute the most controversial category, where the
pretended "rigid dichotomy where certain semantic constructs
are 'paralinguistic' and others are 'linguistic'" (Lieberman,
1975:279) appears to be totally unfounded. They are egressive
and ingressive single or compound sounds, articulated or not,
produced or shaped in the areas covered by the supraglottal
cavities (nares, nasal chamber, nasopharynx, mouth, pharynx),
the laryngeal cavity, the infraglottal cavities, the diaphragm,
and the abdominal muscles; they do not affect the verbal
utterance, but are modified by primary qualities, qualifiers
and kinesic activity, and occur either isolated or alternating
with verbal language and kinesic constructs. In an impressionistic way, I would loosely describe them--as space limitations preclude a detailed analysis--as sighs, throat clearings,
clicks, pharyngeal ingressions and egressions, egressive
frictions, hissing sounds, nareal frictions, moaning sounds,
closed- or open-lip sounds, meaningful silences, etc. Each
language, each culture or social community possesses a great
number of them, perfectly encoded and decoded, as they constitute a true lexicon used constantly in personal interaction
and as systematically as dictionary items, which some are
already. They deserve, therefore, a much higher status in
linguistics as well as in any disciplines dealing with communication, and the following basic facts must be considered:
(a) that they differ radically from other paralinguistic
phenomena because of their lexical value, that is, their
segmentality; (b) that they cannot be regarded any more as
'nonspeech' or 'marginal' sounds just because many are not
constructed with phonemes from the best known languages; (c)
that they play important roles in the mechanism of interaction, with as high a frequency rate as verbal items, and
often with an even clearer semantic and regulatory function,
e.g., an apicoalveolar click + pharyngeal ingression as a
turn-claiming cue, or signifying 'Don't say that; (d) that
they seem to form, more than 'words,' the greater part of the
communicative repertoire each culture utilizes for the

interaction of man and domestic animals (see, e.g., Bynon,
1976); (e) that their articulatory peculiarities should be
given serious thought in glottogenetic studies and with
respect to the phylogeny of the Basic Triple Structure; and
(f) that we need to largely increase the present limited
system of phonetic symbols, labels (i.e., verbs and nouns),
and written forms, as we have for a few ('H'm,' 'Psst,'
'Er,' 'Uh-hu'). While professional writers (e.g., Huxley
in Point Counterpoint) make their description of alternants
a characteristic of their insight and literary style, they
also, like the layman, try very hard to represent them.

REFERENCES

Austin, W. M.   (1965).   Can. J. Ling., 11:31-39.
Bynon, J.   (1976).   The Hague, Mouton.
Crystal, D.   (1971).   185-206.   London, Tavistock Publica-
    tions.
Crystal, D.   (1974).   265-295.   The Hague, Mouton.
Lieberman, P.   (1975).   227-284. The Hague, Mouton.
Pittinger, R. E. and Smith, H. L.   (1957).   Psychiatry,
    20:61-78.
Pittinger, R. E., Hockett, C. F. and Danehy, J. S.   (1960).
    Ithaca, N. Y., Paul Martineau.
Poyatos, F.   (1975).   285-314. The Hague, Mouton.
Poyatos, F.   (1976).   Oswego, N. Y., N. Y. St. Eng. Coun.
Poyatos, F.   (1977).   Semiotica, 20:197-228.
Poyatos, F.   (1978a). München/Salzburg, Wilheim Fink Verlag
    (in press).
Poyatos, F.   (1978b). Semiotica (in press).
Trager, G. L.   (1958).   Stud. Ling., 13:1-12.

SEGMENTAL	verbal constructs	alternants	silences	kinesic constructs	
NONSEGMENTAL	intona. features, primary qualities	qualifiers	differentia- tors	kin. intensity, range, velocity	

FIGURE 1

SILENCE WITHIN THE BASIC TRIPLE STRUCTURE

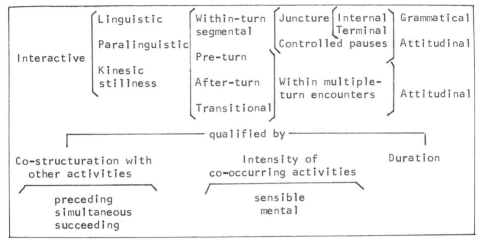

FIGURE 2

LANGUAGE	PARALANGUAGE	KINESICS
Weeell,	high volume, drawl, comma for falling junction and tone-group pause	raised brows, then stillness
what did	lower pitch and volume lower pitch and volume	lowering brows lowering brows
you	higher volumn and pitch	slightly knit brows + narrow-angle head nod + gazing at co-interactant
think of	lower volumn and pitch same	same same
that!	same volume, lower pitch + tone-group falling terminal juncture	lateral head tilt, then stillness

FIGURE 3

INTERACTIONS BETWEEN INTENSITY GLIDES
AND FREQUENCY GLISSANDOS

MARIO ROSSI
Université de Provence

There is an abundant bibliography of studies on the interactions between frequency and intensity. As far as we are aware, however, there has been no study of the inter-actions between intensity glides and frequency glissandos in speech. Nonetheless, the findings of Zwicker (1962), Maiwald (1967), Feth (1972), and Moller (1974) on the interaction between AM (amplitude modulation) and FM (frequency modulation) are of immediate interest to our study. Our aim is the study of intensity glides in speech: their mde of perception and their action on frequency glissandos.

PROCEDURE

Experiment 1: Falling Frequency Glissandos

The stimuli consist of synthesized vowels, (a) with a duration of 20 ms, which are presented to the subjects in pairs. The experimental design consists of five tests (see Fig. 1):

Test 1 - Standard stimulus: static intensity; F_0 static at 155 Hz. Variable stimulus: static intensity; falling glissando (see Fig. 2 for values). The two vowels of each pair are separated by a silence of 600 ms; each pair is separated by a silence of 3 sec. The pairs are presented in random order and form 10 series of 10 stimuli: each pair

thus appears 10 times in the test. The listening level is
fixed at 70 dB SPL. The subject, placed in an anechoic
chamber in front of a keyboard with two keys is required to
indicate which vowel of each pair has the largest fall in
pitch: his task consists in making a decision as quickly
as possible. In all, nine subjects took part in the experiment. The test is run automatically, the reaction time
being measured by the external clock ($F = 1$ kHz) of a T 1600
calculator: the number of responses in each category appears
opposite the values of the variable. This test makes it
possible to determine the threshold for glissandos by the
method of discrimination.

Test II - Standard stimulus: F_0 static at 155 Hz; Intensity:
slope of -8 dB. Variable stimulus: as for test 1. Test
conditions: as for test 1. The average threshold for the
discrimination of an intensity glide (Δ Gt.I) is 12 dB/200
ms (Nabélek and Hirsch, 1969); for some subjects, however,
the lowest value for Gt.I is around 8 dB. We chose this
value in order to test Zwicker and Maiwald's hypothesis that
modulations of frequency and of amplitude, close to the
threshold, are detected by the same mechanism. This test
aims to determine the mode of perception of an intensity
glide; the comparison of I and II will show whether a slope
of - 8 dB has any influence on the threshold of glissando
and if so in which direction.

Test III -. Standard stimulus: static intensity; F_0:
negative slope of 23 Hz, close to the threshold (Møller,
1974). Variable stimulus and test conditions as for test I.
(Fig. 3).

Test IV - Standard stimulus: intensity glide of -8 dB;
Fo: glissando of - 23 Hz. Variable stimulus and test conditions as for Test I. The aim of this test is to determine
the influence of a negative intensity slope on a frequency
glissando. The comparison of III and IV will show whether a
slope of -8 dB facilitates or masks the perception of a
glissando (Fig. 3).

Test VI - Standard stimulus: positive intensity glide of
+8 dB; Fo: glissando of -23 Hz. Variable and test conditions as for Test I. The aim of this test is to determine

the influence of a positive intensity slope on the perception of a falling frequency glissando. The comparison
of III and VI will show whether a slope of +8 dB facilitates
or masks the perception of a falling frequency glissando
(Fig. 3).

Experiment 2: Rising Glissandos

This experiment also consists of five tests analogous
to those of the previous experiment, with, however, a rising
glissando on the various stimulus (see Figs. 1, 4 and 5).

Test I - Standard stimulus: static intensity, static Fo.
Variable: static intensity; rising glissando ranging from
0 to +26 Hz by average steps of 3 Hz.

Test II - Standard stimulus: Intensity = slope of -8 dB;
Fo static. Variable: Intensity static; glissando ranging
from 0 to +26 Hz.

Test III - Standard stimulus: intensity static; rising
glissando near threshold of 19 Hz. Variable: Intensity
static; glissando ranging from 0 to +38 Hz.

Test V - Standard stimulus; Intensity = positive slope of
+8 dB, rising glissando of 19 Hz. Variable: Intensity
static; glissando ranging from 0 to 41 Hz.

RESULTS

Experiment I: Falling Glissandos (Figs. 2 and 3)

The five sigmoids obtained from the mean values of the
responses for the nine subjects are given in Figures 2 and 3.
An analysis of variance shows the difference to be significant between (I, II) and (III, IV); $F_{(3;8)} = 139$, p 0.01.
The subjects behaviour was different depending on whether
they were judging a static tone or a perceptible glissando
of 23 Hz. The intensity factor was also significant but
its effect on Fo was different depending on whether it was
combined with a static tone of a glissando.

An intensity glide of -8 dB added to a static Fo was
perceived as a glissando of -16 Hz; the glissando threshold, for static intensity, was 14 Hz. The intensity glide
facilitates the perception of the Fo slope and lowers the
threshold. In this case the factor of Intensity was less
significant (F (1;8) = 6.5, 0.05 p 0.01). Indeed for two
subjects whose threshold was 8 dB, the intensity glide had
no effect on their behaviour, for the other subjects, the
effect of the intensity glide was very slight and shows that
for them 8 dB is in fact close to their threshold value.

An intensity glide of -8 dB together with a falling
glissando of 23 Hz is perceived as a glissando of 19 Hz.   In
this case the effect of the intensity slope is reversed: it
diminishes the value of the glissando which is perceived and
hinders the identification of the slope of Fo for all the
subjects. The factor of intensity is significant here
(F (1,8) = 6.4; 0.05 p 0.01).

A positive intensity glide of +8 dB associated with a
falling glissando of 23 Hz is perceived as a glissando of
25 Hz. In other words, contrary to the negative slope, the
positive slope of intensity increases the sensitivity of the
ear for the perception of a falling glissando. A complementary test shows that the subjects do not perceive a linear
slope but a convex tone (Fig. 6b).

Experiment 2: Rising Glissandos (Figs. 4 and 5)

An intensity glide of +8 dB associated with a static
Fo is perceived as a rising glissando of 17 Hz; the glissando
threshold, with static intensity, was 12 Hz. The factor of
intensity was extremely significant: (t = 3.87, p 0.01). It
seems from these results that a positive intensity glide
has more effect than a negative glide of the same value.

A rising glissando of 19 Hz, together with a negative
intensity glide of -8 dB is perceived as a glissando of
16.5 Hz (t = 2.32; p = 0.05). A negative intensity glide,
consequently, whether associated with a rising or a falling
glissando always decreases the sensitivity of the ear. The
interaction between the two modulations seems statistically
stronger in the case of a falling glissando of frequency.

A rising glissando of 19 Hz together with a positive intensity slope is perceived as a glissando of 22 Hz (t = 2.95, 0.05 p 0.02). In all cases, then, a positive slope of intensity increases the sensitivity of the ear and facilitates the perception of a glissando whether rising or falling. A complementary test seems to show that subjects assimilate the glissando in this case to a concave tone (Fig. 7).

DISCUSSION

The results of tests I and II (negative and positive glides perceived respectively as frequency glissandos above the threshold) seem to confirm Zwicker and Maiwald's hypothesis that the coding of frequency and amplitude variations close to the threshold are carried out by the same mechanism. This hypothesis, however, predicts that a negative intensity slope together with a falling Fo glissando should increase the sensitivity of the ear and lower the glissando threshold (Zwicker, 1962); in fact our results show just the opposite since this association hampers the perception of the glissando which is perceived as a fall of 19 Hz instead of 22 Hz. Conversely, a positive slope of intensity together with a falling glissando of Fo should decrease the sensitivity and raise the threshold since the two modulations are of opposite phase. Above we have seen, however, that the interaction of intensity and Fo is, in this case, the opposite of what would be predicted by the model, since we have shown that a positive slope of intensity always has the effect of lowering glissando threshold so that in our test a fall of 22 Hz is perceived as a fall of 25 Hz. Zwicker adds, furthermore, that the interaction between AM and FM takes place even for sub-liminary values of modulation: this effect is confirmed by our results since the slope of intensity used (8 dB) is lower than the threshold we have defined elsewhere. In general, though, the model proposed by Zwicker and Maiwald in incapable of accounting for our results. The criticisms of this model made by Feth seem justified.

Another hypothesis which might explain the results we obtained for falling glissandos concerns the positive effect

of the decrease in intensity on the impression of pitch,
an effect which has often been described and has recently
been confirmed by Terhardt. According to this hypothesis
the perceived value of the end of the falling glissando on
the standard stimulus is raised by the decrease in intensity
compared with the variable stimulus; a modulation from 155
Hz to 132 Hz (-23 Hz) is consequently perceived as a glissando from 155 to 135 Hz., which does in fact correspond
to the results obtained. While this hypothesis
accounts for the results obtained for falling glissandos
the opposite effect is obtained for rising glissandos: a
decrease in intensity far from raising the perceived value
of the end of the rising glissando and increasing the sensitivity in fact does the reverse.

   Two models can account for all the interactions between
intensity and Fo in our experiments. The perception of a
glissando could be based on the evolution of the first
formant: not on the change of frequency of F1, which is
stable, but on what we might call harmonic rotation in the
spectrum. In a falling glissando with a range of approximately 20 Hz, for example, the centre of the formant is
represented by the 6 th H.at the beginning of the vowel and
by the 7 th H.at the end. The gradual decrease of intensity
on the 6th H.together with an increase on the 7th H.could
constitute two cues for the perception of a glissando. It
is also possible that the increase in intensity on the central harmonic of F1 at the end of the vowel, here the 7th H.
constitutes the principal cue; this would imply that a comparison is made in short-term memory between the two states
of this harmonic at the beginning and the end of the vowel.
If this hypothesis were correct, we could account for all
the types of interaction observed in the course of our
experiments. Indeed, the negative slope of intensity decreases the central harmonic of F1 by about 8 dB at the end
of the vowel; the state of this harmonic is consequently
the same at the end of the vowel as at the beginning: this
would satisfactorily explain the decrease in sensitivity
when the glissando (rising or falling) is associated with a
negative glide of intensity. Increases the difference
between the initial and the final state of the harmonic
under consideration; and in this case the glissando is more

easily perceived (Figs. 6). This model, however, can be
nothing but an extremely tentative explanation, based as
it is on an unverified hypothesis.

The following model is more reliable in that it is
based on verified and verifiable psychoacoustic data. It
is known that the pitch of a linear frequency glissando
(Nabélek and Hirsch, 1969; Rossi, 1971; Rossi, in press)
can always be represented by the frequency situated at two-
thirds of the slope, irrespective of whether the slope is
positive or negative. The loudness of an intensity glide,
on the other hand, is represented by the sound level of the
first third of a slope when the slope is negative and the
last third when the slope is positive (Fig. 9); in other
words the loudness is determined by the zone of maximum intensity (Rossi, in press). It is noticeable that in all
cases where the points of loudness and pitch coincide, the
perception of the glissando is improved: these points
always coincide when a positive intensity slope is associated with a rising or falling glissando; on the other
hand when the points of loudness and pitch are out of phase,
that is situated at different ends of the stimulus, the
resulting glissando is less well perceived: the association
of a negative slope of intensity and a rising or falling
glissando always brings about a separation of the two
points. The only example of a negative slope lowering the
threshold is when it is associated with a static frequency:
in this case, indeed, there cannot be separation of the
loudness point and the pitch point since there is no single
point of pitch in the signal.

The temporal separation also produces an appreciable
masking effect since the maximum point of intensity is
always, in these cases, situated near the beginning of the
signal. The reinforcement of the final part of the signal
by the temporal co-occurrence of the points of intensity
and pitch does not disturb the perception of the beginning
of the signal which is perceived like a variation of low
amplitude which is integrated as static. It is perhaps this
which causes the glissando to be perceived as a convex or
concave tone and facilitates its identification. Contrary
to what might have been expected, the perceptual contra-
diction responsible for the decrease in sensitivity to

the slope is not caused by the reversal of the intensity
glide and frequency glissando, but by the temporal separation
of the points of loudness and pitch.

CONCLUSION

The results we have just discussed have a direct consequence on the interpretation of prosodic phenomena. The
interaction of a negative slope of intensity and a falling
glissando would seem to indicate that at the end of a sentence a fall in pitch on the stressed syllable is badly perceived, and that it consequently has no intonative function in
neutral statements. This type of organization of prosodic
phenomena is to be met with in the realization of unmarked
terminal intonemes. The association of static intensity, or
a positive glide together with a falling glissando improves
the perceptibility of the glissando and creates, in the second
case, a convex perceptual pattern. These two patterns correspond to the organization of prosodic cues in marked terminal
intonemes (particularly implication and categorical affirma-
tion). For interrogative sentences, the intonation rise is
associated with an intensity slope which is either negative,
null or positive. The first case, where the sensitivity to
the slope is diminished, corresponds to an unmarked form of
question. The parallelism with the terminal intoneme is
obvious. The other two types of organization, which seem
to be the manifestation of marked intonemes, imply respectively an increased perceptibility of the slope and a concave tone. It remains to be seen what relationship exists
between convex and concave patterns created by a modulation
of intensity and those caused by a variation of Fo. The
interaction of variations of intensity and Fo demonstrates
that intonation is constituted by a pluriparametric organization; it also demonstrates the importance for intonative
studies of the perceptual level.

Delattre (1966) had concluded that the interrogative intoneme was represented by a concave Fo pattern. Di Cristo
(1978),however has shown that this type of pattern is not
typical of neutral questions. It is, however typical of marked questions. Delattre, apparently, had not distinguished between neutral and implicational questions. While it is true

that the latter are perceived as a concave pattern, this pattern does not appear in the signal, but is caused by a parallel rise of Fo and the intensity. Delattre had reproduced this subjective pattern synthetically by a concave Fo variation. As we have just seen the intonation features and cues defined by Delattre do not necessarily correspond to the acoustic signal since having been isolated by synthesis, they correspond to our perception of the interaction of parameters. We may consequently conclude that it is not possible to interpret intonation correctly without a perceptual conversion of the objective data.

BIBLIOGRAPHIE

Delattre, P.   (1966).   French Rev., 40:1-14.

Di Cristo, A.   (1975).   Trav. l'Inst. Phon. d'Aix, 5 (in press).

Feth, L. L.   (1972).   Acust., 26:67-77.

Maiwald (von), D.   (1967).   Acust., 18:81-93.

Møller, A.R. (1974).   Berlin, Springer, 227-240.

Nabélek, I. and Hirsch, I. J.   (1969).   J. Acoust. Soc. Am., 45:1510-1519.

Rossi, M.   (1971).   Phonet., 23:1-33.

Rossi, M.   J. Phon., 5, (in press).

Rossi, M.   Phonet. (in press).

Terhardt, J.   (1974).   Berlin, Springer, 353-360.

Zwicker, E.   (1962).   J. Acoust. Soc. Am., 34:1425-1430.

	Gt. I	
	+	−
+	IV, V, VI	III
−	II	I

Go. F

FIG. 1.   PLAN D'EXPERIENCE, Gt. I = GLISSEMENT D'INTENSITÉ; Go. F = GLISSANDO DE FRÉQUENCE

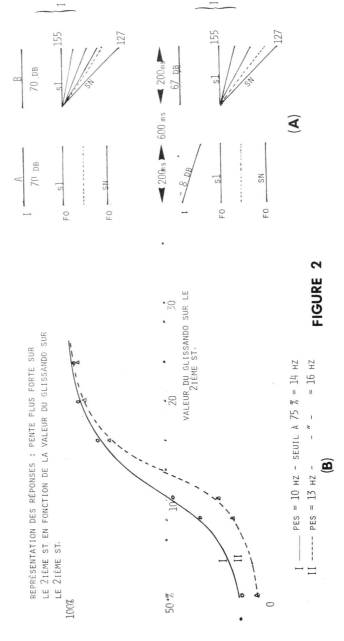

EFFET D'UN GLISSEMENT NÉGATIF D'INTENSITÉ SUR LE
SEUIL DE GLISSANDO DESCENDANT

REPRÉSENTATION DES RÉPONSES : PENTE PLUS FORTE SUR
LE 2IÈME ST EN FONCTION DE LA VALEUR DU GLISSANDO SUR
LE 2IÈME ST.

I —— PES = 10 HZ - SEUIL À 75 % = 14 HZ
II ----- PES = 13 HZ - " - = 16 HZ

FIGURE 2

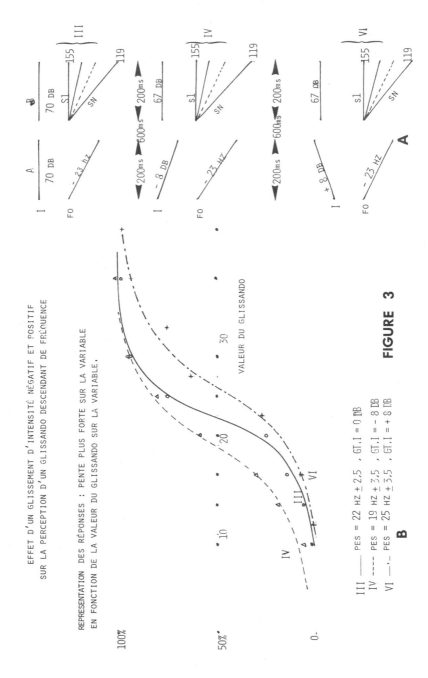

EFFET D'UN GLISSEMENT D'INTENSITÉ NÉGATIF ET POSITIF
SUR LA PERCEPTION D'UN GLISSANDO DESCENDANT DE FRÉQUENCE.

REPRESENTATION DES RÉPONSES : PENTE PLUS FORTE SUR LA VARIABLE
EN FONCTION DE LA VALEUR DU GLISSANDO SUR LA VARIABLE.

III ——— PES = 22 HZ ± 2,5 , GT.I = 0 DB
IV ---- PES = 19 HZ ± 3,5 , GT.I = - 8 DB
VI —·— PES = 25 HZ ± 3,5 , GT.I = + 8 DB

FIGURE 3

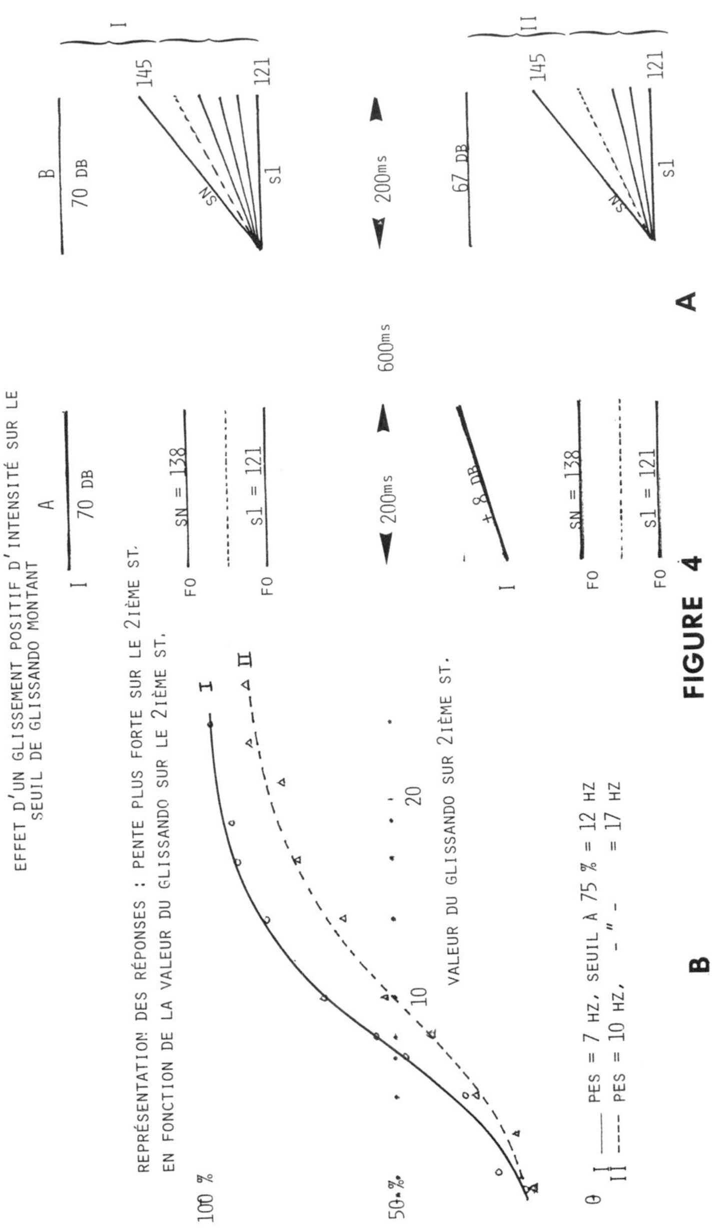
EFFET D'UN GLISSEMENT POSITIF D'INTENSITÉ SUR LE SEUIL DE GLISSANDO MONTANT
A
I
70 DB
FO
SN = 138
s1 = 121
200ms
600ms
+ 8 DB
B
70 DB
145
121
Ns
s1
200ms
67 DB
I
II
A
REPRÉSENTATION DES RÉPONSES : PENTE PLUS FORTE SUR LE 2IÈME ST. EN FONCTION DE LA VALEUR DU GLISSANDO SUR LE 2IÈME ST.
100 %
50 %
0
10
20
VALEUR DU GLISSANDO SUR 2IÈME ST.
I —— PES = 7 HZ, SEUIL À 75 % = 12 HZ
II ---- PES = 10 HZ, - " - = 17 HZ
B

FIGURE 4

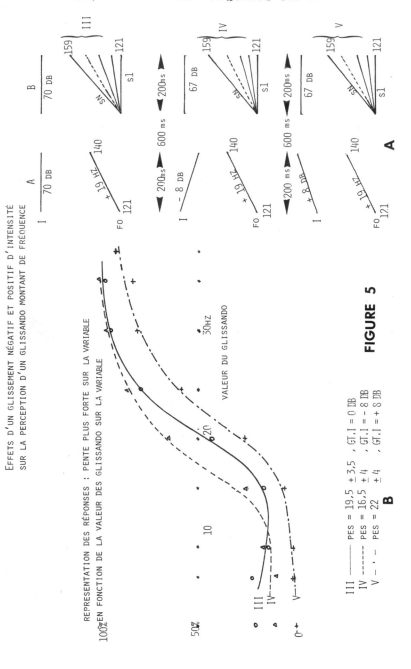

EFFETS D'UN GLISSEMENT NÉGATIF ET POSITIF D'INTENSITÉ
SUR LA PERCEPTION D'UN GLISSANDO MONTANT DE FRÉQUENCE

REPRESENTATION DES RÉPONSES : PENTE PLUS FORTE SUR LA VARIABLE
100% EN FONCTION DE LA VALEUR DES GLISSANDO SUR LA VARIABLE

VALEUR DU GLISSANDO

III ———— PES = 19,5 ± 3,5 , GT.I = 0 DB
IV ------ PES = 16,5 ± 4   , GT.I = - 8 DB
V - · - PES = 22   ± 4   , GT.I = + 8 DB

B

A

FIGURE 5

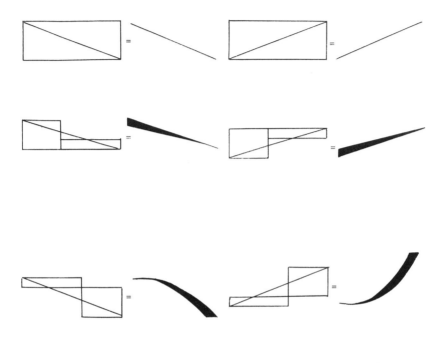

FIGURE 6 (A)   FIGURE 6 (B)

Perception schématisée d'un GoFo descendant   Perception schématisée d'un GoFo montant
  (a) en haut avec GT.I = 0   avec un GT.I ordonné comme en A.
  (b) au milieu avec GT.I = - 8 dB   Les rectangles sont une schématisation du
  (c) en bas avec GT.I = + 8 dB.   poids relatif de chaque partie du contour.

LA FUSION DES VOYELLES EN FRONTIERES INTER-SYNTAGMATIQUES ET INTRA-SYNTAGMATIQUES

LAURENT SANTERRE
Université de Montréal

On examinera la résistance a l'harmonisation qu'opposent les traits de nasalité, d'ouverture et de postériorité des voyelles qui se rencontrent de part et d'autre des frontières inter-syntagmatiques et intra-syntagmatiques. Le corpus a l'étude est composé de plus de 1300 cooccurrences de voyelles tirées de deux conversations libres du corpus Sankoff en francais de Montréal (Sankoff, 1976).

Ce corpus a été analysé sur les plans syntaxique, phonétique et perceptif. L'analyse syntaxique a consisté à indexer les mots selon les types de syntagmes et selon les catégories grammaticales auxquelles ils appartiennent; les frontières inter-syntagmatiques sont marquées par #, et les frontières intra-syntagmatiques, par +. L'analyse phonétique comprend les contextes phonologiques, la durée, l'accent sousjacent, l'accent de surface, les variations de l'intonation et de l'intensité, la transcription phonétique, le débit, la position dans l'énoncé, la position par rapport à l'accent, enfin le type de comportement segmental et suprasegmental. Au moyen de l'analyse acoustique et des tests de perception, on a jugé de la nasalisation, de l'ouverture et de la postériorisation. Pour plus de détails sur cette analyse, voir Santerre 1978. L'interet de ce travail est de voir si les traits segmentaux de nasalité, ouverture et postériorité passent les deux sortes de frontières avec la même facilité, et s'ils les passent avec la même facilité dans les deux sens, régressif et progressif. On devrait par là être un peu plus renseigné sur la nature des frontières et sur les traits segmentaux eux-mêmes.

LA NASALITÉ

Le tableau no 1 illustre, dans sa partie supérieure, les
résultats des cooccurrences de voyelles orales suivies de
voyelles nasales de part et d'autre des frontières inter et
intra-syntagmatiques, et dans sa partie inférieure, les cooccurrences des voyelles nasales suivies de voyelles orales,
i.e. en sens inverse, toujours selon les types de frontière.
Remarques sur le tableau 1. (1) Le trait de nasalité parait
à peu près irréductible, puisque l'on constate que sur les
444 occurrences de voyelles dont l'une est nasale, il n'y a
que 10 cas de perte de nasalité, soit seulement 2.2%. (2) Le
transfert de nasalité, ou l'assimilation nasale, est nettement
plus grand à travers les frontières intra-syntagmatiques
(comparer 27.4% et 24% pour les frontières #, contre 43.1% et
54.6% pour les frontières +). (3) Aux frontières +, l'ordre
(+nas) (-nas) semble, plus que l'inverse, favoriser l'assimilation, soit 54.6% contre 43.1%.

L'OUVERTURE

Le tableau 2 montre les résultats de l'analyse du trait
ouverture-fermeture à travers les frontières. Remarques sur
le tableau 2. (1) Sur 638 cooccurrences, il y a 354 cas
d'assimilation, soit 55%. Sur ces 354 cas d'assimilation,
76.8% se font par ouverture, et 23% par fermeture. (2) C'est
l'ordre (-bas) (+bas) qui favorise le plus l'ouverture, soit
62.7% dans cet ensemble, contre 23.5% dans l'ensemble de
l'ordre inverse. (3) Les frontières intra-syntagmatiques
permettent beaucoup plus les assimilations des deux ordres
que les frontières inter-syntagmatiques; comparer 34.6% et
9% pour les frontières #, contre 72.6% et 28.1% pour les
frontières +. (4) Dans les frontières #, la 2ème voyelle de
la séquence ouvre la 1ère qui se trouve pourtant sous l'accent
(34.6%). Quand la voyelle ouverte se trouve elle-même sous
l'accent, donc en 1ère position, l'assimilation par ouverture
n'est pas plus favorisée; l'ordre importe donc plus que
l'accent pour l'assimilation d'ouverture.

LA POSTERIORISATION

Le tableau 3 montre dans quelle mesure les voyelles
antérieures, non labialisées, ont tendance à se postérioriser

lorsqu'elles sont en cooccurrence avec une voyelle postérieure.
Les (a) sont exclus de cette compilation et ont fait l'objet
d'un traitement séparé, parce qu'ils sont souvent le résultat
d'une règle de postériorisation du /a/ en francais québécois.
Remarques sur le tableau 3. (1) Sur les 210 cooccurrences en
cause, on observe 107 cas de postériorisation (51%), 28 cas
d'antériorisation de la postérieure (11.4%), et 13 cas de
centralisation des deux voyelles (6.2%); le reste, soit 29.5%
n'a pas bougé à la frontière. C'est donc la postériorisation
qui est le phénomène dominant. (2) L'ordre le plus favorable
à l'assimilation par postériorisation est, comme pour l'ouverture, celui qui place la voyelle postérieure en 2ème position,
soit en dehors de l'accent dans les frontières #; comparer
56.8% pour (-pos) (+pos) contre 46.1% pour l'ordre inverse.
Quand il y a antériorisation, c'est surtout dans les cas où
l'antérieure est en 2ème position, soit 15.2% contre 1.7% dans
les frontières #; il est évident que la position l'emporte sur
l'accent. (3) L'ordre favorable (-pos) (+pos) est plus efficace
à travers les frontières +, i.e. à l'intérieur des syntagmes,
qu'à là frontière des syntagmes, (65.5% contre 43.2%). L'ordre
défavorable à la postériorisation, (+pos) (-pos), est plus
permissif de la postériorisation aux frontières # qu'aux
frontières + (51.5% contre 43.9%).

RÉSULTATS

     Les frontières inter-syntagmatiques opposent beaucoup
plus résistance au transfert des traits segmentaux que les
frontières intra-syntagmatiques. C'est ce à quoi on pouvait
s'attendre, puisque les frontières majeures sont rarement
annulées, mais protégées par les traits suprasegmentaux de
variation d'intensité, d'intonation et de durée en même temps
que par les traits segmentaux. Les frontières majeures ne
tombent que dans une proportion inférieure à 2%, tandis que
les frontières mineures peuvent tomber dans au-delà de 25%
des cas. Les frontières mineures sont protégées surtout par
les traits segmentaux, et elles sont beaucoup plus facilement
perméables. Pour plus de détails, voir Santeere 1978.

     Le trait de nasalité est à peu près irréductible et il
s'est transmis, à travers les deux types de frontières et dans
les deux sens, dans une proportion globale de 40.75% dans notre

corpus. Le trait d'ouverture domine sa contrepartie de fermeture et il s'est imposé à travers les frontières dans une
proportion globale de 42.63%. Quant à la postériorité, elle
l'emporte sur l'antériorité et elle a dominé dans 51% des cas
possibles. Même si ces compilations ne font que comparer
les effectifs comportant un trait avec ceux qui ne le com-
portaient pas, sans tenir compte par exemple des degrés
d'ouverture dans la nasalité ou la postériorité, ni de la
postériorité dans la comparaison des degrés d'ouverture ou de
fermeture, il semble bien que le trait le plus lourd et le
plus apte à s'imposer à travers les frontières, donc à les
annuler, soit la postériorité; dans l'ordre viendrait ensuite
l'ouverture, et enfin la nasalité. Mais il n'est pas impossible que l'analyse d'un corpus assez considérable pour per-
mettre des décomptes séparés pour tous les lieux d'articulation
aboutisse à un ordre différent.

On a vu que l'ordre des segments le plus favorable à la
pénétration des frontières et à l'assimilation était progressif pour la nasalisation, et régressif pour l'ouverture
et la postériorisation, du moins pour les frontières intra-
syntagmatiques. On en a conclu que la position du trait
assimilateur importait plus que son accentuation. L'ordre
régressif d'assimilation est connu comme le plus naturel au
francais; c'est celui de l'anticipation articulatoire. Quant
à l'assimilation par nasalité, elle est plutôt progressive
parce que le voile du palais ne s'abaisse pas avant l'arrivée
du phonème nasal; il impose même un retard à la nasalisation,
et une fois abaissé il est ensuite lent à s'élever. Le retard
à nasaliser et à dénasaliser entraîne l'assimilation du segment qui suit plutôt que de celui qui précède la voyelle nasale
Il en est ainsi du moins en francais québécois (Charbonneau
1971) où l'anticipation de nasalité est rare, tandis que le
retard de nasalité est constant.

CONCLUSION

La perméabilité des frontières nous renseigne sur la
cohésion dans la chaîne parlée des constituants en regard.
Le comportement des paramètres acoustiques est le reflet en
surface de l'organisation syntactico-sémantique des structures
profondes. Il me semble, sur la foi de cette recherche

préliminaire, que les traits segmentaux sont plutôt régis par les contraintes que leur imposent les frontières intra-syntagmatiques, tandis que les traits suprasegmentaux ont des fonctions plus importantes aux frontières inter-syntag-matiques.

BIBLIOGRAPHIE

Sankoff, D. et al. (1976). Montréal, Press l'Univ. Québec.
Santerre, L. et Villa, D. (1978). Paris, Didier.
Charbonneau, R. (1971). Paris, P.U.L. Québec.

VOYELLES DE SURFACE

Voyelles Sous-jacentes	N	V + V (+nas) + (-nas) N	V + V (+nas) + (-nas) %	V # V (+nas) + (-nas) N	V # V (+nas) + (-nas) %	V + V (-nas) + (+nas) N	V + V (-nas) + (+nas) %	V # V (-nas) + (+nas) N	V # V (-nas) + (+nas) %
V # V (-nas)(+nas)	62	17	27.4			45	72.6		
V + V (-nas)(+nas)	188	81	43.1	5	2.6	102	54.2		
Total	250	98	39.2	5	2.0	147	58.8		
V # V (+nas)(-nas)	75	18	24.0	2	2.7			55	73.3
V + V (+nas)(-nas)	119	65	54.6	3	2.5			51	42.9
Total	194	83	42.8	5	2.6			106	54.6

Tableau 1. La Nasalité.

Voyelles Sous-jacentes	N	VOYELLES DE SURFACE							
		V # V (+bas) N	V (+bas) %	V # V (-bas) N	V (-bas) %	V # V (-bas) N	V (+bas) %	V # V (+bas) N	V (+bas) %
V # V (-bas)(+bas)	81	28	34.6	3	3.7	50	61.7		
V + V (-bas)(+bas)	230	167	72.6	5	2.2	58	25.2		
Total	311	195	62.7	8	2.6	108	34.7		
V # V (+bas)(-bas)	78	7	9.0	7	9.0			64	82.0
V + V (+bas)(-bas)	249	70	28.1	67	26.9			112	45.0
Total	327	77	23.5	74	22.6			176	53.8

Tableau 2.   L'ouverture.

Voyelles sous-jacentes	N	V # V (+pos)+(+pos)		V # V (-pos)+(-pos)		Centralisation des deux segments		V # V (-pos)+(+pos)		V # V (+pos)+(-pos)	
		N	%	N	%	N	%	N	%	N	%
V # V (-pos)(+pos)	37	16	43.2	3	8.1	2	5.4	16	43.2		
V + V (-pos)(+pos)	58	38	65.5	1	1.7	2	3.4	17	29.3		
Total	95	54	56.8	4	4.2	4	4.2	33	34.7		
V # V (+pos)(-pos)	33	17	51.5	5	15.2	3	9.1			8	24.2
V + V (+pos)(-pos)	82	36	43.9	19	23.2	6	7.3			21	25.6
Total	115	53	46.1	24	20.9	9	7.8			29	25.2

VOYELLES DE SURFACE

Tableau 3. La Postériorité.

SPECULATIONS ON A CONTACT-INDUCED PHONOLOGICAL CHANGE IN GALLO-ITALIAN

GLADYS E. SAUNDERS
Pennsylvania State University

Attempts to establish a theory of sound change have prompted linguists to revert to the question of causality. It has been argued (Lyle Campbell, 1976) that in framing a theory of linguistic change we must take into account not only the internally motivated changes, i.e., those changes attributable to the physical properties of the sound, but also the externally motivated changes, including those changes brought about by language contact. I agree in general with this thesis and will offer further support for the argument in the discussion that follows.

Within the last two centuries literary Italian has exerted a strong superstratum influence on Bolognese. This is evident in Bolognese phonology where modifications due to literary Italian interference have been far-reaching. One such modification will concern us here, namely, the loss of nasality. Modern Bolognese, as spoken by the average speaker under the age of sixty-five, has no nasal vowels. Yet there is evidence that nasal vowels did exist (phonemically distinct from oral vowels) in earlier stages of the dialect. Why should a language once characterized by the feature of nasality lose such a feature? Why hasn't the change also affected the phonology of neighboring mountain dialects--dialects in which vowel nasality still prevails? I shall argue that the modification which has taken place in modern Bolognese, as regards nasality, is the result of a language contact situation in which existing phonological

material of a dominated language shifted its phonetic value
due to the interference of a dominant, prestige language.
This discussion must not be construed as an argument against
phonetically motivated changes, or so called natural pro-
cesses--quite the contrary. It should be interpreted as an
attempt to answer this fundamental question: assuming that
there are a number of possibilities for directions of change,
what determines, in the final analysis, the particular
direction that a change pursues? Several clues suggest the
reconstruction of nasal vowels for Bolognese, among which
are: (a) the presence of a velar /ŋ/ in the modern dialect;
(b) the development of stressed vowels before nasals in
contrast to their development before non-nasals; (c) historical comparative evidence from related languages (French and
other Gallo-Italian dialects) and (d) impressionistic remarks
made by early dialectologists.

Modern Bolognese has four nasal consonants /m, n, ñ, ŋ /.
In terms of underlying features or systematic phonemes, the
labial, dental and palatal nasals present no problem: they
should be treated as phonemes. (See examples in Table 1.)
The status of /ŋ/, however, is precarious. To begin with,
the /ŋ/ has a very limited distribution. Whereas the other
nasals occur initially, medially and finally, the velar
nasal is restricted to syllable final position. In his 1970
structural study of Bolognese, Coco maintains that /ŋ/ is
not a phoneme, but rather an allophone of /n/. To support
his analysis he provides a complex phonetically conditioned
statement, with a jumble of exceptions, that will presumably
predict the occurrences of /n/ and /ŋ/. I do not concur. I
find no compelling reason to suppose that I do not in fact
have four nasal phonemes--one with a peculiar distribution.
But let me return to Coco's analysis and show where it
disappoints. He assumes that /n/ and /ŋ/ are mutually
exclusive. An abbreviation of his statement regarding the
occurrence of /n/ and /ŋ/ is as follows: /n/ → ŋ / V̆
__ (C)#; elsewhere, /n/ → n. (The phoneme /n/ is realized
as a velar nasal in syllable final position, when preceded
by a short stressed vowel and followed by an optional consonant; elsewhere, /n/ is realized as a dental nasal.) This
statement precludes the occurrence of a dental nasal in
syllable final position when the immediately preceding vowel
is short and stressed. But is this statement accurate? If

one takes into consideration the morphophonemics of Bolognese
(which Coco does not do), one encounters, in exactly the
environment restricted to /ŋ/, occurrences of /n/. That is,
Bolognese has a morphophonemic rule which derives certain
feminine plural forms from their corresponding singular forms
by deletion of the final /-a/, e.g.

Singular	Plural	
vá:ka	vá:k	'cow, -s'
a:sa	á:s	'axe, -s'
fója	fój	'leaf, -ves'
suláta	sulát	'sole, -s'
pána	pán	'feather, -s'

Here we see that /pán/ 'feathers' exemplifies the occurrence
of a dental nasal /n/ in syllable final position, immediately
preceded by a short stressed vowel. Since the two phones
/ŋ/ and /n/ do occur in the same environment, as illustrated
by the minimal pair /pán/ 'feathers' /páŋ/ 'bread,' they
must be considered phonemically distinct. But it is not my
intent to debate the phonemic hypothesis at this time.
Rather, I would like to examine the circumstances which
gave rise to the velar segment to begin with.

Historically, the /ŋ/ in Bolognese must be seen as a
vestige of a denasalization process. I have outlined this
process in Figure 1. Here, Roman I represents summarily
the vowels inherited from Western Romance. At this pre-
Bolognese stage, the vowels show no effects of nasalization.
The stage designated by Roman II represents three centuries
of developments--from the end of the 10th century up through
the 13th century. During this period we may assume that
Bolognese had a rule of regressive nasal assimilation--not
unlike that of Old French--which specified that stressed
vowels nasalized when in the environment of a following nasal
consonant: V → Ṽ / __ N; e.g., grand → grãnd 'big.'
Obviously all stressed vowels did not automatically become
nasalized at the same time. Rather, the vowels became
nasalized in turn. It is likely that the low vowels became
nasalized before the high ones.

Roman III in Figure 1 represents the stage in which the loss of nasal consonants in certain environments (for example, at the end of a syllable) led to restructuring: nasality is no longer moored to nasal consonants. That is, in syllable final position we now find an underlying nasal vowel (as opposed to an underlying oral vowel plus a nasal consonant in other positions): N → ∅ / ___ #; e.g., /vĩ/, /vĩ:/ 'wine' but /luna/, /lũ:na/ 'moon.' This stage probably stretched over two centuries; then further developments set in. Nasality led to vowel lowering (cf. Roman IV, Fig. 1). The mid vowels probably began to lower first, while the high vowels lowered last. This process must have continued throughout the 17th century, or even later, with the lowering of /ũ/ to /õ/.

Roman V shows the rise of an epenthetic velar nasal in the environment of a preceding nasal vowel: ∅ → ŋ / Ṽ ___; e.g. lõ:na → lõŋna 'moon.' I assume that the epenthetic /ŋ/ is a development subsequent to the vowel lowering process mentioned above--though a case could be made for the converse order of developments. In seeking motivation for the rise of the velar nasal, one is tempted to draw a parallelism with the denasalization stage cited in the evolution of nasal vowels in French. Such an analysis would perhaps interpret the /ŋ/ of Bolognese as a preliminary or initial phase of the denasalization process. But the question that comes to mind immediately is why should the nasal vowels begin to denasalize, i.e., why should a process that had taken several centuries to come into effect reverse its direction, unexpectedly? The cause cited frequently for the denasalization process in the history of French is the tendency, on the part of a language, to dismiss a redundant feature--the redundant feature being the co-occurrence of non-conditioned nasalized vowels (which resulted from the effacement of syllable final nasal consonants) and environmentally conditioned nasalized vowels. Nasal vowels which appeared before intervocalic nasal consonants consequently denasalized. For Bolognese, I maintain that the motivation just mentioned for the denasalization process in French is not adequate. An explanation of the rise of the velar nasal in Bolognese must be sought elsewhere. However, before going further into the explanation of this change, let me return to Figure 1

and briefly comment on the final stage (Roman VI), as this
stage marks an extension of the change in question.

Roman VI represents contemporary Bolognese, which
is characterized by the absence of vowel nasality and by
the presence of a seemingly ubiquitous velar nasal consonant.
This latter can no longer be called epenthetic because the
conditioning environment (vowel nasality) has disappeared.
That is to say, a restructuring in Bolognese phonology has
taken place.

To return to the question of causality raised above,
my theory is that the /ŋ/, which must reflect a step in the
denasalization process, arose in response to a language contact situation. More specifically, I assume that, up until
the early 18th century, Bolognese still possessed underlying
nasalized vowels (which occurred only in syllable final position, and which could contrast with oral vowels in exactly
that position), along with environmentally conditioned nasal
vowels (intervocalic nasal consonants had not ceased to
nasalize preceding stressed vowels). Nasality is a prominent feature of Bolognese during this period. As Tuscan,
the literary language, became more and more identified as the
language of prestige, and as more and more Bolognese speakers
encountered the literary language and attempted to imitate
it (either consciously or perhaps unknowingly), nasal vowels
in Bolognese became more than ever before stigmatized. If
we suppose that Tuscan speakers ascribe lower class status
to speakers who show a high proportion of nasalized vowels,
and that the pronunciation of non-nasalized vowels is the
mark of prestige, then speakers who show a high proportion
of pronunciations without nasalized vowels would be ascribed
higher social status. The effort, on the part of the
Bolognese speakers, to deaccentuate the characteristic
feature of nasality must have led to the development of the
epenthetic velar nasal consonant and to the eventual denasalization of the vowels. This is illustrated by:
$\tilde{V}: \rightarrow \tilde{V}^{\eta} \rightarrow V^{\eta}$; e.g., $\text{gr}\tilde{a}\text{:d} \rightarrow \text{gr}\tilde{a}^{\eta}\text{d} \rightarrow \text{gra}\eta\text{d}$ 'big.'
Perhaps this change originated in the speech of middle class
Bolognese speakers--those who would have been more aware of
and concerned about language differences than, for example,
the poorer members of the society. Once underway, the change

would then be transmitted to the children, who were learning the dialect. In time, the denasalized vowels would be the general case rather than the exception.

Impressionistic remarks made by Coco in his 1970 study, when compared with those made by Trauzzi (Ungarelli, 1901), shed some interesting light on the denasalization process in Bolognese. While Coco maintains that the average Bolognese speaker does not have nasal vowels--though he admits, in a footnote, that such can be heard on rare occasions when talking with the oldest members of society--Trauzzi, in speaking of the complexity of Bolognese vocalism notes that the language is characterized by overtly marked nasal vowels. Hence, the former, a recent study, accentuates the similarity of Bolognese to Italian, while the latter, an older study, accentuates the differences between the two languages.

Nearby mountain dialects (cf. Nonatola) still show underlying nasal vowels--the presumable archaic feature (see examples in Table 2). The speakers of these dialects would not have much to gain by imitating literary Italian (a person close to the soil, so to speak, is hardly concerned about the prestige aspect of a language). Furthermore, because of their relative geographical isolation, they would not have a great deal of contact with the literary language. Whether or not the mountain dialects will eventually follow the path of denasalization described above is a difficult question to answer--only time can tell.

To sum up, the Bolognese-Italian contact situation provides an example of the manner in which a dominant language can, in certain sociological contexts, alter the phonology and affect the sound system of a less prestigious, dominated language. I hope that the above investigation of the loss of vowel nasality in Bolognese will have some implications for the theory of language change which takes into account external factors as well as internal (phonetically conditioned) factors.

REFERENCES

Campbell, L. (1976). 181-194.
Coco, F. (1970). Bologna; Forni Editore.
Kristeller, P. O. (1946). Word, 2:50-65.
Pope, M. K. (1952). Manchester, University Press.
Ungarelli, G. (1901). Bologna.

Table 1. Distribution of nasal consonants in Bolognese.
(I = word initial; II = intervocalic; III = pre-
consonant, nonfinal; IV = post-consonant, nonfinal;
V = pre-consonant, final; VI = word-final.)

	/m/		/n/	
I.	mánt	'mountain'	nó:v	'nine'
II.	ó:men	'man, men'	lέ:na	'wool'
			pána	'feather'
III.	fámna	'woman'	Kandájla	'candle'
IV.	stmέ:na	'week'	maznέ:r	'to grind'
V.	stámg	'stomach'	---	
VI.	rá:m	'copper'	a:n	'year'

	/ñ/		/ŋ/	
I.	ñó:l	'whimper'	---	
II.	véña	'vineyard'	---	
III.	---		pjáŋta	'plant'
			vaŋna	'vein'
IV.	sñáwr	'sir'	---	
V.	---		gráŋd	'big'
VI.	láñ	'wood'	páŋ	'bread'
			véŋ	'wine'

Table 2.   Nasal Vowels in the Nonatola Dialect.
           (I = underlying nasal vowels; II = oral vowel
           followed by nasal consonant; III = nasal vowel
           followed by nasal consonant.)

I		II		III	
pĩː	'full' (masc.)	piːna	'full' (fem.)	galẽːna	'hen'
vẽː	'wine'	pɛna	'feather'	duzˈẽːna	'twelve'
bõː	'good' (masc.)	pɛn	'feathers'	lũːna	'moon'.
pãː	'bread'	bɔːna	'good' (fem.)		
Kãː	'dog'	veːna	'vein'		
ũː	'one'	an	'year'		

Figure 1. DEVELOPMENT OF STRESSED VOWELS BEFORE NASALS.

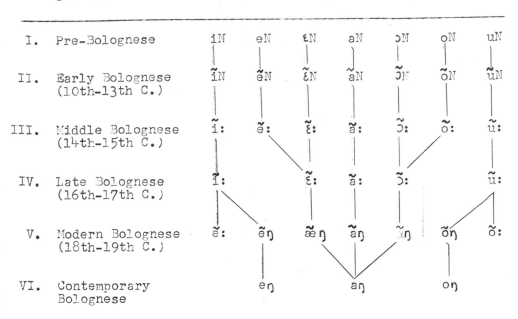

	'moon'	'wine'	'chain'
I.	luna	vin	kadena
II.	lŭna	vĭn	kadĕna
III.	lũːna	vĩː	kadẽːna
IV.	lõːna	vẽː	kadɛ̃ːna
V.	lõŋna	vẽŋ	kadæ̃ŋna
VI.	loŋna	veŋ	kadaŋna

A SHORT MEMORY STRATEGY WITH DISTINCTIVE FEATURES

JAMES MONROE STEWART AND CAROL BARACH
Tennessee State University

Speech researchers have identified a number of variables which can be manipulated to determine the ultimate composition of the phoneme, and these variables coupled with computer technology have led to the extraction of the criterial attributes in speech perception. The study undertaken here reflects the perceptual strategies of adult listeners when a psychophysical method is applied in combination with a short memory task. The scope of the investigation at a microlevel of speech perception was to evaluate certain perceptual responses and their underlying strategies. The goal is to identify and describe some of the underlying strategies of distinctive-feature utilization associated with speech stimuli. The specific purpose of the study was to determine whether a hierarchical structure exists within the phonological domain of distinctive features. The secondary purpose was to determine whether the Chomsky and Halle (1968) Distinctive Feature System is relevant to and descriptive of the perceptual domain of the listener in a speech processing mode. The strategies applied for eliciting responses have been utilized successfully in studies involved in the identification of the psychological units of speech. The evaluation of the responses was obtained through the discrimination in similarity of paired-dyadic stimuli with the Friedman (1937) two-way analysis of variance as the criterion measure for the relative amount of similarity of the paired dyads. The basic unit of input was the CV syllable with the unit of analysis as the judgement between two minimally distinct pairs of disyllables.

PROCEDURES

Subjects. Subjects were from four classes (N = 68)
randomly selected from the two divisions of the Department
of Communication at Tennessee State University. Groups 1,
2, and 3, which consisted of 17, 16, and 18 subjects,
respectively, were comprised of 51 students taking a university requirement in speech. Group 4 was comprised of 17
speech pathology majors with some knowledge of phonetics
(see Black, 1974 and Peters, 1963). A screening evaluation
was given to each student to ascertain whether hearing was
impaired and to determine whether speech was defective. No
subject participated who manifested any type of minimal hearing or speech problem.

Discriminative Stimuli. A discrimination item (or a
stimulus set) consisted of two pairs of dyads spoken with
equal stress contrasting minimally on one of four distinctive
features proposed by Chomsky and Halle (1968). For each
disyllable the two phonemes were paired and identical except
for one feature and, in addition, the two dyadic pairs contained a common phoneme and contrasted two features. For
example, one dyad consisted of /b/ and /p/ and the second dyad
consisted of /b/ and /m/; the first dyad differs on the voicing dimension while the second differs by nasality. The two
disyllables pairs contain /b/ as the common phoneme and contrast the features of voicing and nasality. The stimulus sets
were recorded with the vowel /a/ in the context of a CV syllable. The voicing versus nasality stimulus sets were also
recorded with the vowels /i/ and /u/. Chomsky and Halle's
distinctive feature system includes thirteen features, however, only four features met the requirement of minimally
distinct across pairs as well as within pairs. The four
features included in the study were: voicing, nasality,
stridency, and coronal.

A female who spoke General American English recorded the
sixty-eight stimulus sets with a chest microphone feeding a
Wollensak 6256 high-fidelity stereo tape recorder. The tape
recording was done in a sound-treated room with the stimulus
syllables peaking 0 on the VU meter. There were five seconds
between stimulus sets for subject responses with one second

between pairs in a set. Prior to presentation, the stimulus
tape was evaluated by two persons competent in phonetics to
ascertain the intelligibility of the items. The four classes
were each tested during their regular class hour. The test
was conducted in the same classroom with the stimuli being
presented via sound-field at a comfortable loudness level.
The playback recorder was the same one utilized in recording
the stimuli.

RESULTS

Voicing vs. Coronal Contrasts. Figure 1 shows the order
of presentation of the feature contrasts on the abscissa and
the pooled sample's preferential judgements of similarity in
percent on the ordinate. The figure shows for order 1 the
percentage of similarity judgements associated with the presentation of the voicing contrast first and the coronal
contrast second. In order 1, the subjects judged voicing
more similar 71 percent of the time as to the 29 percent of
the coronal contrast. The figure shows for order 2 the percentage of similarity judgements associated with the presentation of the coronal contrast first and the voicing contrast
second. In order 2, the subjects judged the similarity of the
coronal contrast 46 percent of the time as to the 54 percent
of the voicing contrast. In either presentation order, the
voicing contrast appears more similar. For purposes of information, the figure shows the combined totals of similarity
judgements across both presentation orders. In this total,
the voicing contrast was judged more similar 62 percent of the
time as to the 38 percent of the coronal contrast.

Stridency vs. Coronal Contrasts. Figure 2 shows the
order of presentation of the feature contrasts on the abscissa
and the pooled sample's preferential judgements of similarity
in percent on the ordinate. The figure shows for order 1 the
percentage of similarity judgements associated with the presentation of the stridency contrast first and the coronal contrast second. In order 1, the subjects judged stridency more
similar 75 percent of the time as to the 25 percent of the
coronal contrast. The figure shows for order 2 the percentage
of similarity judgements associated with the presentation of
the coronal contrast first and the stridency contrast second.

In order 2, the subjects judged coronal more similar 30 percent of the time as to the 70 percent of the stridency contrast. In either presentation order, the stridency contrast appears more similar. For purposes of information, the figure shows the combined totals of similarity judgements across both orders of presentations. In this total, the stridency contrast was judged more similar 73 percent of the time as to the 27 percent of the coronal contrast.

Voice vs. Stridency Contrasts. Figure 3 shows the order of presentation of the feature contrasts on the abscissa and the pooled sample's preferential judgements of similarity in percent on the ordinate. The figure shows for order 1 the percentage of similarity judgements associated with the presentation of the voicing contrast first and the stridency contrast second. In order 1, the subjects judged voicing more similar 55 percent of the time as to the 45 percent of the stridency contrast. The figure shows for order 2 the percentage of similarity judgements associated with the presentation of the stridency contrast first and the voicing contrast second. In order 2, the subjects judged the similarity of the stridency contrast more similar 45 percent of the time as to the 55 percent of the voicing contrast. In either order of presentation, the voicing contrast appears more similar. For purpose of information, the figure shows the combined totals of similarity judgement across both presentation orders. In this total, the voicing contrast was judged more similar 55 percent of the time as to the 45 percent of the stridency contrast.

Voicing vs. Nasality Contrasts. Figure 4 shows the order of presentation of the feature contrasts on the abscissa and the pooled sample's preferential judgements of similarity in percent on the ordinate. The figure shows for order 1 the percentage of similarity judgements associated with the presentation of the voicing contrast first and the nasality contrast second. In order 1, the subjects judged voicing more similar 60 percent of the time as to the 40 percent of the nasality contrast. The figure shows for order 2 the percentage of similarity judgements associated with the presentation of the nasality contrast first and the voicing contrast second. In order 2, the subjects judged the

similarity of the voicing contrast more similar 45 percent
of the time as to the 55 percent of the nasality contrast.
In this stimulus set, the order of presentation appears
important. For informative purposes, the figure shows the
combined totals of similarity judgements across both presentation orders. In this total, the voicing contrast was
judged more similar 52 percent of the time as to the 48
percent of the nasality contrast.

DISCUSSION

The short memory paradigm utilized to judge the
similarity of feature contrasts of two pairs of dyadic
syllables appears to reveal results consistent with related
studies. As early as 1963, Peters addressed linguistic
concerns relative to group versus individual differences,
as well as the experienced versus the naive listener. Peters
(1963) found that "the responses of the subjects in the non-
phonetic group were more like the responses of the subjects
in the phonetic group. . . ." Mohr and Wang (1968) found
significant correlations between the groups on their internal
consistency of similarity judgements, although the experimental task differed slightly with the three groups of subjects, who differed relative to linguistic backgrounds. The
current study supports the findings of these studies in that
the three groups of novice listeners and the one group of
students with some phonetic training revealed comparable
responses on their judgements of similarity. Black (1974)
used only novice listeners because he felt experienced
listeners, based upon a pilot procedure, provide no new information, that is they have biases toward learned labels
or classes of phonetic sounds. However, this observation/
finding is not inconsistent with the current or previous
studies. In addition, the nonsignificant result of the
within-order presentations in the current study supports the
finding of Mohr and Wang in that order of presentation is
insignificant.

From earlier studies, some question has arisen regarding
the effects of different vowels in nonsense syllables. The
current study utilized the vowels /i/, /a/, and /u/ in the
voicing versus nasality contrast in order to address the issue.

In this epoch, the three vowels manifested nonsignificance.
Black (1968, 1969, 1974) does not address the issue with
his use of five vowels. Singh and Black (1966) found the
vowel /a/ to yield slightly better discrimination in their
stimuli than the vowel /i/ for the English-speaking listeners. Wang and Bilger (1973) found /u/ to out-perform
/a/ in all their syllable sets; "The effects of the vowel
/i/ on consonant intelligibility, however, depended on
consonant position." However, as an additional point, these
two studies utilized signal distortion.

The between-order findings are of major importance in
this study. The feature contrasts of voicing versus coronal,
stridency versus coronal, and voicing versus stridency, and
voicing versus nasality were all significant. Figures 1, 2,
and 3 reflect a graphic presentation of the saliency of the
feature contrasts. These figures show the greater similarity
of voicing, stridency, and voicing, respectively. Only the
voicing versus coronal contrasts of Figure 1 reveal a dramatic change in the number of similar responses as a function
of order. Figure 2 reflects five percent change with order
in the stridency versus coronal contrasts, while Figure 3
reveals a constant response tendency in the voicing versus
stridency contrasts. Figure 4 appears to reflect a somewhat
stable relationship between voicing and nasality relative to
response judgements of similarity, much like that of voicing
versus stridency. However, in this stimulus set, the judgement of similarity appears to be a function of the order of
presentation. The reason for this is open to speculation.
One possible answer is that voicing and nasality may have
equal perceptual saliency. A second possibility is that the
structure of the paradigm called for not a similarity contrast
between voicing and nasality, but minus nasality versus plus
nasality. This second speculation is based upon the redundancy of voicing in nasality in English and the insignificance
of the within-order of presentation.

REFERENCES

Black, J. W. (1968). Columbus, Ohio State Univ. Res. Found.
Black, J. W. (1969). Columbus, Ohio State Univ. Res. Found.
Black, J. W. (1974). Columbus, Ohio State Univ. Res. Found.

Chomsky, N. and Halle, M.   (1968).   New York, Harper and Row.

Friedman, M.   (1937).   J. Amer. Stat. Assoc., 32:675-701.

Kruskal, W. H. and Wallis, W. A.   (1952).   J. Amer. Stat.
     Assoc., 47:583-621.

Mohr, B. and Wang, W. S.-Y.   (1968).   Phon., 18:31-45.

Peters, R. W.   (1963).   J. Acoust. Soc. Amer., 35:1985-1989.

Siegel, S.   (1956).   New York, McGraw-Hill.

Singh, S. and Black, J. W.   (1966).   J. Acoust. Soc. Amer.,
     39:372-387.

Wang, M. D. and Bilger, R. C.   (1973).   J. Acoust. Soc. Amer.,
     54:1248-1266.

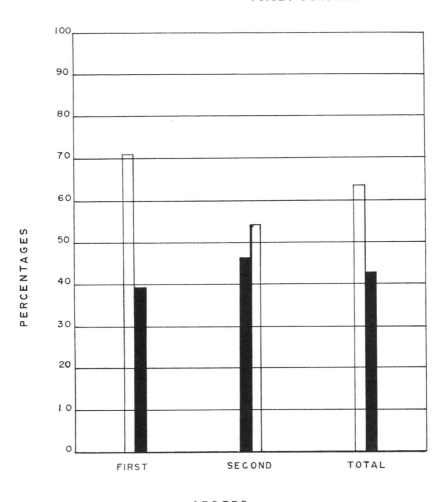

FEATURE   CONTRASTS

VOICE / CORONAL

☐ VOICING

■ CORONAL

Figure 1

BAR GRAPH SHOWING THE ORDER OF PRESENTATION OF THE FEATURE CONTRASTS
ON THE ABSCISSA AND THE POOLED SAMPLS'S PREFERENTIAL JUDGEMENTS OF A
SIMILARITY IN PERCENT ON THE ORDINATE.

FEATURE CONTRASTS
CORONAL / STRIDENT

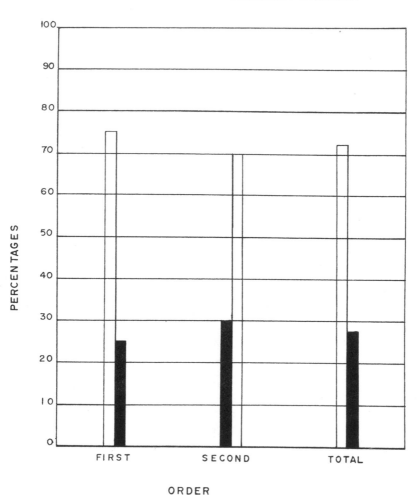

STRIDENCY

CORONAL

Figure 2

BAR GRAPH SHOWING THE ORDER OF PRESENTATION OF THE FEATURE CONTRASTS
ON THE ABSCISSA AND THE POOLED SAMPLE'S PREFERENTIAL JUDGEMENTS OF
SIMILARITY IN PERCENT ON THE ORDINATE.

FEATURE   CONTRASTS

VOICING / STRIDENCY

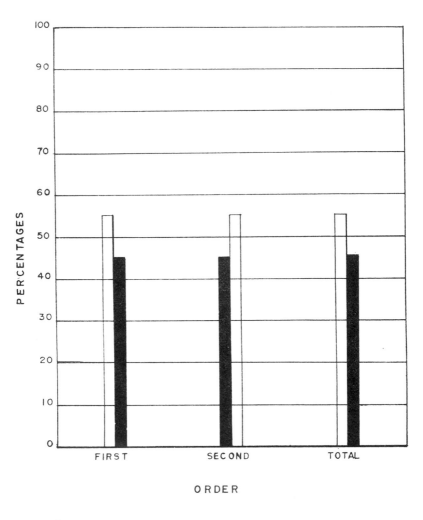

ORDER

☐   VOICING   **Figure 3**

■   STRIDENCY

BAR GRAPH SHOWING THE ORDER OF PRESENTATION OF THE FEATURE CONTRASTS
ON THE ABSCISSA AND THE POOLED SAMPLE'S PREFERENTIAL JUDGEMENTS OF
SIMILARITY IN PERCENT ON THE ORDINATE.

FEATURE CONTRASTS

VOICING / NASALITY

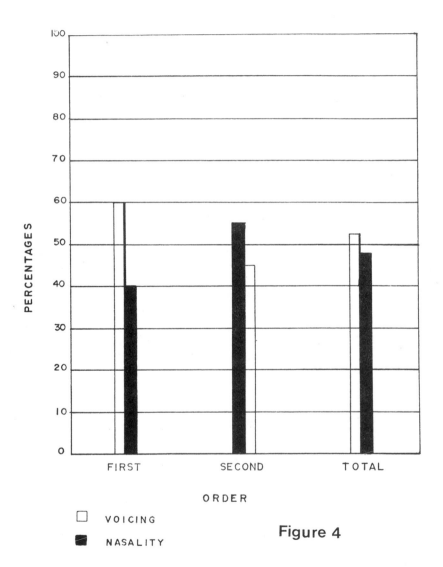

ORDER

☐ VOICING

◤ NASALITY

Figure 4

BAR GRAPH SHOWING THE ORDER OF PRESENTATION OF THE FEATURE CONTRASTS
ON THE ABSCISSA AND THE POOLED SAMPLE'S PREFERENTIAL JUDGEMENTS OF
SIMILARITY IN PERCENT ON THE ORDINATE.

THE ANALYSIS OF THE COMBINATIONS OF
DISTINCTIVE SOUNDS

ANA TATARU
University of Mannheim

This paper presents a new method of analysis based on
contrastive study of the pronunciation of Rumanian and
English. It refers to the combinations of distinctive
sounds, within speech units, in the standard pronunciation
of these languages. The clusters of special interest are
the Rumanian and English /pr,pl,br,bl,tr,tl,dr,dl,kr,kl,gr,
gl/ and also the Rumanian and English diphthongs, as all of
them undergo different combinations in the two languages
influencing their specific pronunciation: the differences
can be distinguished by simple ear training. My idea that
there necessarily must exist differences according to the
mode and intensity of combination (kind and degree of combination) of distinctive sounds has been initially backed
by a short sentence in Jones (1960): ". . .while in other
cases, e.g., in cats. . .the two sounds are pronounced
together in more or less intimate combination" and he adds:
". . .it is often difficult to draw a line of demarcation
between an affricate and an intimate combination of two
sounds."

My contrastive study of the pronunciation of Rumanian
and English includes along with a general comparison of their
systems, also a special analysis of their occlusive consonants. In it I included an analysis of the combinations
of consonants. The special comparison gave a detailed

contrastive description of the Rumanian and English occlusive
consonants (stops and nasals) within words, according to an
original model: we gave first a parallel detailed description
of the articulatory features of the Rumanian and English
plosives, i.e., their own characteristics followed by the
changes resulting from the mutual influence between the
plosives and the contiguous phonemes. This parallel
description was complemented by a contrastive analysis of
the similarities and differences between the Rumanian and
English plosives relative to articulation, combination,
distribution, and spelling, and by a chapter on pronunciation
problems which are caused by interference from the native
language in articulation, combination, distribution and
spelling. The same analysis of the nasals then followed.

Our reason for such a complex analysis was to offer more
than we found usually included in phonemic analyses. According to our view, the description of the phonetic realizations of isolated phonemes, followed by the description of
some phenomena of connected speech, and by that of stress
and intonation--which is what classical outlines of phonetics
usually give--are very necessary but they do not suffice to
indicate the specific character of the pronunciation of different languages. There still remain many 'blanks' to be
filled in. By our complex analysis we tried to fill some of
these 'blanks,' without claiming to have filled all of them.
Nevertheless, our combination analysis is a new analysis,
already verified in practice during our long teaching experience with adult learners. It proved to be efficient not
only in their achieving some better knowledge of the mutual
interactions of speech sounds within speech units, but also
in improving their pronunciation of the foreign language.

THE THEORETICAL BASIS OF THE SOUND-
COMBINATION ANALYSIS

It was long ago stated that sounds do not stand isolated
from one another within speech units; there is coarticulation
or a so-called speech chain of the sequences of distinctive
sounds. As a result, assimilation, elisions, etc. may occur
in rapid or colloquial speech, changing some pronunciation
features of sounds at or in the vicinity of word boundaries.

Our combination analysis essentially differs from a coarticulation analysis as it was not focused on incidental and irregular results of coarticulation but on the usual and regular results of the interconnections of distinctive sounds (we called them 'combinations') within words in standard pronunciation. They are practically of considerable importance to the learners of a given language, especially as a foreign language. As for our combination analysis, it does include this aspect but also much more than that. It includes a complexity of aspects which can be grouped according to the mode and intensity or kind and degree of combination.

Taking into consideration the fact that any combination of two things in any branch of science, art, or human life, must not necessarily form or result in a coherent new unit, I adapted my concept of the sound combinations to this reality and admitted that the combinations can be tighter or less tight or very tight. The intensity (degree) of combination can thus vary between the two extremes: a simple sequence of two distinctive sounds, a simple connection with unimportant combination features, and the very intimate combination of two sounds into a new unit. Although more degrees of combination could be accepted, we have used only three degrees in our analysis: first-grade combinations or loose combinations, second-grade or tight combinations, and third grade or very tight combinations.

According to our opinion, loose combinations usually occur when, in a sequence of two sounds, one sound transmits one of its features to the other sound, or vice versa, but this feature has little influence on the quality of that given sound, e.g., the lip-rounding common to some English or Rumanian vowels transmitted to the neighbouring consonant; the length of the English 'long' vowels reduced under the influence of the following fortis plosive, etc. Tight combinations usually occur when in a sequence of two sounds there is a more intimate combination between their individual features and the sounds are closer to each other than in loose combinations, e.g., the Rumanian palatal allophones of /k,g/ influenced by /i,e,j/; the English allophones of /t,d/ with lateral explosion under the influence of a following /l/, etc. <u>Very tight combinations</u> usually occur when in a sequence of two sounds there is such a strong and imtimate combination that the individual characters of the two sounds melt together, more frequently forming a new unit, e.g., the Rumanian and the English affricates, the English diphthongs, etc.

As for the <u>mode</u> of combination, we established that in some combinations one element dominates the other and its influence is decisive, e.t., <u>the former influencing the latter</u> or <u>the latter influencing the former</u>. Besides, there are other combinations in which the give-and-take process occurs in both directions resulting a <u>reciprocal influence</u>, that is, an almost equal influence between the two elements.

Our research could establish the following: (1) It is implied a certain difference (a) whether the analyzed sounds belong to the same syllable or not, because their combination can be tighter if they are in the same syllable than if they are in different syllables, e.g., the combination of the sequence /tl/ is tighter in <u>settle</u> than in <u>settling</u>; (b) whether the analyzed sounds can occur in both the same and different syllables, or just in different syllables, because the sequences which can occur according to the former possibilities prove to be more flexible within the pattern and can undergo different degrees of combinations, while the others, due to their one-sided character, can less contribute to the specific variety of the given sound-pattern; e.g., the Rumanian sequences /pn,tn/ can occur only in different syllables and are neither typical of nor usual in the Rumanian pattern. (2) The degree of combination also depends on the points of articulation of the two sounds: the combination can be tighter if their points of articulation are the same or near than if they are far apart, e.g., English /tn,dn/ combinations are tighter than English /kn,gn/ combinations also because their points of articulations are the same and not far apart. (3) The mode of articulation is considerably influenced by the position and individual power of the distinctive sounds within the system, which allow them more or less flexibility within the combinations (see the above (b) differentiation), as well as more or less combination possibilities or more or

less influence upon the occurrence of other distinctive
sounds in their vicinity. Besides, some phonemes can more
or less dominate over the adjacent phonemes, and their
presence can exclude some adjacent phonemes from certain
sound-patterns. (4) In our view, the specificity of each
language lies also in the fact that its phonological system
includes individual units owning along with their specificity
also more or less power within the system. In other words,
we can establish, beside the relevant character of each distinctive unit, a particular and natural hierarchy among the
phonemes typical of the phonemic system of each language.
Therefore, some phonemes have a stronger individuality in
one language than their correspondent phonemes in another
language; they are also more viable and more powerful than
other phonemes; they can be of more frequent occurrence and
belong to more patterns than others; they can exert a
stronger influence--in certain circumstances--upon others,
and are more resistent to sound change in unstressed positions than others. Moreover, some phonemes can go together
and can be loosely or tightly combined, while others exclude
themselves from certain patterns according to the specificity
of each language. For instance: the semivowel /j/ has a
stronger position in the Rumanian than in the English phonemic
pattern, which is also proved by its very frequent insertion
between and in front of vowels in Rumanian, i.e., <u>este</u>
/'jeste/, <u>fiinţă</u>ə/'fi-jintsə/, while a similar insertion
would be improper in a similar English pattern, i.e.,
<u>Esther</u> /estə/, <u>seeing</u> /si:-iŋ/. Likewise, an English
sequence as /tn/ with a syllabic /n/ is typical of some
word-endings in English, while the same sequence is impossible in the Rumanian sound-pattern, though a syllabic
/ŋ/ occurs in Rumanian as well.

We may conclude that all the above enumerated factors
must necessarily be guided by some internal rules of the
phonological systems of languages, which, unfortunately have
been little mentioned and studied up to now. Among the
general internal rules of the phonological systems of
languages we have inserted a rule which we called 'harmony
of pattern.' It ultimately seems to decide upon the existence of combinations of sounds and upon the fact that some
phonemes match together, while others exclude one another

in certain languages. We observed that the harmony of
pattern facilitates the existence of certain combinations
in one language, which are different in another language or
even impossible to occur in other languages. Thus, the
harmony of pattern guides the sound-patterns according to
the specificity of each language.

THE PRACTICAL APPLICATION OF THE SOUND-COMBINATION ANALYSIS

The following instances of sound-combination analysis
have been included in the chapter of differences between
the Rumanian and English plosives; the clusters belong to
the three degrees of combination and occur in both languages.
We chose, as examples, such words which have similar or
partly similar phonological compositions in Rumanian and
English in order to better illustrate the pronunciation
differences between the two languages determined by the different combination features.

The Combination Features of the Sequences. Rumanian (R)
and English (E) /pl,kl/ +vowel. For R, first grade combination of a voiceless plosive with a lateral consonant having
different points of articulation: /p/ bilabial, and /k/
velar + a dental apical/l/. They are joined by linked
articulation stages. (By 'linked" articulation stages we
mean the relatively simultaneous articulation of two stages
of the two sounds, i.e., the release of the former and the
onset of the latter.) In this way the lateral character of
/l/ has a reduced influence on the plosives: although the
release of the plosive is shortened and closely followed by
the release of /l/, each of them keeps its typical character,
the former being medial and the latter, lateral, which is
clearly audible. In addition, the voiceless plosive has no
devoicing influence on /l/.

For E, a second grade combination of a voiceless plosive
with a clear allophone of /l/, having different points of
articulation: /p/ bilabial, and /k/velar+ /l/alveolar.
They are joined by knitted articulation stages. (We mean
by 'knitted' articulation stages the relatively simultaneous

articulation of four stages of the two sounds: the hold
of the former with the onset or the hold of the latter, the
release of the former with the hold or the release of the
latter.) Because of their knitted articulation stages
the stream of air cannot escape medially through the mouth
for the release of the plosives, but through the lateral
passage already made by the tongue for the release of /l/.
Thus, the release of the plosive occurs laterally and is
rapidly and closely followed by the shortened release of
the lateral /l/. The lateralized plosion of the plosive
consonant is clearly audible. As the influence is reciprocal, while /l/ transmits its lateral character to the
release of the plosive, the voiceless plosive considerably
devoices /l/ (Gimson, 1970). Therefore, the combination is
based not only on knitted articulation stages but also on
devoicing.

    The R and E /tr,dr/. There is a very considerable
difference in the combination of these clusters of the two
languages. For R, a first grade combination of a dorsal
dental plosive with an apical dental-alveolar rolled sonant.
They are joined by linked articulation stages. The plosion
of /t,d/ is weakened and is rather rapidly followed by the
rolled release of /r/, but two distinct releases are heard,
although the consonants have almost the same points of
articulation; i.e., the tongue has to pass from a dorsal
dental articulation of /t,d/ to an apical dental-alveolar
articulation for /r/. For E a third grade combination of
an alveolar plosive with the post-alveolar fricative /r/.
There is a reciprocal influence between the two elements of
this very tight combination, but the influence of /r/ pre-
dominates. The main changes: the plosives adopt the post-
alveolar articulation of /r/, i.e., the main part of the
tongue is placed as for /r/ and the tip of the tongue is
brought to touch the back part of the teeth-ridge; they
also adopt the somewhat rounded-protruded position of the
lips, typical of /r/; their release is no longer distinctly
explosive because the tongue is removed not too rapidly
from the teeth-ridge; while /t/ loses its aspiration, the
/r/ becomes partly or entirely voiceless. But this is not
all: there is not only a fusion of some articulation

stages--as in first or second grade combinations--but
rather a simultaneous articulation of the two elements
with a common release. It is the very tight combination of
the two elements which make a new complex, close-knit unit,
an affricate. The characteristic of the articulation of
these units is that the stream of air is first completely
stopped and then slowly released with friction,--voiced or
voiceless--but it seems to be less fricative than in
/tʃ,dʒ/. The English affricates /tr,dr/ must be distinguished from the sequences /t+r,d+r/ which also occur in
English and are second grade combinations.

The R and E /ts/. For R, a third grade combination of
a voiceless plosive with a voiceless fricative having the
same points of articulation. Their very tight combination
makes a new, complex, close-knit unit, an affricate. (See
the above described E. affricates.) There is a simultaneous articulation of the two elements of the cluster:
the stream of air, which is first completely stopped, is
then released rather slowly and with friction. The qualitative difference between the R./ts/ and the E./t+s/ can
be caught by a normal ear. For E, a second grade combination of an alveolar voiceless stop with an alveolar voiceless fricative. They are joined by knitted articulation
stages. The former element influences the latter insofar
as it allows only a voiceless morpheme to be added (see
the harmony of pattern). In spite of their common articulation place, two releases are audible, with the characteristic that the release of the plosive is rather short and
without aspiration. In this respect, the difference between
the Rumanian and the English /ts/ clusters is perfectly
audible (Tătaru, 1975).

Pronunciation Problems Caused by Differences in Sound-
Combinations. The different grades of sound-combinations
within words can also cause some real pronunciation problems
and pronunciation errors. Even if referring just to the
few examples presented above, we could underline the following pronunciation problems (Rumanian will be discussed first).
Rumanian students learning English will be inclined to make
combinations in many English clusters less tight than they
should be: (1) they join English clusters like /pl,kl/ and

/bl,gl/ with linked articulation stages, so that the plosive
is not lateralized, which sounds strange in English words
like plop, clean, blond, glass; (2) they use loose combinations and linked articulation stages to join English clusters like /kr,gr,pr,br/ and even /tr,dr/ in words as train,
drug, prune, brad, crude, grade; they also overlook the
fact that E./r/ has a strong influence upon the articulation
of the plosives within these clusters; they even replace
the English fricative /r/ by the Rumanian rolled /r/; (3)
sometimes Rumanian students replace a tight combination by
a very tight combination in English words with the sequence
/t+s/, e.g., brats, prints, being used to their very tight
combination of the affricate /ts/, e.g., braţ, prinţ.

English students learning Rumanian will be inclined to
make the combinations in some Rumanian clusters tighter
than they should be: (1) they join the Rumanian clusters
/pl,kl/ and /bl,gl/ with knitted articulation stages, i.e.,
tight combinations, and thus lateralize the release of the
plosive, which sounds strange in Rumanian words like plop,
clin, blond, glas ; (2) they join Rumanian clusters like
/pr,br,kr,gr/ by knitted articulation stages, and they even
replace the Rumanian rolled /r/ by the English fricative /r/
in words as prun, brad, crud, grad; they often transform
the Rumanian loose combinations of /tr,dr/ into very tight
combinations and replace them by the English affricates
/tr,dr/, in words like tren, drag; (3) sometimes, English
students replace a very tight combination by a tight combination in Rumanian words with /ts/, as they fail to
distinguish the difference between their /t+s/ sequence
and the Rumanian affricate /ts/; compare R. braţ, with
E. brats, and R. prinţ with E. prints.

In conclusion, we find it obviously of no little importance whether we join sounds by loose combinations, where
both sounds keep their quality almost unchanged, or whether
we join them by tight combinations, in which important
changes take place, or even by very tight combinations,
which imply such considerable changes as to give rise to
new distinctive units.

REFERENCES

Gimson, A. C.   (1970).   London.
Heffner, R. M. S.   (1950).   Madison, Univ. Wisconsin Press.
Jones, D.   (1960).   Heffer, Cambridge.

Tataru, A.   (1975).   Printed Ph.D. diss., Univ. Bonn.

LA SPECTROGRAPHIE ET LA SEGMENTATION ACOUSTIQUE AU SERVICE DE LA POÉTIQUE EXPÉRIMENTALE--DES ANALYSES FONDÉES SUR LE DICTIONNAIRE DE POÉTIQUE ET DE RHÉTORIQUE DE HENRI MORIER, ÉDITION DE 1975

SIBYLLE VATER
Université de Geneve

Du point de vue expérimental, l'ouvrage auquel cette étude se réfère examine les phénomenes de la prosodie essentiellement à l'aide d'oscillogrammes, de mélogrammes et d'intensigrammes. A présent, nous nous proposons d'analyser, moyennant la spectrographie et la segmentation acoustique, quelques-uns des effets traités dans ce dictionnaire et reproduits dans les Documents sonores complementaires par la voix du professeur Henri Morier.[1] Les exemples suivants montreront combien la mise en évidence de structures acoustiques peut, à son tour, éclairer la composition rythmique de certains vers.

C'est d'abord le rebondissement vocalique[2]) qui va retenir notre attention.
 "Un rythmique sabbat, rythmique, extrememement;
 Rythmique...VERLAINE, Paysages tristes, "Nuit
 du Walpurgis classique" (DPR, p. 884).

Le spectrogramme (Fig. 1) révèle nettement, dans des paires constituées d'une syllabe brève et d'une allongée, la structure diffuse et répétitive des voyelles /i/ en alternance avec les formants compacts des deux /a/. N'insistons pas sur le rebondissement plus effacé des /ɛ/. Quant à celui des consonnes bilabiales sonores /m - b - m - m - m - (m)/, il agit, par rapport aux timbres vocaliques relancés, comme une sourdine précieuse. A part l'harmonie extérieure du vers, Verlaine a donc été hautement sensible a l'accord "génétique" des voyelles vedettes en réussissant ainsi une parfaite osmose du sens, de l'arrangement linéaire du vers et de sa texture sonore intrinseque: le poete a créé un rythme essentiel.

L'examen au spectrographe d'un vers d'Aragon (Fig. 2) fait reconnaitre une acuité poétique semblable:
"Lès quàis gàis comme en càrnàval; Vont au devant de la lumière." Pour demain (DPR, p. 884).

La structure aérée des trois e successifs /ĕ - ĕ - ē/, convient tout à fait à l'idée exprimée et, à la fois, elle s'oppose aux formants plus "masqués" des trois a ultérieurs /ă - ă - ā/, qui, à leur manière, s'accordent au sémème carnaval. D'autre part, comme Verlaine, Aragon associe au rebondissement vocalique un rebondissement consonantique, mais ici moyennant quatre explosions de consonnes momentanées.

Passons de l'homophonie à la multisonance embrassée[3]:
"C'est qu'à l'orgue l'orage a détruit la voix d'ange /(k) a.'l ɔr/(gə) 1 ɔ.'ra://" ARAGON, Les Yeux d'Elsa, "Plus belle que les larmes," str. 2 (DPR, ibidem).

L'inversion des timbres vocaliques et de leurs satellites se produit indépendamment de la structure rythmique des cellules, qui elle reste stable: /(ʊ) ʊ '-/ (ʊ) ʊ '-/. De plus, devenant croissante, la consonne /R/ change, dans la seconde séquence, de voyelle associée. On a donc les syllabes: /(k)a + 'lɔ·R /... l ɔ +'Ra : // /. Les inflexions et les durées des formants vocaliques en question se ressentent de ces inégalités et, de ce fait, le jeu des timbres se perçoit moins aisément que sur les graphiques précédents (Fig. 4). Ici les enveloppes spectrales se révèlent particulièrement utiles. Etablies pendant la tenue des phonemes, elles permettent d'identifier, d'un coup d'oeil, les structures vocaliques interverties.

Lors du rebondissement et de la multisonance, le timbre en soi de la voyelle se maintient. En revanche, quand à la reprise celui-ci est modifié, il s'agit d'une apophonie.[4]

Il pleure dans mon coeur--/(pl) œ :, (k) œ :/. Comme
il pleu sur la ville; (pl) ø. VERLAINE, Romances
sans paroles, "Ariettes oubliées," III (DPR, p. 120).

Par rapport aux deux premieres voyelles accentuées, les
formants Fl et F2 du timbre correspondant fermé /ø/ ne sont
guere plus écartés (Fig. 4). Ainsi nous voyons combien
l'apophonie est un effet discret et léger, expression d'une
sensibilité poétique subtile.

Verhaeren évoque des "lucarnes rapiécées," qui,
secouées par le vent,
Ballottent leurs loques falotes
 a   ɔ   œ   a   ɔ
De vitres et de paper. Les Villages illusoires,
p. 58 (DPR, ibid.)

Un petit schéma d'Henri Morier illustre comment sont
coordonnées les apophonies /a - ɔ/ et /œ - ɔ/. Certes, pour
chacune des trois cellules rythmiques, le spectrogramme (Fig.
5) confirme ces légères oppositions de timbre et il met en
évidence le rôle particulier qui, dans l'ensemble, revient
à la voyelle œ. Mais comme, par définition, l'apophonie
ne peut se réaliser que dans la chaine parlée, le graphique
montre aussi combien cet effet prosodique rapproche modification et assimilation de timbres vocaliques.

Les phonèmes rebondissants bien définis, les timbres
subtilement modulés ou ingénieusement opposés à d'autres
ne sont pas les seuls à pouvoir appuyer opportunément le
sens des mots. Un simple e atone, placé a propos, s'avérera
pareillement efficace.[6] Sans pouvoir examiner ici de maniere
approfondie la valeur acoustique de cette voyelle faible en
prosodie, nous désirons présenter un exemple où l'e atone se
charge d'une telle expressivité sonore que, pour ainsi dire,
sa réalité se confond avec celle de l'objet évoqué, en
l'occurrence, avec une goutte tombant sur l'eau:

"...Une feuille meurt sur // ses épaules humides,
Une goutte tombe // de la flûte sur l'eau, Et le
pied pur s'épeu://re comme un bel oiseau Ivre
d'ombre ..." Paul VALÉRY, Poésies, "Episode" fin.
(DPR, p. 790).

Dans chacun de ces vers, le verbe se conçoit différem-
ment par rapport à la césure et ce fait important se ré-
percute dans les cellules pré- et postcésurielles. Le
second vers retiendra notre attention particuliere. Avec
Henri Morier,[7] nous apprécions la syncope qui allonge la
voyelle interictuelle / ɔ̃:/, et qui, dans la syllabe /-bə/,
entraine une chute expressive de la voix. Sur notre spectrogramme (Fig. 7), l'e atone final d'hemistiche, étiolé,
s'oppose à trois autres bien constitués, situés dans les
syllabes 2, 4 et 7. Mais ce qui nous frappe presque
davantage est l'effet de la coupe enjambante effectuée
entre les deux premieres cellules du vers en question:
/y.'nə .' 'gu/tə .'tɔ̃:.'bə // .../. L'e atone précédant la
syncope et pris entre les explosions de deux t devient si
délicatement résonnant[8] que, soutenu par ces bruits consonantiques, il évoque à la perfection la goutte se détach-
ant de la flûte et heurtant la nappe d'eau[9]. Cet effet est
d'autant plus réussi que la voyelle atone est contigüe à la
phase audible du premier t mais séparée de celle du second.
Ainsi la resonance vocalique s'epanouit et, ensuite, s'amor-
tit jusqu'au silence interrompu par la deuxième explosion
consonantique. L'enregistrement isolé de la cellule rythmique /.'tə tɔ̃:bə .'// / nous a permis de percevoir encore plus
distinctement le phénomène analysé. Le timbre neutre et
plus ou moins diffus de l'e atone convient sans doute au
concept de goutte limpide. Associant à la voyelle un rebondissement consonantique, la séquence //tə t....'/ repré-
sente donc une véritable métaphore phonétique.[10] De plus,
cette expressivité nous semble être corroborée par le fait
que, dans l'alexandrin en question, cinq syllables sur douze
se composent d'une occlusive croissante et d'un e atone. Et
sans revenir à la syllabe /-bə/, qui, privée par la syncope
de pertinence acoustique, devient signifiante à sa maniere,
il n'est certes pas fortuit que, dans chacun des hémistiches,
la syllabe /-tə/ occupe la quatrieme place et qu'elle fasse
partie d'une coupe enjambante. En revanche, sur douze
syllabes le vers précedent n'en contient que trois du type
consonne + e atone et le vers suivant ("Et le pied pur ...")
n'en compte que deux. Aucune des consonnes en question n'est
occlusive.

    Jusqu'ice les timbres vocaliques ont été présentés,
dans leurs relations avec d'autres phonèmes, comme des

unités. Actuellement, nous voulons penetrer la structure
acoustique de la voyelle et voir dans quelle mesure les formants se plient à certaines contraintes prosodiques.

> "Ou nous aimerons-nous, / l'un l'autre D'un
> parfum ... / d'une saveur?" VIELE-GRIFFIN,
> $\simeq$ 4   4
> OEuvres, II, p. 130 (DPR, p. 27).

    Pour sauvegarder l'isométrie du dernier vers, la syllabe
/-'fœ̃/ doit être allongée de sorte que la nasale prenne la
valeur d'une voyelle double.[11] Le spectrogramme correspondant nous montre trois phases: une première dont les formants sont intensément développés, une deuxieme, centrale,
ou la structure acoustique s'effiloche et une derniere pendant laquelle ne se maintiennent que les basses fréquences.
Meme si une voyelle orale sait mieux résister à l'usure par
allongement, chez elle aussi, de quelque manière que ce soit,
la phase finale s'atténuera.

> "Dans l'effort / de ma jeunesse / et de ma joie
>   dã lefɔ̃-ɔ:R /"
>   4   4   4
> VIELÉ-GRIFFIN, OEuvres, II, p. 157 (DPR, pp.
> 27, 548 et 886). (Fig. 7)

    Les sept spectrogrammes suivants (Fig. 8-14) illustrent
le redoublement vocalique que, pour assurer quatre syllabes
au groupe rythmique initial de ce vers, Henri Morier a
réalisé dans le cadre de l'article accent.[12] L'ensemble
/ɔ̃-ɔ:/ est réparti en trois phases facilement reperables par
deux "bosses" d'harmoniques.[13] Dans ce contexte, Henri
Morier parle, suivant Aragon, d'un "hoquet lyrique" ou d'un
"hoquet d'émotion."[14] Les formants de la première voyelle
/ɔ̃-/, syncopée et donc interictuelle, sont, par un sursaut
pathétique de la voix, resserés dans la verticale. C'est
une phase de grande intensité comme le prouvent l'enveloppe
spectrale établie en plein coeur ainsi que l'intensigramme.
Suit une certaine accalmie avant l'attaque de la seconde
voyelle plus longue. Dans la diction retenue, la partie
redoublée débute par une sorte d'ictus naturel de la voix
(la deuxième élévation des formants,[15]) nettement audible
dans plusieurs de nos segments acoustiques. La durée de la
phase ictuelle /-ɔ:/ égale pratiquement celle de la voyelle

accentuée de jeunesse. L'intensigramme et les enveloppes
spectrales successives montrent que, jusqu'à l'attaque de la
seconde voyelle, l'amplitude ne décroît guère. En revanche,
dans la phase vocalique longue, elle s'affaiblit sensible-
ment.[16]

   Quelques-uns des graphiques comportent à la base des
repères de segmentation acoustique. Nous avons enregistré
sur bande magnétique les segments suivants: (1) ceux qui
incluent partiellement ou intégralement la voyelle verticale:
(a) l'ensemble vocalique entier /ɔ̆-ɔ:/, v. spectrogramme[17]
no 8, repère de base, (b) segment s'étendant du sommet de la
voyelle initiale au dernier tiers de la finale, c'est-à-dire
la section comprise entre les bases verticales de deux
enveloppes spectrales du graphique no 9, (c) la première
voyelle exclusivement, de son début jusqu'à la base verticale
de l'enveloppe spectrale du graphique no 10, (d) la première
voyelle et environ la moitié de la section transitoire
/ɔ̆-··/, v. sp. no 11, (e) la première partie et la section
intermédiaire jusqu'au second sommet mélodique /ɔ̆-ˇ/, v.
sp. no 12, (f) la voyelle initiale intégralement, la transition et approximativement deux tiers de la voyelle finale
/ ɔ̆-ɔ /, v. sp. no 9; (2) les segments qui excluent la
voyelle verticale: (a) segment comprenant la transition et
la voyelle redoublée /-ˇ ɔ:/, v. sp. no 13, and (b) la
voyelle redoublée à partir du second sommet mélodique /ˈɔ:/,
v. sp. no 14.

   Entre autres, l'audition permet d'opposer l'intensité
prédominante de la voyelle verticale dans les segments du
premier groupe à l'amplitude nettement réduite des segments
qui excluent ce timbre interictuel.

   La diction que nous venons d'analyser peut être confrontee
avec deux prononciations complémentaires, également effectuées
par Henri Morier.[18] La première d'elles est accompagnée d'ictus frappés. A leur tour, les spectrogammes correspondants
(Fig. 16-17) confirment la présence de trois phases vocaliques, distinctes par la durée, l'intensité et la hauteur
mélodique: voyelle interictuelle forte et brève, transition
dans le meme timbre, voyelle ictuelle moins intense et
longue. La diction finale nous semble avoir réussi le
meilleur élancement de la voyelle verticale, comprimé dans
environ 0.11 s.

POÉTIQUE EXPÉRIMENTALE: SPECTROGRAPHIE

Dans le vers examiné, le redoublement vocalique ne plaide pas seulement en faveur de l'isométrie, il est en même temps le moyen optimal pour exprimer phonétiquement l'idée d'effort.

Rebondissement vocalique et consonantique, multisonance, apophonie, expressivité de l'e atone, redoublement vocalique—que l'analyse acoustique de ces effets puisse avoir contribué à sensibiliser lecteurs et auditeurs à la densité du langage poétique!

FOOTNOTES AND REFERENCES

1. Au cours de ce travail, nous citerons le dictionnaire en question et les Documents sonores de la maniere suivante: DPR et DS.
2. DPR, p. 883 sqq.
3. DPR, pp. 776.
4. DPR, pp. 120-122.
5. H. Morier a prononcé une voyelle svarabhaktique à l'intérieur du groupe consonantique initial de pleut.
6. V. DPR, pp. 378-388.
7. DPR, pp. 790, 1054-1055.
8. Résonnant au sens de la poétique et résonant au sens de l'acoustique.
9. L'on peut aussi interpréter les explosions consonantiques comme deux petits heurts successifs de la goutte contre la surface de l'eau.
10. Cf. DPR, pp. 688-689 et 1051.
11. DPR, pp. 26-27 et, sous allongement vocalique, p. 85.
12. DPR, p. 27 et DS.
13. Cf. aussi le mélogramme et l'intensigramme correspondants.
14. DPR, respectivement pp. 27 et 886.
15. Cf. la diction complémentaire soutenue par des ictus et reproduite par le graphique no 16.
16. V. graphique no 9.
17. Par la suite, abrégé: sp..
18. DPR, pp. 548 et 886.

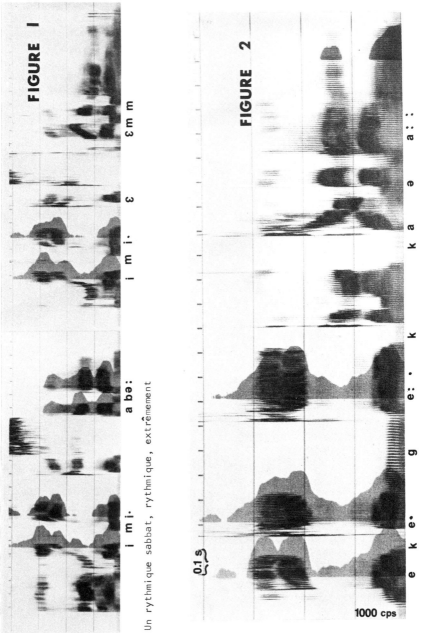

FIGURE 1

i m i·   a be: i m i·   ε m i·   ε   i m i·

Un rythmique sabbat, rythmique, extrêmement

FIGURE 2

e   e ke·   g   e:·   k   k   a   ə   a::

0.1 s

1000 cps

Les quais gais comme en carnaval

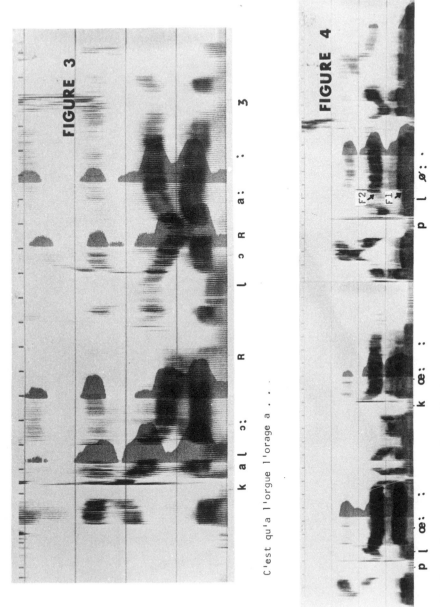

FIGURE 3

k a l ɔ: R   l ɔ R a: :   ɜ

C'est qu'a l'orgue l'orage a . . .

FIGURE 4

F2   F1

p l ø: .

p l œ: :   k œ: :

Il pleure dans mon coeur   Comme il pleut sur la ville

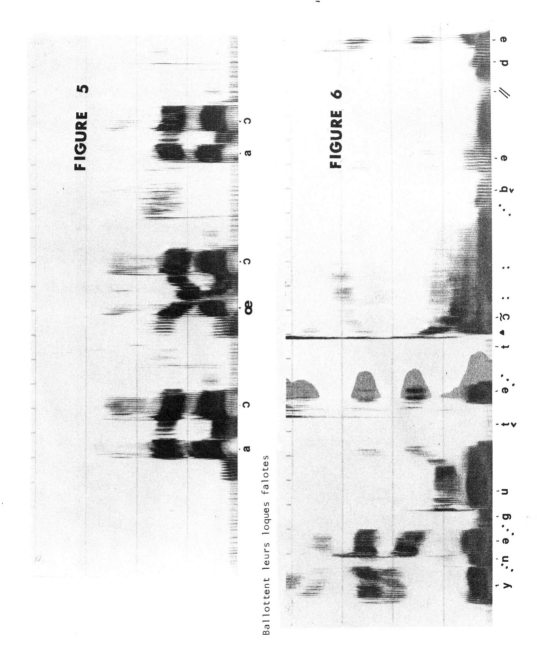

FIGURE 5

FIGURE 6

Ballottent leurs loques falotes

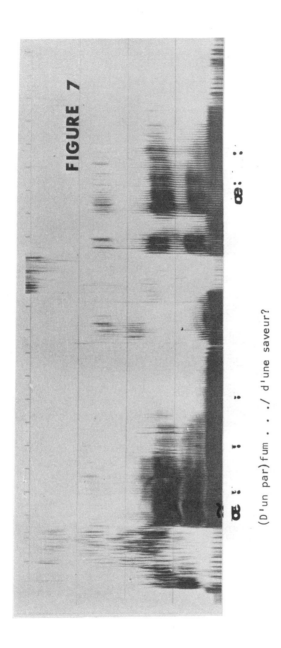

FIGURE 7

(D'un par) fum . . . ./ d'une saveur?

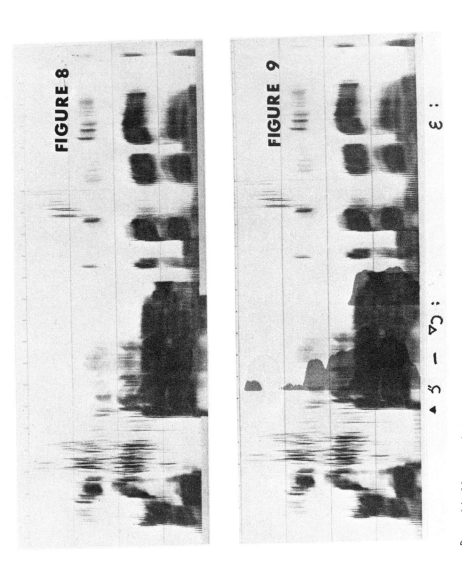

FIGURE 8

FIGURE 9

: ε

: Cᴧ — ʃ ᴧ

Dans l'effo-ort / de ma jeunesse / et . . . .

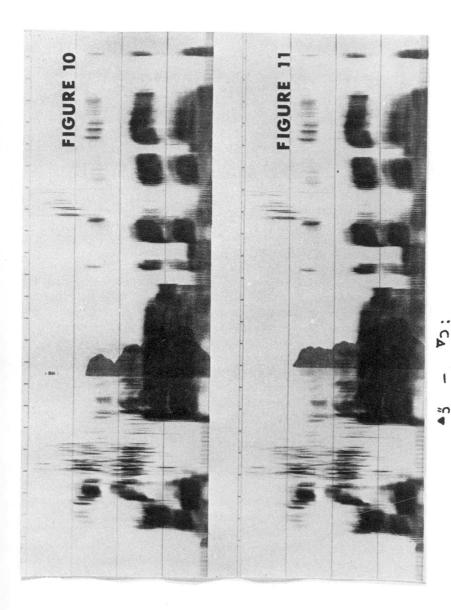

Dans l'effo-ort / de ma jeunesse / et . . . .

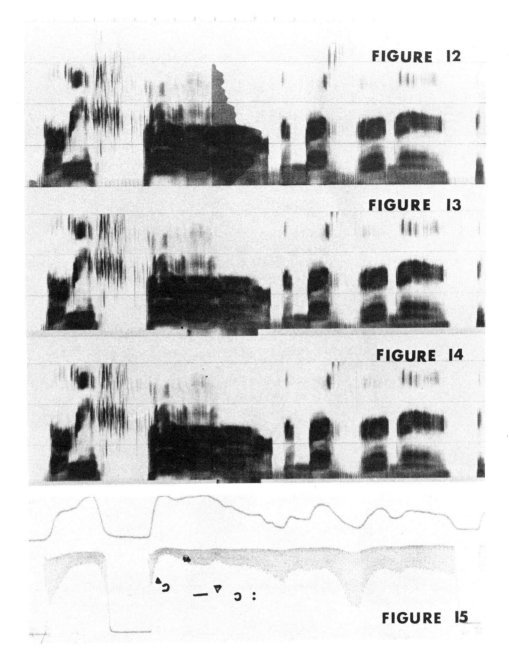

Dans l'effo-ort / de ma jeunesse / et . . .

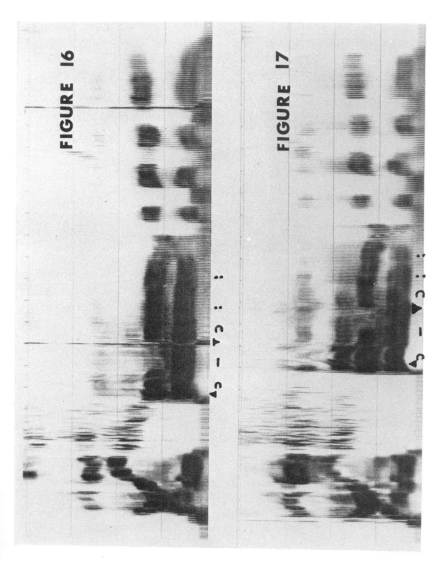

Dans l'effo-ort / de ma jeunesse

PROSODIC FEATURES AND SPEECH ACTS

ARETA VORONIUC
University of Iasi

The topic of this report has been challenging us for quite a long time because the relation between the terms implied, though very often associated by theorists, has never been the subject of any empirical, detailed study, and also because its investigation seemed to be at all easy. The great number of studies devoted to the English imperative shows that it is an important topic, if not a key one, for syntactic, semantic and pragmatic analyses, because elements from all of them are necessary to explain it and also because it is used to explain facts in all of them. In syntax it is analysed to demonstrate the subject/object-verb relation, and it is the subject/object-verb relation that can be used to analyse the imperative (Postal, 1964). The imperative is a language structure which expresses socio-cultural relations, and intonation, rhythm, pause, voice quality may take the place of some verbal components of some imperative forms.

Although an 'imperative' may be such a simple sentence that every speaker can utter and understand it without the least effort, it is a very complicated event that cannot be explained under a fractionated approach; that is, an approach (or approaches) that studies independently of any other approach its different aspects. The basic idea of all language studies should be "language is a phase of human activity which must not be treated in essence as structurally divorced from the structure of nonverbal human activity... Verbal and nonverbal activity is a unified whole and theory and

methodology should be organized or created to treat it as
such" (Pike, 1954).

        This, I think, should be understood that some aspects
of the language should prevail in any study, at least for
the sake of proportion. When we read an imperative sentence
such as 'Close the door' out of any context, it is absolutely colourless. But when we hear it shouted out on a
high level tone and with great force on both 'close' and
'door' we, not only, do not need any context to get some
colour to it, but also it tells us a lot about the situation,
about the speaker and hearer, and about their personal and
social relations. As many of these aspects as possible
should be included in language analyses.

        In this research we start from the assumption that speech
is a unified verbal and nonverbal (Crystal, 1969) activity
and that pitch, stress, rhythm, and the whole range of voice
qualities carry a great part of the meaning of the utterances; that is, they form an illocutionary force indicating
device. We try to analyse to what degree verbal and nonverbal elements interlock in the speech act of imperative,
and what variables can be distinguished. We make the assumption that sentences like 'come here' are not full sentences,
but fragments of sentences of the type 'I order you to come
here' or 'I ask you to come here,' or 'I invite you to come
here,' and that sentences like 'come here please' etc. are
complex (Voroniuc, in press) imperative sentences, but not
full (or complete) imperative sentences. So, the hierarchy
is: (1) full (complete) imperative sentences: I order you
to come here. (2) complex imperative sentences: Come here,
please. (3) simple imperative sentences: Come here. Our
assumption also is that the simple imperative sentences are
used with a great number of interpretations, while the complex imperative sentences have a small set of semantic
interpretations, and that the semantic non-finite interpretations of the simple imperative are signalled in speech
by a varied range of pitch, stress, rhythm, pause, voice
quality, while the nonverbal information that the complex
imperatives carry is less varied.

We do not make the complete imperative sentences a subject of our analysis because they are not often met in everyday speech; they are analysed as the deep, underlying structure of the other imperatives. According to our point of
view, expressed on page two, we are not going to deal with
all the aspects of language analysis. We shall take the
purely syntactical and semantical aspects for granted, which
is no loss with the data we are using, and investigate only
the pragmatic meaning or information carried by the prosodic
features of the imperative sentences in the data.

PROCEDURES

We proposed the following sentences: (1) Come here.
(2) Please, come here. (3) Come here please. (4) Just
come here. (5) Please come here, will you? (6) Come here,
will you? (7) Come here please, will you? (8) Do come
here, will you? and (9) Will you just come here? and we
asked Nina and John to pronounce them into the microphone
in the anechoic room in the Phonetic Lab of the Linguistic
Department of the University of Michigan in as many possible
ways those sentences could be used by native speakers in
different situations. Both speakers had to pronounce the
sentences in the same condition of lack of any context. The
informants were asked not to improvise too much, but to give
the variants that they usually used. In this way we tried
to avoid artificial utterances.

We processed the utterances through the spectrograph, the
mingograph and, a few of them, both of Nina and John, through
the computer. We obtained 35 narrow band spectrograms and
mingograms and five images from the computer. The result was
the visible pattern of the utterances in three fundamental
dimensions--frequency, intensity and time. The narrow band
spectrograms showed the harmonic structures very clear and
we could identify the first formant that is important in
establishing the height of the pitches in intonation. We
could distinguish the rising and falling inflections of the
voice by following the rising and falling of the resonance
band, the intensity of the vocal cord activity by the
intensity of the shade of darkness. We could establish the
frequency from the number of harmonics on the vertical line
and the time distribution on the horizontal line of the

·pectrograms. The mingograms provided us with parallel
images of the voice activity, pitch trace and amplitude
trace. All these could be easily correlated. We devised
a scale that helped us in determining the height of the
pitches. The force line trace and the voice activity image
showed where the stress on the voiced sounds was. We could
determine what the most contrastive pitches were, where the
pauses were, and what the rhythm was. The analysis done on
the computer was very reliable. The computer traces and
figures, that give the exact and correct time duration in
ms., the pitches in hz., and the amplitude in db., saved a
lot of work and gave us the certitude of correctness.

We analysed all these traces and images while listening
over and over again and interpreting parts of, or whole
utterances by means of the loop tape. By perceptual auditive analysis we could appreciate and correlate the characteristic of speech that we were interested in, to the degree
that they can be perceived by the human ear and leave aside
the unnecessary details given by the mechanical devices. In
establishing the contours and in interpreting all the prosodic
features which resulted from our analysis we followed Pike's
theory and terminology (Pike, 1945). In order to determine
the general characteristics of the intonational contours of
the imperative sentences in English we carried out a variety
of statistical analyses.

RESULTS AND CONCLUSIONS

In almost every respect the assumptions we made proved
to be correct. Our analysis supports them in the sense that
in the conditions in which the material was recorded - lack
of any visual and auditive context - the simple imperative
sentences can be given a great number of intonation patterns
(nine for one simple sentence), while the complex imperatives can be given only a small number of intonation patterns
- that is uses or meanings - (1.73 for every sentence in our
case).

The distribution of the pitches and that of the voice
quality, of the rhythm and pauses combine in extremely different ways and make the job of the analyst not very easy.
We made different attempts at classifying and establishing

hierarchies. First we tried to find out frequencies: what precontours and what contours were more frequently used. In this we followed the basic part of the imperative analysed - come here - and then the words and the phrases that make it complex. Out of the 35 utterances of both Nina and John the beginning of the primary contour falls five times on 'come' and thirty-five times on 'here,' which means that the speakers were interested to give prominence to the place not the action desired. The greatest number of the primary contours are falling (i.e., 23), nine are rising and three are level. This shows that the most characteristic contours of the imperative sentences are the falling contours, which is unanimously recognized, but that the rising contours occur at a quite high frequency, too. As can be seen from Table 1, the most frequent falling contours are '2-4 -eight times in Nina's recording, and '1-4 -seven times in John's recording. It should be noted that these are the most frequent contours in the group of utterances 1 (1-6 in Nina's recording and 1-3 in John's recording), that is the simple imperatives, which is intriguing because it seems to be contrary to what we are arguing here for. This fact does not weaken our assumption at all. Important is that out of the 35 utterances analysed, only one is similar to another one (Nina 5.1.5. is the same as her 4.1.4), all the others are different from each other in all respects. The difference comes to a very great extent from the other prosodic features than pitch and stress, especially the rate of speech and the general pitch of the voice, the key, which are not represented graphically by any system that we know of, plus a lot of voice characteristics, besides the voice quality features mentioned in Pike's book (1945), that are very personal and have not been described in terms of any theory, and which we termed as 'voice modulation' (we think now that this term should have been used more often than it was). And, also, we must not forget that 'intonation' is not the only illocutionary force indicating device that adds meaning to utterances. Additional vocabulary is important, too.

In analysing the frequency of the contours on the words that make the simple imperatives complex ones, we distinguished between their use at different points in the

entences: at the beginning, at the end, or in the middle
of the sentences. 'Please' in initial position is pronounced with all pitches except pitch 4, and in quite a great
number of variants, but pitch 2 is predominant. In final
position 4-3 is the recurrent contour. In middle position
it appears only once and the contour is 3 (4)-4. 'Just' in
initial position has pitch 2 in two of the cases and pitch 1
in one case; in middle position it appears with pitch 1 in
the two cases of Nina's recording and with pitch 2 and 3 in
the two cases in John's recording. No occurrence in final
position. 'Will you' occurs only in initial and final
position and in most of its occurrences it takes pitch 4 as
the beginning point of its contour. In initial position
this phrase makes only precontours. 'Do' occurs only in
initial position and its most frequent pitch is 2, although
it takes pitch 1 and 3, too.

As a result of the statistical correlation between the
use of the additional vocabulary, its intonational (prosodic)
patterns and the distribution of the utterances they occur
in on the scheme of variables of the semantic interpretation
of the imperative sentences in English we came out with these
conclusions: 'please' in any position takes the utterances
in which it appears above the line of neutrality unless
there is an emphatic stress on it in which case the utterance
goes below the line; 'just,' which in fact appears only in
initial position, it is always in front of 'come here,' is
almost always emphatically stressed and draws the utterances
in which it appears below the line, though, when there are
no significant contrasts in the intonation pattern of the
utterance, it may go above the line, too (N.11); 'do' always
takes the utterance in which it appears above the line in
spite of the fact that it is always stressed; 'will you' is
a most intriguing additional phrase because it appears in
utterances at all levels in the semantic scheme; we have quite
enough evidence to conclude that its meaning contribution is
very small and that there are other lexical or intonational elements in the utterance which contribute to the
determination of the meaning; the recurrence of the same
contour in almost all cases in which it appears is the best
argument for its neutrality.

PROSODIC FEATURES AND SPEECH ACTS

The additional vocabulary used with imperative senten usually add meaning to the basic sense of the sentence in this way then: 'do' forces the utterances to one of the speech acts above the line of neutrality in our scheme; 'just' forces them down the line, 'please' and 'will you' work both ways. Whatever the word the speaker uses, if the intonation pattern is level, they add very little to the basic meaning of the utterance, the utterance stays at 'O,' but if the intonation pattern presents significant contrasts in more or only one prosodic parameter then the meaning is no longer the neuter one; it becomes marked for the different variables up or down the line of neutrality in our scheme. The language has infinite possibilities of creating significant intonational contrasts, some of them have not been adequately described, others have not been distinguished, yet, though we feel that they are there. Here are some notes on the semantics of the nonverbal (but vocal) activity in the English imperatives: (1) low pitches at the end make them final (down the line); (2) low pitches in the middle make them mild and polite (up the line); (3) high pitches at the beginning and in the middle make them sharp orders (down the line); (4) high pitches at the end make them mild, nonfinal, polite or questioning (up the line); (5) high pitches, strong stress(es), high rate, wide intervals in one and the same utterance make it a sharp command (down the line); (6) low pitches, narrow intervals, slow rate, make the utterance a request, emphatic but mild; the speaker may have a deliberate attitude but is somehow confidential (both ways); (7) emphatic stresses force the utterance to the limits of the scheme (both ways); (8) repeated pauses and jerky rhythm make the utterances rough; (9) low general key is always mild, familiar, confidential and encouraging; (10) high general key is either cheerful or exasperated; (11) precise articulation is characteristic of imperatives of speakers in superior social position with the hearer; and (12) slurred articulation is characteristic of imperatives of speakers in equal social position with the hearer.

We think we must make it clear that the 0 line, the line where the neutral, or normal or unmarked imperative is does not mean complete lack of pitch contrast. As we have seen the unmarked or normal for Nina is 2-4 and for John it

1-4 while Nina's 16.7.3. and John's 3.1.3 are marked by
ck of large pitch contrasts. This again is the result,
nd at the same time points out the complexity of the spoken
language and the necessity of multi-level description of
language.

We think that in this article we have made great steps
towards finding out an adequate, though eclectic, method of
describing the systematic distribution that language makes
of all its possibilities, verbal and non-verbal, in order to
convey meaning, and thus ensuring the non-verbal aspects of
language their deserved place in theoretical linguistics.
In few words, the different variables in our scheme are in-
tonationally marked in this way: 0 - various moderate falling contours, moderate stress and rate, low key, low amplitude, repeated pauses and jerky rhythm; 1 up - rising contours and low key; 2 up - moderate contrasting gliding,
falling-rising or non-final falling contours, slow rate and
high key; 3 up - complex rising contours, high key, low
amplitude; 1 down - falling contours, large intervals, low
key (great differences between Nina's and John's utterances);
2 d - emphatic stress, precision and narrow intervals;
3 d - great pitch contrasts, emphatic descending stress
series, high key, wide intervals, regular pauses.

REFERENCES

Austin, J. L.   (1962). Oxford Univ. Press.
Crystal, D. (1960). Cambridge Univ. Press.
Pike, K. L. (1945). Ann Arbor, Univ. Michigan Press.
Pike, K. L. (1954). The Hague, Mouton.
Posner, R. (1972). Poetica, 4.
Postal, P. M. (1964). Harvard Ed. Rev., 34:2.
Searle, J. R. (1969). Cambridge Univ. Press.
Voroniuc, A. (1976). In press.

Table 1. The frequency of intonational contours in Nina's and John's utterances.

Precontours on 'come'		Primary contours on 'come'		Primary contours on 'here'		
pitch	times	pitch	times	pitch	times	
A. Nina's Utterances						
3	4	'3-2	1	'2-4	4	simple imp's
2	2	'2	1	'3-2-4	1	
				'4-3	1	
3	7			'2-4	3	complex imp's
2	4			'4-3	3	
1	1			'3-4	2	
				'3-3	1	
				'1-3	1	
				'4-4	1	
				'2-1	1	
B. John's Utterances						
2	1	'2	2	'1-4	2	simple imps
3	1			'4-2	1	
4	1					
3	8			'1-4	5	complex imp's
2	4			'4-2	3	
4	2			'3-4	2	
				'4-3	1	
2	1			'2-4	1	
1	1			'3-1	1	
				'2-2	1	

Table 2.   The frequency of other words or phrases in complex
           imperatives of both Nina and John.

	Beginning		Middle		Final	
	cont.	times	cont.	times	cont.	times
please:	'2	3	'3-4	1	'4-3	2
	'3-2	2			'2-4	1
	'3-1	1				
	'1-3	1				
	'1	1				
just:	'2	2	'1	2		
	'1	1	'2	1		
			'3	1		
will you:	4	2			'4-2	7
	3	1			'4-1	2
	2-3	1			'3-1	1
do:	'2	2				
	'1	1				
	'3	1